"Beautifully written, *Through the Dark Field* draws the [...] conversion. Susie Paulik Babka effortlessly weaves together diverse sources—phenomenology, expressionist art, and Christian theology—in a way that disrupts privileged certainty with compassionate vulnerability. Echoing the artists she engages, her constructive retrieval of the doctrine of the incarnation refuses easy answers to life's difficult questions, challenging the comfortable to do more than look at suffering. This is truly a stunning example of interdisciplinary Christian theological scholarship! Don't miss it!"

> —Elisabeth T. Vasko
> Associate Professor of Theology
> Director of Undergraduate Studies in Theology
> Duquesne University

"*Through the Dark Field* is a grace-filled indictment of any easy answer to catastrophic suffering. Susie Paulik Babka's call for each one of us to open to an absurd sort of excess, an overflowing of not knowing, of disorienting vulnerability, the abyss between me and you, is poetic and haunting. In the end, Babka creates a theology of the incarnation that witnesses to the suffering other. Even in our failures, and there are many, we are called to witness to the incarnation by witnessing to all others' suffering, ultimately emptied for the other. This witness is made urgent by Babka's passion for the promise of the visual arts and her sophisticated command of continental theory."

> —Michele Saracino
> Professor and Chair of the Religious Studies Department
> Manhattan College

"A truly profound and thought-provoking study that probes the meaning and existential significance of the incarnation via a gripping engagement with systematic, philosophical, and comparative theology, drawn together via the medium of aesthetics. A highly original work that will prove an invaluable addition to any class in such fields. This stunning monograph will transform how you think and feel alike."

> —Gerard Mannion
> Amaturo Chair in Catholic Studies
> Georgetown University

"The doctrine about incarnation is not the real thing. How, then, do we approach the presence of a God so self-emptied as to appear absent? The way must involve encounter, engage the muscle of the mind that makes images, and transcend the images. Susie Paulik Babka leads us on this way, accompanied by Masaccio's bringing God into our space, by Chagall's association of Jesus with ravaged Jews throughout history, by Rothko's mystical negation of representation itself. This meditative, analytical, affective, personal, penetrating, philosophically learned, aesthetically astute, dialectical, and elegantly written approach to God through the visual arts breaks new ground and should inspire the whole field of constructive theology in our present age."

    —Roger Haight, SJ
    Union Theological Seminary

Through the Dark Field

The Incarnation through an Aesthetics of Vulnerability

Susie Paulik Babka

A Michael Glazier Book

LITURGICAL PRESS

Collegeville, Minnesota

www.litpress.org

A Michael Glazier Book published by Liturgical Press

Cover design by Ann Blattner. *Trinity Pietá* by Master of Saint Laurenz, 1415–30. Wallraf-Richartz Museum, Cologne. Courtsey of Wikimedia Commons.

Marc Chagall, *Le Crucifix (entre Dieu et le Diable)*, 1943. Gouache on cardboard, 68 x 43 cm. Collection of Modern Religious Art, Vatican Museums.

Throne of Mercy, miniature in the Cambrai Missal, ca. 1120. Cambrai, Bibliothèque municipal ms. no. 224.

Masaccio, *Trinità*, circa 1426–1428. Basilica of Santa Maria Novella. This work is in the public domain. Image by John T. Spike, https://commons.wikimedia.org/wiki/File:Masaccio,_trinit%C3%A0.jpg.

Claude Clark, *Slave Lynching*, 1946. Oil on canvas, 13.25" x 16.5". Art Gallery, University of Maryland. Used with permission of Claude Clark estate.

Excerpts from documents of the Second Vatican Council are from *Vatican Council II: Constitutions, Decrees, Declarations; The Basic Sixteen Documents*, edited by Austin Flannery, OP, © 1996. Used with permission of Liturgical Press, Collegeville, Minnesota.

Scripture texts in this work are taken from the *New Revised Standard Version Bible*, © 1989, Division of Christian Education of the National Council of the Churches of Christ in the United States of America. Used by permission. All rights reserved.

Excerpt from "Descent from the Cross," from *In the Illuminated Dark: Selected Poems of Tuvia Ruebner*, translated and introduced by Rachel Tzvia Back, © 2014. Reprinted by permission of the University of Pittsburgh Press.

The lines from "Diving into the Wreck," from *Diving into the Wreck: Poems 1971–1972* by Adrienne Rich. Copyright © 1973 by W. W. Norton & Company, Inc. Used by permission of W. W. Norton and Company, Inc.

"Lightning" from *American Primitive* by Mary Oliver. Copyright © 1983 by Mary Oliver. Used by permission of Little Brown and Company.

Carl Phillips, "Steeple," in *Reconnaissance: Poems* (New York: Farrar, Straus and Giroux, 2015).

1   2   3   4   5   6   7   8   9

Library of Congress Cataloging-in-Publication Data

Names: Babka, Susie Paulik, author.
Title: Through the dark field : the incarnation through an aesthetics of vulnerability / Susan Paulik Babka.
Description: Collegeville, Minnesota : Liturgical Press, 2016. | "A Michael Glazier book."
Identifiers: LCCN 2016007175 (print) | LCCN 2016024256 (ebook) | ISBN 9780814680735 (pbk.) | ISBN 9780814680988 (ebook)
Subjects: LCSH: Christianity and art. | Art—Philosophy. | Aesthetics. | Incarnation. | Suffering—Religious aspects—Christianity.
Classification: LCC BR115.A8 B33 2016 (print) | LCC BR115.A8 (ebook) | DDC 261.5/7—dc23
LC record available at https://lccn.loc.gov/2016007175

Contents

For my father, Lawrence John Paulik (May 16, 1942–June 7, 2016)
In gratitude for your passion for justice and holiness

Every fragile beauty, every perfect forgotten sentence,
you grieve their going away,
but that is not how it is.
Where they come from never goes dry. It is an always flowing spring.
—Rumi

In remembrance of the four other cyclists who were also killed
on June 7, 2016:
Tony Nelson, Debra Bradley, Melissa Fevig Hughes,
and Suzanne Sippel
To the man whose actions took their lives: your life is forever tied
to the lives and memories of those who remain. Through our grief,
we labor toward compassion. We seek to widen our hearts.

Out beyond ideas of wrongdoing and rightdoing,
there is a field.
I will meet you there.
When the soul lies down in that grass,
the world is too full to talk about.
—Rumi

Lightning

The oaks shone
gaunt gold
on the lip
of the storm before
the wind rose,
the shapeless mouth
opened and began
its five-hour howl;
the lights
went out fast, branches
sidled over
the pitch of the roof, bounced
into the yard
that grew black
within minutes, except
for the lightning—the landscape
bulging forth like a quick
lesson in creation, then
thudding away. Inside,
as always,
it was hard to tell
fear from excitement:
how sensual
the lightning's
poured stroke! and still,
what a fire and what a risk!
As always the body
wants to hide,
wants to flow toward it—strives
to balance while
fear shouts,
excitement shouts, back
and forth—each
bolt a burning river
tearing like escape through the dark
field of the other.

—Mary Oliver[1]

1. Mary Oliver, "Lightning," from *American Primitive* (1983), in *New and Selected Poems* (Boston: Beacon Press, 1992), 146–47.

INTRODUCTION

The Landscape of the New

When I say that it is possible to encounter God in your age as in mine, I mean God really and truly, the God of incomprehensibility, the God past all grasp, the mystery beyond speech, the darkness that is light only to those who let themselves be swallowed by it unconditionally, the God who is now beyond all names. But equally it was just this God, no other, that I experienced as the God who descends to us, who comes near to us, in whose incomprehensible fire we do not in fact burn up, but rather come to be for the first time, and of eternal value. The ineffable God promises himself to us; and in this promise of his ineffability we become, we live, we are loved and we are of eternal value; through God, if we allow ourselves to be taken up by God, we are not destroyed but given to ourselves truly for the first time. The vain and idle creature becomes infinitely important, inexpressibly great and beautiful, because God endows the creature with Godself.

—Karl Rahner, "Ignatius of Loyola Speaks to a Modern Jesuit"[1]

1. Karl Rahner, "Ignatius of Loyola Speaks to a Modern Jesuit," in *Ignatius of Loyola*, trans. Rosaleen Ockenden (London: Collins, 1979), 17. I borrowed the "God-past-all-grasp" from the translation by Philip Endean in *Karl Rahner: Spiritual Writings* (Maryknoll, NY: Orbis Books, 2007), who adds the footnote, "*Unbegreiflich* and its cognates are generally translated in this selection with expressions centered on 'past all grasp.' Rahner is drawing on the vocabulary here of the German mystics; it seems appropriate for an English translator to use a phrase of Hopkins: 'past all/Grasp God'—("The Wreck of the *Deutschland*," stanza 32)." See p. 37n2.

I'm eighteen and in my first theology class at the University of Notre Dame. We're on the second floor of the Cushing Hall of Engineering, the classroom a dismal, stone gray, the northern Indiana sky stone gray as well, through a wall of grid windows, another in a string of cloudless, blueless, sunless gray days common to the Midwest; we're reading the work of Karl Rahner (1904–1984), and I am absolutely enthralled with the words above. Meeting God in a place without the constraints and formalism of theology, without the constraints and formalism of religion, without the pain of belonging to a church that denies women ordination: this was the "darkness" I sought, in a hunger for what Rahner understood as "grace." Gazing out the window, I longed to be "swallowed" by this darkness, to be lost in the "incomprehensible fire," his words sparking like embers against the gray.

Although I was not fully aware of it at the time, Rahner was a kindred spirit—one who all his life considered himself a pilgrim, who longed for God, for Mystery, for Beauty, without satisfaction. Today, decades later, I still find him to be a true visionary, one who offers a rare awareness that humility is necessary in any theological assertion, and while the multidimensionality and complexity of earthly reality is often terrifying, it is still the arena of what he called God's grace, of God's "self-gift." For Rahner, God's openness to us creatures—essential to the identification of God as personal—only makes sense when it is met with our openness to God in God's incomprehensibility. Rahner changed the perspective with which I had viewed God. "God" is symbolic for the beginning of humanity constituted in its dynamism toward an infinite horizon of inquiry: here "God" may be *both* personal *and* impersonal, emptiness *and* being, possible *and* impossible, without restriction or categorization. Here the void, the nothing, the absent, melts the conceptual. For all his dense and formal "serious" theological writing, Rahner was at heart a poet and lifelong lover of poetry, someone willingly familiar with the darkness, the abyss, the void, that which is usually an illegitimate source of knowing. For Rahner,

> [T]his monstrous, silent void, which we experience as death, is in truth filled with the originating mystery we call God, with God's light and with God's love that received all things and gives

all things; and when then out of this pathless mystery the face
of Jesus, the blessed one, appears to us and this specific reality
is the divine surpassing of all that we truly assume regarding
the past-all-graspness of the pathless God.[2]

The void is a meeting place where life emerges from emptiness. It
is a place of incarnation, where conventional boundaries are eliminated, a dark field where things grow. Such darkness is the locus of
detachment, the place in which there is no direct path to the God
beyond our hold, the God who will eternally remain as elusive to
grasp as a beam of light.

Why was I so enthralled with these words that, decades later, the
memory of discovering them is still so vivid? I wouldn't call the
classroom encounter with Rahner's thought, that day or any other,
a "religious experience" as described by Rudolf Otto: there was neither the "burst in sudden eruption up from the depths of the soul
with spasms and convulsions," nor the "intoxicated frenzy," nor the
"hushed, trembling, speechless humility of the creature."[3] Otto's
attempt to bring Kantian philosophy into conversation with nonver-
bal religious experience doesn't describe what Rahner meant to me
that day, or what his thought still means. Rather, the attraction to
Rahner's thought was more emotionally subdued, confirming instincts about my faith that I had not yet articulated. Or, more ac-
curately, it was an intellectual lightning bolt, as Mary Oliver's poem
describes above, in which there is fire and risk when radically new
ideas appear on the landscape.

The landscape in which the "new" appears is dark, resolutely
unfamiliar. A field on a moonless night, a pathless field, an expanse
of shadow. Stepping onto this dark field is a risk: such is its exhila-
ration, as the naturalist John Muir found when he climbed trees to
witness lightning storms. Willing to risk the drastically, even dangerously new is the way the discipline of academic theology—the critical

---

2. Karl Rahner, quoted by Ronald Rolheiser in "Reflections on Death," November 6, 2005, http://ronrolheiser.com/reflections-on-death/#.Vd4mrPlViko.
3. Rudolf Otto, *The Idea of the Holy*, trans. John W. Harvey (Oxford: Oxford
University Press, 1950), 12–13.

evaluation of belief—will not only survive but also thrive in the present age, an age in which deconstruction, demythologization, and the tearing down of presumptions, assumptions, and centuries-old power structures, seems to negate everything "sacred."

The fear that drives this age, in which we see more insidious growth in racism, homophobia, xenophobia, and sexism and increasing retreat into rigid ideologies and religious fundamentalism, is a self-protective fear investing in certainty. The "certainty" that perpetuates self-protection is defined through a finality and security that the changing world will never afford us. Yet we still pursue the illusion that we can be certain about anything, which often means rejecting the risk of the strange and the stranger, the new, the Other. The self-protective cloak of certainty mitigates fear of the strange; but it will not prevent fear from manifesting in violent self-protection. The Enlightenment notion of reason as an instrument of power led to the identification of truth and certainty; claims to certainty became the way to justify acts that perpetuate the apparatus of power. Violence often masks the fear of the unknown, and so also the openness to truth, taking refuge in the futile attempt to be invulnerable. Indeed, violence is defined in the refusal to be vulnerable, the refusal of any form of weakness or poverty which often justifies itself as "self-defense." Violence against the stranger, the "Other," rears from the misguided attempt to protect the self at all costs, to maintain the security of the individual. Violence results from the desire for certainty outmaneuvering the openness required by the initial stages of intellectual or personal encounter.

Encounter requires a self-emptying of the concepts which led to it, otherwise there is no encounter. Concepts, and the words that house them, are merely placeholders as we grope through this field, markers on the pilgrimage, the scrawled graffiti of those who have been here before. Wanderers who placed symbols in chalk on the fence posts. We need to learn how to inquire and not expect definite answers in return, not to expect anything but another placeholder, another marker for the way. A temporary sign that can be abandoned for another. We need to learn to accept our essential vulnerability before the incomprehensible Other, to sleep in the open air, without shelter, to take the risk that a predator will come, to live with a borderless field or space (*lieu*) in which a belief, affirmation, or question can appear as "other than itself to itself," as Jacques Derrida described, where difference is unearthed in a glimpse and disappears again.

The metaphors and phrases Rahner uses—"darkness," "fire," "swallowed up"—are more common to biblical language than the language of academic theology; these images constituted a welcome moment in the gray dullness of that day. Perhaps these phrases touched a poetic nerve in me, at a vulnerable time in life, so that the thrill of discovering them became itself religious. Rahner's genius navigates both the passionate language of faith (of *kerygma*, proclamation) and the formal language of academic theology; such demonstrates his belief that all theological language begins and ends in the Holy Mystery of God, the *reductio in mysterium*, the return to the mystery. Indeed, the chance and privilege of studying theology was (and still is) an opportunity that of its nature awaits the unexpected. Hopes for it. Having recently finished Anselm's *Cur Deus Homo* in that theology class, I wanted an interruption in the monotony of stale ideas about the incarnation as a substitutionary debt to God for human sin. Perhaps the assertion "Jesus died so our sins could be forgiven" should finally be emptied into a repository for desiccated doctrines. It is a tired theodicy—a justification of catastrophe as associated with the goodness of God—that belongs to a time when God was thought to control the events of history, when God was viewed as the One to Be Appeased. The "God who descends to us, who comes near to us" would not will, expect, require, or need Jesus' death to forgive human sin. Perhaps Anselm's God of serfdom, the heavenly Lord of legal recompense, is the God who died when Nietzsche's madman announces his glorious obituary in the town square, and over a century later we are still "not ready." The plusses and minuses that pull and push in language that approaches the bearing and being of God gives theology life, emerging from a fissure in the argument.

This book investigates the doctrine of the incarnation as an expressive poetics or symbolic language that indicates the emptiness by which God is "God"—by which God may be glimpsed but never grasped—a divine kenosis or self-emptying that is continually poured out for the fulfillment of the Other in the sphere of time and space.

God's emptiness is an openness to the material world, a devotion to the world's vulnerability that makes the created world the embodiment or enfleshment, the incarnation, of the divine life. This emptiness and embodiment is glimpsed in the person of Jesus and is enlivened in Jesus' appeal that we see the divine in all who suffer. Sensibility to the vulnerability of the suffering Other is therefore the gateway to the meaning of the doctrine of the incarnation. Kenosis is then necessary on both "sides" of the divine equation: the creator creates by withdrawing, in the thought of Rabbi Isaac Luria,[4] and the divine becomes incarnate and enters fragility, suffering, and mortality by self-emptying. Our human subjectivity is constituted by our openness—understood as exposure or vulnerability—toward the suffering Other, according to Emmanuel Levinas. The withdrawal or contraction of "self" is also an indispensable prelude to both the making of and the experience of art, requiring that we contract in order to communicate and withdraw in order to witness.

Chapter 1 relies on the thought of Maurice Blanchot and Levinas to propose an aesthetics of vulnerability. Because I consider "aesthetics" as both a category of experience and as necessarily tied to the arts, I explore Blanchot's relationship between art and the void, between art and emptiness, in terms of the power of art to summon the sacred, as well as the failure of art—which is somehow also its accomplishment *as* art—to contain the sacred. Levinas was close friends with Blanchot but did not explicitly share Blanchot's devotion to art; Levinas's thought is instead devoted to critiquing the program of philosophy which did not prevent the horror of the Shoah. Levinas cautions against anything that distracts from the primordial sensibility that directs us for the Other. Since vulnerability is the locus of the relation to the Other, denial of this vulnerability in a vain attempt to overcome it breeds violence. Taken together, Blanchot and Levinas offer a wider scope of the sensibility to the outside, to the void, to the alterity of the Other and the consequent responsibility to the Other. In the exposure of vulnerability we may articulate the self-emptying that assists what it means to say "God becomes incarnate"

---

4. See Maurice Blanchot, *The Writing of the Disaster*, trans. Ann Smock (Lincoln, NE: University of Nebraska Press, 1995), 13.

or "the Word became flesh" (John 1:14). Chapter 2 considers Christology through an aesthetics of vulnerability, in an effort to reimagine the metaphysical categories in which the doctrine of the incarnation initially developed. The ability of theology to respond to catastrophe in the present age means undermining "onto-theology," the classical metaphysical logic on which traditional theology relies, specifically the substance ontologies that have so identified Western thought that it was difficult for even Einstein to accept the implications of his own theories of relativity. Onto-theology is the naming of God as the "highest Being" abstracted from the material world, the God of the "omnis"—the omnipotent God of theodicy, for example, for whom catastrophic suffering is justified, or the immutable God who is remote to the suffering of the poor. Because I see visual culture and the arts as sources of the interruptions necessary to heighten sensibility to the vulnerable, chapter 3 studies issues in theological aesthetics, including the commodification of art and religion, in an effort to argue for the integrity of art and its value irrespective of the marketplace; chapter 4 traces the meaning of art, beauty, and the imagination as resources for theology.

We will then apply two distinct motifs in visual art as a resource for considering divine incarnation: the first motif, described in chapter 5, is the *Gnadenstuhl*. The term *Gnadenstuhl*, translated as "Throne of Grace" or "Mercy Seat," is thought to have originated from Martin Luther's 1534 translation of both Exodus 25:21-22 and Hebrews 4:16 in reference to the lid on the Ark of the Covenant. The original Hebrew term is *kapporeth*, meaning "to cover," not only as a noun, as in "lid," but also, based on the Hebrew root from which it was derived, as a verb, meaning "to pardon," or "to atone for," as in "to cover a debt." Thus, although it can be translated as simply "cover," *kapporeth* is used exclusively in the Hebrew Scriptures to refer to the "Mercy Seat" which resides over the ark, the throne of God's dwelling. The term *Gnadenstuhl* was then used to describe the medieval motif in visual art that depicts God the Father enthroned, supporting the crucified Son in his lap or on the cross. The Spirit, appearing in the form of a dove, either joins the Father and Son or is among them, elsewhere in the composition. The *Gnadenstuhl* motif is characterized by an insistence that the three divine persons each participate in the crucifixion event, although not in the same way. Only the second person of the trinity dies, but the tangible sorrow often found on the Father's face expresses the anguish of the loss of a child, and the placement of the Spirit often echoes either the bond between the Father and the Son or their separation at the moment of the Son's death. Also present in compositions of the *Gnadenstuhl* motif is symbolism referring to the shared grief of heaven and earth; much of this is derived from Jewish throne-chariot or *Merkabah* mysticism found in the visions of Ezekiel, Isaiah, Daniel, and the author of Revelation. The earliest known appearance of the motif is in a missal illumination from Cambrai in the twelfth century; the *Gnadenstuhl* soon becomes part of the Gothic renovation of Saint-Denis in Paris, travels through the Netherlands and Germany, and becomes a popular feature of the Florentine Renaissance, as in the phenomenal Masaccio *Trinity* at Santa Maria Novella, ca. 1427.

Chapter 6 will consider the doctrine of the incarnation through the dynamic interplay between the presence and absence of the sacred, reflected in art created during a time in which figuration was assumed to have been exhausted in its relevance—the Abstract Expressionism of the mid-twentieth century. Associated with artists such as Jackson Pollock, Mark Rothko, and Barnett Newman in the beginning and Ad Reinhart, Robert Motherwell, and Helen Frankenthaler soon after, this movement took place principally in the United States from the mid-1940s into the early 1970s. The movement away from representation reveals a way to envision and express the radically new in the wake of the failures of modernity: the tragedies of technology and industry, the wars and environmental degradation. Abstract art abandons previously held expectations of what art is for, reconceiving color, shape, form, and perspective in startling ways, which is what theology must also risk. Theology may regard abstract art as participating in new forms of inquiry, which in turn shapes new appreciations of the meaning of incarnation in a world marked by catastrophe and the absence of God.

Standing before a work from another century, or a recent work more obviously abstract—any work born of the particular perception of the artist, the lens through which the artist sees the world and which by definition I do not share—provides immediate alterity in the space of the unfamiliar: the "dark field" in which I must rethink what I think I know and be willing to discard what I think I believe. This is what Richard Kearney calls "an aesthetic openness to the gracious and strange," and what André Gide called a "disposition to receive *(une disposition á l'accueil),*" since religions are "imaginary works" that depend on the symbol, story, and image to witness the transcendent.[5] The power of the experience of art, whether creating or appreciating it, offers the occasion for the doing of theology, the articulation of the experience of the divine, toward a "space" in which "God is the sphere of which the center is everywhere and the circumference is nowhere."[6]

5. Richard Kearney, *Anatheism: Returning to God after God* (New York: Columbia University Press, 2010), 14.

6. Georges Poulet, *The Metamorphoses of the Circle*, trans. Carley Dawson and Elliot Coleman (Baltimore: Johns Hopkins University Press, 1966), xi; see also Kevin Hart, *The Dark Gaze: Maurice Blanchot and the Sacred* (Chicago: The University of Chicago Press, 2004), 2.

CHAPTER ONE

Theology, Vulnerability, and Art as the Consciousness of Grief

We live with a deep secret that sometimes we know, and then not.

—Rumi

Theology is constantly striving for an appropriate grammar in which to express the inexpressible. Language is then both the tool and the torture of theologians; we are aware of the need for deconstruction and revision of creedal and doctrinal formulae and also retrieval of the forgotten corners of the tradition, as much as we are aware of the eventual ineffectiveness of any statements we make. Such absurdity in pursuit of saying something regarding the being/life/identity/possibility of God does not deter us. Theologians tend to be a loquacious bunch. My friend and colleague Mary Doak tells the story of bringing her young daughter Sarah to one of her classes and then afterward asking Sarah what she thought. Sarah replied with her usual directness: "All you do is talk! Blah-blah-blah, *God*, blah-blah-blah." That's actually about right, for any of us who make a living talking about God. There are times in class when I lecture and am suddenly hit with the realization, as Thomas Aquinas is supposed to have realized, that this talk is all so much straw. But I keep talking; my blah-blah-blahs also punctuated occasionally with "God." So I am grateful for Derrida's insight that writing is anguish, "the restricted passageway of speech against which all possible

1

meanings push together, preventing each other's emergence"[1]—I am grateful that I will never be responsible for the last word, and that this small effort will be unsaid by better thinkers.

What gives theology (and most theologians) pause to silence, however, is catastrophe;[2] when faced with the horrors of the Shoah, the despair of Syrian refugees and thousands drowned when boats capsize with the weight of the hopeful, the devastation of AIDS and the resurgence of Ebola in West Africa: theology is appropriately rendered mute until lamentation can be channeled into expression. But "the disaster ruins everything, all the while leaving everything intact,"[3] wrote Maurice Blanchot. Etymologically, Blanchot reminds us, "disaster" refers to the separation from the star, from the compass of security. Negotiating the geography of expression and silence when faced with devastation is beyond mere theology or any "God-talk," and so beyond the limits of language. It seems we need more ways to enter these realities and more ways to impart what we witness. How might we do theology in such a way that the disaster, the catastrophe, leaves nothing intact, detaching our security from the star?

Through the artistic drive, we may explore what it means to consider God in detachment from the secure categories of the past, in the wake of disaster. Blanchot notes that it isn't just "knowledge of the disaster, but knowledge as disaster" that "disorients the absolute," displacing what masquerades as knowledge.[4] Art's detachment from certainty or objectivity may be why Theodor Adorno cautiously recommended "the idea that art may be the only remaining medium

1. Jacques Derrida, "Writing and Difference: An Essay on the Thought of Emmanuel Levinas," *Writing and Difference*, trans. Alan Bass (Chicago: The University of Chicago Press, 1978), 9.

2. J. Matthew Ashley writes that it is the *Leidensfrage*, the "question of catastrophic, massive and systemic suffering" that provides the context for Metz's later work. Based on the usage by Ashley and Metz, I have adopted the term "catastrophic suffering." Ashley, in *Interruptions: Mysticism, Politics, and Theology in the Work of Johann Baptist Metz* (Notre Dame, IN: University of Notre Dame Press, 1998), vii.

3. Maurice Blanchot, *The Writing of the Disaster*, trans. Ann Smock (Lincoln, NE: University of Nebraska Press, 1995), 1.

4. Ibid., 3–4.

of truth in an age of incomprehensible terror and suffering."[5] The motivation to navigate meaning, to create and express experience through the arts can be argued as concurrent with the religious impulse in human beings: both art and religion require an abstract or transcendent dimension of mental activity willing to examine what is known or believed in new forms, willing to turn what is experienced into metaphor and myth, symbol and story. The process of creating a work of art, and the process of envisioning the invisible, involves submission to the imagination, the muscle in the mind responsible for creating the images by which we shape the world.

The viewer of art, on the other hand, is a witness to this newly disclosed reality. Art assumes a sacred character when the artist releases a new way of seeing or hearing something that touches us in terms of the weight of existence, even if in the perception of art we cannot articulate it as such. We may feel moved before a work of art but be unsure as to why. That's all right, of course; art is also about enjoyment, appealing to our aesthetic intelligence, to what "pleases the senses"; etymologically, this is the original definition of "aesthetics," perceived sentiment. Aesthetics is also a critical, philosophical stance that addresses the appeal to the senses, attempting to articulate the often indescribable experience of something beautiful, or moving, or even something ugly and repellant. Joseph Parry and Mark Wrathall write that art functions as "A way of directing us to important phenomena and helping us to understand them in their own terms."[6] Since sight is often the most immediate sense experience we have, visual art and culture will be our primary source of experience in this book, but we will rely on poetry as well. "Visual art, especially painting," note Parry and Wrathall, "has a particular power to bring us into contact with the world that we study and in which we study because it can convey what the world itself gives us to perceive 'in full innocence,' as Merleau-Ponty famously declared."[7]

---

5. Theodor Adorno, *Aesthetic Theory*, ed. Gretel Adorno and Rolf Tiedemann, trans. C. Lenhardt (London: Routledge, 1984), 27.

6. Joseph D. Parry and Mark Wrathall, introduction to *Art and Phenomenology*, ed. Joseph D. Parry (London: Routledge, 2011), 1.

7. Ibid., 2.

This "innocence," or way that the world gives, is also a matter of its vulnerability, which is symbolized in the naked exposure of one to another. If we consider the sensibility required to appreciate what is outside the self, the bodily sensibility by which we "take in" the outside world, then the aesthetic is the faculty of appreciation and recognition through sensibility, and here particularly through the sensitivity by which we may appreciate the vulnerability and alterity of the Other. The Other, and the art object, must be considered in their alterity, in their integrity, independent of the interpretation I may want to impose, otherwise I disregard this vulnerability, and perhaps even the Other or the art object itself. Although the phenomena of a painting's color, texture, and line work together to present a face, "a painting doesn't merely represent reality"—even if the technique used is photographic realism, as in the portraits of faces by Chuck Close—rather, paintings "re-stage the meanings that make up and structure our most basic experience as human perceivers in the world,"[8] such that within this re-staging is a creative and responsive disturbance of the ego-based tendency to gaze only at my own reflection of the world. As Levinas argues, the Other—and I would add, the artwork—are interruptions, ruptures of the narcissistic response toward which we usually yield. Our aesthetic sensibility is our openness to appreciating the vulnerable Other, as well as our openness to the creative discourse that occurs through the arts.

A Double Mouthful of Silence: Toward an Aesthetics of Vulnerability

Great art discloses *more* than pleasure, and *more* than sentiment; it is, however, notoriously difficult to name or say what the "more" is. This is because great art has always been connected to the sacred or ineffable dimension of the weight of human existence. The French critical essayist and experimental novelist Maurice Blanchot (1907–2003) comes close to describing this "more," this intensity of the experience of existence, in *The Space of Literature*:

8. Ibid., 3. See also Martin Heidegger, *On the Essence of Truth*, in Martin Heidegger, *Basic Writings*, ed. D. F. Krell (San Francisco: Harper Collins, 1993).

[T]he brilliance, the explosive decision—this presence or "light-ning moment"—let us acknowledge that such a dazzling affirma-tion arises neither from the assurance of stable truths nor from the clarity of the day which we have conquered and where living and being are accomplished in actions whose limits are familiar to us. The work brings neither certitude nor clarity. It assures us of nothing, nor does it shed any light upon itself. . . . Just as every strong work abducts us from ourselves, from our ac-customed strength, makes us weak and as if annihilated, so the work is not strong with respect to what it is. It has no power, it is impotent: not because it is simply the obverse of possibility's various forms, but rather because it designates a region where impossibility is no longer deprivation, but affirmation.[9]

Blanchot was raised in a devout Catholic family but identified as an atheist, primarily, it seems, because of exasperation with institutional religion's totalizing and absolutist tendencies.[10] But the vestiges of Catholicism's sacramental imagination may have remained a tacit background to his musings on sacred realities in the wake of the modern experience of the absence of God, even if he himself did not explicitly make the connection. He was fascinated by "the inhuman, the nonpresent, the divine that is present and activating . . . and yet is also hidden and as if unrecognized."[11] As you may guess from the above passage, he is famous for making positive and negative state-ments about the same thing at the same time: here the technique comes close to illuminating the experience of great art as disclosing

9. Maurice Blanchot, *The Space of Literature*, trans. Ann Smock (Lincoln, NE: University of Nebraska Press, 1989), 221–22.

10. Blanchot understood that atheism of the postwar era was devoid of the means to overcome the fascist tendencies in religion. Despite his rejection of Catholicism, and religion in general, Blanchot appreciated Judaism as a religion that disdains idolatry and tries to overcome superstition. He sees in Judaism "the recognition of an ethical order manifesting itself in respect for the Law"; Blanchot writes that the reason Hitler wished to eliminate the Jews was because the Jews consider myth as subordinate to the ethical. See Blanchot, "Intellectu-als Under Scrutiny: An Outline for Thought," in *The Blanchot Reader*, ed. Michael Holland (Oxford: Blackwell, 1995), 221.

11. Blanchot, *The Space of Literature*, 229.

a sacred reality—a reality "set apart and forbidden," according to Emile Durkheim—that is both an affirmation and a negation at once, strong and weak, possible and impossible, each interpenetrating the other. Hence, it seems Blanchot realized that the experience of the sacred, and specifically the experience of the sacred through art, gives way to an appreciation of the non-dual (neither one nor many but not-two[12]) or mutually interdependent poles of paradox found in Buddhist thought. Blanchot reminds us that we are assured of nothing, whether in the possible communication of the written text or the plastic arts. But through these, we have the designation of the affirmation of the void, the impossible emptiness of existence that permeates, limits, and also liberates the human condition. Only by attending to the void, to the unknowing and unsaying necessary to any discussion of the sacred, can we possibly approach the parallel realities of art and religion. Shouldering the void contains the possibility of self-annihilation when we are confronted with alterity, with otherness, with the "blessed unforeseen."

Art, Blanchot muses above, brings nothing that is certain, reassuring, permanent, or stable to the intellect or the emotions: its greatness, its endurance, and its allure are in its ability to shift the ground beneath us, to hint at a transcendence of limits within the limits of matter (canvas, pigment, bronze, marble) and time. This transcendence that is also the void, "a region where impossibility is no longer deprivation, but affirmation," refers to "infinity" for Blanchot and his close friend, the Jewish Lithuanian philosopher Emmanuel Levinas (1906–1995). "God" represents this infinity, this "Holy Mystery" for Rahner because "God" is transcendent and not the object of my interpretation or the imposition of my perception; the same is true for Levinas. The God beyond the narrow confines of my desire is transcendent Other; but I also desire that which is beyond the confines of my desire. I desire to be swallowed by that which I cannot name. I yearn for what is Other than these bound-

---

12. I am relying on Paul Knitter's use of Raimon Panikkar's way of expressing non-dualism: "God and creation are not two, but neither are they one," Knitter, *Without Buddha, I Could Not Be a Christian* (London: Oneworld, 2013), 22.

aries, lost in the dark field, a void in which to be passive before the unknown.

Such is also the case for the artist Mark Rothko. Rothko writes that what distinguishes "art" from an "illustration" pertains to matters "heroic": art "must provide the implications of infinity to any situation."[13] Rothko's color field paintings thrive in the boundary-less boundaries of ethereal rectangles and the limits of the canvas. They are fields of color both brilliant and brooding, both stable and wandering. Rothko applies "heroic" to art frequently in his writings; for this he relies on Friedrich Nietzsche, one of the first modern thinkers who had the courage to be untethered from the modern illusions of both permanence and progress. Nietzsche credits the Greeks with translating tragedy into an art form; without art to make sense of tragedy, Rothko observes, life would have been unendurable for the Greeks, as it would be for us. Nietzsche, writes Rothko, understood that "the entire function of art is to produce an intelligible basis for the endurability of man's insecurity."[14] Indeed, the only values Nietzsche could tolerate in a world he saw as uninhibited by objective meaning are artistic and aesthetic values, which celebrate life when we are confronted with the banality of death.

According to Kevin Hart, Blanchot draws out Nietzsche's aphorism, "We possess art lest we perish of the truth" toward understanding art as that which "takes us to the abyss where truth can find no traction."[15] "Truth," in Nietzsche's aphorism, refers to what he understands to be a characteristically Christian emphasis on a spiritual realm *opposed* to a material realm. Christians have made the mistake of staking a claim on the spiritual as though it is not only *contained* in the revelation of Jesus Christ but also prioritized above and against the material world. For Nietzsche, art is to be valued because it maintains the human commitment to the sensuous, dangerous, unpredictable world. Hart reminds us that here, art reveals

13. Mark Rothko, *The Artist's Reality: Philosophies of Art*, ed. Christopher Rothko (New Haven, CT: Yale University Press, 2004), 95.

14. Ibid., 36.

15. Kevin Hart, *The Dark Gaze: Maurice Blanchot and the Sacred* (Chicago: The University of Chicago Press, 2004), 65.

the space of impossibility for Blanchot.[16] The "impossible" refers "to what is 'outside' the world, and it expresses the profundity of this outside bereft of intimacy and of repose. . . . [A]rt has its origin, not in another world but *in the other of all worlds*."[17] Hence, what Blanchot referred to as the *dehors*, the "outside," the "impossible," the "other" of all worlds, is the one we do not imagine or expect, but one which we are urged to have the courage to risk. The "outside" is a risk because it challenges the boundaries of what is safe, or easy, such when we cling to dualistic thinking in an effort to escape complexity and nuance. Blanchot, however, asserts, "Art is not religion . . . but in the time of distress which is ours, the time when the gods are missing, the time of absence and exile, art is justified, for it is the intimacy of this distress: the effort to make manifest, through this image, the error of the imaginary, and eventually the ungraspable, forgotten truth which hides behind this error."[18] Art, then, is a means to make tragedy *endurable* as Rothko and Nietzsche attempted to do, because art emerges in a time when the gods are missing in the midst of tragedy, when the star has become separated. Making tragedy "endurable," however, must never be to justify it: tragedy is neither defensible as a means to redemption nor as a necessary conduit to great art, whether in the mental torture Van Gogh experienced, or in the depression that plagued Rothko for most of his life and finally claimed him at the end. Ultimately, Rothko could not make his own tragedy endurable, but his art leaves us with this hope.

The space in which we may be open to the impossible, open to the void as permeating existence, refers to the condition and intention of art, even if it means imagining a world in which we live in proximity to the sacred rather than close to the distraction, willing

16. "What he calls 'the space of literature' is the place, or better, nonplace where discontinuity reigns and everything we encounter is strange, and it is in questioning literature and approaching this space that we are led to figure being human by way of the impossible as well as the possible." Hart, *The Dark Gaze*, 8.

17. Blanchot, *The Space of Literature*, 74. Emphasis mine.

18. Ibid., 83.

to risk what Blanchot called the "consciousness of unhappiness," faithful to the "demands of grief."[19] For Levinas,

> Opening is the stripping of the skin exposed to wound and outrage. Opening is the vulnerability of a skin offered in wound and outrage beyond all that can show itself, beyond all that of essence of being can expose itself to understanding and celebration. In sensibility "is uncovered," is exposed a nude more naked than the naked of skin that, form and beauty, inspires the plastic arts; nakedness of a skin offered to contact, to the caress that always . . . is suffering from the suffering of the other.[20]

For Levinas, subjectivity emerges through openness to vulnerability, a willingness to be exposed to what is outside my ego. Living in proximity to the sacred, to the alterity that is a trace of the transcendence of God, means living in proximity to the grief that comes when we shun distraction and escape, when we enter the pain that vibrates from every headline and "Butcher's Bill" of catastrophe. Entering the pain of another, a willingness to live with a consciousness of the grief of another, is a willingness to make oneself vulnerable and fragile for the sake of another, a voluntary poverty. Such a voluntary vulnerability, awareness of the openness to the Other, reverses the violence of triumphalism, imperialism, absolutism, and control. Living in proximity to the sacred is living in proximity to the work that must be done to meet this pain and commit to being agents of, and so responsible for, its transformation. Art is the consciousness of grief because grief is the activity of witness to suffering, the activity of loss, the despair of the disrepair of the world; "[art] describes the situation of one who has lost himself, who can no longer say 'me,' who in the same movement has lost the world, the truth of the world, and belongs to exile, to the time of distress when, as Hölderlin says, the gods are no longer and are not yet,"[21] writes Blanchot. Theology must adopt the weight of the consciousness of

19. Ibid., 74.

20. Emmanuel Levinas, *Humanism of the Other*, trans. Nidra Poller (Urbana, IL, and Chicago: University of Illinois Press, 2006), 63.

21. Blanchot, *The Space of Literature*, 74.

grief if it is to retain its integrity and critical function. The weight of this world, the heft of its suffering, must especially accompany those privileged to benefit from this world.

Derrida writes that mortality binds us all "to the experience of compassion, to the possibility of sharing the possibility of this non-power, the possibility of this impossibility, the anguish of this vulnerability and the vulnerability of this anguish."[22] Vulnerability is the first experience of being alive, and it is the last experience of being alive: it is the essential component of compassion, because no one born into mortality will escape suffering: "From the moment of sensibility, the subject is for the other. . .nothing is more passive than this challenge prior to my freedom, this pre-original challenge, this sincerity."[23]

Because great art often accompanies great suffering, it becomes necessary in witness to great art that we be vulnerable witnesses to catastrophic suffering. In other words, none of us will ever feel deeply the art or pain of another unless we are willing to deny the imposition of the ego upon it. Art brings us closer to the reality of the suffering Other insofar as we are each willing to be open to the alterity of the Other, to refrain from dismissing what is offered, to allow it to affect us. Such a kenosis or emptying of self happens when one is vulnerable before the Other, laid bare, refraining from the tyranny of the imposition of ego—the "in my opinion"—that tends to be the first impulse in the presence of the new. From the standpoint of *witness*, great art encourages the faculty of awareness and the cultivation of perceptual acuity when one withdraws the self; similarly, from the standpoint of *creativity*, great art occurs when an artist avoids the

---

22. Jacques Derrida, "The Animal That Therefore I Am (More to Follow)," trans. David Wills, in *Signature Derrida*, ed. Jay Williams (Chicago: The University of Chicago Press, 2008), 410. Derrida writes this essay to displace the anthropocentrism that occupies Western discourse; I use him here in a similar vein, since a recovery of vulnerability is essential to displacing all oppressive power structures. For an excellent investigation of this essay regarding non-human animal rights, see Aaron S. Gross, "Sacrificing Animals and Being a Mensch," chap. 5 in *The Question of the Animal and Religion: Theoretical Stakes, Practical Implications* (New York: Columbia University Press, 2015).

23. Levinas, *Humanism of the Other*, 64.

affection, sensibility, a passivity more passive still than any passivity, an irrecuperable time, an unassemblable diachrony of patience, an exposedness always to be exposed the more, an exposure to expressing, and thus to saying, thus to giving."[28]

It is this vulnerability that I read into Blanchot's "demands of grief." As aesthetic markers, the expressive potential of the arts provides a way to articulate the consciousness of vulnerability. Thus vulnerability gives rise to the signification, which Levinas names as prior to being, the "hither side of or beyond essence."[29] The hither side—the "outside"—is the other of all worlds, beyond the tidy claims I have staked in my attempts at individuality. For Levinas, vulnerability is "a defecting or defeat of the ego's identity. And this, pushed to the limit, is sensibility, sensibility as the subjectivity of the subject. It is a substitution for another, one in place of another, expiation."[30] Such an excess of sensibility is where the aesthetic may play, where vulnerability makes the expression in language and image possible. Hence, the exposure of one to another is the necessary precondition of the "signifyingness of signs": "The plot of proximity and communication is not a modality of cognition. . . . It is in the risky uncovering of oneself, in sincerity, the breaking up of inwardness and the abandon of all shelter, exposure to traumas, vulnerability."[31] When one can dismantle the shelter of the ego, art and language are possible; disclosing this vulnerability is always conscious of, and so "faithful to," the demands of grief.

In turn, I am concerned to emphasize that the viewing of great art prepares one to dismantle the shelter of the ego by altering one's perception and offering a glimpse of alterity "embodied," so to speak. I am far from the first to consider art's ability to alter perception, but just as Levinas argues that language and communication are possible when the self is emptied, emerging from the primordial vulnerability that is openness to the Other, we should remember the potential of art to empty the self of what it thinks it knows or understands when

28. Ibid., 50.
29. Ibid., 14.
30. Ibid., 15.
31. Ibid., 48.

art offers a new dimension of reality. Art negotiates between the vulnerability that is primordial openness and the transformation of the subject that takes place when one is laid bare before the experience. There is therefore a profusion of meaning on either side of art's equation—both audience/witness and artist—a profusion that may be described as "emptiness" through the lens of what Buddhism indicates as *sunyata*, a term which describes the interrelatedness of all things. "Emptiness" points to interdependency out of which all things are manifest. That the divine could be glimpsed through the complex paradox between emptiness and plenitude indicated by *sunyata* is a refrain that reverberates in the paradox of what Blanchot describes in *Thomas the Obscure* as "this void which contemplates."

While it was not Blanchot's intention to "do theology" and, as Kevin Hart cautions, it would be "dishonest in the extreme" to read Blanchot as having an implicit theological intention or "an oblique rapprochement with the Christian or Jewish God,"[32] it seems to me that such "demands of grief" ask whether in the dismissal of the positive naming of God or the positive (and exclusivist) claims of religion, we may retain concepts such as "transcendence," "mystery," even the "divine" with the discipline of negation and paradox in the unworking (*désoeuvrement*) or unsaying of language. "Transcendence" is how the temporal and finite "names" the "beyond": the impossible beyond of another's pain, the impossible beyond of a God I can never comprehend, but both of which are still as near to me as my own breathing. The beyond of an Other and the beyond of the infinite represent parallel displacements of my perspective. But the human relationship—the interhuman encounter—is where the displacement of perspective refers to an infinity that has the divine as its term of transcendence. This relationship in the here and now is the space of the sacred: although I am engaged in the life of another person, I must never make the mistake of assuming that even that which occurs in the temporal, material, and finite could ever be comprehensible or exhaustible. The relationship, the encounter, is past-my-grasp while I grope for it; such makes it sacred. This relationship displaces the ego I have carefully protected until our encounter.

32. Hart, *The Dark Gaze*, 230.

For Blanchot and Derrida, the encounter that displaces occurs through art and in language; for Levinas such was less the case, as he privileges the actual encounter and physical relationship. Between language and art, Levinas privileges language. But I hope to show that visual culture, whether photography, visual media, or visual art—all aspects of visual witness—serve to widen the scope of impact by the Other whom I will never physically meet. The image as essential to visual culture invites us to witness, invites us to move beyond the familiar, and heightens sensibility, which heightens perception.

When I look into the eyes of Finda Fallah,[33] a woman who lost three of her six children, and her husband, mother and sister to the Ebola virus—all of whom died in her arms—and picture her sleeping with her children on the streets of West Point, the most densely populated neighborhood in Monrovia, Liberia, in the cold mud, because the clinic had no room for them, the weight of the demands of grief are more than I can tolerate. Art serves to negotiate this burden; the visual culture involved in witnessing her testimony preserves it. I must carry her with me, as powerless as I am. I must never forget her. This "must never" is an indictment of my infinite responsibility to those who suffer, where a glimpse of the divine infinite is possible, but only if it is an interruption and not an assimilation, what Blanchot calls "an interruption escaping all measure."[34] Although I may never meet Ms. Fallah in person, "here is the strangeness of this strangeness—such an interruption (one that neither includes nor excludes) would be nevertheless a relation; at least if I take it upon myself not to reduce it, not to reconcile it, even by comprehending it, that is, not to seek to consider it as the 'faltering' mode of the unitary relation."[35] Her face interrupts my life; how can I maintain this interruption without reducing it, without reconciling it, without *comprehending* it? For Blanchot, God is not

33. From "Outbreak," PBS *Frontline*, episode produced by Dan Edge and Sasha Joelle Achilli, directed by Dan Edge, aired May 5, 2015, http://www.pbs.org /wgbh/pages/frontline/outbreak/.

34. Maurice Blanchot, "The Relation of the Third Kind (Man without Horizon)," chap. 7 in *The Infinite Conversation*, trans. Susan Hanson (Minneapolis, MN: University of Minnesota Press, 1993), 68.

35. Ibid.

an explicit aspect of this relation; Levinas, however, sees a trace of the divine within this infinite difference that is "nevertheless a relation." The relation is established where my power ceases, where self-protection descends; Blanchot explains, "I have in this relation a relation with what is radically out of my reach; and this relation measures the very extent of the Outside."[36]

The demands of grief recognize that the "truth is nomadic"[37]— truth wanders and evolves, and hides again, behind affirmations that open into emptiness, when every question is shadowed by another: "[T]hat which is concealed without anything being hidden, which asserts itself and remains unexpressed, which is there and forgotten: That what was there should have been always and every time a presence, was the surprise within which thought fulfilled itself, unsuspected."[38] "Presence" for Blanchot and Levinas is always at the same time an absence, a proximity that carries the weight of an infinite distance. Asserting the weight of distance intends to obstruct any violence I might perpetrate by assuming that I can ever know the Other or understand the suffering of an Other, or can make any claim to "my" God. The interplay of light and shadow, the hazy shapes of persons in the field of vision of one nearly blind: such is the truth of the sacred that persists through interhuman encounter. That which inspires religious thought begins in the context of relationship.

According to Blanchot and Levinas, "otherness" refers to that which draws us outside ourselves, into this *lieu*, this space. Levinas writes, "[I]t appears as a movement going forth from a world that is familiar to us, whatever be the yet unknown lands that bound it or that it hides from view, from an 'at home' (*chez soi*) which we inhabit, toward an alien outside-of-oneself (*hors-de-soi*), toward a yonder."[39] Such occurs, notes Blanchot, in the "frankness of a gaze,

---

36. Ibid., 69.
37. Maurice Blanchot, "The Conquest of Space," in Holland, *The Blanchot Reader*, 271.
38. Maurice Blanchot, "Waiting," in Holland, *The Blanchot Reader*, 278.
39. Levinas, *Totality and Infinity*, 33.

in the nakedness of an approach that nothing prevents."[40] Weaving verse from the poet Paul Celan, Blanchot observes,

> [T]he I is not alone, it turns into *we*, and this falling of the one with the other joins together what is falling, even into the present tense. . . . [W]e are foreigners, having to bear in common this distraction of distance which holds us absolutely apart. We are foreigners. Just as, if there is silence, two silences fill our mouths: Let us remember this, if we can: a double mouthful of silence.[41]

The quality of witness, of interhuman encounter in which there may be a trace of the divine, is that we are both ultimately silent in mutual reflection. We are each incomprehensible to the other, which means that the encounter will never be exhausted, an intimate distance. Our mutual vulnerability renders us silent. This space of the "outside" for Blanchot is neither interior nor exterior; it is borderless, indeterminable by geography. But neither is the *dehors*, the "outside," solitary; and although we are foreign one to the other, in the depths of other perspectives, other experiences, other worlds, we fall into this distance together, in the proximity of silence. Through the other, "Other" "in an eminent sense,"[42] we open ourselves to the "impossible," the *dehors*, through the suffering of the Other, and through art and the ethical commitment of responsibility for the Other, we meet this suffering, witness to it, enter into it, and are passive before its alterity so as not to reduce it to the familiar, to my "self," my ego, and my suffering.

We must therefore empty ourselves of ego or "self" (*kenosis*, "self-emptying") in order to refer to this space, this "outside." There is no primacy of subject here; for Blanchot and Levinas, the subject is always under construction, in a state of becoming, forged through

---

40. Blanchot, "Knowledge of the Unknown," chap. 5 in *The Infinite Conversation*, 54.

41. Maurice Blanchot, *Une voix venue d'ailleurs* (Gallimard, 2002), p. 87, quoted in Leslie Hill, " 'Distrust of Poetry': Levinas, Blanchot, Celan," *Modern Language Notes* 120, no. 5 (December 2005): 995.

42. Levinas, *Totality and Infinity*, 33.

ekstasis (Greek for displacement), standing beyond or beside the self and the body's boundaries, toward the Other. That the self may be lost in the Other determines the "me" that I am: the Other is the sculptor, chipping away at the marble, and I recognize my subjectivity through seeing how the encounter with otherness releases the "me." I do not come to the Other complete, a finished statue, so to speak. Self-emptying, then, is not merely negation, otherwise a some-*thing* would have to be negated; rather, the activity of self-emptying, of detachment from self as origin, releases a space where the subject becomes possible. The "I" occurs in the negative space that "makes" the something, the statue (to continue the metaphor). Such kenosis, such exposure, might have emptiness as its analogue, emptiness as its source, emptiness as a nonexistence or potency in the *sunyata* of Mahayana Buddhism. Kenosis as an emptying of the self refers to this potency as an openness without foundation, a pure openness, a passivity; Rahner alluded to this in his notion of "obediential potency."[43] In such we find the kenosis of Jesus Christ, as an action of radical heteronomy, a passivity directed toward the Other. To paraphrase Richard Kearney, the recognition of powerlessness, vulnerability, fragility, brokenness, is where we "find ourselves empowered to respond to God's own primordial powerlessness and to make the potential Word flesh."[44]

Because no language and no art can capture the depth of the suffering Other, and no language and no art can capture "God," we are left with desire. Desire for Levinas is simply the tending toward the outside, "toward something else entirely": this is not "desire" based

---

43. Karl Rahner, following Thomas Aquinas, argued that the human being is constituted in terms of an obediential potency for God: human beings have to be able to receive something of the divine self-communication, or else there is no point in God communicating anything: this is a condition present in the existential structure of the human being, prior to awareness or self-reflection. Rahner discusses this more fully as the "supernatural existential." The hypostatic union of divine and human in Christ is the logical outcome of this: the incarnation is the actualization of the essence of humanity, the "obediential potency" for union with God.

44. Richard Kearney, *The God Who May Be: A Hermeneutics of Religion* (Bloomington, IN: Indiana University Press, 2001), 2.

on need, as though I desire food when I am hungry or companionship when I am lonely. This is rather a "metaphysical" desire, to use Levinas's terminology, a desire that "cannot be satisfied" because it indicates a "just-beyondness" (my term, based on Rahner) of anything that could seemingly complete it.[45] Because it is a desire that can never be complete or fulfilled, it is always in reference to what is further beyond. Desire as that which refers us outside, to the always just-beyond, is an indication of the infinite. We desire the Other; we desire the sacred, which is at the root of what it means to be human. We desire in the manner of Rahner's "incomprehensible fire in which we do not in fact burn up, but rather come to be for the first time."[46] Through this desire, we see that we are both passive before the Other and the "impossible" brought by the difference or alterity of the Other and what it means to be responsible/responsive before the Other.

We are inclined to name or say this experience, to articulate it, express it in images, while also incapable of finally saying anything about it at all. The Other, as well as "God," are not objects of thought, to be seized upon and dissected. Rather, the experience of the space of the ineffable, this dark field in which I clumsily grope, has an infinite horizon: Rahner saw "God" as the term of this horizon; Blanchot saw this horizon in the "sacred"; Levinas saw a "trace of God," so careful was he to avoid naming the divine Other. The "trace" is "the mark of the absence of a presence"[47] for Jacques Derrida, heavily influenced by Levinas, a way for language to fade into erasure while in use. The "trace" may be said to be a presence of an absence as well, as in Rahner's "past-all-graspness"; to use a geographical metaphor, like two lovers separated over thousands of miles but who can only think about each other, the desire between them in the space between them. Even when these lovers reunite, the space remains. A space of no form, no substance, but in which we are swallowed up.

45. See Levinas, *Totality and Infinity*, 34.
46. Rahner, "Ignatius of Loyola Speaks to a Modern Jesuit," 17.
47. Gayatri Chakravorty Spivak, translator's preface to Jacques Derrida, *Of Grammatology* (Baltimore: Johns Hopkins University Press, 1997), xvii.

At the Limit of Being and Non-Being

How do we engage this outside, this impossible, this trace[48] of the infinite? Entering a space for the abstraction of reality reminds us that the ultimate reality, what Paul Tillich called "the ground of being," cannot be expressed in words, concepts, or images. The emergence of abstract art occurs alongside modernism's crisis of representation, when the instability of concepts and the identification of linguistic theory's analysis of the relationship between the signifier and the signified. Modernism began to see that all language and all visual art participate in a type of abstraction; even if a painting attempts a realistic portrayal of something, its removal of the subject matter outside of its time and space constitutes an abstrac-

48. The notion of "trace" will appear throughout this book, especially in reference to Levinas's thought. Levinas relies heavily on "trace" as a signifier for the infinite. Immanuel Kant considered the "trace" a way to discuss the barest sense impression of an a priori concept. Jane Kneller writes, "If we are somehow able to sense or feel that nature had a place for moral beings—that beings with purpose belonged there, and that nature itself had a purpose—then we would have something of the feeling of hope that we need to make following its strict law possible and even natural." She cites Kant's third Critique, section 42: "[R]eason also has an interest in the objective reality of the ideas (for which, in moral feeling, it brings about a direct interest), i.e., an interest that nature should at least show a trace or give a hint that it contains some basis or other for us to assume in its products a lawful harmony with that liking of ours which is independent of all interest (a liking we recognize 'a priori' as a law for everyone, thus we cannot base this law on proofs). Hence, reason must take an interest in any manifestation in nature of a harmony that resembles the mentioned harmony, and hence the mind cannot mediate the beauty of nature without at the same time finding its interest aroused." Translation by Kneller. *Kant and the Power of Imagination* (Cambridge, UK: Cambridge University Press, 2007), 61. Using the term "trace" is a way to evade direct signification or representation. This is true in Derrida's use of the term as well: the meaning of a sign or signifier is related to its difference from other signs, and so any signifier contains a "trace" of what it does not mean, indicating what is never fully present or absent. The "trace" for Derrida is related to the *khôra*, a "place" in "the history of philosophy where the *différance* by which all things are inhabited wears through, where the abyss in things opens up and we catch a glimpse of the groundlessness of our beliefs and practices." Jacques Derrida, *Deconstruction in a Nutshell: A Conversation with Jacques Derrida*, ed. John Caputo (New York: Fordham University Press, 1997), 98.

tion. Artists began to experiment with forms of abstraction in order to set in crisis ways of naming reality which had been unreflexively accepted. Because of its interest to light fires under what is conventional and established, abstract visual art may be a way for theology to train its "mind" toward the vision of the radically new. Although Levinas's own work seldom focuses on art, he understands the potential of abstract art to help us think beyond the nameable: "modern painting re-immerses things in a non-figurative reality. In a profusion of monstrous forms, it seeks the compossibility of the incompossible. No longer does anything impose choice, and imagination discovers its independence from perception, whose categories it shatters."[49]

Because modern art moves beyond the explicitly religious imagery from the Middle Ages through the Baroque, during which time it was believed that the invisible could be made manifest through the visible,[50] modern art asks that we abandon visual expectations, opening a space for spiritual perception and preparation for what is radically Other. Yet the movement between the invisible and manifestation, between kenosis (self-emptying) and incarnation, between potency and expression, is still evident in abstract art, because it is still color, or darkness, or line, or form—the tangible—that enables this space to open. Surrealism was one of the initial movements in modernist art that explicitly saw itself as a bulwark against the narrow confines of rationalism, "heralding a way of thought which is no longer a reducing agent but has become infinitely inductive and extensible,"[51] according to André Breton, one of the framers of Surrealist ideology.

49. Emmanuel Levinas, "Lévy-Bruhl and Contemporary Philosophy," in *Entre-Nous: Thinking-of-the-Other*, trans. Michael B. Smith and Barbara Harshav (New York: Columbia University Press, 1998), 45.

50. Hugh of St. Victor (1096–1141) wrote, "All things visible, when they obviously speak to us symbolically, that is when they are interpreted figuratively, are referable to invisible significations and statements. . . . For since their beauty consists in the visible form of things . . . visible beauty is an image of invisible beauty." *In Hierarcham Coelestem* 2; PL175, col. 949. See also Richard Viladesau, *Theological Aesthetics: God in Imagination, Beauty, and Art* (New York: Oxford University Press, 1999), 109.

51. André Breton, "The Crisis of the Object," in *Surrealism and Painting*, trans. Simon Watson Taylor (Boston: MFA Publications, 2002), 277.

While not self-identified as within the movement as articulated by Breton, Georgia O'Keeffe (1887–1986) provides a vision that transforms the everyday object or scene until it leads to another world. She was fascinated with the spaces created by holes in material objects; her genius depicts these objects from angles that remove their identity. Her *Pelvis Series*, for example, emphasizes the space through which the sky or a landscape that isn't a landscape can be seen; her magnified flowers contain doorways to a dark promise of infinity. Although her paintings abound in saturated color and light, O'Keeffe paints the space between things until the objects themselves no longer seem relevant. The object—the door to Alfred Stieglitz's Lake George, New York home (*Farmhouse Window and Door*, 1929), for example—is identifiable as a door, but the off-kilter position alters its dimensionality, giving it a quality beyond its identity. The object then becomes a gateway to the dimension of emptiness from which the object is born. The object separates—and joins—two worlds, the known and the unknown. The unknown then becomes the catalyst by which the "known" may be not known. We have seen that a simple door, reduced to its rectangular and angular simplicity, when shown through the artist's expression, is always more than a door, and this is more than a residence. As Breton commented in "The Crisis of the Object," objects take on infinite dimensions with the risk of new perspective in Surrealist works: "With this new focus, the same object, however complete it may seem, reverts to an infinite series of latent possibilities which entail its transformation."[52] In this sense, Surrealism is indicative of the fragmentation that often characterizes modernity and so is a portent of the deconstruction and de-centering found in postmodern thought.[53]

For Blanchot, language, poetry, and the arts are not only what we must trust because we have no alternative but also what we must mistrust because we have no alternative.[54] We are caught in the

---

52. Ibid., 280.

53. For this point, I rely on Celia Rabinovitch, *Surrealism and the Sacred: Power, Eros, and the Occult in Modern Art* (Boulder, CO: Westview Press, 2002), 8–9.

54. See Blanchot, *The Writing of the Disaster*, 110–11; see also Hill, "Distrust of Poetry," 1008.

whirlwind. This is especially the case in theology, David Tracy asserts, saying,

> [R]eflection upon limit-questions and limit-situations does disclose the reality of a dimension to our lives other than the more usual dimensions, . . . a dimension which, in my own brief and hazy glimpses, discloses a reality, however named and in whatever manner experienced, which functions as a final, now gracious, now frightening, now trustworthy, now absurd, always uncontrollable limit-of the very meaning of existence itself.[55]

Tracy here reminds us of the "limit-experience" Georges Bataille understood as sacred and Blanchot describes in the experience of writing and art. Kevin Hart explains that this is "experience in its radical sense: the peril of passing from a moment in time to the space of images. It is . . . an experience of experience . . . from that which yields positive knowledge to that which, in not offering itself to the senses, cannot enter the order of knowledge. This is what Bataille urges us to see when he speaks of the new theology as having 'only the unknown as its object.'"[56] The experience of limits, like the heightening of sensibility for witness, or the empowering of a powerlessness that lays bare the "self" for the Other, is activity that mirrors the divine, when God chooses powerlessness in the incarnation. Observes Richard Kearney, "God thus empowers our human powerlessness by giving away [divine] power, by possibilizing us and our good actions—so that we may supplement and co-accomplish creation."[57]

The "brief and hazy glimpses" of a reality that bursts the seams of knowing occurred to me the day I discovered Rahner's imagination; theology can play in the field of the gracious, frightening, trustworthy, absurd, and uncontrollable dimension of a reality none of us can name. Theology at its best reveals a garden of earthly delights,

---

55. David Tracy, *Blessed Rage for Order: The New Pluralism in Theology* (Chicago: The University of Chicago Press, 1996), 108.

56. Hart, *The Dark Gaze*, 27.

57. Kearney, *The God Who May Be*, 108.

knees aching in the dirt, digging holes into the unknown. Theology is reflection on limit-questions—death, meaning, existence, God— and in the discovery of discourse about God that interrupts, in which Rahner's human being is affirmed in the incomprehensibility of God, there was that day in the tedious colorless sky stretched out like time, the heady thrall of being introduced to a fresh spot in this field, where Sr. Corita Kent sees "the garden our life is—a place where questions are scattered like seeds."[58]

Who Is the "Other"?

Who is the "Other" and what is meant by the term? According to Emmanuel Levinas, the "Other" is not a "phenomenon"—not merely something that appears in my experience—but is rather a *disturbance* of my perceptions of the world. To call the Other a "phenomenon" would be to name the Other according to my perceptions, which for Levinas is violent, an activity of domination and mastery. Rather, the "Other" is the one who interrupts and alters my tidy and secure experience of what surrounds me in such a way that I am not human, and certainly not a subject or a self, until I engage the Other as disturbing my perceptions, and not merely as an extension of them. The "Other" reverses the natural order of things; where I should be primarily preoccupied with my own survival (as in evolutionary biology) and my own existence (as in much of existentialist philosophy), the Other's alterity presents an opportunity for holiness, "the certitude that one must yield to the other the first place in everything, from the *après vous* before an open door . . . to die for the other."[59] Levinas calls "alterity" the distinctiveness of another

---

58. From a serigraph artwork by Corita Kent, *The Garden Our Life Is* (1979): "[A] place where questions are scattered like seeds—an atmosphere where answers for a season grow and blossom—then another year of seasons—it is the school the garden our life is," www.corita.org/.

59. Emmanuel Levinas, interview with François Poirié, trans. Jill Robbins and Marcus Coelen, with Thomas Loebel, in *Is It Righteous to Be? Interviews with Emmanuel Levinas*, ed. Jill Robbins (Stanford, CA: Stanford University Press, 2001), 47.

person, the dimension of the Other that is hidden from me, such that even in a one-to-one encounter, there is far more unknown about the other person than is understood and far more which will forever remain beyond my grasp. "The face is present in its refusal to be contained,"[60] Levinas writes. Paradoxically, the hidden dimension of the person refers to the transcendent dimension, that which is indicative of the infinity that indicates "God."

We may feel threatened by the dimension of unfamiliarity and hiddenness revealed by the Other, fear this unknown, distrust it, and even, according to Levinas, try to kill the one in whom alterity resides. More often than not, we fear the Other in such a way that we attempt to preserve an illusion of security, surrounding ourselves with the familiar. This is ultimately futile, since we forget that those closest to us, even those we love the most, are still separate, possessing worlds of perceptions and experience we cannot know, and so are always Other, forever eluding my comprehension. This is what Blanchot and Levinas call the *rapport sans rapport*, the relationless relation; Derrida explains, "Dissociation, separation, is the condition of my relation with the other. I can address the Other only to the extent that there is a separation, a dissociation, so that I cannot replace the Other and vice versa."[61] Levinas forbids us complacency even regarding those with whom we have the longest relationships: to prevent the violence of "totality" or "sameness"—in which I assume the other person is comprehensible and comprehended—the "Other" marks the difference between my ego-driven world and the world beyond the boundaries of my experience.

This is because "to comprehend" entails knowledge as a closed system: I know who you are, I know what you are, I know what you have done and what you will do. But for Levinas, such claims to comprehension of persons are totalizing, conquering, prone to violence. An example of the beyond-comprehension, the beyond-being, is in the Jewish tradition that refers to "God" as *Ha-Shem*, "the Name." Using *Ha-Shem* as a divine reference acknowledges that one can never know the Name of God; the divine identity is unnamable

---

60. Levinas, *Totality and Infinity*, 194.
61. Derrida, *Deconstruction in a Nutshell*, 14.

and so incomprehensible, so a signifier is used. In Exodus, Moses inquires after God's name before the burning bush,

> If . . . they ask me, "What is his name?" what shall I say to them? God said to Moses, "I am who I am." He said further, "Thus shall you say to the Israelites, 'I am has sent me to you.'" God also said to Moses, "Thus shall you say to the Israelites, 'The Lord, the God of your ancestors, the God of Abraham, the God of Isaac, and the God of Jacob, has sent me to you': this is my name forever, and this is my title for all generations." (Exod 3:13-15)[62]

By altering God's answer three times, God explains that the divine Name—which for the early Hebrews signified comprehension of God—is always just beyond our grasp, just further afield. The Hebrew tetragrammaton YHWH, translated as "I am who I am" above or as "I am who I shall be" elsewhere, is unpronounceable in Jewish tradition. But this "just beyond" is a field where the people of this God have gathered, where they remember their heritage, where they tell their stories. That there is such a "beyond" or such a transcendent dimension to alterity is a "shock": the "shock of the divine, the rupture of the immanent order, of the order that I can embrace, of the order which I can hold in my thought, of the order which can become

---

62. John Courtney Murray argues in his famous lecture on the Name of God in Exodus, "Over against the inconstancy and infidelity of the people, who continually absent themselves from God, the Name Yahweh affirms the constancy of God, his unchangeable fidelity to his promise of presence." God's nearness to the world, however, does not exhaust God's mystery; as Murray explains, "The text, thus understood, contains a threefold revelation—of God's immanence in history, of his transcendence to history, and of his transparence through history. God first asserts the fact of his presence in the history of his people: 'I shall be there.' Second, he asserts the mystery of his own being: 'I shall be there as who I am.' His mystery is a mode of absence. Third, he asserts that, despite his absence in mystery, he will make himself known to his people: 'As who I am shall I be there.' The mode of his transparence is through his action, through the saving events of the sacred history of Israel. However, what thus becomes known is only his saving will. He himself, in his being and nature, remains forever unknown to men, hidden from them." John Courtney Murray, *The Problem of God* (New Haven, CT: Yale University Press, 1964), 10–11.

mine, that is the face of the other."[63] Levinas contrasts openness to this "beyond,"—this "alterity" or just-beyondness of the Other, this infinity—with "atheism," the self's maintaining "itself in existence all by itself, without participating in the Being from which it is separated . . . One lives outside of God, at home with oneself; one is an I, an egoism. . . . By atheism we thus understand a position prior to both the negation and affirmation of the divine"[64] in which the "I" is comfortably acceptable as the arbiter of all reality, the "totality."

Levinas arrives at this position based on what he understands as the order of priorities that has structured philosophy in the West, which he argues refers to the "primacy of ontology" within Martin Heidegger's philosophical investigation of Being. For Heidegger, the human being is characterized by inquiry into Being: *Dasein*—German for "being-there"—describes the contextual place of the human person in the world, irrevocably tied to time and place and so conditioned by concrete existence when asking the question of Being. Only human persons inquire into Being, and in doing so they orient themselves beyond their circumstances, beyond their context, toward the horizon of Being. Dasein does not have an essence which determines it, but is its possibility: it fashions its own existence. Dasein is central to Heidegger's project because Dasein is the only being capable of interpreting the world, the beings within it, and the horizon of Being; such interpretive skill gives Dasein existence and makes the things of the world ontologically defined by Dasein.

For Heidegger, Western metaphysics is in error when it names Being, that of which Dasein inquires, "God." Heidegger coined the term "onto-theology" in agreement with Kant against the notion that a Platonic hierarchy of beings necessarily leads to the "Highest Being," or "God." Merold Westphal sums it up well: onto-theology, the designation of "Being" as "God," is "bad philosophy" because it converts the question of Being into the question of *a* being, even if the "Highest Being."[65] From Heidegger's perspective, questions

---

63. Levinas, interview with François Poirié, in *Is It Righteous to Be?*, 48.

64. Levinas, *Totality and Infinity*, 58.

65. Merold Westphal, *Overcoming Ontotheology: Toward a Postmodern Christian Faith* (New York: Fordham University Press, 2001), 259.

about "God" belong in theology, not in philosophy,[66] and to justify the existence of God philosophically rather than religiously is to gut religion of its wonder. Heidegger writes that whereas naming "God" the first cause uncaused (*causa sui*) might work for a philosophical system's desire for order in the chain of causation, "Man can neither pray nor sacrifice to this god. Before the *causa sui*, man can neither fall to his knees in awe nor can he play music and dance before this god."[67] Heidegger argues here that "God" understood as "*causa sui*" is "the right name for the god of philosophy" because the statement is a logical outcome when positing a chain of causation, a fixed point which can be easily identified.[68] Abandoning the "god of philosophy is thus perhaps closer to the divine God."[69]

Levinas agreed with Heidegger that onto-theological tendencies must be overcome. I believe that Levinas also agreed that one can only approach discourse on God through religious thinking; he furthermore follows Heidegger in separating his explicitly religious writings, such as his lectures on the Talmud, from his philosophical project. Levinas, however, argues that two components of Heidegger's thought are misguided: Dasein's fundamental orientation in the particular "mineness," *Jemeinigkeit*,[70] of Being and Heidegger's assertion that Being must be intelligible. His arguments against Heidegger on these points reveal Levinas's own priorities. Levinas argues that ontology—which he defines in terms of Being as a *totality* encompassing all truth—is what distracts us from the metaphysical exposure to the alterity of the Other, which opens to infinity and so to transcendence and so makes it possible for us to exist, to be subjects. The structure of Levinas's understanding of subjectivity (for Heidegger, the "I" that determines existence) pertains to a primordial exposure

66. See Martin Heidegger, "Kant's Thesis about Being," in *Pathmarks*, ed. William McNeill (Cambridge, UK: Cambridge University Press, 1998), 340.

67. Martin Heidegger, *Identity and Difference*, trans. Joan Stambaugh (Chicago: The University of Chicago Press, 2002), 72. See also Westphal, *Overcoming Ontotheology*, 261.

68. Heidegger, *Identity and Difference*, 71.

69. Ibid., 72.

70. Martin Heidegger, *Being and Time*, trans. John Macquarrie and Edward Robinson (San Francisco: Harper and Row, 2008), par. 9, H. 42, p. 68.

to the Other; the inescapable and infinite alterity of the Other and the response I make to the Other fashions my existence.

Heidegger's philosophical emphasis, however, is first on Dasein's own solitary obligation to decide what and how to be. While Dasein does depend on others in the world, Dasein is not affected by others in the particularity of Dasein's own possession of—or Dasein's activity as a "clearing" (the noun meaning "open space") for—Being, and so Heidegger does not prioritize the ethical obligation to the Other as primordial to Dasein. Acting authentically for Heidegger means acting with full awareness of responsibility to the self, until death, the loneliest, but most "mine" experience one can have. In this sense, allowing others to determine one's existence is "inauthentic." While Heidegger argues that being-in-the-world entails being-with-others, the structure of Dasein's being is not fundamentally for the Other: "'[I]n the first instance' this entity is unrelated to Others, and that of course it can still be 'with' Others afterwards."[71] Dasein is first being which is concerned with its own being.

Neither does Heidegger want to equate or otherwise refer to "God" when discussing Being (such he names as the mistake of the onto-theological trajectory of Western metaphysics since Plato and Aristotle): as we see above, Heidegger preferred to bracket or suspend faith in God from philosophical inquiry. Heidegger wished to consider the primacy of Being without "God" getting in the way, and so Heidegger is against "metaphysics" as built on the traditional Western trajectory. Hence, Heidegger wants to change the way *ontology* is done. But where Heidegger misses the mark for Levinas is in making Being and my possession of Being the fundamental matrix of existence, which (although not Heidegger's concern) can lead to the danger of reducing "God" to Being or subsuming "God" under Being. Furthermore, for Levinas, Heidegger makes the Greek metaphysical mistake of assuming that Being is intelligible.

The presumption that one can possess or know Being at all is described by Levinas as "one sole thesis" in Heidegger's *Being and Time*:

---

71. Ibid., par. 117, H. 121, p. 156.

> Being is inseparable from the comprehension of Being; Being is already an appeal to subjectivity. . . . [T]o affirm the priority of Being over existents is to already decide the essence of philosophy; it is to subordinate the relation with someone, who is an existent (the ethical relation) to a relation with the Being of existents, which, impersonal, permits the apprehension, the domination of existents (a relation of knowing).[72]

Although Levinas readily acknowledges not only Heidegger's influence on his work but also that Heidegger is "one of the greatest philosophers in history,"[73] Heidegger's anti-Semitic practices[74] were for Levinas evidence that his description of Dasein is deficient. Levinas located Heidegger's Nazism—he joined the party in 1933—in the components of his philosophical trajectory independent of the needs of the Other, toward "autonomy" or the freedom of the self in the *Jemeinigkeit* of Being. This freedom "maintains oneself against the other, despite every relation with the other, to ensure the autarchy of an I," thus suppressing alterity. Levinas, perhaps in the memory of the deaths of his parents and brothers shot by Nazi soldiers, fashions an arrow straight to the heart of Heidegger's philosophy: "Ontology as first philosophy is a philosophy of power. . . . Heideggerian ontology, which subordinates the relation with the Other to the relation with Being in general, remains under obedience

72. Levinas, *Totality and Infinity*, 45. See also Westphal, *Overcoming Ontotheology*, 261.

73. Levinas, interview with François Poirié, in *Is It Righteous to Be?*, 32.

74. Heidegger was also deeply anti-Semitic, according to his own philosophical diaries, the "black notebooks." He writes in the summer of 1941: "World Judaism is ungraspable everywhere and doesn't need to get involved in military action while continuing to unfurl its influence, whereas we are left to sacrifice the best blood of the best of our people." He seems to have believed the Jewish people were a key factor in the modern age's "abandonment of Being." See Peter E. Gordon, "Heidegger in Black," *The New York Review of Books*, October 9, 2014, http://www.nybooks.com/articles/archives/2014/oct/09/heidegger-in-black/. These notebooks begin in 1931 and end in the early 1970s, filling thirty-four volumes. The volumes written during the Nazi regime are currently only available in German in their entirety. See *Überlegungen* 2–15, ed. Peter Trawny (Frankfurt am Main: Klostermann, 2014).

to the anonymous, and leads inevitably to another power, to impe-rialist domination, to tyranny."[75]

This tendency in the modern West to steamroll everything different or Other into a mere extension of the self is totalizing: reductionistic, ego driven, and perhaps even the basis for imperialistic tendencies in Western thought. Levinas calls this tendency toward autonomy, the "law of the self," "an odyssey wherein all adventures are only accidents of a return to self."[76] The tendency of the self to take what is disturbing about the Other and the newness represented by the Other and inte-grate this into what is familiar, what is "at home," what is "the Same," is problematic because it makes the self the measure of all things. This begins in Platonic philosophy: as Michael Morgan points out, in the *Sophist* and the *Timaeus*, "the same" refers to the self, to the mind or reason; "the other" refers to that which is beyond or outside the self.[77] What is "other" is contrasted with "the same"; what is Other is Other relative to the self. But in the modern age, when the "self" became the locus of "truth" rather than the receiver of it, the "self" and the lust for autonomy took the sublimation of the Other into the self as the melting pot of difference. In this way, the "self" of modernity lost its sense of the infinite when it reveled in its totalizing autonomy.

The only way out of this totalizing odyssey of the Same is to radicalize openness to the Other, to replace autonomy/freedom with heteronomy, by which the "law of the other" becomes the *source* of "being me": "The putting into question of the self is precisely a welcome to the absolutely other. . . . [T]he epiphany of the Abso-lutely Other is a face by which the Other challenges and commands me through his nakedness, through his destitution . . . from his humility and his height. . . . [T]o be I signifies not being able to escape responsibility."[78] "Responsibility" is the ethical response to

75. Levinas, *Totality and Infinity*, 46–47.

76. Emmanuel Levinas, "Transcendence and Height," in *Basic Philosophical Writings*, ed. Adriaan T. Peperzak, Simon Critchley, and Robert Bernasconi (Bloomington, IN: Indiana University Press, 1996), 14.

77. Michael L. Morgan, *The Cambridge Companion to Emmanuel Levinas* (Cambridge: Cambridge University Press, 2011), 89.

78. Ibid., 17.

the command the Other makes in disturbing my bubble of autonomy. "Freedom" for the autonomous self isn't really free because it doesn't lead to existence, which should increase and develop beyond the confines of the totality of Being. What does free the subject seems paradoxical: freedom of the subject consists in the infinite obligation to the Other, even to be "held hostage" by the needs of the Other in an asymmetrical relationship.[79] Only through radical openness to the otherness, the difference of the Other, can the subject exist, and so go *beyond* Being.

This to Levinas is central to the phenomenological project: consciousness is an intentionality always in contact with objects outside itself, with that which is Other than itself.[80] In phenomenology, human consciousness is never merely pure cognition with no object of intentionality—it rather moves toward something outside itself and then reflects on it as meaningful. Such is the "lived experience" which Levinas thought Heidegger neglected: the value of interrelationship between human persons that is an irrevocable and primordial aspect of being-in-the-world. The historical and contextual conditions that frame the particularity of being-in-the-world are unintelligible without attention to our relationships and social interaction. According to Levinas, Heidegger's mistake is to neglect the fundamental importance of these relationships; in this way, Heidegger is aligned with the very Western concepts he sought to overcome. To overcome the Western reliance on autonomy, we must adopt the ethical or biblical perspective that transcends the Greek philosophical emphasis on the intelligibility of Being. Levinas asserts,

> [T]he theme of justice and concern for the other as other, as a theme of love and desire which carries us beyond the finite Being of the world's presence. The interhuman is thus an interface: a double axis where what is "of the world" qua phenomenological intelligibility is juxtaposed with what is "not of the world" as ethical responsibility. It is in this ethical perspective that God

79. See Levinas, *Otherwise than Being*, 112.
80. See Richard Kearney's interview with Emmanuel Levinas, *Dialogues with Contemporary Continental Thinkers* (Manchester, UK: Manchester University Press, 1986), 50.

must be thought and not in the ontological perspective of our being-there or of some Supreme Being and Creator. . . . God, as the God of alterity and transcendence, can only be understood in terms of that interhuman dimension which emerges in the phenomenological-ontological perspective of the intelligible world, but which cuts through and perforates the totality of presence and points toward the absolutely Other.[81]

The ethical relation to the Other is prior to the relation with the self or even to the things of the world and our historical contextuality. Levinas here argues that a both/and approach is necessary to flesh out the conundrum of personhood: the phenomenological description of comprehension as moving outside the self is meaningless without the ethical matrix of interhuman obligation that makes justice/heteronomy more important than freedom/autonomy.

How can being bound to the Other be liberating? How can being "held hostage" to the vulnerability of the Other open to the infinite? For Levinas, within this command or summons of the nakedness of the Other is the possibility of life, of existence, since the self is constructed in response to the acknowledgment of the Other's difference and in meeting her needs. This disturbance places what I think I know into question, and so it is precisely this disturbance that contains the possibility that I may be open to the alterity of the Other, which is an invitation to live in this openness, and therefore, exist. Fr. Zosima, whose character in *The Brothers Karamazov* is based on a monk who helped Fyodor Dostoyevsky heal after the death of his three-year-old son, teaches this as well:

> When he realizes that he is not only worse than others, but that he is responsible to all people for all and everything, for all human sins, national and individual, only then the aim of our seclusion is attained. For know, dear ones, that every one of us is undoubtedly responsible for all people, and everything on earth, not merely through the general sinfulness of creation, but each one personally for all humanity and every individual. . . . Only through that knowledge, our heart grows soft with infinite, universal, inexhaustible love. Then every one of you will have

81. Ibid., 56–57.

the power to win over the whole world by love and to wash away
the sins of the world with your tears.[82]

Here, the language is effulgent, like water luxuriously spilling out of
the tiers of a fountain. The secret to love is more than what is required
or expected or necessary; far, far more. I am responsible even for the
sins of others. Every yapping tendency to shut down this excess, to
shut off the water supply, with claims that "I can't—it is beyond me"
circle back to "the I," which isn't "mine" (if *Jemeinigkeit* can ever be
said) until it is shrugged off, the self that is no-self. The assertion that
one cannot be infinitely responsible for the Other is a failure of the
imagination, a failure of the aesthetic and sensitive acknowledgment
of the Other's vulnerability, and a failure to recognize the human
potential for the incarnation. Dostoyevsky's poetic prose resonates
with anyone familiar with biblical language: it is "all and everything."
The horizon of infinity, of the infinite in the finite. Dostoyevsky repeats the theme of interpersonal responsibility throughout the novel;
Levinas is fond of quoting "I more than the others am responsible
for all"[83] throughout his own corpus.[84]

The vulnerability of the Other and consequent "summons to respond" is the foundation of subjectivity, the locus of "self." Levinas
further describes this responsibility as "infinite" because the need
of the Other as other will never cease. Recognition of the Other's
alterity will never end; otherwise, I would have subsumed the Other
into my self-identity, and the potential for infinity is diminished. The
unsettling constant disturbance, the helplessness to ever fulfill the
task the alterity of the Other presents, is a "surplus of being" and
"existential exaggeration that is called *being me*."[85] The human potential for infinity is the "being me" that is exercised through the
responsibility to the Other that will never end.

82. Fyodor Dostoyevsky, *The Brothers Karamazov*, trans. Constance Garnett
(New York: Barnes and Noble, 2004), pt. 2, bk. 4, chap. 1, pp. 155–56.

83. Ibid., pt. 2, bk. 6, chap. 2, p. 274.

84. See, for example, Levinas, *Otherwise than Being*, 146.

85. Levinas, "Transcendence and Height," 17. Emphasis his.

Because of the infinite character of this alterity, God, Levinas asserts, is encountered through the disturbance in our worldview offered by the Other. The very disturbance we often try to ignore, deny, or assimilate is where the divine may be glimpsed. Human beings seek order, and order is referential to the self's imposition of what is familiar. The very forces of an imperialist Christianity that replaced imperialist Rome, which enervated and undermined what was a shocking Gospel of divine attentiveness to the destitute, vulnerable, and naked Other, continue to be active in the ecclesial power structures of today, clothing Jesus in robes of wealth, privilege, whiteness, and patriarchy.

For Levinas, the willingness to be challenged by the Other, to be displaced and altered by the Other, especially the suffering of the Other, is essential to the meaning of being human and to the making of the subject. Levinas provides a revolutionary and challenging philosophical system in which compassion is constitutive of the subject. I believe his thought sheds important insights on the meaning of the incarnation as characteristic of divine activity: the value of the doctrine of the incarnation in a world of catastrophic suffering is that the Judeo-Christian-Muslim "God" does not merely "comprehend" or remain tangential to the suffering of the Other—whether of human beings or indeed the entirety of the suffering world—but enters fully into it, assuming the needs of the Other, becoming the God *who* suffers in solidarity out of love, as well as the God who provides the summons to mitigate and eliminate such suffering.

The instinct of the early Christians to believe that Jesus embodied the divine, that Jesus represented God's intimate dwelling with a suffering people, involves the understanding that divine activity in relationship to the suffering Other assumes—shoulders, carries—that suffering as much as possible precisely because one is responsible for the Other. Similarly, God's infinity is located in God's responsibility to us and to creation as a whole; it is useless to speculate about divine infinity apart from the human beings who cry out to God from the places where God's absence is most acutely felt. The doctrine of the incarnation must be an affirmation that the cry of those beset by catastrophe has been heard, based on the life of Jesus, whose message and work centered on the care of the destitute, forgotten, and outcast. It is precisely in the heteronomy of his being that he manifests what was appreciated by his followers as revelatory of the divine. Jesus' life and work manifest the inescapable intertwining of human and divine, such that it is impossible to think of one without the other, or at least of one who does not yearn for the Other.

Hence, this project proceeds with the idea that it is in the disturbance of being, in the "lightning strike" that interrupts complacency, that we may "meet the God past-all-grasp." The significance of the incarnation, in which those who met Jesus in history believed that his disturbance, through action and word, was dangerous to the established order, is considered here in terms of the disturbance made through the arts and the visual, and the way we may be brought to our existence through attentiveness to the Other. That there is alterity that exceeds human consciousness, pointing toward a responsibility for each other that exceeds our finite limitations; such may provide new ways to approach the doctrine of incarnation, in which God becomes the vulnerable, suffering Other, and through which God must experience the perpetual command of the Other as a human being. The arts provide ways to transcend the limits of language and, especially, the limits of propositional language. The idea and possibly the doctrine of "incarnation" may be approached more as the outpouring of the divine, through the sensitivity of the visual, which gives us our existence by first disturbing our complacency. Art in all its forms, but specifically here considered in terms of the visual, is the human self-expression with the potential to manifest the divine self-expression, the glimpse of the divine through openness to the radically Other, and as such is a medium for conceiving and encountering new ways to comprehend the Christian doctrine of the incarnation.

By examining "incarnation" as the belief that the divine breaks into the lonely monotony of human life and energizes it for something more incomprehensible than our reason can capture—whether we refer to the life and work of Jesus in the first century or the Spirit's empowerment of those who seek justice, we see openness to the Other, to the radically new, to peeling away the layers of the familiar. The provoking of discomfort and disquiet, is beyond any linguistic formula. As James Cone puts it, "[T]o be Yahweh's servant not only means that God will strengthen and help you and 'will uphold you with my victorious right hand' (Isa. 41:10); it also means that Israel suffers with Yahweh in the divine establishment of justice in the land. There is no divine election without the call to suffer for justice."[86] For Levinas, subjectivity is unachievable without the summons to justice.

But perhaps the idea of "incarnation" should not be confined to the Christian worldview, or even to the explicitly religious worldview: perhaps "incarnation" is a linguistic signifier that would benefit from a dispersal into the visual imagination that illuminates the work of the creative, wild Infinite, work that manifests the surprise and shock and excess of the divine. Perhaps "incarnation" should be approached not in the Christian confidence that the divine *has been* represented, in a once-for-all historical finality, but as a signifier that the divine *cannot* be represented, cannot be contained, that there is no defining enfleshment. In this sense, to say that Jesus is God "incarnate" may refer to Jesus' own emptiness of self, his turn to the Other as the locus of existence, an Other that is beyond representation. Since it is Jesus who is described by his earliest followers as "kenotic," the dialectic between emptiness and form, between historical moment and the illusion of time, is energized in non-duality. The Buddhist Heart Sutra, "form is emptiness and emptiness is form," helps Christians to appreciate this dialectic. As soon as "incarnation" becomes a fixed truth that stops with itself, we have failed to approach the holy ground of the infinite, the holy ground where the bush burns but is not consumed—where the flesh of Jesus suffers and dies but death is not the end. In other words, if what Christians mean by "incarnation" is that the divine *can* be represented, and *is* represented only and uniquely in Jesus Christ, then Christians are not speaking of the "divine" after all. The divine is unpresentable, unrepresentable; Jesus is the "way" to God because, as Jean-Luc Marion writes, Jesus gives himself over to "the excessiveness of the invisible that enters into visibility through infinite depth," who "speaks this infinite depth,

---

86. James Cone, *God of the Oppressed* (Maryknoll, NY: Orbis Books, 1997), 159.

where the visible and the invisible become acquainted."[87] "Incarnation" has the potential to be appreciated in excessive, effulgent ways through creative and artistic endeavor, as the process that uncovers the radically new through openness to the Other.

87. Jean-Luc Marion, *God Without Being,* trans. Thomas A. Carlson (Chicago: The University of Chicago Press, 2012), 22.

CHAPTER TWO

Christology Positive and Im-positive

Diving into the Wreck

I came to explore the wreck.
The words are purposes.
The words are maps.
I came to see the damage that was done
and the treasures that prevail.
I stroke the beam of my lamp
slowly along the flank
of something more permanent
than fish or weed

the thing I came for:
the wreck and not the story of the wreck
the thing itself and not the myth
the drowned face always staring
toward the sun
the evidence of damage
worn by salt and sway into this threadbare beauty
the ribs of the disaster
curving their assertion
among the tentative haunters.

—Adrienne Rich[1]

1. Adrienne Rich, "Diving into the Wreck," in *Diving into the Wreck: Poems 1971–1972* (New York: W. W. Norton & Company, 1973, repr. 2013), 22–24.

Adrienne Rich (1929–2012) wrote this poem neither about the search for Jesus nor about the search for God, so it seems an odd choice to head a chapter on Christology. The poem illustrates what it means to live as a woman in a world dominated by patriarchy, in which the attitudes and symbol systems concerning sexuality and gender are rigid and yet so tacit that most of the time we are unaware of how they affect every aspect of experience. From a religious standpoint, the images and language of a male God are so pervasive that Christians fail to recognize that "maleness" is symbolic, a metaphor, a social construct. Carol Christ, in a remarkable and celebrated essay, refers to the anthropologist Clifford Geertz to argue for the necessity to include more fluid gender references for the divine. "Religion is a system of symbols which act to produce powerful, pervasive, and long-lasting moods and motivations" in a culture;[2] a "mood," she reminds us, is Geertz's term for a psychological attitude such as awe, trust, or respect, while a "motivation" is the social and political trajectory created by a mood that transforms mythos into ethos and symbol system into social and political reality.[3] Symbol systems reach deep into the psyche; even those who no longer consider themselves "religious" may revert to familiar symbols of religious significance in times of crisis. Religions centered on the worship of a male God create "moods" and "motivations" that legitimate male authority, whether in the church or in secular government influenced by Christian culture, creating the impression that female power can never be fully legitimate.[4] Christ reminds us that images and language organized around the symbol of a male God facilitate an environment in which women may see themselves in the image of God only when they deny their own sexual and gender identity in favor of a universal and generic humanity. For Rich, "diving into the wreck" means having to navigate the mythos and ethos which has created a paradigm so totalizing that we hardly realize we are swimming in it.

---

2. Carol P. Christ, "Why Women Need the Goddess: Phenomenological, Psychological, and Political Reflections," in *Womanspirit Rising: A Feminist Reader in Religion*, ed. Carol P. Christ and Judith Plaskow (San Francisco: HarperCollins, 1992), 224.

3. Ibid.

4. Ibid., 275.

Christianity has totalized Western culture in more ways than one. The "wreckage" of history has piled up, to use the words of Walter Benjamin, into "one single catastrophe"—the dominance of the many by the few—"which keeps piling wreckage upon wreckage and hurls the 'storm of progress' that maintains itself in violence."[5] Ta-Nehisi Coates calls this storm of progress "the Dream," meaning the "American Dream"; but this Dream could describe the Western steamroller of a conviction that there are some who deserve the power that accompanies privilege, who are protected by it, but are secretly terrified that it is illusory, and so increase violence both

---

5. See Walter Benjamin, "Theses on the Concept of History," in *Illuminations*, ed. Hannah Arendt, trans. Harry Zohn (New York: Schocken Books, 1969), 257. Benjamin owned a print by Paul Klee, *Angelus Novus*, that Benjamin contemplates as the angel of history: "A Klee painting named *Angelus Novus* shows an angel looking as though he is about to move away from something he is fixedly contemplating. His eyes are staring, his mouth is open, his wings are spread. This is how one pictures the angel of history. His face is turned toward the past. Where we perceive a chain of events, he sees one single catastrophe which keeps piling wreckage upon wreckage and hurls it in front of his feet. The angel would like to stay, awaken the dead, and make whole what has been smashed. But a storm is blowing from Paradise; it has got caught in his wings with such violence that the angel can no longer close them. The storm irresistibly propels him into the future to which his back is turned, while the pile of debris before him grows skyward. This storm is what we call progress." *Angelus Novus* is referenced by Gershom Scholem in a poem written in honor of his close friend Benjamin's twenty-ninth birthday: "My wing is poised to beat/but I would gladly return home/were I to stay to the end of days/I would still be this forlorn." "Greetings from Angelus," trans. Richard Sieburth, *The Fullness of Time: Poems* (Jerusalem: Ibis Editions, 2003), 145. Scholem, the great scholar of Jewish mysticism, also here references the *Merkabah* imagery examined in chapter 6. Scholem kept the print for Benjamin in 1921 when he wrote the poem. In an essay, "Walter Benjamin and His Angel," Scholem explains that Benjamin was fascinated with the angels of the Kabbalistic tradition, who are formed and then disappear before God, and so "'pass away as the spark on the coals.' To this, however, was added for Benjamin the further conception of Jewish tradition of the personal angel of each human being who represents the latter's secret self and whose name nevertheless remains hidden from him. In angelic shape, but in part also in the form of his secret name, the heavenly self of a human being (like everything else created) is woven into a curtain hanging before the throne of God." Scholem, *On Jews and Judaism in Crisis: Selected Essays* (Philadelphia: Paul Dry Books, 2012), 213.

explicit and implicit to maintain it. Those entranced by the spectacle of Dream and "progress" fear those whose black and brown bodies historically marginalize them from this Dream. And so, writes Coates, "[B]ecause the Dream rests on our backs, the bedding made from our bodies,"[6] the edifice of the Dream may fall on those who try desperately to keep it from imploding, as in Barnett Newman's sculpture *Broken Obelisk,* examined in chapter 6.

How has Christianity contributed to this wreckage, this storm, this Dream? Can it ever recover from its culpability? Even today, Christianity is almost unrecognizable without the garb of imperialism; as Catherine Keller notes, "With its imperial success, the church . . . absorbed an idolatry of identity: a metaphysical Babel of unity, an identity that homogenized the multiplicities it absorbed, that either excluded or subordinated every creaturely other. . . . God was cast in the image of this ontological identity, infused with a power that could only be—lacking all receptivity and reciprocity—all-controlling."[7] This homogeneity is the hallmark of imperialism, the attempt to level all multiplicity and difference into "the Same." Such imperialistic control of the symbols that reference the divine attempt to deny women access to God and people of color access to power. The symbols "God" and "Lord" became so aligned with imperialistic control based largely on Greco-Roman philosophy and political structures that categories of divine "perfection" in the development of Christian theology rarely suggest the vulnerability and self-emptiness of love but rather, as Keller notes, are "lacking all receptivity and reciprocity." The language and imagery of Christianity's historical preference for Greco-Roman thought infuse rituals, worship, doctrinal claims, and, of course, reference to Jesus as "Lord." This is the "God" within onto-theology, the God whose symbols are defined through sovereignty and jurisdiction, through courts and basilicas, such that "omnipotence" must mean more power to control and more power to intervene, even if violently, to protect the righteous. The omnipotent God acts according to what God "wills," the wise

6. Ta-Nehisi Coates, *Between the World and Me* (New York: Spiegel and Grau, 2015), 10.

7. Catherine Keller, *God and Power: Counter-Apocalyptic Journeys* (Minneapolis, MN: Fortress Press, 2005), 115.

parent (Father), who imposes on us the suffering that is best for us, even the suffering of his only Son. Such is the attempt, according to Richard Kearney, "to reify God by reducing [God] to a being—albeit the highest and most indeterminate of all beings."[8]

If we want to change course, to transform the very structures of Christianity which contribute to the racism, violence, and imperialism of history, to invert the power of these structures to oppress, then we must remember that "the words are maps"; the traditions, doctrines, and rituals all must be re-imagined in light of a desire to eliminate vestiges of triumphalism, hierarchy, and imperial forms of power. The journey is dangerous. In the opening verses of the poem, Rich prepares us: "checked the edge of the knife-blade,/I put on/the body-armor of black rubber/the absurd flippers/the grave and awkward mask." We aren't sure what we will find or what will emerge. Rich's poem illuminates what it feels like to peer out over the totality of the water in which we swim: she writes from the perspective of one who explores the depths of patriarchy from the outside, diving deep toward the foundations of the jagged edges of exclusion and exclusivism. Are we Christians able to explore these depths when the totality that excludes and oppresses is already part of our mythos and ethos? When the Christian tradition was constructed in and by power structures that enslaved, murdered, and repressed? Womanist and feminist Christians may be able to take a step back from the Christian totality to probe its depths for something liberating, some piece of the wreckage that is valuable, which we can polish and see in a new way. Womanist and feminist methodologies incorporate such retrieval because it is highly motivating to correct injustices generated under a patriarchal worldview, such as the Vatican's refusal to consider ordaining women or use inclusive language in the lectionary. These are distinct and obvious rallying cries: we try to satisfy the lack in order to generate a more just order. But what do Christians do with doctrines that are usually termed irrevocable or untouchable? No Christian doctrine escapes the vestiges of imperialism and the authority of Greco-Roman categories of thought, including that of a "pre-existent" Logos in the incarnation

---

8. Richard Kearney, *The God Who May Be: A Hermeneutics of Religion* (Bloomington: Indiana University Press, 2001), 24.

of Jesus; and so no Christian doctrine escapes the rigor of interpretation involved in a hermeneutics of suspicion, since, as Paul Ricouer said, all hermeneutics involve suspicion.

Rich illuminates the danger inherent in diving into the wreckage of something that lies beneath the surface and yet manipulates all that surrounds it. We know enough today to know that we live in a "wreck": slavery and colonialism were devastating assaults on human and environmental dignity, and patriarchy and racism continue that trajectory of misery and violence. The influence of power structures that emerged from Western and church-sponsored colonialism, however, their remnants in economic oppression, elitism, heterosexism, and other practices of exclusion, extend in ways that are still unacknowledged, awaiting exploration. The metaphor drawn in Rich's poem is analogous to problems in Christian theology that have become so normative, so assumed in Christian belief, that they are difficult to investigate and analyze. But the suspicion or elimination of metaphysical or ontological truth claims in postmodernity and the acquisition of insights from globalization and interreligious dialogue are indicative of a climate in Christian theology that must dive into the wreckage of a Christianity that is no longer the center of Western civilization. Absolutist claims that locate a definitive and final revelation of God within language describing the divinity of Jesus exclusive of truth claims in other religious and faith traditions are no longer satisfactory for many Christians. Even those who belong to marginalized communities must contend with the totalization of the Christian attitude legitimating the particularity of divine revelation in Christ which excludes divine revelation in non-Christian sources, communities, texts, and persons. Along these lines, even those Christians who themselves suffer from racism or economic oppression may profess the same absolutist claims that dismiss the thought, beliefs, and practices of other religious traditions or of other marginalized communities, such as when churches from economically disadvantaged communities stand against LGBT rights or promote Islamophobia. In other words, the existence of absolutist claims in one area of Christian belief may be replicated in another area of belief.

Specifically, the doctrine of the pre-existent Logos who becomes incarnate in Jesus of Nazareth has been misapplied to legitimate a single interpretation of Christian faith, as in *Dominus Iesus*: "it must be *firmly believed* that, in the mystery of Jesus Christ, the Incarnate Son of God, who is 'the way, the truth, and the life' (John 14:6), the full revelation of divine truth is given. . . . Only the revelation of Jesus Christ, therefore, 'introduces into our history a universal and ultimate truth which stirs the human mind to ceaseless effort.'"[9] Christians must inquire the way in which absolutist and exclusivist claims such as these became aligned with repressive power structures, thereby losing the original message of inclusion and justice promoted by Jesus. Has such an interpretation of the doctrine of the incarnation been wielded as a weapon or even as a seemingly innocuous velvet rope, separating those inside from those outside "salvation"? How has the belief that the unique incarnation of the Logos or Word of God in Jesus of Nazareth developed into arguments that there could be no other incarnations, or that the eternal salvation of all human beings is tied to this singular event? In other words, "salvation" has been located in a pre-existent Son/Logos/Word becoming incarnate to the exclusion of other revelations of divine being.[10] Even when the development has been generously extended in universal proportions, such that the salvation effected by Jesus applies to *all* human beings, even those who aren't Christian, or when the proposition is that *all* creation is re-created in the singular moment of incarnation, Christians must inquire into the latent power structures behind these developments and examine the extent to which this generosity may be a form of supersessionism disguised by a thinly veiled claim of doctrinal certainty. The "cosmic" character of Christ may even be extended to the corners of the universe (saving extraterrestrials?).

The "universal" or "cosmic" character of eternal salvation through Jesus Christ would mean that even those who are not Christian may

---

9. Declaration of the Congregation for the Doctrine of the Faith, *Dominus Iesus*, par. 5, http://www.vatican.va/roman_curia/congregations/cfaith/documents/rc_con_cfaith_doc_20000806_dominus-iesus_en.html.

10. The clearest statement on this point is made in *Dominus Iesus*, par. 4: "The Church's constant missionary proclamation is endangered today by relativistic theories which seek to justify religious pluralism, not only *de facto* but also *de iure* (*or in principle*). As a consequence, it is held that certain truths have been superseded; for example, the definitive and complete character of the revelation of Jesus Christ, the nature of Christian faith as compared with that of belief in other religions."

benefit from it, as Karl Rahner claimed in his famous argument for "anonymous Christians."[11] This is indeed a charitable extension of the exclusivity of salvation through Christ, but it doesn't solve the problem of privileged access and the dangerous positivistic claim it makes on the incomprehensible Mystery of God. Rather, Rahner's notion of anonymous Christians puts an intellectual "band-aid" on the situation: Christians who wish to maintain the positivistic character of the incarnation of the Logos of God but are troubled by the supersessionism and exclusivism it implies bandage the wound with

11. Rahner's argument for "anonymous Christians" is found throughout his work, reflecting both his theological anthropology that argues for a relationship with God that is inherent in the universal human condition, regardless of religion, and also his Christ/Logos-centered theology which affects all human persons because of the pre-existent second divine person who became incarnate as Word made flesh. Usually understood as a leading example of the inclusivist model of a theory of religious diversity, the terminology "anonymous Christian" argues that one has "accepted of his freedom this gracious self-offering on God's part through faith, hope, and love, while on the other he is absolutely not yet a Christian at the social level (through baptism and membership of the Church) or in the sense of having consciously objectified his Christianity to himself in his own mind (by explicit Christian faith resulting from having hearkened to the explicit Christian message). We might therefore put it as follows: the 'anonymous Christian' in our sense of the term is the pagan after the beginning of the Christian mission, who lives in the state of God's grace through faith, hope and love, yet who has no explicit knowledge of the fact that his life is oriented in grace-given salvation to Jesus Christ." Rahner, "Observations on the Problem of the Anonymous Christian," trans. David Bourke, *Theological Investigations* 14 (London: Darton, Longman & Todd, 1976), 283. Rahner expands on this argument in "Anonymous and Explicit Faith," trans. David Morland, *Theological Investigations* 16 (London: Darton, Longman & Todd, 1979). Rahner's argument was intended to extend salvation beyond the Catholic Church and beyond Christianity; it was not intended as a complete and systematic response to the problems of pluralism but rather as a way for Christians to understand the universal salvific will of God demonstrated in the activity of revelation or divine self-communication in general and the activity of God in sending the Son and Spirit in particular. We find the spirit of his argument influencing the Second Vatican Council's attitude toward other religious traditions, as in *Lumen Gentium* 16: "Those who, through no fault of their own, do not know the Gospel of Christ or his church, but who nevertheless seek God with a sincere heart and, moved by grace, try in their actions to do his will as they know it through the dictates of their conscience—these too may attain eternal salvation."

the assumption that Christ is latently present wherever there are "good people" who seek the divine.

Of course, there are truth claims in every religious tradition, and perhaps it was inevitable, as John Hick acknowledges, for the church as it was becoming more monolithic and institutionalized to solidify the excessive language of praise and experience of religious fulfillment found in the Christian Scriptures into the "language of absolutes."[12] What has been particularly problematic, however, is the historical willingness to describe the eternal life of the divine *prior* to the historical life of Jesus of Nazareth. The early Christian experience of the divine in Jesus developed into a dangerous doctrinal presumption that we can *know* or *explain* the life of God *prior* to divine revelation (even prior to the act of creation), thereby absolutizing a particular historical event into one that is cosmically necessary for salvation after death.

Once the various ways of expressing divinity in Jesus became solidified and absolutized in Nicene language against Arius, the preexistent Logos/Son of God came to be understood as *homoousios* with God the Father, and so "eternally begotten," not "created," originating independently of time. Here, the scope of the early Christian understanding of God narrowed to the myopic confidence that the life of God could be known apart from divine activity in the material world, the world of human experience. It was perhaps inevitable that such confidence would not only become authoritative and normative but also draw a line between those who know God and those who do not have the fullness of divine revelation. Paul Knitter points out,

> [A]ll religions claim to have experienced or discovered something that is universal—which means something that is potentially meaningful for others, able to connect with them,

---

12. Hick writes, "What seems to have happened during the hundred years or so following Jesus' death was that the language of divine sonship floated loose from the original ground of Jewish thought and developed a new meaning as it took root again in Graeco-Roman culture. This language was pitched to the level of the reality which was to be expressed. For whenever men and women encounter God something of absolute importance has happened, something which can only be expressed in the language of absolutes," *God and the Universe of Faiths: Essays in the Philosophy of Religion* (Oxford: Oneworld, 1993), 116.

something that cannot be contained fully in any one language or culture. It is this "something," this mystery for which we will never find the "right" name or symbol that, according to Levinas, gives the "face of the other" its power and attraction over us. . . . In the face of this religious other I see or sense the face of the Other that shines within and beyond us all.[13]

Are there ways to re-imagine the symbols that reflect the totalizing attitude of the Same? Can Christians abandon the band-aid thinking that merely casts a wider net of "salvation" while ignoring the essential root of the problem, a failure to recognize the humility and vulnerability that is perhaps the meaning of "incarnation" understood through the lens of the self-emptying/self-negating activity of divine being in the material world? May we see divine power located in vulnerability for the sake of the Other rather than in the architecture of the reward of salvation that occurs only after death? Can Christians ever really be open to Other revelations, Other covenants, Other scriptures, as legitimate, as affecting their own?

If we are willing to plumb the ocean for what may be both disconcerting and wonderful ways to do theology, pursuing the limit-questions of which Tracy, Blanchot, and Bataille speak, we need new ways to witness the intersection between self, Other, and God. This chapter seeks to consider these questions through an aesthetics sensitive to the vulnerability of the Other. Despite the many characterizations of God in the Judeo-Christian Scriptures, a consistent portrayal of divine power from the prophets to the gospels is invested in the vulnerable. Divine power is vested in neither triumph nor control but rather the sensibility toward and care of the vulnerable.

Christians may describe divine power in terms of "incarnation" because it is through attention to the vulnerable that the trace of God is experienced. This is how Jesus' followers recognized divine power through and in him, and this is how Jesus empowered those around him for the impossible: Jesus calls Peter to venture out on

---

13. Paul F. Knitter, "Is the Pluralist Model a Western Imposition?," in *The Myth of Religious Superiority: A Multifaith Exploration*, ed. Paul F. Knitter (Maryknoll, NY: Orbis Books, 2005), 39–40.

the water; Jesus recognizes the woman with a hemorrhage has ventured toward her own healing. We are all called to be healers and conduits of divine power, through the responsibility for the Other that exceeds the boundaries of what is reasonable or even possible. It is precisely because I am utterly unable to fulfill the needs of another—even my child, whom I must welcome as the stranger—but that I still *desire* to attempt to fulfill those needs that God is glimpsed in the moment between awakening to the Other and living life for the Other. For Levinas, we must not seek the basis for the relationship with God in knowledge, because theoretical thought is not decisive in religious sensibility.[14] Rather than the certainty aligned with positive truth claims, we must appreciate the uncertainty within our infinite responsibility to repair the rifts created by violence and injustice. Here we may glimpse what it means to witness the symbol of incarnation. Jesus' embodiment meant a limited geographical scope—even Jesus did not, and could not, heal all those who suffered while he was physically alive. For the work that remains to be done, he would hardly limit incarnation to his person alone.

This chapter will not treat the specific issues involved in interreligious and interfaith encounters, but such concerns should always accompany us on the journey, as necessary in widening the scope of Christology. So that we may be prepared for the event, cautiously optimistic for the lightning strike of something new, I raise the problem of totality and absolutism here because it is the duty of Christian theology to examine the implications of positivistic truth claims such that even the central claims of Christian faith are critiqued. How can we be surprised by alterity when we do theology, as Richard Kearney puts it, in a "hall of mirrors"? How will we ever "meet" God, how will we ever follow Jesus, unless we are open to what is beyond the seemingly endless reflections of our own Christian categories? How will we ever learn from the wreckage of history, a wreckage for which Christians are often culpable? If we wish to maintain that it is God's Logos or Word which becomes incarnate, what does that mean for other "words" of God? As Roger Haight inquires,

14. See Renée D. N. van Riessen, *Man as a Place of God: Levinas' Hermeneutics of Kenosis* (Dordrecht: Springer, 2007), 180.

Why is Jesus not one of many symbolic actualizations of God's loving presence in humankind? Cannot "more" of God be revealed in other "incarnations"? There is no hard reason why God could not approach humankind in a variety of ways and in more than one medium, so that such a restriction seems inappropriately predicated of God. In principle a Logos Christology is open to this view, but its tendency has been to tie God's saving action in history exclusively to Jesus as its unique cause.[15]

Have the Christian symbols of Logos and incarnation become so beholden to their status as "representations" of the divine that they are indeed idols? I do not presume to even scratch the surface of what is implied in these questions; better thinkers have done more scratching. My concern is simply to keep asking—the question is always more important than an answer—in hope that we may discover new contexts and new images with which to formulate critique of doctrine, to cast out idols, to traverse this dark field, and then to be grateful that these same contexts, images, and symbols will be replaced in a later time. We will attempt these questions from the standpoint of an aesthetics of vulnerability, such that the arts in general, and the visual arts in particular, attract openness to the sacred *dehors* which haunts us like a whisper in the dark, a vulnerability that serves as corrective to the absolute certainty and triumphalism that has plagued Christianity in some regard for the better part of its history.

The Christ "Event"

The meaning we may glean from a doctrine, like the interpretation of a work of art, is neither independent of contextual frameworks that cultivate language nor entirely dependent on them; the meaning tends to oscillate between a culturally and historically conditioned interpretive framework and the attempt to show a purity of form, as in Kasimir Malevich's *White Square* or Ad Reinhardt's black paintings. The same is true for how Christian theology attempts to articulate something of the meaning of Jesus Christ, over two thousand years after the death of those who were his witnesses.

---

15. Roger Haight, *Jesus: Symbol of God* (Maryknoll, NY: Orbis Books, 1999), 433.

Jackson Pollock's *The Deep*,[16] one in the series of paintings he created shortly before his death in 1956, reminds us how thick and tenuous is the process of peering into the inky unknown, shuffling through the luminous wreckage, the white feathery down ripped apart. The artistic process, Blanchot realized, is like the experience of loss because the self is dissipated; Pollock also loses himself in the act of painting, the act of reaching limits and then transgressing them.

> When I am in my painting, I'm not aware of what I'm doing. It is only after a sort of "get acquainted" period that I see what I have been about. I have no fear of making changes, destroying the image, etc., because the painting has a life of its own. I try to let it come through. It is only when I lose contact with the painting that the result is a mess. Otherwise there is pure harmony, an easy give and take, and the painting comes out well.[17]

The deeper Pollock descends into the process of painting, the less the traditional instruments of painting are important to him: he discards the easel by stretching canvases on a cold barn floor; brushes become inconsequential, replaced by preferences for sticks and such materials as sand and broken glass to manipulate and transform the fluidity of the paint. In her book on Pollock, Elizabeth Frank places a passage from Melville's *Moby Dick* alongside *The Deep*: "Hither and thither, on high, glided the snow-white wings of small, unspeckled birds; these were the gentle thoughts of the feminine air; but to and fro in the deeps, far down in the bottomless blue, rushed mighty leviathans, sword-fish, and sharks; and these were the strong, troubled, murderous thinkings of the masculine sea."[18]

We creatures are the raw material for divine expression of divine life; Rahner first articulated this for me. We are empty vessels for the self-emptying of God. The creative process, both a passive submission—"When I'm in my painting, I'm not aware of what I'm

---

16. Pollock, *The Deep*, 1953; oil and enamel on canvas, 220.4 x 150.2 cm, Musée national d'art moderne, Centre Georges Pompidou, Paris.

17. Jackson Pollock, "My Painting," in *Jackson Pollock: Interviews, Articles, and Reviews*, ed. Pepe Karmel (New York: Museum of Modern Art, 1999), 18.

18. Cited by Elizabeth Frank, *Jackson Pollock* (New York: Abbeville Press, 1983), 97.

doing"—and an active engagement—"when I lose contact with the painting, the result is a mess"—highlights the channels and flow of this expression. Creativity is the breakthrough of the new, in acquaintance with the void. Blanchot wrote, "To live is always to take leave, to be dismissed and to dismiss what is. But we can get ahead of this separation and, looking at it as though it were behind us, make of it the moment when, even now, we touch the abyss and accede to the deep of being."[19] Blanchot is here speaking of the recognition of death as a part of the creative process, as is the desire for transformation; he comments on Rilke's statement, "Whatever closes itself into staying the same is already petrified." Over two thousand years ago, belief that the God of Israel had become incarnate in a human being was like a hole punched into the world, a disturbance of the obvious; and here in the hole Pollock wields, we see tragedy, tempest, "our promptness for disappearing, our aptitude for perishing, our fragility, our exhaustion, our gift for death,"[20] the impossibility of God occupying vulnerability, the state of dying and woundedness, while remaining transcendent.

The recognition of Jesus as somehow incarnate of God is a foundational subject of discourse for Christians, exploring what it means to articulate the belief that God enters time and material reality in a new moment or event. John Caputo references the way Derrida explains an "event": as both something "coming" and something "to come," an event may "simmer" in the present but is not finished in the present.[21] An event takes us by surprise, the way our lives are reinvented for us in our exposure to the future over which we have limited control; we cannot make events happen, but we can make ourselves available to their future.[22] Caputo calls a "prophet" a "functionary of the event," who can see the consequences of the future;[23]

---

19. Maurice Blanchot, *The Space of Literature*, trans. Ann Smock (Lincoln: University of Nebraska Press, 1989), 141.

20. Ibid., 140.

21. See John D. Caputo, *Truth: The Search for Wisdom in the Postmodern Age* (London: Penguin, 2013), 75.

22. Ibid.

23. John D. Caputo, *The Weakness of God: A Theology of the Event* (Bloomington: Indiana University Press, 2006), 31.

the prophet calls us to stay awake for what is to come and to begin the work of what is coming *now*. The "Christ event," observes Roger Haight, is "the generating source of Christian faith. . . . [T]he central piece in the Christian vision."[24] The "vision" of Jesus Christ's person and work is key to discipleship, but how do Christians articulate it? How may we put this vision into words, when images may be more appropriate to the emotional resonance that draws us more deeply into the non-knowing that brings us to the "outside," the *dehors*, the space of the Other? If the "self" is understood as a being-for-the-other, as we have seen in the thought of Emmanuel Levinas and Maurice Blanchot, how does this impact the traditional Christian use of the term "person" when we say that God is "personal" or that a divine "person" becomes human?

Through an aesthetics of vulnerability, metaphysical claims about the pre-existence of the Son are subordinate to recognizing that Jesus' teaching and life reveal something about the identity of the divine who liberates human beings from injustice and sin to offer communion and wholeness. This is salvation understood in the original meaning of *salvus*, Latin for "health" or "wholeness." Salvation experienced through Jesus is described in biblical language pertaining to the kenosis or emptiness of the divine in the person of Jesus, the divine who empowers human beings for infinite responsibility toward the establishment of justice and the promotion of compassion and peace.

As we have seen, adopting an aesthetics of vulnerability requires scrutiny of the positive character of metaphysical language on which the doctrine of the incarnation often relies. The positive character of divine presence in the incarnation of Jesus Christ is often referred to, for example, as his "saving particularity," Jesus' relationship with God the Father that *only* he can have. The "only" is used to point to Jesus' salvific achievement: because he is God, *only* he can lead humanity to God. Does Jesus possess the fullness of divine being in such a way that human consciousness may seize upon it, claim it, and from there go out to all the nations?

If divine "presence" and divine "being" are connected in a positive way, it is hard to disengage them. This was Heidegger's critique:

24. Haight, *Jesus: Symbol of God*, 16.

onto-theology reduces the divine to a "thing," even if the highest "thing." To locate the "presence" in one place and not in another is to reify it, to "thing-ify" it; Derrida would add that the "not there" associated with "presence" is then the "absence" of the thing. Concretizing presence leads to naming, knowledge, even ownership. As Richard Kearney explains, "Unless we let go of God as property and possession, we cannot encounter the Other as radical stranger."[25] Balancing the historical context of the doctrine of the incarnation with confidence in the ontological categories in which this doctrine is usually articulated is difficult without slipping into an identification of *God* with these categories. Joseph O'Leary asserts, "The God of the Bible is constantly shattering the fixated, idolatrous images his worshippers form of him, and the Johannine language of God as Spirit, light, love, locates God in a dynamic realm of communal contemplation from which it would be difficult to distill a well-defined divine substance suited to metaphysical analysis."[26]

The Greek philosophical project that made metaphysical categories such as "eternity," "immutability," and "impassibility" intelligible guided the positive relationship between language and reality in articulating Christian doctrine. When the "truth" of Greek philosophical theology of the incarnation frames a *privilege* of proximity to the Christian "truth" in terms of a positive presence, a thingness, or reification, of the Absolute, and if this privilege in access to the truth is what is meant by "tradition," then the tradition has deviated

---

25. Richard Kearney, *Anatheism: Returning to God after God* (New York: Columbia University Press, 2010), 64.

26. Joseph O' Leary, "Emptiness and Dogma," *Buddhist-Christian Studies* 22 (2002): 165. John Keenan and Linda Keenan echo O'Leary's sentiment about John's gospel: "John veils the beginning in mystery and maintains a sense that . . . we do not know much about this God at all. John's mystic vision serves not to elaborate upon God, but rather to expose our primal ignorance," John P. Keenan and Linda K. Keenan, *I Am/No Self: A Christian Commentary on the Heart Sutra* (Leuven: Peeters, 2011), 87. The "Word became flesh and dwelt among us" in John's Greek "reflects the more transient and impermanent meaning of 'to tent,' that is, 'to pitch a tent.' . . . [T]his is more like the Witness Tent that accompanied and went before the Israelites in their wilderness wanderings . . . a shelter for people on a journey, not a fixed habitation. . . . [T]he Word, now enfleshed, tents with us," ibid.

from the original vision of those who first sang of divine self-emptiness when they worshiped Jesus. Such is the quandary of onto-theology, the "conceptual idolatry" that at once claims both divine ineffability and a designation of what constitutes being itself.[27]

Christians do not have privileged access to the fullness of divine presence or "truth," and any "truth" we claim is a function of the way it has been manifested to us, as a "persecuted truth," a vulnerable truth that rises from the experience of the oppressed. The "impossible" idea that the Infinite could shimmer through the vulnerability of the Other is not only central to the Gospel but also found throughout Christian tradition. As Oscar Romero taught, "The poor tell us what the world is and what service the church can offer the world. . . . [W]e are incarnated in the poor. . . . [E]very time we come closer to the poor, we discover the true face of the suffering servant of Yahweh. There we come closer to knowing the mystery of Christ who becomes human and becomes poor through us."[28]

Given Jesus' commitments to the destitute poor, the form of truth manifest in the idea of an incarnation is a "persecuted truth" in which the Other is the form of directionality of the self. Levinas writes, "[I]n divesting the ego of its imperialism, the hetero-affection establishes a new undeclinability . . . the self involved in the *gnawing away at oneself* in responsibility, which is also incarnation"[29]—a way that the self gives until there is nothing left. The "self" is enacted, performed, through the incarnation of infinite responsibility. Hent de Vries writes that Levinas thus provides another meaning of incarnation, "that of a carnage in the flesh; that the infinite leaves this intrigue in the finite is just another way of saying that responsibility eats its way in and through the flesh, infinitely," and that by turning "itself" "inside out," the self is capable of giving.[30] The incarnation

27. See Kearney, *The God Who May Be*, 24.

28. Oscar Romero, *A Martyr's Message of Hope: Six Homilies* (Kansas City, MO: Celebration Books, 1981), 82.

29. Emmanuel Levinas, *Otherwise than Being: Or Beyond Essence*, trans. Alphonso Lingis (Pittsburgh, PA: Duquesne University Press, 1998), 121.

30. Hent de Vries, "Adieu, à dieu, a-Dieu," in *Ethics as First Philosophy: The Significance of Emmanuel Levinas for Philosophy, Literature and Religion*, ed. Adriaan T. Peperzak (New York: Routledge, 1995), 215.

reveals what is divine in its burning away of the imperialistic ego. The "image" becomes imageless, the representation becomes unrepresentable. "Thing"-ness dissipates into abstraction. "Incarnation" is embodiment turned outward, the "self" that empties.

This notion of humility as a modality of the "truth"—a persecuted truth—is sometimes conflicted in Levinas's thought when applied to God. We must keep in mind that Levinas's ethical project is singular and unyielding: as soon as one waivers from the radical alterity of the Other to presume similarity, one is subject to the violence of the Same. But Levinas asserts that the only possible modality or form by which divine transcendence manifests in the world is in humility: "The idea of a truth whose manifestation is not glorious or bursting with light, the idea of a truth that manifests itself in its humility, like the still small voice in the biblical expression—the idea of a persecuted truth—is that not henceforth the only possible modality of transcendence?"[31] That God could be in exile with the mar-

---

31. Emmanuel Levinas, "Un Dieu Homme?" "A Man-God?," in *Entre-Nous: Thinking-of-the-Other*, trans. Michael B. Smith and Barbara Harshav (New York: Columbia University Press, 1998), 55. Renee van Riessen argues that Levinas follows Kierkegaard on this point. J. Aaron Simmons notes that there is a conflict in Levinas's reading of Kierkegaard when Levinas criticizes Kierkegaard for not taking ethical priority far enough. On Levinas's use of the phrase "persecuted truth," which Levinas mentions in the essay "Kierkegaard: Existence and Ethics" as well as in "A Man-God?" Simmons notes that Levinas's reading of Kierkegaard is "highly selective" and that, while the two share a common interest in critiquing Hegel's totalizing vision, they differ in terms of what constitutes the concept of religion. Where Kierkegaard sees a radical interiority of human subjectivity as that which dethrones Hegel's triumphalism, Levinas sees a deviation from the ethical project, something that makes the Kierkegaardian subject fundamentally defined as being "for itself." Simmons disagrees with this as a description of Kierkegaard's thought. Kierkegaard, asserts Simmons and Merold Westphal, sees the essential kerygma of Christianity as *kenosis*; the self is therefore essentially relational. But, Simmons rightly points out, the Other with whom the Kierkegaardian subject is engaged is *God* and not necessarily another human person. I believe that this reversal of foundational ethical priorities is intolerable for Levinas, since for him we are only aware of God as a *trace* in the Other through the infinite responsibility toward the Other. The consideration of the self in direct relationship with God such that the human Other can be bypassed is a red flag that Levinas cannot abide. Levinas finds such presumptuousness

ginalized, enslaved, and forgotten is key to the Jewish image of God and also key to Levinas's thought: God *chooses* exile, as in the Kabbalah; God chooses the vulnerability of the suffering Other as God's own modality.

Jesus lived this "turned-out," "gnawed-out" life, a life in which the ego was finally burned away for the sake of the desperate and destitute. Human subjectivity is impossible apart from relationship; the paradox of subjectivity is that the subject is constituted by a

---

endemic in Christian thought insofar as Christians believe that they have direct access to God through Christ's accomplishment of reconciliation, making the Other unnecessary to salvation. "Persecuted truth is an idea that Levinas can wholeheartedly support," argues Simmons; "Unfortunately, right at the moment when it seems that he is beginning to see the connection between his and Kierkegaard's thought, he goes in the opposite direction. . . . [T]he main split between Levinas and Kierkegaard is their different loci of relational priority. Although Levinas will champion the new modality of truth opened by Kierkegaard, . . . Levinas ultimately returns to the charge of egoistic subjectivity when he considers the priority that Kierkegaard gives to the religious sphere," J. Aaron Simmons, "Existential Appropriations: the Influence of Jean Wahl on Levinas' Reading of Kierkegaard," in *Kierkegaard and Levinas: Ethics, Politics and Religion*, ed. J. Aaron Simmons and David Wood (Bloomington, IN: Indiana University Press, 2008), 47–48. Because I agree with Simmons that Levinas can and does champion the notion of a "persecuted truth," and because Levinas is uncompromising in his ethical vision, unfortunately at times to the detriment of his scholarly balance, I rely on Levinas's use of the notion of "persecuted truth" here. The essays to which Simmons refers, "A Propos of 'Kierkegaard Vivant" and "Kierkegaard: Existence and Ethics," were first published in 1963 and 1966, respectively. Both essays appear in the volume *Proper Names*, trans. Michael B. Smith (Stanford, CA: Stanford University Press, 1996). In 1968, Levinas first publishes the essay *Qui est Jesus-Christ? Un Dieu Homme?* after a presentation given during the Week of Catholic Intellectuals held in Paris. The ideas of "persecuted truth" and humiliation as the modality of truth appear more favorable in this latter essay (perhaps in deference to his audience), which I also feel justifies my use of this notion here. In Levinas's *Otherwise than Being* (first published in 1974), "persecution" appears as an ethical term: "[T]he other . . . before being an individuation of the genus man, a rational animal, a free will, or any essence whatever, he is the persecuted one for whom I am responsible to the point of being a hostage for him" (p. 59), and "The persecuted one is expelled from his place and has only himself to himself, has nothing in the world on which to rest his head" (p. 121).

"hemorrhage that bleeds my own comfort for the sake of the Other."[32] A way to approach the mystery of the incarnation refers to this enfleshment that is a carnage of the flesh, a burning away of the flesh for the sake of the suffering Other. Jesus' heteronomy, his life lived for the Other, thus reveals that the particularity of embodiment cannot be turned in on *itself*, turning Jesus' person into a restricted or private place for God to dwell. Indeed, Jesus as indicative of divine closeness to creation follows a long tradition of recognizing the divine relationship to creation in the Hebrew Scriptures. Terence Fretheim writes, "To suggest that God first entered into time and history in the Christ event is to ignore this wide swath of Old Testament material. God's act in Jesus is an intensification of this already-existing trajectory of God's way of being present in and relating to the structures of the world."[33]

Levinas acknowledges that Judaism has no analogue for what Christians understand as the incarnation of God; but regarded through the lens of kenosis, the "humility of God who is willing to come down to the level of the servile conditions of the human," he sees precedent in the Hebrew Scriptures, "describing a God bending down to look at human misery or inhabiting that misery."[34] Levinas examines the Jewish understanding of kenosis by pointing to several examples in the Hebrew Scriptures, such as Psalm 147, "God who heals the broken hearted and binds their wounds" also "counts the number of the stars and gives them all their names." "There is an inseparable bond between God's descent and God's elevation," writes Levinas: wherever we find the power of the Holy One, we find God's humility, the proximity of God to human suffering.[35] The conjunction of elevation and descent is also found in Isaiah 57:15, "Says the High and Lofty One

---

32. Levinas, *Otherwise than Being*, 74; see also William Edelglass, "Levinas on Suffering and Compassion," *Sophia* 45, no. 2 (October 2006): 54.

33. Terence Fretheim, "Christology and the Old Testament," in *Who Do You Say That I Am? Essays in Christology*, ed. Mark A. Powell and David R. Bauer (Louisville, KY: Westminster John Knox Press, 1999), 209; see also Roger Haight, *The Future of Christology* (New York: Continuum, 2007), 170.

34. Emmanuel Levinas, "Judaism and Kenosis," in *In the Time of the Nations*, trans. Michael B. Smith (New York: Continuum, 2007), 101.

35. Ibid., 102.

who inhabits eternity and whose name is Holy: I dwell in the high and holy place, but I am with whomever is of a humble and contrite spirit, to revive the spirit of the afflicted." God's greatness is thus precisely in God's kenosis, a humility that provides a space—*tzimtzum*—that accepts our questioning of God's holiness in a world incapable of restricting itself to the light of divine revelation.[36] The space opened by God for us, while honoring our difference from God as creatures, also subordinates God's infinite being to the human. We as human are Other from God such that our alterity provides the "necessary conditions for the association of God with the being of the worlds."[37] Human otherness from God is not described as a dualism, however, or a gap that cannot be bridged; rather, alterity is described as the condition of interdependence, the condition, perhaps, of non-duality:

> [E]verything depends on humanity . . . located within the order of action and work, at the level of matter. Everything depends on the human, even the outpouring of God, which confers being and light on the entire hierarchy of worlds. The last to be created and raised to the highest by the divine breath that gives life, humanity carries within their being a residuum of all the levels of the creature. . . . [T]he human is in affinity with the totality of the real.[38]

God's self-emptying makes it possible for the human to exist at all levels of reality, from the material to the spiritual; but even more important, writes Levinas, God's self-emptying makes a space for human beings to affect more than our present circumstances. Our being ensures the holiness in the "other than myself" such that we are answerable for the holiness of the universe. This responsibility is found in the microcosm of human relationship as well as in the macrocosm of the interaction of humanity with the plurality of worlds. The meaning of being is responsibility for the Other, which is an infinite responsibility originating from God's kenosis.

36. Ibid., 105.
37. Ibid., 109.
38. Ibid., 110.

Form of a Slave

The referential meaning of the doctrine that "God became human" entails that God somehow and in a moment of interruption of time as the flow of consciousness—an event that raises the messianic specter of novelty—manifests an opportunity for a way out of the chaos that is the suffering world. God becomes an ordinary (whatever that means) human being who just so happens to live a life that made enough of an impact that it led to his death, as well as enough of an impact that one who should have remained nameless would be remembered. Weighing the impact gets tricky, to be sure: it takes a fair amount of discipline to shackle the tendency magnified in our culture by American superhero mythology to avoid saying that Jesus had superpowers—that his "divine nature" elevated his "human nature" into something that no longer makes Jesus one of us. It takes a fair amount of discipline to envision the messianic as coming from the powerless and impotent within a first-century worldview which understands power as Roman garrisons and the rich as receivers of divine favor or within a present-day worldview which understands power as tanks and guns or as white skin and stock options.

It may be a worthwhile thought experiment to imagine that Jesus as a carpenter would have built something crooked, or as a teacher would have lost his train of thought. He had to have snapped at his parents as a moody adolescent or reneged on a promise. Imagine: there were those who brushed past him in the street, who didn't see a golden-haired Apollo dropped from the heavens or the definitive savior to end all would-be saviors. There were those who met him during his lifetime who thought of him as merely "that carpenter from Nazareth." (Nice boy, when will he get married?) These musings on the particularity of the incarnation are ways to imagine its historical and embodied character. Here's where the notion of "particularity" works to make the incarnation what it is: God becomes one of the nameless who just so happens to be remembered because he believed in and lived out the overwhelming love of God for the nameless.

Art can help us imagine Jesus as one of the destitute poor of first-century Palestine, as an antidote to the mountain of images, especially those from the eighteenth to the twentieth centuries, that portray him well-scrubbed, well-coiffed, and well-fed. Images which bring Jesus into modern art are willing to bend these "Jesus rules" that had dominated Christian art, "rules" that diminished his humanity. Often, those artists who are most perceptive about Jesus' human reality—in terms of his Jewish identity, the bleakness of his destitution, and the ambiguity regarding his mission with which he wrestled in the desert, among other things—are those artists who themselves struggled with conventional Christianity.

Käthe Kollwitz (1867–1945) used etching as a medium to portray the stark reality of the poor; her triptych *The Downtrodden* (1900) shows a horizontal figure which recalls Hans Holbein's *The Body of the Dead Christ in the Tomb* (1520–1522)[39] as the centerpiece of three groupings of figures. On the right, a mother's face grimly vacant, her palm gently supporting the head of a child. The father can neither touch nor look upon the child and buries his head in his arm. We are given the moment that the child has just died, her skin having now fallen a ghostly white, in glaring contrast to the shadows that enclose her family. The figures to the right, twisted in agony, seem to be allegorical for the desperation displayed here. The emaciated, spent body of the Christ-figure lies in horizontal association between the current situation and the mythologies of the past. Here Christ is not a savior, and the work provides neither the hope of resurrection nor resolution of the sorrows of the present. The triptych, commonly used in altarpieces of the Middle Ages, gives a certain religious weight to the work while also mocking the fact that religious faith has not alleviated this tragedy.

Kollwitz lost her son Peter in World War I and a grandson in World War II; keenly astute to the hardships of the working class, she was a committed pacifist and socialist. Christianity never satisfied her desire for answers to the depth of suffering and loss that welled in and around her, but her work often reflects Christian themes, such

39. Hans Holbein the Younger, *The Body of the Dead Christ in the Tomb*, 1520–1522. Oil on wood, 30.5 cm × 200 cm. Öffentliche Kunstsammlung, Basel. It should be noted that this painting so transfixed Fyodor Dostoyevsky that his wife was worried that he would endure another epileptic seizure in the gallery. Holbein's life-size depiction of Christ's decomposing body, gangrene spreading from his wounds, his mouth agape and his eyes open, haunted Dostoyevsky for the rest of his life.

as the pietà, as in the searing *Woman with Dead Child*,[40] and she names as "prayer" the channeling of her grief into *Mourning Parents*,[41] the memorial she created for her son: "I am praying when I remember Peter. The need to kneel down and let him pour through, through me. Feel myself altogether one with him. It is a different love from the love in which one weeps and longs and grieves. When I love him in that way I do not pray. But when I feel him in the way which I want to make outwardly visible in my work, then I am praying."[42]

Fritz Eichenberg (1901–1990), who revered Kollwitz and worked with Dorothy Day, placed *Jesus in a Breadline*, after the line that formed outside the Catholic Worker house in New York.[43] The figure of Jesus is discernible, in silhouette in front of the sun, a halo that is the work's light source. Jesus joins the hungry as they wait to be fed; he does not miraculously feed them but is hunched over in the way they are, a bit ashamed, perhaps, uncomfortable, clutching a cloak around him in the cold as the others do. This is not the Christ of the "already" of the reign of God; this is the Jesus of the "not yet," awaiting bread with the rest. Born Jewish, Eichenberg was a young man in Germany during World War I. When he openly opposed Hitler, he left Germany for New York. He had a nervous breakdown after his wife suddenly died in 1938. He turned to Zen Buddhism and later became a Quaker, soon assuming a vocation through Day's mission to the poor. He remained associated with the Catholic Worker for forty years. Eichenberg's portrayal of Jesus continued throughout the rest of his life; *Black Crucifixion*, a woodcut print from 1963, responds to the civil rights movement by showing Jesus on the cross, in the traditional contortions and traditionally accompanied by Mary and John, but with black skin.

---

40. Käthe Kollwitz, *Woman with Dead Child*, 1903, etching, National Gallery of Art, Washington, DC.

41. Käthe Kollwitz, *Die trauernden Eltern, Mourning Parents*, 1931. Marble, Vladslo, Belgium, grave of Peter Kollwitz.

42. Levinas, "A Man-God?," 64.

43. Fritz Eichenberg, *Jesus in a Breadline*, 1953, woodcut. Work commissioned by *The Catholic Worker*; for a collection of Eichenberg's prints, see *Fritz Eichenberg: Works of Mercy*, ed. Robert Ellsberg (Maryknoll, NY: Orbis Books, 1992).

Claude Clark, *Slave Lynching*

Claude Clark's *Slave Lynching*[44] gives vivid expressionist clout to a modern crucifixion. The scene could have taken place anywhere in America, the crowd a sea of smeared faces observing the horrific flogging of a naked slave, his hands tied to a crossbeam, his body splayed on a dais, his deep brown skin glowing with sweat and blood. We cannot see his face. The last view the slave sees is of a crowd who looks on, silently approving of this torture. The slave's fists are clenched, anticipating the whip, and we, on the other side of the painting, shielded from this history, are left in terrible suspense, since we know what will happen next. James Cone writes of Jesus as the subject of Black Theology "because he is the content of the hopes and dreams of black people. . . . [H]e was their Truth, enabling them to know that white definitions of humanity were lies."[45] Clark paints these lies here. Clark steadfastly incorporated Southern

44. Claude Clark, *Slave Lynching*, 1946. Oil on canvas, Art Gallery, University of Maryland.

45. James H. Cone, *God of the Oppressed* (Maryknoll, NY: Orbis Books, 1997), 30.

folk art and African art as a way to show the dignity and cultural integrity of persons of color. Cone reminds us of the resistance of the black slaves against the attempts of white slave masters' intentions "to present a 'Jesus' who would make the slave obedient and docile. Jesus was supposed to make black people better slaves, that is, faithful servants of their white masters,"[46] but the slaves chose to make Jesus the basis of their struggle: "Through Jesus Christ they could know that they were people, even though they were bought and sold like cattle. Jesus Christ was that reality who invaded their history from beyond and bestowed upon them a definition of humanity that could not be destroyed by the whip and pistol."[47] The truth of the black slave reflects the manifestation of the divine in and through humility, the taking of the "form of a slave": such is the import of "kenosis."

Paul includes the famous kenosis hymn in his Letter to the Philippians:

> Let the same mind be in you that was in Christ Jesus, who, though he was in the form of God, did not regard equality with God as something to be exploited, but emptied himself, taking the form of a slave, being born in human likeness. And being found in human form, he humbled himself and became obedient to the point of death—even death on a cross. Because of this, God also highly exalted him and gave him the name that is above every name, so that at the name of Jesus every knee should bend, in heaven and on earth and under the earth, and every tongue should confess that Jesus Christ is Lord, to the glory of God the Father. (Phil 2:6-11)

While biblical scholarship makes varied conclusions on the meaning and significance of this hymn, especially concerning the issue of whether this hymn points to a belief in the preexistence of Christ,[48]

---

46. Ibid., 29.

47. Ibid., 31.

48. The literature on this debate is extensive. Ralph P. Martin, in *Carmen Christi* (Cambridge, UK: Cambridge University Press, 2005), argues that the hymn was used as an "ode" to Christ in three phases: first the preexistent, next the incarnate and humiliated, and last the triumphant. James D. G. Dunn argues that the hymn

scholars agree that these verses, having already been in use by the early Christians, were inserted, rather than invented, by Paul. This epistle to the Philippians is considered to have been written by Paul himself while in prison in Rome, in the early 60s. Paul was appreciative of the contributions by the church at Philippi and was attempting to provide solace in his suffering and in theirs, expressing trust that his suffering reflects that of Christ's suffering: Christ's humbling in the hymn is akin to the "humiliation" of being human in a hostile world (Phil 3:21). Knowing both how to be humble and how to enjoy the world is an effort with which Paul is familiar and which he attributes to Christ's example (Phil 4:11-13).

The hymn likely originated much earlier than the epistle and so predates the Prologue to John's gospel, which displays a more developed sense of the preexistence of the Logos who becomes incarnate. Even if the sophistication of a propositional statement of a preexistent Son of God is not worked out in the *kenosis* hymn, it shows that for some in the early Christian community, the Lordship of Christ is worshiped alongside God the Father. The borrowing of phrases from Isaiah 45:23, "every knee shall bow, every tongue shall swear," shows a reading of Isaiah that, according to Larry Hurtado, presupposes the early devotional connection between Christ and God.[49] The use of these phrases underscores submission to God as well, which reflects Jesus' humility on what is asked of us. In the same way that Luke sets up the paradox that "the first shall be last and the last shall be first," humility and exaltation go together. Hurtado advises we read Philippians 2:6-8 as a narrative sequence: Jesus' earthly obedience in 2:8 is the apex of a set of self-emptying actions which are answered by divine exaltation in 2:9-11.[50]

---

is simply an Adamic description of Christ's life, death, and resurrection, without reference to preexistence (Dunn, *Christology in the Making: A New Testament Inquiry into the Origins of the Doctrine of the Incarnation* [Grand Rapids, MI: Eerdmans, 1996]). The hymn is therefore a description of what God intended Adam to be and what is now personified in Christ. J. Jeremias, O. Cullmann, and M. Hengel all agree that Philippians 2:5-11 contains the blueprint for the trajectory of worship of Christ *lex orandi, lex credendi*. See Martin, *Carmen Christi*, xix.

49. Larry W. Hurtado, *Lord Jesus Christ: Devotion to Jesus in Earliest Christianity* (Grand Rapids, MI: Eerdmans, 2003), 388–89.

50. Ibid., 123.

From a theological standpoint, the hymn connects the act of self-emptying with something divine, whether a divine helper to God or God Godself; this hymn is celebratory and, as such, is excessive and abundant in its language. God is praised in the divine humiliation which becomes an exaltation, a celebration of the divine in our midst. Such should be sung. That the humiliation of God recognized in Jesus was expressed in an early hymn means that it was not composed in isolation, a lonely scholar bent over books in a lonely cell. The hymn of kenosis was sung in a community; more specifically, the hymn was sung in a community of persons who had endured great hardship and humiliation themselves. Hurtado argues that *Kyrios* (Lordship) "designates Jesus as the recipient of corporate devotion."[51] Because its origins are in the context of worship and community, kenosis is significant to the early Christian regard of the way God is in God's relationship to the world, such that through humility is the paradox of the presence and absence of God.

Kenosis as a modality of humiliation and a self-emptying does not point to God ceasing to be God but rather to a way in which God is glimpsed: in the movement toward the Other that preserves the alterity of the Other. In the kenosis hymn, God preserves the "otherness" of human beings ("taking the form of a slave, being born in human likeness") and in this specific activity, Jesus' humiliation is exalted as divine. The encounter between God and humanity in the activity of kenosis refers to God's making the Other the matrix of God's own existence, the way God is God. If the doctrine of the "incarnation" is language meant to describe God's attempt to bring those who suffer into the recognition and care of the divine will, then kenosis describes the movement of the eternal and boundless through the vulnerable, temporal, and finite, making vulnerability a modality of divine being and emptying any definitive duality between divine and human. Kenosis is a term that emerges from the significance of paradox: how can the changeless change? By referring to "emptiness" as the origin of non-duality, the origin of the "not-one but not-two." The "love" by which Christians understand divine activity in becoming incarnate

51. Ibid., 117.

has its referent in emptiness, in which Buddhists find the elimination of dualism—or selfhood, or the distinctiveness of substances—that allows relationship to be the primary ontological category.

If Jesus is "God," then God takes the form of a slave, the form of one waiting for soup and bread, the one shot in the back as he runs from a police officer. If, however, Jesus' humanity is understood as substantively greater than our humanity, whether in ability,[52] knowledge, freedom, or in degree of suffering, if we understand Jesus as above sexual desire (as though celibacy is a "higher" vocation than marriage), or if we believe Jesus to be in command of the forces of nature in a way that no other human being is capable, then Jesus is

---

52. The underlying question regarding the "difference" between Jesus' humanity and the humanity of all human beings pertains to the ubiquity of sin. Jesus as a first-century Jew would have been subject to the same structures of ethnic-based racism and religious exclusivism that were prevalent at the time. Elisabeth Vasko has made an excellent case for the demonstration of this in the story of Jesus' encounter with the Syro-Phoenician woman in Mark 7:24-30, when Jesus first dismisses the woman, "Let the children be fed first, for it is not fair to take the children's food and throw it to the dogs." Vasko writes: "The passage calls Christians to remember that even the body of Christ can become inscribed in structural sin, something that privileged interpreters often miss. Our idealization of Jesus has led privileged interpreters to excuse and overlook the ways in which Christological discourse was never meant to be a monologue, an all-encompassing totality of divine Truth, preoccupied with matters of religious and doctrinal purity. Rather, it must be a living dialogue informed by the wisdom of those who occupy marginal sites." Vasko, *Beyond Apathy: A Theology for Bystanders* (Minneapolis: Fortress Press, 2015), 170. Does Jesus "sin" when he uses a racial slur? The woman's dignity and boldness challenging Jesus' racism ("Sir, even the dogs under the table eat the children's crumbs") turns the tables on him, turning master into student; notes Vasko, "What is remarkable about this biblical narrative is that the word of an 'unclean' woman not only interprets a 'christological word,' but it also effects a change in Jesus," ibid., 175. That Jesus was open to recognizing his weaknesses—that he was capable of learning from his mistake—brought him to a deeper sense of his own teaching on the reign of God. While Vasko wants to discuss Jesus as subject to the structural sin of racism in first-century Palestine, she does not call Jesus' initial dismissal and insult of the woman a "sin." Had he walked away from her, scorning her entirely, and never altered his own views on those marginalized within his own marginalized society, perhaps his action toward her would more clearly constitute "sin."

a *tertium quid*, a "third thing"—neither "fully" human nor "fully" divine and so inadequate to describe the non-dual relationship between divine and human in "incarnation."

Arius, the early fourth-century troublemaker, could not envision Jesus as equal to God because the divine nature can neither be differentiated nor suffer. Much of the Christological response since Arius has tended to overcompensate for Arius's arguments, prompting affirmations of Jesus' superhuman "humanity." Such makes Jesus an alien dropped into our environment for the purpose of intervening in the lives of a few to save them from damnation or the mediator who negotiates between the distant God and the lowly planet. But the historical persistence of maintaining the "fully human" side of the Chalcedonian equation must pertain to the hope that God occupies/becomes what is authentically, genuinely human, not clothed in the appearance or veneer of humanity.[53] Fidelity to the belief that God becomes incarnate in Jesus does not necessitate that God elevates Jesus' humanity above our own. Rather, such fidelity should redirect our gaze toward the significance of the humanity we all share, since it *is* our very humanity, as well as the very particularity in each of us, that God "becomes."

Christians may thus see Jesus not as an angel or an alien, or as a hybrid of matter and spirit, or as the "reconciliation" of divine and human (which isn't necessary if divine and human aren't opposed), but as the one in whom his followers and friends saw a moment in the history of God's covenant, in an event that provides a dimension to the God-world relationship which continues to surprise us and in which the exile of God with the oppressed is re-imagined. This innovation in the prophetic tradition, this lightning strike, does not supersede the moments of divine revelation previous to the life of the historical Jesus and neither does it deny the potential of future moments of disclosure: rather than a linear progression of moments, this is God's "time"—or "eternity"—in time's multivalence, such that past and future are interdependent, like rays emanating from the same source. Perhaps the meaning of awaiting the "second com-

53. For more on this point, see Susie Paulik Babka, "Arius, Superman and the *Tertium Quid*: When Popular Culture Meets Christology," *Irish Theological Quarterly* 73, no. 1 (2008).

ing" of the incarnation refers to the novelty to come, because the center will always shift; "God is new each moment," as Edward Schillebeeckx taught. If revelation comes from the infinite, then there is always more to come. Judaism, Christianity, and Islam are not each static moments in the life of God but reveal different dimensions of divine life in all the social, political, cultural, and historical manipulations of language and image that condition our inquiry. Consequent to "newness" is "openness" to a future previously unimagined: "We have to leave God his freedom in being new with regard to us. . . . I prefer to see God not as an unchangeable and unchanging God but rather as eternal youth. . . . God is a constant source of new possibilities."[54] The emergence of new possibilities does not require that any one moment be definitive, exhaustive, or even superior to the previous. Joseph O'Leary remarks,

> The Christ we have known is only a limited historical manifestation of Christ; the Christ whom faith holds to be universal is not yet manifest. The former is the seed which must fall in the ground again and again and die if the full dimensions of the incarnate phenomenality of God are to become apparent. The entire language of pre-existence, resurrection and exaltation names this hidden dimension of Christ towards which Christian faith is always underway, losing Christ again and again in order to find him in his fullness.[55]

There is no finality to divine self-disclosure; the new moments will continue, in ways and places we never anticipated. If God can be thought to submit to the agony of the cross like so many thousands in the ancient world, like the thousands hung from lynching trees in the new world, then God *is*, precisely where we are not tempted to abuse the power of "finding" God or claiming divine presence for our *selves*. The trace of the divine is in and through those deemed unworthy of our attention, until the visual compulsion shatters complacency and we are brought to the meaning of "God

54. Edward Schillebeeckx, *God Is New Each Moment*, with Huub Oosterhuis and Piet Hoogeveen (Edinburgh: T & T Clark, 1983), 29.

55. Joseph S. O'Leary, *Questioning Back: The Overcoming of Metaphysics in the Christian Tradition* (Minneapolis: Winston-Seabury, 1986), 211.

incarnate." The infinite ethical summons takes place on a visual plane. Faithfulness to Schillebeeckx's "God of surprises" means constant vigilance at the door of the wedding banquet, vigilance traversing the dark field, in openness to the manifestation of infinite responsibility, for the ever-new moment.

Jesus and the Aesthetics of Vulnerability

Reimagining the doctrine of divine incarnation in light of an aesthetics of vulnerability recognizes interdependency as the condition of existence. For Emmanuel Levinas, subjectivity is meaningless, barren of existence, without the face of the Other to summon a response. Jesus shows that attentiveness to the Other is the primary locus of subjectivity, of the existence of a "self," which is never a terminus. The "self" in an aesthetics of vulnerability is that which carries the wounds of the Other, which is the locus of inclusion, the "Desire that is not a lack," that transcends separated, non-dual being and is accomplished in the exponential character of a "Desire that is accomplished" but never satisfied, "In transcending itself, in engendering Desire."[56] Such is similar to John Zizioulas's observation, "Communion does not threaten personal particularity: it is constitutive of it."[57] There is only the particularity broken open by the encounter with the Other; there is only existence as pertains to a life lived for others, a life emptied (kenosis) of "self." "Salvation" as a docile reliance to "be saved by" Jesus is not relevant if my fundamental concern is whether and how I fulfill the needs of the Other. Salvation is then linked with our response to the Other even *before* it is an explicitly religious response, even before it is an explicit response to God. When we regard the incarnation within the orientation of the human toward God and God toward the human (or creation toward God and God toward creation), from which emerges the reign of God, the divine heteronomy displayed in the incarnation has the potential to be fulfilled in each of us.

56. Emmanuel Levinas, *Totality and Infinity: An Essay in Exteriority*, trans. Alphonso Lingis (Pittsburgh, PA: Duquesne University Press, 2008), 269.

57. John D. Zizioulas, "Human Capacity and Human Incapacity: A Theological Exploration of Personhood," *Scottish Journal of Theology* 28 (1975).

The turn to the Other is then already a turn to God, even if implicitly; Christians see this embodied in Jesus Christ, and according to Levinas, Jews see this embodied in Torah. The turn to the stranger, the Other refers to the Other as the trace of God. The stranger, Richard Kearney explains, is the outsider, the uninvited, who has nowhere to live unless we provide a dwelling;[58] as Jesus illustrates in Matthew 25:34-46:

> Then the king will say to those at his right hand, "Come, you that are blessed by my Father, inherit the kingdom prepared for you from the foundation of the world; for I was hungry and you gave me food, I was thirsty and you gave me something to drink, I was a stranger and you welcomed me, I was naked and you gave me clothing, I was sick and you took care of me, I was in prison and you visited me." Then the righteous will answer him, "Lord, when was it that we saw you hungry and gave you food, or thirsty and gave you something to drink? And when was it that we saw you a stranger and welcomed you, or naked and gave you clothing? And when was it that we saw you sick or in prison and visited you?" And the king will answer them, "Truly I tell you, just as you did it to one of the least of these who are members of my family, you did it *to me*."[59]

In a Levinasian reading, this passage becomes the premier text of the significance of the incarnation: its requirements, to give food to the hungry and drink to the thirsty, to welcome the stranger and clothe the naked, to care for the sick and visit the imprisoned, are so important that they are repeated in entirety four times in Matthew 25. But what gives this a remarkably incarnational import is that "the king," or God, claims to be incarnate in the hungry, the thirsty, the stranger, the naked, the sick, and the imprisoned. We are not asked to do these things "for" God, or in the name of God, or in the name of religious obligation, or as some moral duty, but *to* God. Here is the crux of incarnational thinking that is turned toward the reign of God: we do these things, we make concern for the stranger the primary locus of being, because the stranger is where God is.

58. Kearney, *Anatheism*, 21.
59. *New Revised Standard Version*, my emphasis.

Levinas himself often referred to this passage from Matthew 25 with admiration:

> The other concerns me in all his material misery. It is a matter, eventually, of nourishing him, of clothing him. It is exactly the biblical assertion: Feed the hungry, clothe the naked, give drink to the thirsty, give shelter to the shelterless. . . . This holiness is perhaps but the holiness of a social problem. All the problems of eating and drinking, insofar as they concern the other, become sacred.[60]

Such is the blueprint of the reign of God. Jesus used parables as illustrations to encourage the imagination; everyone loves a good story, and these stories had the particular quality of inviting the hearer to participate in completing the story. Matthew 25 contains three significant parables or illustrations of the reign of God: the Ten Bridesmaids, the Talents, and the Great Judgment, the "capstone of Jesus' teaching," according to Robert Farrar Capon. In each of these parables, we see the reign of God visible in the tension between what is given and what is coming, between faith and ethical action. The subjects of these parables are waiting—on the slim ledge of anticipation—for something to happen, and only those who also act in their waiting, who act without certainty of outcome, who invest, prepare, and attend to the needy, are rewarded. Those who willfully choose blindness, ignorance, and neglect are not. Capon points out that the righteous in 25:34-46 didn't realize they were already in relationship with God "when they ministered to the least of his brethren, any more than the cursed knew they were despising the King when they didn't so minister."[61]

According to Levinas, our ethical obligation to the stranger metaphysically precedes the explicitly religious obligation. Michael Himes notes this as well: "Not one doctrine, not one specifically religious act of worship or ritual turns out to be relevant to the criterion for

---

60. Jill Robbins, ed., *Is It Righteous to Be? Interviews with Emmanuel Levinas* (Stanford, CA: Stanford University Press, 2001), 52.

61. Robert Farrar Capon, *Kingdom, Grace, Judgment: Paradox, Outrage, and Vindication in the Parables of Jesus* (Grand Rapids, MI: Eerdmans, 2002), 508.

the last judgment. . . . [N]ot only are religious acts beside the point, so are specifically religious motives. The point is not that you love your brothers and sisters for Jesus' sake, but simply that you love your brothers and sisters."[62] Widening the imagination for the reign of God, Jesus takes us beyond the laundry list of religious obligations and gives a new, reflexive dimension, a metaphysical dimension in which existence emerges consequent to the ethical summons to the Other. For Levinas, the ethical summons takes place on a visual plane: "ethics is an optics."[63] "Ethics" as attention, "a mode of consciousness without distraction, without the power of escape through dark underground passages,"[64] to the just-beyond-our-grasp of the infinity glimpsed in the needs of the Other: such is a new lens through which to see life in the world.

Jesus' artistry in illustrating this vision of new life and new society, of seeing God in welcoming the stranger, recasts the prophetic exhortation in a poetics that fires the imagination. The images that summon us to stay awake, to be sensitive, attentive; to refrain from burying our talents in the ground, to regard service to the Other as the foundational impulse of existence itself: such images promote what Oscar Wilde called "a width and wonder of imagination that fills one almost with awe." In *De Profundis* ("from the depths I cry to you, O Lord," Psalm 130), a letter Wilde wrote to Lord Alfred Douglas during his incarceration for "gross indecency," Wilde praised Jesus as an artist, whose actions were the creative expression of his teaching: "To the artist, expression is the only mode under which he can conceive life at all. . . . [H]e took the entire world of the inarticulate, the voiceless world of pain, as his kingdom, and made of himself its external mouthpiece."[65] Wilde, the celebrated author and

---

62. Michael Himes, *Doing the Truth in Love: Conversations about God, Relationships, and Service* (New York: Paulist Press, 1995), 51.

63. Levinas, *Totality and Infinity*, 23.

64. Emmanuel Levinas, "Paul Celan: From Being to the Other," in Smith, *Proper Names*, 43.

65. Oscar Wilde, *De Profundis*, in *The Collected Works of Oscar Wilde*, ed. Ian Small (Oxford: Oxford University Press, 2000), 114. See also Simon Critchley, "Oscar Wilde's Faithless Christianity," *The Guardian* 15 (January 2009), http://www.theguardian.com/commentisfree/belief/2009/jan/14/religion-wilde.

playwright, whose attendance at parties was adored, whose peacock-like style was cheered, was relegated to a damp prison cell of "hard labor, hard fare, and a hard bed" and found a kindred spirit in Jesus. This probably surprised Wilde himself more than anyone, as religion was no solace for Wilde: "When I think of religion at all, I feel as if I would like to found an order for those who cannot believe: the Confraternity of the Faithless, one might call it, where on an altar, on which no taper burned, a priest, in whose heart peace had no dwelling, might celebrate with unblessed bread and a chalice empty of wine."[66] Wilde found solace in the power of the artistic endeavor, and he saw Christ's incarnation as pertaining to the truth of art, "the inwardness of suffering in outward form, the expression of deep internality in externality,"[67] according to Simon Critchley. Wilde saw in Christ "the incarnation of love as an act of the imagination, not reason, the imaginative projection of compassion onto all creatures."[68] Only the imagination can regard the possibility of compassion for all, even the enemy, even the ugly, even the one covered in disgusting sores; ethics is this optics.

The visual in particular is characterized by an inclination exterior to the self, constituted by what Hagi Kenaan describes as a "strong directionality"; the visual is not a neutral or formal domain that simply contains the totality of what encounters the eye but rather is what pertains to one's social location, "where one can find and lose, be close, closer, far, infinitely far," a space of appearance wherein the question of orientation is already an essential component of what appears.[69] Hence, attention to the visual, expressive, and artistic dimensions—in which the self and the Other can be close but never collapse into a totality that eradicates alterity—assists in widening the imagination for the incarnate among us.

66. Oscar Wilde, *De Profundis*, in Simon Critchley, "Wilde Christianity," excerpted from "The Faith of the Faithless," the *Montreal Review*, July 2012, http://www.themontrealreview.com/2009/The-Faith-of-the-Faithless.

67. Ibid.

68. Ibid.

69. See Hagi Kenaan, *Ethics of Visuality: Levinas and the Contemporary Gaze*, trans. Batya Stein (London: I. B. Tauris, 2013), xi.

Marc Chagall's Still Point

My mother is an artist who works in the arduous technique of using watercolors in a hyper-real manner; my uncle is an abstract artist who teaches painting classes at a university, so art museums were common excursions in my childhood. While I looked forward to these excursions, I have no memories of any one work making a significant impression. Perhaps I wasn't ready, or mature enough; I remember strolling along, listening to my uncle's erudite explanations, nodding my head dutifully. The tumblers hadn't kicked into place yet.

The same year I discovered Karl Rahner, I also visited the Art Institute of Chicago. I had visited previously many times, remembering enormous canvases in serene white spaces filled with light. Seeing Marc Chagall's *White Crucifixion* (1938) that day, however, was the key that undid the lock in one of those elevated moments that overcomes the ordinary markers of memory. Chagall's penetrating blue stained-glass windows (*America Windows,* 1977) marked a lifelong love of Chagall and the intense bright blue that frequently appears in his work, a blue which recalls the celestial blue of the Russian icons which occupied the culture of Chagall's heritage. But *White Crucifixion* interpreted Jesus' suffering in a way I had not yet encountered in theological studies or liturgy. This painting uncovered a new journey on the well-traveled paths of Christian discourse; even more astonishing to this cradle Catholic was that this new way of imagining came from the passion of a Jewish artist who happened to have a particular affinity for the meaning of Jesus' cross for Jews rather than for Christians.

White Crucifixion discloses the recognition (stunning, at the time, to me) that Jesus' cross is not a necessary, divinely required sacrifice. Jesus here is rather one more of those deemed disposable, amid centuries of brute suffering caused by the ideologically justified violence of those who kill under the guise of promoting "civilization." Historically, Jesus died as one of the thousands who were crucified as collateral of the tenuous *Pax Romana*; Chagall depicts him as one of the more famous Jews who have died because their lives were deemed expendable. Also purposeless are the relentless displacement of persons from homes and histories, the destruction of peaceful communities in smoke and ash. The painting is similar in composition to a Russian icon, in which a central figure is surrounded by depictions of related stories. In *White Crucifixion*, Jesus is surrounded by scenes from the persecutions of Jews in the 1930s, such that, as Ziva Amishai-Maisels observes, "it seems that both they and Christ occupy the same time and space."[70]

Jesus' face is the still point of the painting, a promise of peace amid the "turning world"; "Neither flesh nor fleshless, neither from nor towards," in T. S. Eliot's *Four Quartets*.[71] The face of the murdered, even though finally relaxed from the spasms of pain, is a turning on the still point, a disjunction, the death that falls on life. Jesus does not here represent the distant, divine drama of substitution and ransom. Rather, Jesus is one of the murdered, one of the dispossessed. As is the case with any murder, crucifixion can never be good or holy; to believe that Jesus' murder was divinely willed and therefore salvific is rendered absurd when we witness the destruction of lives and homes in the painting. Jesus' murder didn't solve the crimes of humanity; Jesus' murder *is* one of the crimes of humanity. Jesus' murder is displayed at the center both because it led to a chain of historical developments that amplified oppression and because it was, after all, the murder of a righteous man. Situating Jesus' murder within the larger historical patterns of genocide and persecution, Chagall speaks specifically to the Christian persecution of European Jews and illuminates that most frustrating of paradoxes for the Christian, that the Christian savior died while championing the very people whose blood is now on Christian hands.

Chagall begins work on the *White Crucifixion* in late 1938, likely completing it in 1939. But by maintaining its date as 1938, he deliberately recalls the 1938 of Nazi Germany: the census, the marking of Jewish businesses, the forced adoption of the names Abraham and Sarah, the stamping of "J" ("Jude") in Jewish passports—culminating in the horrific *Kristallnacht* of November 9 and 10.[72] Chagall grew

---

70. Ziva Amishai-Maisels, "Chagall's *White Crucifixion*," *Art Institute of Chicago Museum Studies* 17, no. 2 (1991): 139.

71. From T. S. Eliot's "Burnt Norton," in the *Four Quartets* (Orlando, FL: Harvest Books, 1971), 15.

72. Ziva Amishai-Maisels, "Chagall's *White Crucifixion*," 140.

up in Vitebsk, Russia, knowing both a closely knit, humble community that provided some of the nostalgic symbolism seen in the scope of his work as well as a place of terror in the pogroms he witnessed as a child; the burning synagogue in *White Crucifixion* refers to a personal memory for him.

Jesus' Jewish identity—emphasized by the replacement of the traditional loincloth with a tallit, or prayer shawl, the replacement of the traditional crown of thorns with a headscarf, and the inscription above him, Aramaic rendered in Hebrew script: "Jesus of Nazareth, King of the Jews"—is the central feature of *White Crucifixion*, but only insofar as his Jewishness makes him a member of a persecuted community, not its messiah, the one who would end the suffering. The juxtaposition is ominous: between the catastrophe that continues through history and Chagall's implicit response to the Christian investment in an accomplished salvation inaugurated by their messiah. The concept of messiah as "the person who comes to put a miraculous end to the violence in the world, the injustice and contradictions which destroy humanity but have their source in the nature of humanity"[73] does not satisfy us, observes Levinas. "One cannot lay claim to the prophetic vision of truth, and go on to participate in the values of the world. . . . [T]here is nothing more hypocritical than the messianic prophetism of the comfortable bourgeois."[74]

Jesus, his innocence obvious and shared by those who surround him, is not the beginning of the end of the suffering for Chagall and so is not a symbol or harbinger of salvation; rather, Jesus is the one who embodies the divine mark of the *tav* (Hebrew)/*tau* (Greek) and so reveals the Lord's favor of the oppressed, shown by Chagall's choice of a *tau*- or T-shaped cross that recalls the mark of Ezekiel, when God instructs: "Go throughout the city of Jerusalem and put a mark on the foreheads of those who grieve and lament over all the detestable things that are done in it" (Ezek 9:4). Those who grieve and lament, represented in the painting by the patriarchs and Rachel

73. Emmanuel Levinas, *Difficult Freedom: Essays on Judaism*, trans. Sean Hand (Baltimore: Johns Hopkins University Press, 1990), 59.

74. Ibid., 96. Perhaps it should be noted that Levinas is speaking of the hypocrisy of his fellow Jews here, although Christians should take heed.

above the cross, as well as those who remain in the raw midst of their agony, are marked by God as under God's particular concern—an idea articulated in liberation theology's "option for the poor."

If there is a messianic figure in *White Crucifixion*, perhaps it is the mother in the lower part of the painting, to the right of the candelabrum[75] at the foot of the cross. Of all the figures, she is the only one in the painting who looks directly at the viewer. She implores me and I can do nothing for her. I am paralyzed outside her space; I am reminded of my own paralysis when catastrophe occurs in worlds away from me. She is in anguish, desperate. Clutching a child, the child's face touches her face. She runs toward us from the chaos, her haste cutting most of her body from the canvas: She is the child's refuge in a world without relief, leading to the impossible possibility of another world. Her attention and courage will lead the way out. Perhaps we may even hope she has escaped. Chagall repeats this motif of the mother as a fortress for her child, as the preservation of an idea of home, throughout his work, as he repeats the motif of crucifixion and the brilliant blue in numerous works. The initial viewing of *White Crucifixion* stayed with me as Rahner's thought had—both offer something profoundly, compulsively *new* in discourse about God and the meaning of Jesus' death for Christians.

A little-known work of Chagall's in the Collection of Modern Religious Art at the Vatican Museums, *The Crucifix (Between God and the Devil)*, from 1943, depicts the crucified Jesus and the fleeing mother with child as figures of the same size and occupying the same space. This work is rougher in form than *White Crucifixion*, less finished, but it indicates Chagall's preferred use of these figures in repeated works: the fleeing mother and the dying prophet belong

---

75. It is unclear why Chagall depicts what appears to be a menorah with six branches at the foot of the cross. The menorah with seven branches is the menorah of the temple in Jerusalem, the holy symbol of Judaism, which the Talmud declares must never be removed from the temple. The menorah with nine branches (eight plus a servant candle for lighting the others) is for celebrating Hanukkah. Another menorah lies desecrated outside the burning synagogue, but it is difficult to count the branches.

Mark Chagall, *The Crucifix (Between God and the Devil)*

together in Chagall's oeuvre. Here the pairing is especially manifest: one murdered by the oppression he opposed, the other a protective and nurturing reference to the divine, as she is cloaked in the celestial blue Christians associate with Jesus' mother. Both the prophet and the mother are greater in size than the burning houses in the distance; both are also larger than the goat in the corner, symbolic of the devil. The painting is more hopeful than *White Crucifixion*; the expression on the mother's face hints at a joyful future. She has reason for hope. Her back is turned away from the crucifix: she has left it, is running from it and the cruel finality of death that it represents. Her child, however, looks back toward the mutilated body in wonder: Jesus' face a smeared grimace against the yellow fires in the distance with gray; the child's small mouth is open, and he guards a small light.

The verse by Emily Dickinson, "This World Is not Conclusion,"[76] came to mind as I viewed this painting. This broken, bloody world, in which the slow tortuous death of crucifixion is too common, is not the world of divine peace and wisdom, the world of God's desire. The mother provides hope that the world of violence and oppression is not final; anticipation persists for the divine world, the reign of God, even when hope is marginalized. But the responsibility lies with us. The messianic does not wait, according to Blanchot and Derrida. Derrida tells Blanchot's story: The Messiah, dressed in rags, was at the gates of Rome unrecognized until one asks him, "When will you come?" "The messianic does not wait," Derrida asserts, "the responsibilities that are assigned to us by this messianic structure are responsibilities for the here and now."[77] For Chagall, the suffering of the cross and the refuge the mother provides for the future are equivalent realities, such that with imagination and persistence, one day our work building a world of refuge for all will eliminate catastrophic suffering. Chagall's perception of the divine persistence in the midst of the broken world does not come from academic theology and textbooks; is comes from raw creativity and the optimism of intense belief.

The Incarnation as Lightning Strike

Creativity is the agency of "the new"—the innovative determination that widens the scope of the possible. Creativity is the arena of the God who does not hold back, who, as the pervasive energy of being, animates the drive of creative expression in the brief and hazy glimpses of life captured by the poet and the painter. I read Mary Oliver's poem "Lightning" as a metaphor for the incarnation of God into human history and reality, proclaimed in Christian witness: a union of earth and electricity, ozone and dust, which enters consciousness in the mundane sweep of time, a welcome storm for a

76. Emily Dickinson, poem 501; see *Emily Dickinson's Poems as She Preserved Them*, ed. Cristanne Miller (Boston: Belknap Press, 2016), 169.

77. Jacques Derrida, *Deconstruction in a Nutshell: A Conversation with Jacques Derrida*, ed. John Caputo (New York: Fordham University Press, 1997), 24. Maurice Blanchot tells the story in *The Writing of the Disaster*, trans. Ann Smock (Lincoln, NE: University of Nebraska Press, 1995), 141–43.

parched ground. Lightning tearing through "the dark field" is a symbol of incarnation to which I refer repeatedly in this project because it describes the impact of the new and different, the unusual and strange, upon the mundane perceptions with which we normally operate. "The new" is the source of amazement, of wonder, the place where openness to what is possible meets the impossible, where mystery is not a problem to be solved in language but rather stretches and deepens its reach in us.

Audre Lorde said that "the master's tools will never dismantle the master's house": can we imagine the shock of a lightning strike, an idea or a vision of "incarnation," with new wine in old wineskins—bygone terminology that has to be shrugged off like snakeskin or discarded like an obsolete raft, every millennia or so? Can we critique the concepts and beliefs of the Christian tradition with the same concepts and beliefs, just shuffled around? Sometimes theology feels like an elaborate card game. Wittgenstein remarked, "The master of the language is the master of us all"; in the formulation and pedagogy of doctrine this is especially accurate. With absolutes in the language of doctrine come boundaries, fixity, attempts to control, to normalize, to "produce effects at the level of knowledge." "[P]ower produces knowledge," notes Michel Foucault. He continues, "There is no power relation without the correlative constitution of a field of knowledge, nor any knowledge that does not presuppose and constitute at the same time power relations."[78] Theology must then continually explore ways in which "incarnation" can be more effectively understood as a linguistic signifier that empties and opens a space for the impossible, that in its own performance of what is true, "incarnation" may be approached by way of a trace, a beacon, a light in the distance.

The advent of "the new" is explained by John Caputo, following Derrida, who was influenced by Levinas and Blanchot, as the event that shatters the horizon of possible experience, the horizon of what is expected in the Kantian sphere of what we are capable of experiencing. For Immanuel Kant, the domain of knowledge is only what can be experienced with the senses, when perceptions (from our

---

78. Michel Foucault, *Power/Knowledge: Selected Interviews*, ed. Colin Gordon (New York: Pantheon, 1972), 58–59; see also Margaret Miles, *Image as Insight: Visual Understanding in Western Secular Culture* (Boston: Beacon Press, 1985), 20.

senses) join with conceptions (the *a priori* categories from the mind or reason, independent of experience and universal to all rational human beings). The focus of *metaphysical* knowledge, knowledge outside sense experience, can only be named according to the constitution of the human understanding that actively imposes categories on sense information, which, along with the imagination, constitutes the object in the first place. This means the end of saying that we can *know* anything about ideas which are outside the boundaries of sense perception, such as immortality, justice, love, freedom, or "God." None of these are "objects" in the material sense, of course; none of these are "things." "Metaphysics" for Kant pertains to considering how such ideas, through the activity of the imagination, might give unity to human knowledge when sense experience cannot make connections; but "God" after Kant is no longer an object of *knowledge*. Edmund Husserl and the phenomenological method he pioneered followed this line of thought to claim that "God" cannot appear as a thing in the world upon which my intentional gaze might rest but instead appears precisely other than the world and transcendent to it. Husserl claimed we should "bracket" anything not immediately present to the intentional consciousness, hence "God" should be bracketed as outside the immediate immanent mental process of knowing.[79] God's disappearance from the sphere of knowledge, however, does not mean that the spirit and mind of the human being aren't traversing the dark field in the intuition of a presenced absence/absenced presence that lies on the outside of what we think we can or do know. Caputo observes, "[T]o shatter the horizon of possible experience is to be impossible, to belong to an impossible experience. . . . [T]he possibility of the impossible is one of God's most venerable biblical names."[80] To be open to the possibility of the

79. See J. Aaron Simmons and Bruce Ellis Benson, *The New Phenomenology: A Philosophical Introduction* (London: Bloomsbury Academic, 2013), 1591–1600/5691 in Kindle edition.

80. John D. Caputo, *The Insistence of God: A Theology of Perhaps* (Bloomington, IN: Indiana University Press, 2013), 10–11. In his discussion of the "possible impossible," Caputo refers to Jacques Derrida, "Psyche: Invention of the Other," in *Psyche: Inventions of the Other*, vol. 1, trans. Peggy Kamuf and Elizabeth Rottenberg (Stanford, CA: Stanford University Press, 2007), 1–47.

impossible, Caputo locates as prayer: may I be open to the shattering of all that I think I *know*. And may lightning strike.

The impact of Jesus on the destitute of the early first century must have felt like a lightning storm, causing enough upheaval in barely a year of ministry to get him killed. That he was one of the destitute, from their midst, who had been for generations relegated, like the countless nameless in history—to the crowd scenes, the scores of replaceable "extras" in the imperialist drama of the time—must have felt like a lightning strike. Jesus should have died without record—the first thirty years of his life were so unremarkable that there isn't a single reliable historical hint of his life during those years. In his early thirties, he was probably jarred into a calling by the preaching of John the Baptist. His baptism by John in the Jordan was the beginning of his abandonment to a life lived devoted to Judaism, to God, and to leaving behind all else: his village, his family, his trade. Ched Myers describes the social and political meaning of this decisive moment: "In baptism Jesus was declared an 'outlaw,' so to speak; his mission will be to challenge the oppressive structures of law and order around him. A modern analogy to baptism-as-declaration-of-resistance might be public acts of draft card burning";[81] Myers further explains that Jesus' baptism scene in Mark's gospel is outlined by the prophetic voice which had been neglected in the first century by the scribes and rabbis but preserved in the subversive movements quickly suppressed by the Romans.[82]

Jesus soon realized that John's apocalyptic message was no longer fulfilling. He looked more to Isaiah and Ezekiel, who provided the framework of a society based on the reign of God, which could be actively exercised in the present moment rather than unresponsively anticipate a cataclysmic future. Jesus models a society that welcomes those cast out, which levels class distinctions and depends on shared resources. To see Jesus speak to those in authority without fear or self-interest must have startled his followers into new ways of imagining God as more compassionate than absolute, experienced through intimacy and care rather than through domination and violence. Jesus

81. Ched Myers, *Binding the Strong Man: A Political Reading of Mark's Story of Jesus* (Maryknoll, NY: Orbis Books, 2008), 130.
82. Ibid., 125.

provided a vision of a society in which the nameless are sought after like lost treasure, in which we are all responsible for one another, and in which the meaning of human life is in love abundantly given.

Jesus' life and teaching was a sign to his early followers that God opposed the dominance of Rome: "many who are first will be last and the last will be first" (Mark 10:31; Matt 19:30; 20:16; Luke 13:30). Ched Myers points out that there are three confrontations over the meaning of messiahship in Mark, each time Jesus replacing "Messiah" with "Human One"; resisted by the disciples at 8:29-38, rejected by the rebel recruiters at 13:21-26, and ridiculed by the high priest at 14:61-62.[83] Even the Roman soldier who facilitated Jesus' crucifixion is stunned by the recognition—perhaps finally realizing the depravity of the Roman occupation—that Jesus should replace his own emperor with the designation "Son of God."[84]

The radical claim that God was incarnate among the destitute and abandoned and not in the wealthy elite is a claim continuous with every biblical story about God: God surpasses our expectations and assumptions and chooses the weak and vulnerable as the locus of disclosure. As Paul wrote in 1 Corinthians 1:23-25, "[W]e preach Christ crucified—a stumbling block to Jews and foolishness to Gentiles, but to those who are the called, Christ the power of God and the wisdom of God. For God's foolishness is wiser than human wisdom, and God's weakness is stronger than human strength." The history of Christianity would not bear out this statement, however: with the rule of the Holy Roman Empire, the power of domination and violence replaced the "weakness" of turning the other cheek and the "foolishness" of self-sacrifice. Today, we who are Christians are the inheritors of the odd absorption of a Gospel—the central focus

---

83. Myers, *Binding the Strong Man*, 405.

84. I am conflicted on this point. Myers argues that the "confession" of the Roman soldier is really an attempt to show the opposite, and continue the mocking of Jesus begun before the cross: "[A]re we to see the centurion's words as trustworthy? If so, we will have failed to learn one of the most salient lessons of the whole story, which is that those in power indeed 'know who Jesus is,' and are out to destroy him, whereas those who follow him are often unsure who he is, but struggle to trust him nevertheless." Myers, *Binding the Strong Man*, 398. Perhaps I want to believe that the sight of Jesus' agony might have converted the soldier from his own oppression against the Jewish people.

of which is in welcoming the stranger—by a power dynamic that has insulated itself from the stranger. Much of that initial lightning strike has faded, its "fire and risk" sanitized by acclimatization into a comfortable ethos of "the Same."

When calculated, confident rationality in the use of fixed philosophical categories becomes more prized than praise, painting, or poetry, or more valuable than the narrative of Scripture as *narrative*, we cannot approach the abyss that permanently remains an element of human existence. Doctrines should reflect ruptures in the order of theoretical knowledge: rather than positive, propositional, or definitive statements, doctrines are living things, symbols with hope in their composition and faith in their reception. The narrative of Scripture does not intend the sort of controlled, precise litmus test to which it is subjected in today's scientifically positive speech. From Noah's ark to Hebrew slaves as the "chosen people" to Joshua's seven shofar reducing Jericho to rubble: the narrative of Scripture is a poetic narrative that does not end before the composition of the gospels. This language of celebratory excess in the Hebrew Bible mutates into parable and practical hope for the manifestation of the reign of God. The language of the Christian Bible is still excessive through story and parable, but it is no less enigmatic. But the enigma, the ambiguity, is the space of the trace of the infinite, the no-place that is the exile of both God and the wanderer.

This language of excess, this poetry that flirts with the impossible, is the movement of "attraction and withdrawal," as Blanchot put it, painting an image which bleeds through abstraction. The ambiguity of the poetic image, the trace of the obscure, is behind all art forms. This ambiguity is the darkness of the "outside" that Blanchot finds as the space of literature, the space of exile in the country of the wanderer: "Error," writes Blanchot, "is the risk which awaits the poet. . . . [E]rror means wandering, the inability to abide and stay. For where the wanderer is, the conditions of a definite here are lacking. In this absence of here and now what happens does not clearly come to pass as an event based upon which something solid could be achieved."[85] Art and religion are a risk; we risk the life we express

85. Blanchot, *The Space of Literature*, 237.

in the creative and religious endeavor, we risk the undermining of meaning. "Truth" as absolute is neither the revelation nor the goal of art for Blanchot, nor, I dare say, is absolute truth the revelation or goal of the narrative of Scripture. Rather, the excess of language in the Bible or the excess of color and light in a painting draw us out toward the exile to which God commits divine life.

Art is then exile from absolute truth, asserts Blanchot; art affirms our "belonging to the limitless outside" where the secure intimacy of such truth is unknown; in its stead is "the intertwining of the Yes and the No, the ebb and flow of the essential ambiguity."[86] In the Kabbalah, God descends to be in exile with the enslaved despite the admonitions of the angels that God should remain in heavenly glory: the awareness of descent as humility is the very rejection of the glory of absolute "truth." Levinas observes,

> To present oneself in this poverty of the exile is to interrupt the coherence of the universe. To pierce immanence without thereby taking one's place within it. Obviously such an opening can only be an ambiguity. But the appearing of an ambiguity in the seamless texture of the world is not a looseness in its weave or a failure of the intelligence that examines it, but precisely the proximity of God which can only occur in humility.[87]

Entering the exile of the Other, multiplying one's vulnerability by risking the vulnerability of the Other: this is the way God's modality of being is infinite—by endlessly resisting signification as final or absolute truth. "Incarnation" and divine sonship must be understood within this context of vulnerability, as a recognition of the divine in exile with the thousands of migrant peoples desperate and wandering.

Abdullah Kurdi lost his entire family, his wife Rehen and two sons, Aylan and Galip, when they drowned off the coast of Turkey in September 2015, in the horrific no-place between the four-year war in Syria and the traffickers who promised a way out. The photographer who captured the image of little Aylan's body washed ashore

86. Ibid., 239.
87. Levinas, "A Man-God?," 55.

said, "There was nothing to do. And that is exactly what I did. I thought that this is the only way I can express the scream of his silent body."[88] The epiphany of Aylan's lifeless face calls us all toward our collective failure to be fully sensitive, fully aware of the desperation of his people. Seeing enables this sensibility, it opens the abyss, widening it until I fall in with him, and I ache, with memories of holding my little boy and his warmth in my arms. Seeing has brought the imagination to ethical command: imagination provides, according to Maurice Merleau-Ponty, "privileged access to the hidden dimension of Being" which he calls the "invisible [that] pre-exists in the visible," such that every visible dimension is connected to an invisible or imaginary dimension.[89] Prophetic witness coincides with the perception of the order of responsibility to the Other, the divine order by which I am torn from complacency. To answer "Here I am" to the vulnerability of the Other, as the prophets answered the divine call, is the risk taken prior to all theology, writes Levinas in *Otherwise than Being*. "The Infinite is not in front of its witness"; the Infinite is "outside, or on the other side of presence, already past, out of reach,

---

88. Photographer Nilufer Demir, quoted by Ashley Fantz and Catherine E. Shoichet, "Syrian Toddler's Dad: 'Everything I Was Dreaming of Is Gone,'" CNN, September 3, 2015, http://www.cnn.com/2015/09/03/europe/migration-crisis -aylan-kurdi-turkey-canada/.

89. Richard Kearney, *Poetics of Imagining: Modern to Post-modern* (New York: Fordham University Press, 1998), 121, explaining the dialectical imagination of Maurice Merleau-Ponty, a topic Kearney revisits in *Anatheism*: "Phenomenology thus marks the surpassing of traditional dualisms between body and mind, real and ideal, subject and object. This is how Merleau-Ponty describes the enigma of flesh as mutual crossing-over in his posthumously published work, *The Visible and the Invisible* (1964): 'The seer is caught up in what he sees . . . the vision he exercises, he also undergoes from the things, such that, as many painters have said, I feel myself looked at by the things, my activity is passivity,' So much so that 'the seer and the visible reciprocate one another and we no longer know which sees and which is seen. It is this Visibility, this anonymity innate to Myself that we have called flesh, and one knows there is no name in traditional philosophy to designate it,'" *Anatheism*, 89, citing his own translation. For Merleau-Ponty's entire essay, "The Intertwining—the Chiasm," see *The Visible and the Invisible*, ed. Claude Lefort, trans. Alphonso Lingis (Evanston, IL: Northwestern University Press, 1968), 139.

a thought behind thoughts which is too lofty to push itself up front."[90] But we may witness the passing of the infinite through the Other, and we may be exiled wander into the infinite abyss that both frames the artistic process and unfolds every catastrophe. If we say that the invisible, the "Infinite," in Levinas's usage, is here, on this beach, exiled in this little broken body, we must also say that we have failed to be exiled with him if we leave him there, his little person sublimated into a mere anecdote.

So we are left with the ambiguity of our failed responsibility: the exile of God in the visible, the Infinite behind the agonized face, is beyond me. Levinas writes, "The enigma of the Infinite, whose saying in me, a responsibility where no one assists me, becomes a contestation of the Infinite. By this contestation everything is incumbent on me, and there is produced my entry into the designs of the Infinite."[91] We are not given to assurance but to hope that the God in exile may be witnessed in imagination and maybe some of that "frenzy" to which Friedrich Nietzsche often referred: "Frenzy must first have enhanced the excitability of the whole machine; else there is no art"[92]—the frenzy by which I may be for the Other, obsessed with justice.

90. Levinas, *Otherwise than Being*, 149.

91. Ibid., 154.

92. Friedrich Nietzsche, *The Twilight of the Idols*, in *The Portable Nietzsche*, trans. Walter Kaufmann (New York: Penguin, 1976), 518.

CHAPTER THREE

Sensibility to Vulnerability in the Form of Art

The ineluctable: the interruption in the playful order of the beautiful and the play of concepts, and the play of the world . . . a seeking for the Other. A seeking, dedicating itself to the other in the form of a poem. A chant rises in the giving, the one-for-the-other, the signifying of signification. A signification older than ontology and the thought of being, and that is presupposed by knowledge and desire . . .

—Emmanuel Levinas, "Paul Celan: From Being to Other"

Paul Tillich's Moment of Beauty

The fire and risk of lightning tearing through a field: what nature provides in its wildness, its compelling silence and moving shadows, human beings provide in artistic creation, which, according to Paul Tillich, is an "encounter with the power of being itself . . . the astonishing awareness that something is and is not nothing, and that I participate in its power to be."[1] Tillich, born August 20, 1886, in Starzeddel, Germany (now Starosiedle, Poland), was one of the greatest theologians of the twentieth century, an ordained Lutheran pas-

---

1. Paul Tillich, describing his experience before Botticelli's *Madonna and Child with Singing Angels* (1477, Berlin-Dahlem Museum, Berlin), in "Human Nature and Art," lecture given to the Minneapolis School of Art in 1952, in *On Art and Architecture*, ed. John Dillenberger (New York: Crossroad, 1987), 12.

tor who studied existentialist philosophy and sought to correlate its questions with ideas, symbols, and beliefs in Christian thought. His devotion to the importance of culture for articulating these questions and the mode of theological thought for addressing them constitutes a vital moment in the development of the field of theological aesthetics in the twentieth century; no consideration of the possibility of a mutual impact between aesthetics and theology would be complete without acknowledging his contributions.

The year 1919 was a tumultuous one for both Tillich and Germany. The end of the Great War meant dealing with the loss of nearly two million people; the economy was $44 billion in debt and riots turned to shoot-outs in the streets over labor disputes. With the end of his brief marriage, recovering from a second nervous breakdown and having recently accepted a position at Berlin University, Tillich was searching for something to anchor his sense of displacement in the wake of seismic shifts in civilization. When he entered the Kaiser Friedrich Museum in Berlin, he intended to view the paintings he had seen only as reproductions in magazines that kept him distracted from "the mud, blood, and death of the Western Front" during the war.[2] Huddling in dugouts by candlelight, he had hoarded prints of paintings, "studying this new world" as a way to escape the turmoil around and within him. Thus Tillich discovered works of visual art that had eluded him as a boy growing up the son of a Lutheran minister in eastern Germany: "neither at home nor at school was I taught that there is beauty we can see";[3] music was the art on which his father relied.

That day in Berlin, he finally saw Sandro Botticelli's *Madonna and Child with Singing Angels* (1477) and "felt a state approaching ecstasy. In the beauty of the painting was Beauty itself. . . . As I stood there, bathed in the beauty its painter had envisioned so long ago, something of the divine source of all things came through to me. I turned away shaken."[4] Perhaps because the symbols that spoke to Botticelli's

---

2. Paul Tillich, "One Moment of Beauty," in Dillenberger, *On Art and Architecture*, 234.

3. Ibid.

4. Ibid., 235.

audience do not speak as well to us today, the painting, Tillich acknowledges, is "not the greatest. I have seen greater since then"—but
the moment standing before its luminous color after the trenches in
France was "never repeated."[5]

Botticelli's use of the *tondi*, circular paintings usually about one
meter in diameter, was favored for the way figures can be brought
together in an intimate space; Botticelli repeats the composition seen
in *Madonna and Child with Singing Angels* several times with different
figures. The composition brings us face to face with Mary and the
infant Jesus as he prepares to nurse. Her countenance is gentle, and
like many of Botticelli's Madonnas, touched with the gravity of sorrow; wingless angels to the right are singing and to the left are listening. Perhaps the symmetry and harmony soothed Tillich after
witnessing the horrific disorder of battle. Botticelli's finely wrought
details of gold filigree in the costumes perhaps reassured Tillich that
technical skill is capable of achieving an end other than death.

The young Alessandro di Marino Filipepi, nicknamed "Little
Barrel"—Botticelli—perhaps after an early teacher, translated his
own physical frailty into the diaphanous veil surrounding Mary's
face. While not a masterpiece on the scale of his *Primavera* (1478, at
the Uffizi in Florence), the painting was there for Tillich in an especially vulnerable time, and the vulnerability of Mary amid the heavy
child—she can barely support the infant Jesus on her lap—moved
him. As such, Tillich participated in Botticelli's artistic vision, which,
like any work of art, requires the viewer to be complete. The intimate
conversational style of the tondo is echoed in the intimacy of meeting which takes place when we come before a work of art. Hence
Tillich's insight that there is a divine calling in the witness to art on
the order of the divine calling of the prophets: without the witness,
without the hearer, without the response, there is no revelation,
there is no divine self-expression: "I know that no artistic experience
can match the moments in which prophets were grasped in the power
of the Divine Presence, but I believe there is an analogy between
revelation and what I felt. In both cases, the experience goes beyond

5. Ibid.

the way we encounter reality in our daily lives. It opens up depths experienced in no other way."[6]

Tillich realized in this experience that theology and culture had become dangerously separated in the course of the early twentieth century, leaving theology (what discerns the "spiritual" or "unconditioned" or "ultimate" concern) without grounding in the "human situation," the conditioned sphere of culture where the language and symbols of divine revelation may be received. Culture is capable of pointing human beings toward the questions that form theology. "Everything in human culture has a religious dimension if it points to the holy, to that which is the ground and aim of everything that is [and] insofar as it contributes to the answer of the question of the meaning of our existence,"[7] wrote Tillich shortly before his death. Art as a product of its time for Tillich meant that art not only contributes to religious thought but also indicates deficiencies and gaps in theological discourse; this is true even when contemporary works of art no longer explicitly rely on religious stories or symbolism, as they did during Botticelli's time. If works do explicitly rely on religious stories or symbolism, they must be careful to note the contextuality of the symbols themselves, otherwise there is the danger of "a kind of sophisticated primitivism, a limited understanding of the religious symbols as if there were a world above our world, a tripartite world of heaven, earth, hell, and divine beings going from one place to the other. This is supernaturalism in its bad sense . . . it is not *en kairo*: it is not appropriate today."[8] For this reason, Tillich praises painters more contemporary to his time such as Emile Nolde, Georges Rouault, and even Pablo Picasso who are able to translate religious ideas into symbols which are more *en kairo*. Picasso's *Crucifixion* (1930), for example, with its garish colors and alarming displacement of figures, takes inspiration from the crucifixion scene in Mattias Grünewald's Isenheim Altarpiece (1512–1516). But Picasso puts those symbols through a grinder, chewing up the figures in

---

6. Ibid., 235.

7. Paul Tillich, "Religion and Art in Light of the Contemporary Development," in Dillenberger, *On Art and Architecture*, 167.

8. Paul Tillich. "Art and Society," in Dillenberger, *On Art and Architecture*, 38.

Grünewald's masterpiece in a way that better captures the fragmentation experienced in 1930, foreshadowing Picasso's more famous *Guernica* of 1937. *Guernica* is perhaps Tillich's favorite painting; he proclaims it has "religious style in a very deep and profound sense"[9] even though it does not include explicit references to religious symbols. The "religious style" in *Guernica* is what "describes the human situation in its depths of estrangement and despair."[10]

In a faded, wrinkled magazine reproduction of a Botticelli tondo, Tillich on the battlefield glimpsed something ultimate through the arresting gaze of a woman both detached from the terror that surrounded him and yet still melancholy with the premonition of her future sorrow. Even stronger was Tillich's personal witness to the vibrancy of the painting's actuality and the silent power of the figures. Visual art is a resource for doing theology because it expresses the attempt to perceive, reconstruct, reimagine, and transform the often chaotic world. As Tillich describes, however, great art is not merely a reflection of human experience: great art *creates* experience, offering a different entry point into reality, such as in Cubism's attempt to show multiple surfaces at once, or Surrealism's inquiry into the porous boundaries between memory and moment, wakefulness and dreams. Art shows "in symbols taken from ordinary experience a level of reality which cannot be grasped any other way. . . . [I]t is as necessary as knowledge and other forms of human spiritual life."[11]

Symbols and language as symbolic are important to Tillich's theology because the primary concern of the theologian is always the present moment and its existential concerns. The phenomenon of human history can be traced through the replacement of symbols and the evolution of religious language. For Tillich, anything with referent to the ultimate is symbolic except that God is the ground of being, being-itself.[12] The aesthetic function of the human spirit is

9. Paul Tillich, "Existentialist Aspects of Modern Art," in Dillenberger, *On Art and Architecture*, 95.

10. Ibid., 96.

11. Tillich, "Existentialist Aspects of Modern Art," 94.

12. See Paul Tillich: "The statement that God is being-itself is a nonsymbolic statement. It does not point beyond itself. It means what it says directly and

related to the religious function insofar as both aesthetics and religion are patterns of symbols that point to the ultimate. Symbols are "living" because they themselves are not ultimate and are replaced when the cultural and social conditions of human beings shift, in the same way that religious knowledge evolves when conditions shift. It is incumbent on theologians to discern whether and how contemporary art forms contribute to the conditions which shape religious symbols. Tillich's love of the arts relates to his interest in the relevancy of theology to the present situation; for him, art and culture offered meaning where the trenches of Europe offered only death and absurdity. Art and culture provide a place to witness the divine even amid the collapse of traditional language and doctrine about God, as well as soothe a broken psyche and fuel the imagination for what is beyond the mundane.

The Marginalization of Art (and Religion)

The academic discipline of theological aesthetics had been expanding for more than a generation, certainly since Paul Tillich brought the study of visual art and culture from the merely secular to recognizing their indispensable theological value in the mid-twentieth century.[13] Tillich is candid in confessing the power of the personal

---

properly; if we speak of the actuality of God, we first assert that he is not God if he is not being-itself. Other assertions about God can be made theologically only on this basis." Tillich, *Systematic Theology*, vol. 1 (Chicago: The University of Chicago Press, 1951), 238–39.

13. In her 1941 essay "Toward a Christian Aesthetic," Anglican Dorothy L. Sayers asserted that "we have no Christian aesthetic—no Christian philosophy of the Arts. The Church as a body has never made up her mind about the Arts, and it is hardly too much to say that she has never tried." Sayers, *Letters to a Diminished Church: Passionate Arguments for the Relevance of Christian Doctrine* (Nashville, TN: Thomas Nelson, 2004), 141. In the early to mid-1960s, Hans Urs von Balthasar formulated his theology of revelation centered on divine glory along aesthetic lines; Balthasar understands his work as distinctively a Catholic way to be faithful to the analogy of being, in which there is "a genuine relationship between theological beauty and the beauty of the world." Von Balthasar, *The Glory of the Lord*, vol. 1, *Seeing the Form*, trans. E. Leiva-Merikakis, ed. Joseph Fessio and John Riches (San Francisco: Ignatius Press, 1982), 80. In this vol-

experience of viewing art and how it affected his academic efforts. Many have wondered why he did not write a systematic theological aesthetics; perhaps it is because he thought he lacked the scholarly credentials, as he admits in nearly every essay he writes on the relationship between art and religion, "I am far from being considered an expert in the visual arts."[14] His lack of formal expertise aside, Tillich declared

---

ume, Balthasar outlines his project; it is, however, important to note that Balthasar did not understand aesthetics as his primary concern but as a way to answer Karl Barth's rejection of aesthetics. Jane Dillenberger, an Episcopalian, understood aesthetics as a primary concern for religious studies and theology, publishing *Style and Content in Christian Art* in 1965, followed by *Secular Art with Sacred Themes* in 1969, *The Religious Art of Andy Warhol* in 1998, and *The Religious Art of Pablo Picasso* in 2014, just before her death; she was one of the first after Tillich to recognize how fertile the interaction could be and was formally trained in art history. Her ex-husband and sometime collaborator, John Dillenberger, helped found the Graduate Theological Union in Berkeley and published *A Theology of Artistic Sensibilities* in 1986. Since Balthasar, however, little was done in theological aesthetics by Catholic theologians until David Tracy published *The Analogical Imagination* in 1981, which, while not focused on aesthetics, raised the conversation in a pronounced way. In the 1990s, efforts of the Anglican Jeremy Begbie, *Voicing Creation's Praise: Towards a Theology of the Arts* (Edinburgh: T & T Clark, 1991) and the Catholics Richard Viladesau, *Theological Aesthetics: God in Imagination, Beauty and Art* (Oxford: Oxford University Press, 1999) and Alejandro Garcia-Rivera, *The Community of the Beautiful: A Theological Aesthetics* (Collegeville, MN: Liturgical Press, 1999), helped to remedy this lacuna. Since the 1990s, the field of theological aesthetics has grown exponentially, with contributions by Frank Burch Brown, Diane Apostolos-Cappadona, David Bentley Hart, Hans Küng, Robin Jensen, Margaret Miles, Gesa Elsbeth Thiessen, Nicholas Wolterstorff, Anthony Godzieba, Henri Nouwen, and Maureen O'Connell, among others.

14. Paul Tillich, "Art and Ultimate Reality," *On Art and Architecture*, ed. John Dillenberger (New York: Crossroad, 1987), 139. Tillich seems more concerned with establishing the necessity of the relationship between art and religion and with the very human experience of the elevated moment that comes with appreciating the arts than with analysis of the different ages of art and what is disclosed in each age about religious understanding. He did not envision a comprehensive aesthetics. He considered this outside his expertise; his own reflections on specific works of art are limited. For a critique of Tillich's use of art and aesthetics in his theological thought, see Russell Re Manning, "Tillich's Theology of Art," in *The Cambridge Companion to Paul Tillich*, ed. Russell Re

that between "a moment of ecstasy" viewing a Botticelli Madonna and encountering the German Expressionism of Emil Nolde, "I always learned more from pictures than from theological books."[15] Even if what Tillich learned is more implicit than systematically explicit, one can hardly deny the contribution Tillich made in turning the great eye of academic theology toward the significance of culture and the arts in describing the dynamic of human life and existence, between humanity and the creative ground of being, between humanity and what Tillich called the "ultimate concern."

Yet, for all the richness of theological discourse art can provide, the arts are still regarded by many scholars of religion and theology as a luxury, a less intellectually rigorous pursuit, an unnecessary distraction from injustices which require more immediate attention and assistance. In the wider public sphere, increased availability of media for entertainment and information has pushed live performance arts and the visual arts—best experienced in person—toward the back burner. As the novelist and playwright Max Frisch famously observed, "[T]echnology [is] the knack of so arranging the world that we don't have to experience it."[16] Richard Kearney adds, "We live in a civilization of images where the human subject is deemed less and less responsible for the working of his/her own imagination."[17] Indeed, our age is bombarded with images, and education has not been able to

---

Manning (Cambridge, UK: Cambridge University Press, 2009), esp. 164–70; Gesa Thiessen, "Religious Art is Expressionistic: A Critical Appreciation of Paul Tillich's Theology of Art," *Irish Theological Quarterly* 59, no. 4 (1993): 301–11; Kelton Cobb, "Reconsidering the Status of Popular Culture in Tillich's *Theology of Culture*," *Journal of the American Academy of Religion* 63 (1995): 53–84; John Dillenberger, *A Theology of Artistic Sensibilities: The Visual Arts and the Church* (London: SCM, 1987), 221; Jeremy Begbie, *Voicing Creation's Praise: Towards a Theology of the Arts* (London: T & T Clark, 1991), 1–77.

15. Tillich, "Art and Ultimate Reality," 151.

16. Max Frisch, quoted by Robert E. Innis in *Pragmatism and the Forms of Sense: Language, Perception, Technics* (University Park, PA: Penn State University Press, 2002), 200.

17. Richard Kearney, "The Crisis of the Image: Levinas' Ethical Response," in *The Ethics of Postmodernity: Current Trends in Continental Thought*, ed. Gary B. Madison and Marty Fairbairn (Evanston, IL: Northwestern University Press, 1999), 12.

maintain the necessary critical formation in discerning value and meaning in visual culture. Most of my students, for instance, have never been to an art museum, and many have not seen a live theatrical production, so have little interest to go when they travel home or abroad. Their lack of formation likely comes from their parents' lack of formation, since arts education in elementary and high school have been on the decline for at least a generation.[18]

Perhaps this decline is due to a failure to prioritize arts education in public schools; but a lack of parental formation may also stem from the intimidation people often feel regarding the arts, because they assume they won't understand what they are "supposed" to see or experience. Modern art, art of roughly the late nineteenth through the twentieth century, is still largely misunderstood in popular discourse: it seems to require no artistic skill because there isn't anything resembling what is "real," and there may be little pleasing to the eye. Indeed, one of Dada's stated goals as a movement was to liberate the world from art in a negation of the aesthetic. Dada didn't last long, but its impact reverberates through modernist art: there are often distressing political messages or disturbing sexuality, the

18. According to the 2008 Survey of Public Participation in the Arts sponsored by the National Endowment for the Arts, surveys from 1982–2008 show a general trend of declining rates of childhood arts education, particularly among low-income and minority children, which led to a decline of participation in the arts as adults. Childhood arts education declines were found to be associated with reductions in arts programs in school; low-income, African American, and Latinoa children disproportionately saw more of the decline in childhood arts education. Twenty-six percent of African Americans surveyed in 2008 reported receiving any arts education in childhood, a huge drop from 51 percent reporting arts education in 1982; for Latinoa, 28 percent in 2008 represents a decline from 47 percent in 1982. The study also found that those with any arts education were twice as likely to attend an activity as those without any arts education; those educated in two or more art forms were three times as likely to participate in the arts as those without any arts education. See http://www.artsedsearch .org/summaries/arts-education-in-america-what-the-declines-mean-for-arts -participation#sthash.dzlNb8xK.dpuf. An interesting project would examine the relationship between this decline and levels of religious participation, as well as forms of broader sociocultural awareness such as understanding issues in diversity, race, gender, and sexuality.

use of materials such as bodily fluids, in what appears to be blatant hostility to beauty and technique. The dearth of accessible meanings for a wide audience contributes to a popular sense that fine art—art usually displayed in museums—is an elitist endeavor, perhaps even a fraud designed primarily for shock value: How can a urinal turned upside down and displayed on a pedestal be called one of the most important works of art in the twentieth century? How can paint splattered on a canvas the size of a wall be worth millions of dollars (or worth my time)? But do those with such opinions seek to invest the time to overcome their disinclination? The arts require time; in order to appreciate any work of art, one must slow down, allow the work to penetrate. One must give it a chance, devote three hours to a performance: this is something that few of us are conditioned to do in today's unending busyness. Perhaps the reluctance to carve out the necessary time to appreciate the arts similarly comes from a failure in education, since educators are reluctant to foster this sort of silent reflection or to allow students to be discomforted, so we are back where we started.

These concerns attest to both the marginalization and commodification of art in society, living, as religion does in the United States, in primarily the private purview of taste: what one "likes." This is David Tracy's observation: "[W]here art is marginalized, religion is privatized. Indeed, religion suffers even greater losses than art by being the single subject about which many intellectuals can feel free to be ignorant. . . . Religion seems to be the sort of thing one likes 'if that's the sort of thing one likes.'"[19] Crucial to Tracy's point is the relevance of both religion and art to encourage the recognition of symbols and mythmaking to sustain society's ability to be self-critical; religion and art might be topics of intimate parlor conversations among friends, even in American intellectual circles, but they should affect society more than as amusement of the bored elite. The progress of the liberal arts—philosophy, history, poetry, literature, religion, art—has been what Elie Wiesel calls "maddeningly slow, if there has

---

19. David Tracy, *The Analogical Imagination: Christian Theology and the Culture of Pluralism* (New York: Crossroad, 1986), 13.

been any real progress at all"[20] in comparison to the growth of science and technology. Wiesel implies that the failure to take seriously the critical functions of the liberal arts contributed to fascism's foothold in the 1930s; Theodor Adorno echoes this: "[T]he premier demand upon all education is that Auschwitz not happen again."[21] Indeed, today's growing "First World" patience with genocide, preventable disease, mass migration from war-torn nations, extreme poverty and hunger, and the death of a child every three seconds from these conditions is a collapse of all that makes us human. Education that fosters critical inquiry and knowledge of religious symbol systems is necessary to the formation of ethical subjectivity.

Modern Art and the Problem of Displacement

Both art and religion have always had public effects, or effects outside their particular communities, because neither is ideologically neutral—whatever activities occur in service of religion or art have something to say and so demand a response external to a particular group or community. This is most obvious when an act of violence is committed that purports to have a religious motivation; but it is similarly true when the bishop of San Diego presides over Mass at the Mexican–US border and prays for immigration reform laws and justice for undocumented persons. Negotiating the different teachings and ideologies of the different communities to which most people belong is where things can get tricky, however. When an artist uses his own urine to create both a symbolic and chromatic effect, as in Andres Serrano's infamous *Piss Christ* (1987), the response, especially from devout Christians, was vehement, from hate-filled rhetoric to a

20. See his interview with Michaël de Saint-Cheron in *Evil and Exile* (Notre Dame, IN: University of Notre Dame Press, 2000), 19.

21. Theodor W. Adorno, "Education after Auschwitz," in *Can One Live After Auschwitz? A Philosophical Reader*, ed. Rolf Tiedemann, trans. Henry W. Pickford (Stanford, CA: Stanford University Press, 2003), 19; see also Claire Elise Katz, *Levinas and the Crisis of Humanism* (Bloomington, IN: Indiana University Press, 2013), 1.

hammer that damaged the work when on display in Avignon, France, in April 2011.

Serrano's Cibachrome photograph—one of the most difficult types to execute because of its saturated color and glassy surface—is nearly five by three feet and shows a crucifix surrounded by an ethereal fiery glow. The actual crucifix used is a small, plastic souvenir-type, easily purchased in any store that sells religious-themed items; but in the photograph, it assumes a magnitude beyond its humble proportions. Serrano, whose background is Afro Cuban, grew up Catholic and admits an "obsession" with religious-themed objects.[22] Indeed, without the title "Piss Christ," there is little doubt that the work would be admired by the same devout Christians who have taken offense. But the title, of course, is part of the point; Cynthia Freeland observes, "[I]t seems we are meant to be torn between being shocked and musing over an image that is mysterious, perhaps reverential."[23] We see an object used for devotion, taken out of its context in a faith identity, and placed in decidedly profane circumstances: whether the work is in a public venue, such as a gallery or museum, rather than in a church, or when we consider his use of bodily fluids as medium rather than waste.

The work is part of a series Serrano composed featuring the coincidence of bodily fluids and religious subject matter. Reference to bodily fluids in ritual and narrative is endemic through Christian cultural history, stemming from a memorial to Jesus that promises to drink of his blood and eat of his flesh to reenactments of Jesus' crucifixion during Holy Week in the Philippines, when devotees are physically nailed to crosses. In the history of Christian art, there are lactating Madonnas, bleeding statues of Jesus with heads of real hair, depictions of Mary ejecting breast milk into the mouth of Bernard of Clairvaux, and statues and paintings that weep or ooze oil.[24]

22. Robert Hobbs, "Andres Serrano: The Body Politic," in *Andres Serrano: Works 1983–1993* (Philadelphia: Institute of Contemporary Art, University of Pennsylvania, 1994), 18.

23. Cynthia Freeland, *But Is It Art? An Introduction to Art Theory* (Oxford: Oxford University Press, 2001), 19.

24. See David Freedberg, *The Power of Images: Studies in the History and Theory of Response* (Chicago: The University of Chicago Press, 1989), 286–88.

Caroline Walker Bynum notes that all bodily fluids are some form of blood in medieval medical theory; blood is understood as both life-giving and life-identifying, such that "the blood of the passion is the blood of birthing."[25]

Christianity has historically been entrenched in the material reality of the body, even when piety turned its gaze toward the spiritual. The tension between embodiment—with all the body's attendant issues, so to speak—and the "spiritual home" of Christians is played out in the Franciscan and Dominican arguments of the Renaissance era that the fixation of the faithful on the bodily relics of Christ is a misguided focus on the corruptible.[26] Despite this more academic theology, the faithful only increased its zeal during the Renaissance for depicting and experiencing the material humanity of Jesus in as realistic terms as possible, to make him "come to life." David Freedberg points out that this is also the case for other players in the Christian narrative: "[I]mages of the Virgin and saints also frequently demonstrated their vitality," which indicates "the need to render the divine accessible by making it seem familiar, recognizable, able to be grasped."[27] The material body not only witnesses to the vitality of the subject depicted; for Derrida, bodily fluids witness to the discomforting mortality of the body. Bodily fluids are "visible signs of existence," indicating the crossing of boundaries between what is inside and what is outside, "resisting the traditional categories ordering Western metaphysical discourse."[28] From this perspective, *Piss Christ*'s juxtaposition of the majesty and mortality of Christ is well within the trajectory of Christian art.

In Matthias Grünewald's Isenheim Altarpiece (1512–1516),[29] one of the most famous early examples of expressive painting depicting

25. Caroline Walker Bynum, *Wonderful Blood: Theology and Practice in Late Medieval Northern Germany and Beyond* (Philadelphia, PA: University of Pennsylvania Press, 2007), 158–59.

26. See Ibid., 144.

27. Freedberg, *The Power of Images*, 298.

28. K. Malcolm Richards, *Derrida Reframed* (London: I. B. Tauris, 2008), 115.

29. Matthias Grünewald, *Isenheim Altarpiece*, 1512–1516. Oil on panel, 336 x 589 cm. Musée d'Unterlinden, Colmar, France. The graphic nature of Jesus'

the agonizing suffering endured on the cross, Jesus is covered in open, oozing sores and pockmarks, some with thorns still protruding. It remains one of the most graphic depictions of suffering found in art of the crucifixion, in many ways ahead of its time in its willingness to distort the proportions of Jesus' body, abstracting from realism, for expressive effect. Grünewald's depiction had a profound effect on the interpretation of Christ's suffering, influencing Picasso as well as expressionists such as Graham Sutherland and William Congdon. But because of cultural taboos regarding urine, one work still inspires piety while the other inspires a hammer.

Both works are profound depictions of the relationship between vulnerability and the body. In some ways, Serrano's *Piss Christ* is more disturbing in its use of bodily fluids than Grünewald's because it reminds us more of our mortality. The deterioration and waste products of the body tacitly remind us of its eventual demise and decomposition; without the certainty of eternal life, the body's vulnerability can be disturbingly uncomfortable. Freeland notes, "Symbols of pain and suffering that are central to many religions can be shocking when dislocated from their community. If they mix with more secular symbols, their meaning is threatened. Artwork that uses blood or urine enters into the public sphere without the context of either well-understood ritual significance or artistic redemption through beauty."[30] When Serrano's work appears in an art gallery or museum and not in a church, does this mean that the meaning of the symbols shifts? Or can the work help the faithful blur the lines between sacred and secular, such that the secular has the potential to disclose the sacred? Would we want to shut down something with the potential to show us something new?

The potential of art to change perception about so-called boundaries between sacred and secular also belongs to religion in the best sense. John de Gruchy notes that the ability of art "to evoke imagination and wonder" causes us to pause and reflect, thereby opening the possibility of changing our perception and ultimately our lives;

---

sores likely refers to the commissioning of the piece by the monks of St. Anthony in Isenheim, who specialized in caring for skin diseases.

30. Freeland, *But Is It Art?*, 7.

"in this way art serves the cause of human liberation."[31] Tracy argues that this is because in the experience of art "we lose our usual self-consciousness and finally encounter a rooted self—a self transformed into both new possibility and the actuality of rootedness by its willingness to play and be played by that transforming disclosure."[32] In this transforming disclosure of the loss of self is the possibility for community, for public significance, for social responsibility: "liberated from privateness into the genuine publicness of a disclosure of truth . . . it seems fatal to consign [classic works of art] to the privacy of a merely entertaining, tasteful, interesting aesthetic realm of temporary refreshment."[33]

Tracy touches a nerve in the consideration of art as a resource for theology here; as soon as art or religion are understood primarily as forms of "temporary refreshment," mere decorations in the expanse and rush of daily life, art and religion become vehicles for the failure of the imagination rather than the promotion and advancement of it. In American society, art and religion tend to be relegated to the private sphere of what fulfills personal taste, whim, and reassurance; in this sense, the experience of art, like the experience of religion, may reflect values of self-preservation and promotion rather than the sort of interpersonal creative exchange that is possible in the appreciation of art. Art should challenge us out of our "comfort zones" in order to prepare for the experience of an Other; this requires openness toward the perspective and language of an Other. From Blanchot's perspective, as we saw in chapter 1, the truth of art comes from the way it exposes us to the *dehors*, the "outside," the realm of the unknown or of infinite alterity. But when we seek only to have our present perspectives reinforced or soothed, in an interest to continue the trajectory of "the Same," both art and religion become susceptible to the comfort-based commodification common in today's capitalist ethos, as well as to the attendant power structures

31. John W. de Gruchy, *Christianity, Art and Transformation: Theological Aesthetics in the Struggle for Justice* (Cambridge, UK: Cambridge University Press, 2001), 200.
32. Tracy, *The Analogical Imagination*, 115.
33. Ibid.

that promote the interests of the wealthy to extract profit from exploiting what is popular in the marketplace.

Fear of the Other and the Marketplace

Both art and religion are susceptible to the sort of solipsistic sanitizing of the threatening and dangerous Other. If art or religion are to be judged solely on the ability to provide comfort and pleasure, according to the utilitarian, it doesn't matter the work or the source. If a painting from the present day depicts a blond, blue-eyed Jesus with white robes and white skin but provides ease and affirmation of faith in a chaotic world, why can't it be "art"?

The late Thomas Kinkade amassed a multi-million dollar fortune painting exactly what would soothe the jangled nerves of a public exposed to—*quelle horreur!*—artists such as Andres Serrano and Robert Mapplethorpe. Kinkade, the self-trademarked "painter of light," crafted paintings Joan Didion describes as typically featuring "a cottage or a house of such insistent coziness as to seem actually sinister, suggestive of a trap designed to attract Hansel and Gretel. Every window was lit to lurid effect, as though the interior of the structure might be on fire."[34] Those who bought his paintings and assorted merchandise do not regard them this way, of course: some estimates place a copy of one of his works in every twentieth household in America. Sales have been highest of his paintings with Christian themes and biblical verses. Given the enormous commercial success of these paintings, and their deliberately nonthreatening subject matter, can we call these works "art"? Will his paintings lead us to the abyss, to the "outside"? Or do they function as supporting a totality of "the Same"?

Part of the problem in defining Kinkade works as "art" pertains to his motivation to paint his subject matter in unambiguously pretty and entertaining compositions: he knew what would sell and painted accordingly. "The number one quote critics give me is, 'Thom, your work is irrelevant.' Now that's a fascinating comment," muses

---

34. Joan Didion, *Where I Was From* (New York: Random House, 2004), 73.

Kinkade, "Yes, irrelevant to the little subculture, this microculture, of modern art. But here's the point: My art is relevant because it's relevant to ten million people. That makes me the most relevant artist in this culture."[35] Success in the marketplace apparently equals success as an artist. One can hardly blame such confidence arising from the approbation of the dollar, as it is no coincidence that the rise of market-driven pricing, even for avant-garde art in the twentieth century, arose alongside the rise of capitalism. The twentieth century saw few great artists as poor as Van Gogh, who died before profiting from a single painting. Bureaucratic and commercial structures govern more and more areas of social life alongside the growth of the marketplace; the value of a work of art is less innovation and more money-driven. David Cottington sees this phenomenon as part of the concurrent rise of the value of the autonomous individual; Western capitalism affirms the individualism of the artist as it affirms the individualism of the oil magnate.[36]

But none of Kinkade's paintings display an innovative vision or disclose anything about his inner life: his childhood in poverty, his alcoholism and drug dependency, his penchant for strip clubs and public outbursts.[37] There is, in other words, a troubling disconnection between Kinkade as a person and Kinkade as an artist, a lack of attention to his own vulnerability and failures. One could argue that he painted an ideal world, a cottage that encapsulates all the nostalgia for a past that never was, and incorporated symbols of a Christian faith on which he himself could not fully rely. Perhaps his artistic vision consists in avoiding vulnerability, in distancing himself from the mortality that obviously haunted him enough that he drank to escape from it.

Avoiding the discomfort of vulnerability is also endemic to American culture. Indeed, the masses might cry, *don't we need these distractions?*

35. Quoted in Oliver Burkeman, "Dark Clouds Gather over 'Painter of Light,'" *Guardian*, March 25, 2006, http://www.theguardian.com/world/2006/mar/25/arts.artsnews.

36. See David Cottington, *Modern Art: A Very Short Introduction* (Oxford: Oxford University Press, 2005), 5.

37. Burkeman, "Dark Clouds Gather over 'Painter of Light.'"

Isn't the world painful enough? Such demands result in "kitsch," the German word which means "junk" but was used in Munich in the late nineteenth century to describe visual works that were cheaply made and popularly accessible. Milan Kundera proposes that "kitsch" refers to an essential component of the human condition, that which unites human beings in tears, a sentimentalism that can appreciate what we hold in common: "[T]he brotherhood of [humanity] on earth will be possible only on a base of kitsch."[38] He also refers to kitsch as "a folding screen set up to curtain off death."[39] What would Nietzsche say? Didn't Nietzsche prize art's deception for the purpose of celebrating life which cannot otherwise be encouraged?

If we want to examine art for its ability to inspire a sense of responsibility and openness to the alterity of the absolutely Other, to insist on the potential of art to guide through the dark field of the double vulnerability of encounter, then art done purely for the sake of catering to the whims of the marketplace, such as the work of Kinkade, cannot offer the original, unique, and unrepeatable perspective of the artist who resists commodification.

Kantian aesthetics explains the impasse. Kant asserted that what characterizes "art" is "disinterest" in purposefulness or usefulness, which we may see as pertaining to the marketplace. "Beauty" in art refers to what is "purposive without purpose," that is, "presenting that is purposive on its own and that furthers, even though without a purpose." If the "purpose" of a thing pertains to what it was made for, art is made for a purpose that is entirely its own, regardless whether one finds it beautiful or not, or meaningful or not. This is "art for art's sake." As soon as one regards a work of art as valuable because it complements the colors in one's living room couch, one is no longer able to appreciate the work of art for itself, as it is in itself, detached from its utility. But because in our capitalist ethos, objects give pleasure in a fetishistic[40] way, it is difficult to regard a

---

38. Milan Kundera, *The Unbearable Lightness of Being*, trans. Michael Henry Heim (San Francisco: HarperCollins, 1999), 251.

39. Ibid., 253.

40. A "fetish" is an inanimate object that is given animate or lifelike qualities. The term's use originated in anthropological discussions of religion; Karl Marx

work of art simply for its excitement of the imagination and the "free play" of the intellect and senses it elicits. Considering the value of art for theology (and so too the value of art for ethical responsibility), however, it is important to explore what it means to regard as *art* objects deliberately created for the marketplace.

A "commodity" is something that is produced for an economic exchange. Karl Marx observed that the value of a commodity is dependent on its relationship with other commodities and its exchange value in comparison to other commodities. Once wood is made into a table, the natural, sensual value of the wood has been altered into "a thing abounding in metaphysical subtleties and theological niceties . . . which transcends sensuousness."[41] It even becomes "mystical": something to be desired. "Commodification" is a term coined by the Frankfurt School[42] of critical social theorists, which included

---

relies on Charles de Brosses's *The Cult of the Fetish Gods* (1760) when discussing the mystical properties that attract human beings to things in his discussion of commodities. In *Capital*, Marx writes: "A commodity appears at first sight an extremely obvious, trivial thing. But its analysis brings out that it is a very strange thing, abounding in metaphysical subtleties and theological niceties." Karl Marx, "The Fetishism of the Commodity," in *Capital*, vol. 1, trans. Ben Fowkes (London: Penguin, 1976), in *The Visual Culture Reader*, ed. Nicholas Mirzoeff (London: Routledge, 2002), 122. Much has been written on the complex intersections of cultural, social, and aesthetic aspects of the valuations of things; "fetishism" pertains here to the attribution of an inherent value in something that gives one access to the divine or to beauty in a way that substitutes private taste for theological and aesthetic discourse. See *The Social Life of Things: Commodities in Cultural Perspective*, ed. Arjun Appadurai (New York: Cambridge University Press, 1986). Fetishes are laden with mystique as well as the illusion that they are autonomous and therefore independent of the very mystique that makes them attractive, according to Marx.

41. Marx, "The Fetishism of the Commodity," 122.

42. The Frankfurt School, a group that developed from the Institute for Social Research, began in 1930 as a way to confront the growth and influence of capitalism, considers forms of Marxist thought in which the transformation of society was more the responsibility of intellectuals than the proletariat and was concerned with the freedom of the individual to resist the "culture industry," in which the arts are tailored for consumption and as such dull the critical faculties. See David Held's excellent *Introduction to Critical Theory: Horkheimer to Habermas* (Oxford: Blackwell, 1989).

Theodor Adorno and Herbert Marcuse. "Commodification" refers to the production of a thing tailored less for its utility and more for its ability to meet the preference of the consumer, exploiting the "mystical" quality of a thing as Marx described. A thing is desirable because people give it a value that transcends its material sensuousness or usefulness. Marx acknowledges the desire that comes from merely owning the object. The commodification of religious-themed objects—from books to seminars to angel pins and plastic "spiritual warfare" armor for children to equip themselves in "fighting Satan"— and the commodification of art-themed objects, turning Van Gogh masterpieces such as *Irises* into silk ties and dinner plates—are remarkably similar in their ability to engage the marketplace. This is because both sets of products described were deliberately produced to appeal to trends in the marketplace: such products are produced specifically to turn a profit because they will sell.

There are all sorts of commodities, of course, from tables to tomatoes. But "commodification" refers to the conversion of something not created specifically for an economic exchange into something that is. Commodification, then, means transferring the original intention of that on which the product is based into something purposefully suited to the whims and desires of the marketplace. Education, for example, is increasingly being thought of as a "product" that makes students (and/or their parents) into consumers and professors into labor capital; this means that the worth of a college education is directly related to marketability of a particular major or the income a graduate receives in her or his first career placement. The value of the ideas and critical thought generated in the process of higher education is not measured on something like social awareness or the service of the common good but on the monetary value accrued by a college degree. This is just one of the many reasons the liberal arts are devalued, even in colleges which claim to be based in the "liberal arts."

In an example related to the commodification of religious ideas, there has been an extraordinary popularity of products that endorse and extol images and mythology regarding angels, which are relatively insignificant theologically. In the Hebrew Bible, angels act as mediators between God and the people, typically charged with delivering instructions or a message from God. The English word "angel" derives from the Greek *aggelos*, "messenger." While a thorough assessment of the history of angelology and its motivations are not necessary here, we should note that in the development of the Judeo-Christian tradition, belief in God's transcendence and incoherence eventually became understood in terms of divine *distance*. God understood as transcendent "Other" was interpreted to mean that God rarely interacted with the material world. This understanding was supplemented by an increasing hierarchy of entities and saints in a heavenly realm who had more access to God than human beings in the lowly material realm but were not divine and so could interact with the material world. The commodification of angel-themed items means that the tradition of divine transcendence allied to an idea of geographical distance results in the desire of the faithful for talismans (or fetishes) that comfort with the promise of the more direct access to God angels are believed to experience. Recognizing and meeting the demand for religious-themed items that provide this comfort is the delighted work of those more concerned to turn a profit than address the spiritual needs of those who believe God is too remote to care about them. Hence, the guardian angel pin, complete with a prayer to "protect and guide you." In a Möbius-style loop, the deficient theology of a distant and indifferent God is perpetuated by the businesses which answer the demand of the consumer seeking immediate comfort rather than more challenging theology. Commodities then replace critical thought, questioning, and investigation with easy antidotes to an often cruel world. This ease, this availability and accessibility is the foundation of religious "kitsch." Religion becomes more about what is privately and immediately gratifying than about ethical responsibility or a willingness to engage the unknown.

The same has been said for the commodification of art. The power of Vincent van Gogh's *Irises*,[43] painted in the year before his death, pertains to the complexity of a man both keenly attentive to the simplicity and joy in a patch of deep purple flowers and so tortured mentally that he had voluntarily committed himself to the asylum

43. Vincent Van Gogh, *Irises*, 1889. Oil on canvas, 74.3 x 94.3 cm. The Getty Museum, Los Angeles.

of Saint Paul-de-Mausole in Saint-Rémy-de-Provence a week prior
to the painting. Does Van Gogh's anguished longing for the compassion of the long stems of flowers gently bent in a breeze become
trivialized when it becomes a pattern for a scarf or coffee mug? Such
commodities do not appear out of nowhere: read optimistically, such
are answers to a public's desire to tap into Van Gogh's profound
appreciation of the natural world and the reprieve it provided him;
read pessimistically, these objects exemplify the public's desire to
own something that echoes a work of art the market has deemed
expensive and only therefore precious and worthwhile.

The problem is, perhaps, not with the angel pins or the coffee mugs
in themselves (neither would have what Marx called "exchange value"
if they didn't sell): the problem is when the taste or comfort value of
things *substitutes* for engaging the mysterious and often troubling
questions signified in the desire for religious and aesthetic truths
(becoming the "folding screen set up to curtain off death"). Marx
noted this attraction to the mysterious value of things when he discusses the phenomenon of "commodity fetishism"; things, like the
practice of religion itself for Marx, distract persons from their authentic selves and their ability to engage in social relationships with
other persons. When we pay more attention to the acquisition of
things in this regard, then religion and art become trivial and disposable matters of whim and private taste.

David Morgan examines mass-marketed religious images for their
sociological impact; his study of Warner Sallman's famous *Head of
Christ*,[44] which is estimated to have been reproduced over five hundred
million times, investigates the motivations that make devotional
imagery so popular. Morgan is not concerned to critique the theological content of these images but rather examine the emotional
connection and attraction to them.

> Sallman's pictures and a host of mass-produced images by other
> artists were not simply about the private sentiments of those
> who admired them; they were the very means of making con-

---

44. Warner Sallman, *Head of Christ*, 1940. Oil on canvas, 28 1/4 x 22 in. Jessie C.
Wilson Art Gallery, Anderson University, Anderson, Indiana.

crete, uniform and universal the memories and feelings that define the individual. This ubiquity and sameness, this pervasive familiarity will seem militantly boring to those for whom the imagery signifies an alien world, but it is deeply reassuring for an image's adherents. Believers return to the same imagery over and over because it reaffirms what they want to take for granted about the world.[45]

The problem with *Head of Christ* is not that it depicts Jesus in a gentle way, or that its gentleness may inspire the sharing of tears; the problem is the mass-marketing forces (aided, to be sure, by religious leadership) that created a hegemony of ideas about Jesus resulting from the picture's emphasis on a savior with white, blond, Eurocentric features and nonthreatening sentimentality. Furthermore, there is a problem when those who appreciate these images do not regard them as *temporary* respite, or as situated within a *spectrum* of possible depictions of Jesus. Morgan admits that "believers return to the same imagery over and over because it reaffirms what they want to take for granted about the world"; such desire for security in belief and certainty of conviction, however, is misplaced at best and dangerous at worst. If Levinas is accurate when describing the impulse to totalize as dominant in the West, that impulse which suppresses diversity, assimilates all differences into what provides the comfort of a secure isolation from the threatening Other, then we see in the use of visual images not only the creation of communities and personal identity but also, possibly, the very root of violence against the Other.

What seems harmless in the countenance of Jesus gazing upward becomes harmful in the way whiteness is associated with divinity and salvation, especially when we consider that the portrait was fashioned during a volatile time in American history, when black men and women were regularly lynched and the civil rights of all people of color barely existed. Sallman may have been reacting negatively to research on the historical Jesus which was, at the time, gaining momentum (in academic circles, anyway). While it would

---

45. David Morgan, *Visual Piety* (Berkeley, CA: University of California Press, 1998), 17.

be unfair to speculate on his motives, however, Sallman plucked the symbol of the white-skinned European Jesus from a more mawkish nineteenth-century Academicism (since that is its style) and dropped it into a time in which discrimination, segregation, beatings, and worse continued to be blameless, if not actually legal, and the United States was entering World War II with a segregated army.[46]

Sallman's portraits confirm racist attitudes, to be sure; but these attitudes are both exacerbated when invested in imagery that is commodified and justified when associated with religious redemption. Add the phenomenon of these portraits used in military recruitment posters or as pocket-sized talismans sent to soldiers at the front, and these attitudes assume nationalistic dispositions, part of the grand narrative that America is not only a "white nation" but also a "Christian nation." Perhaps, bound to an image, these factors taken together—the commodification pervasive in capitalism plus religious justification plus nationalism—might resemble the imperialistic motives of those Christians who severed millions of Africans from their villages during the centuries of slave trade. While this point may seem hyperbolic, Morgan's extensive work verifies not only the popularity of these images but also their ubiquity, even among those who are not Christian or even religious in any sense. So identified with American Evangelical Protestantism's global missionary outreach, Morgan contends, the portraits of Jesus by Sallman and his ilk are among the most recognizable in the world, part of a religious ethos that sought to be "world-redeeming, as constitutive of a nation that enjoyed a manifest and now global destiny," relying on such visual culture for didactic as well as devotional purposes.[47] "World-redeeming"? Perhaps. Try "world-dominating."

---

46. Edward J. Blum and Paul Harvey note that Sallman's *Head of Christ* was initially accepted in Catholic circles. The painting's "shared use by Protestants and Catholics was part of strengthening relationships across the religious divide," especially during World War II and the subsequent Cold War, as a way to solidify symbols of American nationalism against atheistic Communism. *The Color of Christ: The Son of God and the Saga of Race in America* (Durham, NC: University of North Carolina Press, 2012), 210.

47. David Morgan, *Protestants and Pictures: Religion, Visual Culture, and the Age of American Mass Production* (Oxford: Oxford University Press, 1999), 265.

When religion and art are so privatized as to insulate persons from self-reflexive critique of dearly held ideas, images, and beliefs, when they totalize and universalize experience in such a way that the alterity of the Other is excluded, one may feel the strength of their identity increase while the ethical commitment to the Other decreases. The more I feel my selfhood invested in the hegemonic ideas of a particular population, the less I am able to look beyond that familiarity to what is different. In his "Letter from Birmingham Jail," Martin Luther King observed, "[I]t is an historical fact that privileged groups seldom give up their privileges voluntarily." The perpetuation of the privileges that underlie market-driven ideas, images, and beliefs revel in their ability to universalize their content in such a way that those outside of the content can be easily excluded, ridiculed, or harmed. What purports to merely offer comfort and form refuge from the chaos of the world can result in an ideological form of violence that manifests as racism, sexism, homophobia, and other forms of xenophobia.

Constructive Possibilities of Art as a Resource for Theology

The trajectory on which art and religion can operate, pointing toward a transcendent Other, envisioning the transformation of the world, a future happily incongruous with the present ("the end of the world *as we know it*," as the lads in the rock band R.E.M. sing), is dangerously twisted by the culture industry's determination to level diversity in the marketplace. Only when artworks maintain a dialectical character, as the "social antithesis of society, not directly deducible from it,"[48] as Adorno argues, can art (and religion) point the way forward, out of the sphere of totalizing sameness. Thus, the paradox: art (and religion) can only arise from the world, in the world, by material and fallible means, integrating these components "into their law of form and in this integration at the same time maintain what

48. Theodor W. Adorno, *Aesthetic Theory*, ed. Gretel Adorno and Rolf Tiedemann, trans. and ed. Robert Hullot-Kentor (Minneapolis, MN: University of Minnesota Press, 1997), 8.

resists it and the fissures that occur in the process of integration."[49] Adorno notes that "artworks recall the theologumenon that in the redeemed world everything would be as it is and then wholly other." This dialectic between the identity of art with the world, or conformity to a society that resists alterity and otherness, that resists encountering the strange as strange without sublimating it into "the same" and the "heightened order of existence" achievable by art (and religion), is art's inevitable energy if it is authentically art. Adorno explains,

> [A]s Schoenberg said, one paints a painting, not what it represents. Inherently every artwork desires identity with itself, an identity that in empirical reality is violently forced on all objects as identity with the subject and thus travestied. Aesthetic identity seeks to aid the non-identical, which in reality is repressed by reality's compulsion to identity. Only by virtue of separation from empirical reality, which sanctions art to model the relation of the whole and the part according to the work's own need, does the artwork achieve a heightened order of existence.[50]

This short reflection on the relation of art and religion in the private and commodified sphere of American society reminds us that the power of art and religion to transform and critique is muddled when used to confirm and perpetuate the status quo in society, which often means accommodating the white wealthy elite and the consumer pursuit of comfort and security. Perhaps we may also see that in as much as art and religion may be made to conform to "the Same," artists themselves in every century have seen their work as concerned with religious questions. Even if the academy has often denied the power of art to be a resource for theology, modern artists such as Mark Rothko, Robert Motherwell, and Ad Reinhart regarded their work as exploring themes pertaining to theological discourse and questions of ultimate concern, such as the interaction between being and nothingness and the failures of language and representation to fully articulate the spiritual dimension of the human being.

49. Ibid., 7.
50. Ibid., 4.

May we understand art as that which critiques society in the vein of the prophetic tradition of the Abrahamic religions, in the way that serves to oppose a conforming and comfortable worldview? But what can art do to be both relevant to theology and confront a world in which people are systematically oppressed and murdered? More specifically, what can art do to facilitate the sort of thinking about God in which material and spiritual, vague and particular, contextual and general, abstract and figurative, coalesce into something like an incarnation in order to inspire the ethical enthusiasm to confront a world in which people are systematically oppressed and murdered? Can art's necessary contextual dependence on the historical situation serve a liberating function from the privatization that totalizes the Other into "the Same"?

In his first book, *The Birth of Tragedy*, Friedrich Nietzsche was concerned with Christianity's use of the arts to pander to a morality he describes as a "hatred of 'the world,' condemnations of the passions, fear of beauty and sensuality, a beyond invented the better to slander this life, at bottom a craving for the nothing, for the end. . . . [A]ll this has always struck me . . . as the most dangerous and uncanny form of all possible forms of a 'will to decline'—at the very least a sign of abysmal sickness, weariness, discouragement, exhaustion, and impoverishment of life."[51] Nietzsche's early period is characterized by vehement opposition to any system which impeded the enjoyment of life and the flourishing of art as the only true metaphysical task. This vehemence is perhaps due to his belief in the vanity of Christian values, nihilistic because passively resigned to a supernatural illusion and so incapable of beauty. The unrestrained hedonism and emotion of Dionysius should be allowed to bloom, but he believed this to be unachievable as long as people were numbed by the wet blanket of Christianity. In *Human, All Too Human*, published six years later, he writes, "Art is above and before all supposed to beautify life, thus make us ourselves endurable, if possible pleasing to others. . . . [A]rt is supposed to conceal or reinterpret everything ugly, those painful, dreadful, disgusting things which . . . again and

51. Friedrich Nietzsche, *The Birth of Tragedy*, trans. Shaun Whiteside, ed. Michael Tanner (New York: Penguin Books, 1993), 8.

again insist on breaking forth,"[52] those things that seem to be why Kinkade's paintings are so popular. Not that Nietzsche would have tolerated Kinkade's syrupy sentimentalism. There is a fine line between taking respite from the turmoil in the world and fleeing its responsibilities, escaping a sober awareness of what unrestrained narcissism has created in the social and economic fabric of the age. Nietzsche's mistake was to divorce the beautiful from the ethical, and so creativity from morality, as though ethics and morality are necessarily governed by religious motivation, or worse, that ethics and morality are necessarily governed by reward-seeking religious motivation. Nietzsche had little tolerance for compassion and the idea of self-sacrifice for the sake of another human being (sacrifice for art and intellectual pursuits, however, was fine); Christians had been crying wolf on compassion for too long by the time he watched his father, a pastor, slowly die of cancer. He was through with giving Christianity's promise of hope the benefit of the doubt.

Art in the modern era was compelled to respond to the fragmentation and alienation exacerbated by the repercussions of the assembly line on human identity and the rapid development of technology. Add two world wars that traumatized all of Europe and the landscape of meaning would never be the same. Theodor Adorno asks Jean-Paul Sartre's question, "Does living have any meaning when men exist who beat you until your bones break?" as the question of whether art should exist at all in a spiritually deprived age.[53] While Adorno realizes that both art and language play a role in the generation of the sort of society in which catastrophic suffering becomes normative, he notes that "the abundance of real suffering permits no forgetting . . . what Hegel called the awareness of affliction—also demands the continued existence of the very art it forbids; hardly anywhere else does suffering still find its own voice,

---

52. Friedrich Nietzsche, *Human, All Too Human*, 2.174, trans. R. J. Hollingdale (Cambridge, UK: Cambridge University Press, 2004), 255.

53. Theodor W. Adorno, quoting Jean-Paul Sartre's *The Dead without Tombs*, in "Commitment," trans. Shierry Weber Nicholsen, in *Can One Live after Auschwitz? A Philosophical Reader*, ed. Rolf Tiedemann, trans. Rodney Livingstone, et al. (Stanford, CA: Stanford University Press, 2003), 251–52.

a consolation that does not immediately betray it."[54] In short, we must continue to stretch the idea of art beyond the totalizing proclivities of the wealthy elite, if only to serve as a witness to those who suffer oppression and catastrophe.

Adorno affirms that art may be the last medium of the inexpressible, because art lives through its ability to expose us to the radically new, to what contradicts the "official optimism" of a society that promotes "normalcy" and conformity while at the same time considering human beings "collateral damage" and blurring the distinction between torturers and tortured. "Normalcy," or security in the status quo, threatens the death of the new by its societal proclamation that change is to be feared and squashed. This is because Adorno is passionate about viewing the world from the lens of its redemption, in a nonreligious sense, since for him the persistence of catastrophic suffering means that the world has not yet been redeemed. He writes, "Knowledge has no light but that shed on the world by redemption. . . . Perspectives must be fashioned that displace and estrange the world, reveal it to be, with its rifts and crevices, as indigent and distorted as it will appear one day in the messianic light."[55]

Facing the despair of catastrophic suffering and the willingness to assume the insecurity of the vulnerability of the Other calls for "consummate negativity" toward a normalcy that can never be fully escaped: viewing the world with the perspective of what the world can be is "utterly impossible" because one is always mired in, and must on some level acquiesce to, the very structures that perpetuate the misery of the innocent. Art at least attempts this contradiction, observes Adorno: "Even its own impossibility it must at last comprehend for the sake of the possible."[56]

Art must be cautious to resist the naïve optimism of the "culture industry," because the culture industry dominates and levels all nuance, distinction, and alterity into a totality—"the Same." Adorno writes, "The power of the cultural industry's ideology is such that

54. Ibid., 252.
55. Theodor W. Adorno, *Minima Moralia: Reflections on Damaged Life*, trans. E. F. N. Jephcott (London: Verso, 2005), 247.
56. Ibid.

conformity replaces consciousness."[57] Such power may be under-stood as a brainwashing of sorts, a numbing to the real problems in society, and a failure to be appropriately critical of them. But for Adorno, there is hope for a better world only if art creates a space in which it is possible to imagine the radically new. Notes Lydia Goehr, "Any activity or form of expression that pricks through the ideological web of familiarity is, for Adorno, already radical in the deepest sense and sustains the only hope possible. For radical does not mean revolutionary; more deeply, it implies the sort of reflection that cracks established patterns of self-evidence."[58] Art has the potential to conform to the whims of the totalizing mechanisms of the culture industry (and thereby lose its character as art); art also has the potential to fire the imagination for ways to critique and therefore gain conceptual tools to resist "the Same." Such is required of a moral nature, writes Adorno, "to face the psychological mecha-nisms operating on various levels in order not to become blind and passive victims. We can change this medium of far-reaching poten-tialities only if we look at it in the same spirit which we hope will one day be expressed in its imagery."[59]

Returning to Tracy's original point, "where art is marginalized, religion is privatized," and Adorno's observations that true hope exists where art resists conformity, we may add that hope exists where religion resists conformity to the totalizing numbness that prevents the critique and reform of society's oppressions. Whether or not he would approve of my usage here, Adorno provides a frame-work in which we may explore the authentically social interactions religion and art can offer. I believe that the value of art as a theo-logical resource relies on the ability of art to challenge the viewer, to confront them with an experience of alterity that is so radical that it may at first appear shocking, or frightening, or stupefying, or mad-

57. Theodor W. Adorno, *The Culture Industry*, ed. and trans. Rolf Tiedemann (London: Routledge, 1991), 104.

58. Lydia Goehr, "Dissonant Works and the Listening Public," in *The Cambridge Companion to Adorno*, ed. Tom Huhn (Cambridge, UK: Cambridge University Press, 2004), 235.

59. Adorno, *The Culture Industry*, 176.

dening—but that it can also inspire the quietly surprising, gently prodding, itch one can't scratch, the habituation of mind. Certainly there will always be sentimental value attached to things as well as experiences—Tillich admits as much when discussing his moment of transformation upon seeing the Botticelli Madonna—but the enduring greatness of a work of art or a religious belief or a liturgical practice refers to its ability to engage and enthrall—while also developing and evolving—exposing the endless "outside," every time. This we may also see in the encounter with Beauty, that which breaks through the mundane, orienting toward the vulnerability of the Other, in deeper awareness of what it means to respond in consistent self-donation.

CHAPTER FOUR

Visual Art as a Resource for Theology of the Incarnation

Steeple

Maybe love really does mean the submission of power—
I don't know. Like pears on a branch, a shaking branch,
in sunlight, 4 o'clock sunlight, all the ways we do harm,
or refrain from it, when nothing says we have to. . . . Shining,
everyone shining like that, as if reality itself depended
on a nakedness as naked as naked gets; on a faith in each
other as mistaken as mistaken tends to be, though I have
loved the mistake of it—still do; even now—as I love
the sluggishness with which, like ceremony or, not much
different, any man who, having seen himself at last,
turns at first away—has to—the folded black and copper
wings of history begin their deep unfolding, the bird itself,
shuddering, lifts up into the half-wind that comes after—
higher—soon desire will resemble most that smaller thing,
late affection, then the memory of it; and then nothing at all.

—Carl Phillips[1]

---

1. Carl Phillips, "Steeple," in *Reconnaissance: Poems* (New York: Farrar, Straus and Giroux, 2015), 12.

Aesthetics and the Problem of Beauty

Possibly the most accurate thing we can say about art is that it has been around in one form or other for more than thirty thousand years, once anatomically modern humans replaced Neanderthals. The caves at Lascaux, France, discovered in September 1940 by four teenage boys exploring the woods, provide a magnificent example of the value earliest human societies placed on art. Created during the Upper Paleolithic period (40,000 to 10,000 BCE), the best paintings in Lascaux are from the Magdalenians (from the name of a site), peoples who populated the European continent from 18,000 to 10,000 BCE. These works have unifying characteristics such that the period of Magdalenian art became the first and longest identifiable in human history; evidence of their culture is found in about three hundred caves in southern France and northern Spain. There are approximately two thousand images in the Lascaux cave system; nearly half are animals, and the rest are geometric designs, with only one of a human being, possibly a shaman.[2] What is most striking about the work done in the caves, besides the overwhelming vigor and bearing of the paintings themselves, is that archeologists and anthropologists have determined that the works were not created for the decoration of dwelling spaces. In Lascaux, the first paintings are located sixty-five feet below ground level, where there are no sources of natural light. Some paintings are fourteen feet above the cave floor; since early peoples were much shorter than modern people, this necessitates the design and engineering of scaffolding, assembled and climbed in nothing more than trembling light from a torch or lamp fueled with animal fat and held while the artist went to work. The entire project must have been incredibly dangerous; some were sure to have fallen to their deaths from the scaffolding to the slippery rock below.

Why would early peoples, so focused on survival, venture miles into the cold, damp rock to paint, and not just paint at eye level—that would be too easy!—or paint mere scrawls, but paint accurate like-

2. See Norbert Aujoulat, *Lascaux: Movement, Space and Time* (New York: Abrams, 2005), 257.

nesses of bulls seventeen feet long, working at nearly three times the height of the average Paleolithic person off the ground, in barely any light? Wouldn't the industry and ingenuity have been better spent on gathering and preserving food sources and livable shelter? Karen Armstrong presents the widely accepted theory that the caves were sacred places for ceremony and ritual, sanctuaries in which the "iconography reflected a vision that was radically different from that of the outside world."[3] Increasingly, archeologists are finding evidence of a much closer relationship between primitive religious culture and art, such that these form the fundamental basis for society rather than the other way around. Armstrong notes, "If historians are right about the function of the Lascaux caves, religion and art were inseparable from the very beginning."[4]

For the French philosopher Georges Bataille (1897–1962), close friends with Maurice Blanchot and Emmanuel Levinas, the Lascaux paintings were so significant that he calls the day of their discovery the day of "our birth." Bataille's publication of *The Birth of Art* in 1955, soon after the Lascaux caves were opened to the public, was met with skepticism by scientists for its assertion that the origin of art signals the origin of humanity. There is no evolutionary requirement or biological justification for the works at Lascaux; the desire of those who risked their lives to create more and more fantastic works of art pertain to something like sacrifice. Writes Bataille, "A work of art, a sacrifice contains something of an irrepressible festive exuberance that overflows the world of work, and clashes with, if not the letter, the spirit of the prohibitions indispensable to safeguarding this world. . . . [E]very sacrifice has its cause in the quest for a sacred instant that for an instant puts to rout the profane time in which prohibitions guarantee the possibility of life."[5] This quest, these aspirations: that there was a journey into the unknown dark populated by the mysteries of the commonplace seems eerily analogous today. Maurice Blanchot notes this as well:

3. Karen Armstrong, *The Case for God* (New York: Anchor Books, 2010), 5.
4. Ibid., 7.
5. Georges Bataille, *Prehistoric Painting: Lascaux or the Birth of Art*, trans. Austryn Wainhouse (Geneva: Skira, 1955), 39.

Lascaux should be both what is most ancient and a thing of today; these paintings should come to us from a world with which we have nothing in common, . . . yet they nonetheless make us, regardless of questions and problems, enter into an intimate space of knowledge, . . . confirming our faith in art, in that power of art that is so close to us everywhere, all the more so that it escapes us.[6]

Those who made the initial journeys into the caves after their modern discovery must have felt as though they had entered a birth canal, revealing horses, bison, and a bear writ in glowing hues. The caves might also reveal the birth of religion; Bataille seems to think so.[7] Even the atheist Blanchot cannot resist such awe: "[T]he first spectators must have experienced, as we do, and with as much naïve astonishment, the wondrous revelation; the place from which art shines forth and whose radiance is that of a first ray—first and yet complete."[8] The beginnings of art seem to coincide with the beginnings of recognizing the sacred, perhaps a watershed moment in the becoming human of humanity, a moment "set apart" from the tasks and challenge of survival. As Blanchot muses over Bataille's assertions, early art forms "are probably linked to the movement of effervescence, to the explosive generosity of celebration when man, interrupting the time of effort and work—thus for the first time truly man—returns to the sources of natural overabundance in the jubilation of a brief interlude, to what he was when he was not yet."[9]

The cave art and early temples, such as the 11,600-year-old Göbekli Tepe in the southeastern Anatolia region of Turkey, show that homage to the sacred and art were the organizing principles of

6. Maurice Blanchot, "The Birth of Art," in *Friendship*, trans. Elizabeth Rottenberg (Stanford, CA: Stanford University Press, 1997), 1–2.

7. See Richard White, "Bataille on Lascaux and the Origins of Art," *Janus Head* 11, nos. 1–2 (2009): 323–24. White discusses Bataille's theory that the cave paintings reflect an awareness of the prohibitions of life, such as death and sex, and religious rituals developed to cope with these, setting up boundaries of the forbidden which functioned to order society.

8. Blanchot, "The Birth of Art," 1.

9. Ibid., 4.

the earliest human societies, priorities that surpassed mere survival, since the creation of art and sacred gathering spaces was often dangerous.[10] Art and religion were inseparable from life in the earliest identifiable societies of human beings. Taken further, we may venture that art appears to communicate the experience of the sacred before the formalization of language and the written word. Art therefore precedes Logos. What does this mean for us today? Not only that we have become disconnected from the "explosive generosity of celebration" of the sacred that first made us human but also that we have disconnected from the space of the paradox between absence and presence that appears thirty thousand years ago and has yet to be resolved or overcome. Blanchot continues, "[A]s if the origin, instead of showing itself and expressing itself in what emerges from the origin, were always veiled and hidden by what it produces, and perhaps then destroyed or consumed as origin, pushed back and always further removed and distant, as what is originally deferred." This deference, this distance, this "lacuna" as Blanchot calls it, this space of the impossible, refers to the "hidden meaning of art" which returns to the "non-origin": "art explores, asserts, gives rise to— through a contact that shatters all acquired form—what is essentially before; what is, without yet being."[11]

How does art bring us to the abyss, the "space" articulated by Blanchot, without abandoning us to the despair and ambiguity of

10. Klaus Schmidt was the lead excavator of Göbekli Tepe for over a decade, beginning work in 1995. The site, which shows no evidence of long-term human habitation (for example, Schmidt shows that there is no evidence of buildings or hearths interpreted as domestic; the site had no water source, with the nearest stream about three miles away), led to his conclusion, "first came the temple, and then the city." There are at least twenty installations or temples. Builders were somehow able to extract and transport over two hundred stone pillars weighing ten to twenty metric tons, ranging in height from three to six meters, from quarries hundreds of feet away, using no wheels. Images of animals, from fox to scorpions, were carved into the stones and placed in concentric circles. Schmidt considered it a pilgrimage destination. See J. Peters and K. Schmidt, "Animals in the Symbolic World of Pre-Pottery Neolithic Göbekli Tepe, South-eastern Turkey: A Preliminary Assessment," *Anthropozoologica* 39, no. 1 (2004): 179–218.

11. Blanchot, "The Birth of Art," 10.

the incomprehensible? In Dostoyevsky's *The Idiot*, teenage Hippolyte Terentiev, dying of tuberculosis, mocks Myshkin's sentiment that "beauty will save the world." Alexandr Solzhenitsyn, who spent years as a political prisoner in the Gulag Archipelago, admits the idea is tough to swallow: "When in bloodthirsty history did beauty ever save anyone from anything? Ennobled, uplifted, yes—but whom has it saved?"[12] Myshkin's own condition, epilepsy—a condition from which Dostoyevsky also suffered and which took the life of his son Alyosha—does not deter his purity, his desire to see beauty despite a world racked with pain and confusion. His notion of beauty comes from a hope which in turn comes from his faith. Myshkin hopes that Nastassya Filippovna's beauty will save her from her past, but in the end she refuses Myshkin's help and runs away with a man she knows will destroy her (and he does). Tragically, Hippolyte has lost hope, not just of survival, but that there is any meaning to be found in his short life, lamenting that his impending death impedes his place in the world's order: even the "little fly which buzzes around my head in the sun's rays . . . is a sharer and participator in all the glory of the universe, and knows his place and is happy in it."[13]

"Beauty" is more about hope in Dostoyevsky's final analysis; by the time he finishes *The Brothers Karamazov* (which chronologically follows *The Idiot*), he seems to understand that the practical goods of responsibility for others in the ethical life engender a hope that is plausible in the midst of a world filled with catastrophe. Dostoyevsky also wrestles with the deceptive and constructive aspects of the beautiful in *The Brothers Karamazov*, but this time, the purity and persistence of Alyosha's faith are a beacon for the story rather than its heartbreaking end, as for Myshkin. Fr. Zosima provides Alyosha with the key notions of redemption in the novel, overcoming Dmitri Karamazov's agonized claim that beauty is "fearful and terrible," the "battlefield" upon which God and the devil struggle.

12. Alexandr Solzhenitsyn, "Lecture for the Nobel Prize in Literature, 1970," Nobelprize.org, http://www.nobelprize.org/nobel_prizes/literature/laureates/1970/solzhenitsyn-lecture.html.

13. Fyodor Dostoyevsky, *The Idiot*, trans. Constance Garnett (London: Heinemann, 1913), 414.

> Have no fear of men's sin. Love a man even in his sin, for that is the semblance of Divine Love and that is the highest love on earth. . . . Love the animals, love plants, love everything. If you love everything, you will perceive the divine mystery in all things. . . . There is only one means of salvation. . . . [M]ake yourself responsible for all men's sins. . . . [F]or as soon as you sincerely make yourself responsible for everything and for all men, you will see at once that it is really so, and that you are to blame for every one and for all things.[14]

"Love everything"; as we saw in chapter 2, this is again the language of enthusiasm and excess. To overflow with love for all things, even the ugly, even the repulsive, seems an insurmountable task that mocks human capability. But that's the point: if we are truly to enter the space of the impossible and unexpected, to glimpse the trace of the divine in all that breathes and lives, human capability should be mocked in its silly, paltry timidity. To love even our vulnerability such that the very vulnerability of the Other which disturbs my complacency becomes the locus, the space of God: only the imagination can overcome the limitations reason erects. Again, the Buddhists seem to understand this better: embracing all things, from the plants to the animals to the sinful Other, should be as deliberate as breathing, even while this love is as difficult as fearlessness. Fr. Zosima's exhortation to be responsible even for the sins of others gives Alyosha the practical hope he needs to survive the world that Ivan has outlined for him, a world built out of the horror and violence of human action, a world we will examine more specifically in chapter 5. Alyosha's faith, born of this hope, gives Dmitri the strength to endure his false imprisonment. " 'Beauty will save the world,' " Solzhenitsyn came to realize, is "not a careless phrase but a prophecy. After all *he* was granted to see much, a man of fantastic illumination. And in that case art, literature might really be able to

---

14. Fyodor Dostoyevsky, *The Brothers Karamazov*, trans. Constance Garnett (New York: Barnes and Noble, 2004), Part II, Book 6, chapter 3, 293–95. Please forgive the non-inclusive language; someday, someone will translate this work using inclusive language that remains true to Dostoyevsky's vision.

help the world today."[15] May we also find in the experience of beauty the prophetic hope that saves the world through art?

Beauty has the particular quality of drawing us out of ourselves; its reality pertains to the awakening of attention and desire. The "prophecy" Solzhenitsyn finds within the direction of beauty toward justice is realized through the way in which beauty draws us toward compassion. Aesthetic sensibility is the faculty of recognition; it pertains to the scope by which we are able to experience the world bodily in becoming a subject, which Levinas argues is only meaningful in responsibility for the vulnerable Other. Beauty encountered through the arts (although much of this applies to the beauty of the natural world as well) is relevant to this aim in two ways: first, when our senses and intellect are lit on fire by the experience of something beautiful, we become accustomed to notice more around us than just the painting or just the concerto. An elevation of the senses takes place, as well as a corresponding craving by the intellect to find out more. Second, the cultivation of attentiveness also engenders responsiveness, as long as the attention is toward the external, what is outside the self. But cultivating the attention which draws us outside ourselves is harder than it sounds. "It is not easy to live in that continuous awareness of things that is alone truly living," writes Joseph Wood Krutch, "the faculty of wonder tires easily. . . . Really to see something once or twice a week is almost inevitably to have to try to make oneself a poet."[16] Seeing enables a primordial connection to the world outside us: it is inherently ecstatic, the first movement of exteriority, because there is always an object of the gaze. "Seeing comes before words," asserts John Berger, "seeing establishes our place in the surrounding world; we explain the world with words, but words can never undo the fact that we are surrounded by it. . . . [T]he explanation never quite fits the sight."[17] With the modern age, "seeing" becomes a synthesis, performative,

15. Solzhenitsyn, "Lecture for the Nobel Prize in Literature, 1970."

16. Joseph Wood Krutch, *The Desert Year* (Tucson, AZ: University of Arizona Press, 1985), 37–38; see also Douglas E. Christie, *The Blue Sapphire of the Mind: Notes for a Contemplative Ecology* (Oxford: Oxford University Press, 2013), 10.

17. John Berger, *Ways of Seeing* (London: Penguin Books, 1973), 7.

a sight that operates like a saying, observes Jean-Luc Nancy. Kant provides the outline of the imagination's role in the synthesis between sight and the sort of perception that is constitutive or productive of its object; the imagination for Kant becomes "a purveyor of knowledge," presenting all things, the subject and object, the imaginable and the unimaginable.[18]

Kant and the Imagination

Understanding the interaction between the senses and the intellect through the experience of something beautiful points first to Kant's elucidation of the relationship between the experience of beauty and the imagination and second to the potential of the imagination to recognize and create an ethical vision. Immanuel Kant (1724–1804) was born the same year that his hometown, Königsberg, East Prussia, was formed by the conglomeration of three large towns on the Pregel River. He was raised in a cultural and home-based milieu that valued intuitive experience and feeling as expressed in Pietism, a movement that tried to mitigate what it saw as the Lutheran church's spiritual inertia.

Rather than speculative doctrine, which it saw as primarily related to the interference of the institutional church, Pietism emphasized individual spiritual rebirth and a direct relationship with Christ based on the rigorous study of scripture. While not necessarily hostile to the arts, Pietism was suspicious of the potential for both the natural world and the arts to steer one's attention away from God. Alexander Gottlieb Baumgarten (1714–1762), also raised Pietist, appropriated the term "aesthetics" (from the Greek *aisthetikos*, meaning "sensitive" or "sentiment," the ability to receive sensation) to scientifically describe matters of taste as recognizing the agreement of form and content, which appealed to the intellectual direction of the late Enlightenment.[19]

18. See Jean-Luc Nancy, *The Ground of the Image*, trans. Jeff Fort (New York: Fordham University Press, 2005), 81.
19. See Tanya Kevorkian, "Pietists and Music," in *A Companion to German Pietism, 1660–1800*, ed. Douglas Shantz (Leiden: Brill, 2014), 171.

Kant considered it his duty to harness the capacities of reason that had been gradually inflated throughout the Enlightenment; while he admired Baumgarten's intentions to gird a "science" of aesthetics as a matter of taste with objective, cognitive laws, Kant initially declared this project "futile" in the *Critique of Pure Reason* (1781)[20] by arguing that its rules or criteria are "merely empirical" and so "can never serve as determinate *a priori* laws to which our judgment of taste must conform."[21] In other words, there are no rational principles by which to determine aesthetic experience; but Kant identifies two pure forms of intuition, space and time, that are *a priori* and structure our capacity to receive this experience. Such is the "transcendental aesthetic." By the time the third *Critique*, the *Critique of Judgement*, was published in 1790, Kant had honed the notion of "taste" as the aesthetic subjective response to an experience of an object. Aesthetic judgments pertain to the experience of beauty, which is not merely reducible to what *pleases* the senses, but is not cognitive, either. As Richard Kearney explains, beauty pertains to an "inner finality of form" which "derives from the sense of *autonomous freedom* which the imagination enjoys in beholding it," such that the mind "becomes its own means and its own end, the mirror turned lamp."[22] The autonomous freedom of the imagination means that one can be "disinterested" in the object's utility, seeking instead to appreciate it for its own sake; such subjective "purposiveness

20. Kant chose the term "critique" carefully to distinguish his work from a "doctrine." According to Nicholas Walker, a critique attempts to distinguish between the true and the false with a carefully considered judgment, based on justifying grounds, upon any contested subject; Kant's transcendental philosophy is a *metaphysics of experience* rather than a *transcendent metaphysics* by which we can have knowledge of supersensible objects; hence, it is "an inquiry into the very conditions of the possibility of objective knowledge and principled action." Nicholas Walker, introduction to Immanuel Kant, *Critique of Judgement*, trans. James Creed Meredith (Oxford: Oxford University Press, 2009), x.

21. Immanuel Kant, *Critique of Pure Reason*, trans. Werner S. Pluhar (Indianapolis, IN: Hackett, 1996), A 21, p. 74n23.

22. Richard Kearney, *The Wake of the Imagination* (New York: Routledge, 1988), 172, my emphasis.

without purpose" is, or must be, universally communicable when we wish for others to confirm our experience.

Kant had first written about aesthetics in 1764, with *Observations on the Feeling of the Beautiful and Sublime*, which was focused on categorizing the various feelings involved in aesthetic experience. The Enlightenment had been concerned to relate the "higher" faculties of reason with the "lower" faculties of sensation, perception, and inner feeling; the "imagination" was seen as that which negotiates these.[23] Kant's approach is rather to give imagination a governing role rather than a mediating one; the imagination directs what the experience of beauty inspires, a "free play" between reason (*Vernunft*, the faculty of principles), understanding (*Verstand*, the faculty of rules), and sensation, that which we receive of the outside world through our senses.[24] Kant's assessment of the imagination's role in the mind's activity is complex but is the only aspect of his epistemology that leaves room for the imagination, so to speak, insofar as the imagination contains the possibility of impossibility. To Heidegger, Kant redefined the imagination as the "formative center" of sensible intuition and cognition, insofar as the imagination is presupposed or transcendental and productive, intuiting images which it forms itself rather than relying on representations of perceptions derived from experience.[25]

---

23. See Jane Kneller, *Kant and the Power of the Imagination* (Cambridge, UK: Cambridge University Press, 2007), 1.

24. For Kant, there are three active faculties of the intellect: imagination, understanding, and reason. "Understanding" is not synthetic and so cannot produce principles. "Principles" refer to *a priori* concepts, such as axioms in mathematics. Reason is the domain of principles, heuristic or regulative of particular conceptions, and so operates independently of experience. An "experience" for Kant must have quantity (extension in space and time), make a qualitative effect on our senses, stand in relation to other things, and must be manifest as possible, necessary, or actual. Sense experience is a receptive or passive faculty compared with the imagination, reason, and understanding; the information ("phenomena" or the "manifold") received in our senses is processed by understanding and imagination. Reason, however, cannot explain objects grasped through the senses.

25. See Richard Kearney, *Poetics of Imagining, Modern to Post-modern* (New York: Fordham University Press, 1998), 47.

What is the role of the imagination for Kant? Imagination, as argued in the *Critique of Pure Reason,* is active, like reason, not passive, like sensation. The imagination first apprehends a sense impression of something, then makes an image of the object, and finally recognizes it in a concept; but because the imagination is not itself ordered by rules or concepts, it can form images without the experience or presence of an object. Because it introduces the possibility of reflexivity to the understanding, the imagination is then the *a priori* condition of experience, and so is transcendental, as the active connector, organizer, and unifier of the interdependent categories of understanding and the "sensible manifold": the imagination is an active faculty for the synthesis of the manifold of intuition. "For the imagination is to bring the manifold of intuition to an *image,* it must beforehand have taken the impressions up into its activity, that is, apprehend them."[26] In short, the imagination is the faculty of representing an object in intuition even without the object's presence, or indeed without the aid of sense experience, such as our intuition of time.[27] This was especially exciting for Heidegger; as transcendental, the imagination intuits time as the horizon of possibility.[28] We will get to the "impossibility" in a minute.

According to Mark Johnson, Kant describes the imagination as providing an objective structure to our consciousness, or a transcendental unity of consciousness not derived from empirical experience.[29] Hence, the transcendental imagination, the *a priori* schemata of our understanding, is for Kant "a hidden art in the depths of the human

26. Kant, *Critique of Pure Reason,* A 121, p. 168.

27. Ibid., B 151, p. 191.

28. Kearney, *The Poetics of Imagining,* 47. Kearney notes that Kant's identification of the transcendental imagination was credited by Heidegger as the first modern attempt to interpret being in terms of time; Heidegger saw that Kant's outline led to the imagination as that which forms images of the present, recalls images of the past, and anticipates images of the future. Furthermore, Kant discloses "the ontological character of human being as that which temporalizes itself out of the future" when he gives the anticipatory ability of the imagination priority. See Kearney, *The Poetics of Imagining,* 50.

29. See Mark Johnson, *The Body in the Mind: The Bodily Basis of Meaning* (Chicago: The University of Chicago Press, 1987), 151.

soul, whose true stratagems we shall hardly ever divine from nature."[30] This points to what Kearney explains is Kant's hunch that the transcendental imagination is an *original* power of *production* that underlies both sensation and understanding, a power "so primordial that it operates behind our backs, as it were, unconsciously."[31] The transcendental imagination provides the synthetic unity of intuition and understanding in apperception—the ability to self-reflect—which maintains Kant's desire for autonomy in the human subject; if the intellect cannot be self-reflective, the human being can neither be rational nor moral and furthermore cannot communicate these ideas. This is why Kant had wanted the third *Critique* to connect the first with the second, the *Critique of Practical Reason*, otherwise he has set up a dichotomy in the intellect: the apparently unbridgeable gap between the human being as a casually determined member of the sensible world (of which reason is the benevolent overlord) and the human being as a free member of an intelligible world who can act morally.[32]

It would seem that Kant wanted this gap to be bridged by the transcendental imagination. Johnson observes that Kant's hunch about the transcendental imagination means that

> there can be no meaningful experience without imagination, either in its productive or reproductive functions. As productive, imagination gives us the very structure of objectivity. As reproductive, it supplies all of the connections by means of which we achieve coherent, unified, and meaningful experience and understanding.[33]

The reproductive imagination gives order to the world; but the productive imagination opens the Pandora's Box of freedom and limitless creativity. The reproductive imagination follows Hume's trajectory in the way it connects our various past sense impressions with our current ones. But these connections made by the reproductive dimension of the imagination are subordinate to the synthetic endeavor of the productive dimension of the imagination. Hence,

---

30. Kant, *Critique of Pure Reason*, B 181, p. 214.
31. Kearney, *The Wake of the Imagination*, 191.
32. See Kneller, *Kant and the Power of the Imagination*, 45.
33. Johnson, *The Body in the Mind*, 151.

the productive power of the imagination to relate to the whole of understanding: "the principle of the necessary unity of pure (productive) synthesis of imagination, prior to apperception, *the basis for the possibility of all cognition,* especially of experience."[34] The productive imagination is the "common root" of both sense experience and understanding, and not merely their mediator, as Enlightenment philosophy had previously assumed. Furthermore, Kant was able to show that perceptions necessary to human autonomy, derived from the intelligibility of both consciousness and self-consciousness, are subsumed here under the transcendental imagination. The productive synthesis of my perceptions must be joined to my consciousness of myself as the ultimate source of unity, Kearney observes, "[F]or it is only because I ascribe all perceptions to *one consciousness* (i.e., original apperception) that I can say of my perceptions that I am conscious of them."[35] Here we see what Kant saw: the potential of the productive imagination to surpass the limits to reason he has so carefully constructed. "Hidden art," indeed.

Alas, this was not to fully flower by the publication of the *Critique of Judgement*; the potential of the imagination to creatively form the self as well as all knowledge or cognition was curbed significantly and was made subordinate to the understanding. Some of this is already evident in the 1787 second edition of the *Critique of Pure Reason,* observes Jane Kneller.[36] Kneller points to the possibility that Kant was ultimately unable to develop a faculty that on the transcendental level was not governed by laws and on the empirical level could not be muddled by the body and its desires.[37] He was cautious about the excesses of enthusiasm: "passion as such deserves censure."[38] Kant's strict limitation of the creative role of the imagination and its poten-

---

34. Kant, *Critique of Pure Reason,* A 118, p. 166. Emphasis mine.

35. Kearney, *The Wake of the Imagination,* 170.

36. See Kneller's analysis of the B passages of Kant's *Critique of Pure Reason* in *Kant and the Power of the Imagination,* 99–103.

37. Ibid., 120.

38. Immanuel Kant, *The Conflict of the Faculties,* trans. Mary J. Gregor (Lincoln, NE: University of Nebraska Press, 1979), 155; see also Kneller, *Kant and the Power of the Imagination,* 120.

tial freedom in the *Critique of Judgement*, compared to what he describes as the fundamental role of the transcendental imagination in the first *Critique*, incited the ire of Nietzsche and Heidegger. Heidegger's frustration with Kant's failure to follow through with the implications of the transcendental imagination from the first *Critique* in the *Critique of Judgement* is palpable. Heidegger concluded that Kant "saw the unknown; he had to draw back."[39]

Like Heidegger, Richard Kearney faults Kant for dissociating reason from imagination but allows Kant's description of the sublime as something of a compensation. It seems that in the third *Critique*, Kant can't resist a peek into the Pandora's Box he set up in the first place. What is the difference between beauty and the sublime? How might the sublime refer to the impossible, to the pure creativity that has no referent? While both are "pleasing," "beauty" is more limited and limiting an experience, concerned with form and referring to the *understanding*, while the sublime for Kant provokes "limitlessness," referring more to the universal aspects of human *reason*, as he writes in the third *Critique*: "[T]he sublime is to be found in an object even devoid of form, so far as it immediately involves, or else by its presence provokes a representation of limitlessness (*Unbegrenztheit*), yet with a super-added thought of its totality."[40] Mark C. Taylor argues that the beautiful and sublime are codependent for Kant: what beauty grasps by the form or figure of a thing, the sublime dis-figures and un-forms, subverting the boundaries set by attempts at articulation: "What cannot be articulated cannot be represented; it can, however, reveal itself by hiding itself in and through the process of disfiguring seemingly stable figures. Disfiguring presents the unpresentable without which representation is impossible."[41]

The "sublime" is a "serious matter in the exercise of the imagination" (rather than "play"); it is a "negative pleasure" (where beauty

---

39. Martin Heidegger, *Kant and the Problem of Metaphysics*, trans. James S. Churchill (Bloomington, IN: University of Indiana Press, 1962), 166; see also Kearney, *The Wake of the Imagination*, 195.

40. Kant, *Critique of Judgement*, pt. 1, bk. 2, p. 75.

41. Mark C. Taylor, *After God* (Chicago: The University of Chicago Press, 2007), 123–24.

refers to a "positive pleasure"), "a momentary check to the vital forces followed at once by a discharge all the more powerful . . . not simply attracted by the object, but is also alternatively repelled";[42] the sublime subverts the harmony that beauty elicits. The sublime is the unimaginable; "it is productive of itself even unto its failure, productive of its limit and of the surpassing of its limit,"[43] Jean-Luc Nancy writes. Simply in our apprehension of something that "excites the feeling of the sublime," it may appear that this excitement contravenes "the ends of our power of judgement, to be ill-adapted to our faculty of presentation, and to do violence, as it were, to the imagination, and yet it is judged *all the more sublime* on that account."[44]

Perhaps the sublime's ability to simultaneously elevate and negate the imagination is related to its "horror" from Kant's *Observations*, from 1764:

> The sight of a mountain whose snow-covered peak rises above the clouds, the description of a raging storm, or Milton's portrayal of the infernal kingdom, arouse enjoyment but with horror. . . . Night is sublime, day is beautiful . . . the sublime moves, the beautiful charms. The mien of a man who is undergoing the full feeling of the sublime is earnest, sometimes rigid and astonished. . . . [I]ts feeling is sometimes accompanied with a certain dread, or melancholy; in some cases merely with quiet wonder. . . . [T]he first I shall call the terrifying sublime, the second the noble, and the third the splendid.[45]

What is this quality that it is more pronounced when it negatively impacts the imagination, when it unsettles all the carefully constructed scaffold of the way we know, the way we think, the way we act, setting up the possibility of impossibility? Could this be from the same man who was so regular in his daily walks that the people of Königsberg would set their watches by him? The ideas excited by the sublime are those of which the imagination *cannot* form images,

42. Kant, *Critique of Judgement*, pt. 1, bk. 2, p. 76.
43. Nancy, *The Ground of the Image*, 81.
44. Kant, *The Critique of Judgement*, pt. 1, bk. 2, p. 76, emphasis mine.
45. Immanuel Kant, *Observations on the Beautiful and Sublime*, trans. John T. Goldthwait (Berkeley, CA: University of California Press, 2003), 47–48.

cannot be represented in visible or even sensible forms.[46] The sublime refers to what is *beyond* sense experience. The abyss is again open for business.

Kearney notes that in Kant's account of the sublime, the "imagination displays its power by betraying its own powerlessness; it surpasses the self-sufficient limits of beauty and points to a vastness which it is unable to embody."[47] Thus the vulnerability in the wake of the infinite, on the edge of the abyss: even Kant realized that the imagination is capable of indicating the pleroma, the field of the supersensible. Kearney is confident that the arts are capable of the expression of this for Kant: "Art becomes sublime to the extent that it produces 'symbols' (analogues to the ideas of reason) which signify something which our mind cannot actually grasp . . . but the precise identity of this mysterious greatness is left in suspension."[48] That Kant, for all his stuffed formality and painstaking efficiency—this was someone who developed a technique of breathing only through his nose to avoid catching a cough and never took a companion on his daily walks for fear that conversation would force him to breathe through his mouth in the open air[49]—could glimpse this vastness, this darkness, ungraspable and yet distinctively indicated, is a joyous occasion.

Kant gave us other ideas about beauty that still persist in aesthetics: his argument that beauty cannot be a property of a thing (as of course existence cannot be a property of God, which anticipates the demise of onto-theology). Beauty and the sublime pertain to our response to something, specifically a "disinterested interest," the experience of ecstasy, awe, before a work of art or even something in the natural world does not spring from an object's utility or because of personal self-interest. "Disinterest" for Kant pertains to a response that is not self-directed but is, rather, a way to be interested without self-satisfaction, even if the feeling aroused by the artwork or the forest is satisfying.

46. See Kearney, *The Wake of the Imagination*, 175.
47. Ibid., 176.
48. Ibid.
49. See Immanuel Kant, *The Conflict of the Faculties*, in *Religion and Rational Theology*, trans. Allen W. Wood and George Di Giovanni (Cambridge, UK: Cambridge University Press, 1996), 323–25.

Kant's recognition of the other-directedness of aesthetic judgments is important to his intentions to maintain a moral structure to the human person. He just didn't follow through on the implications set up by his epistemology. On one hand, as Kneller points out, Kant writes about an imagination powerful enough to envision new worlds; it would seem that the power of the imagination (especially as a schemata) could also connect the postulates of reason (God, freedom, immortality) to human beings in a contingent world, thereby producing the rational ground for our hope in the possibility of bringing about the highest good, of transforming nature.[50] She argues that for Kant, the existence of a moral world presupposes agency that can bring it about, and the command by reason to seek it presupposes that we can believe it possible to create by our own agency; representing such a world in the creativity of the imagination would show us the possibility of a moral world in this world and in ourselves as creators of that world.[51] Art, it would seem, would enable the creative expression of this vision, allowing for the communication necessary in the social dimension of morality; but Kant keeps the Pandora's Box closed this time. Interest in beautiful art, while it may cultivate civility, does not prove inclination to morality.[52]

Yet, in the same section of the third *Critique*, in which he disparages art because it may be deceptive, he argues that the *intellectual* experience of the beautiful in nature is more immediate, showing a trace or a hint that it contains an orderliness that may be conducive to the state of justice we morally desire.[53] When we follow through the interest which Kant sees as intrinsic to the experience of something beautiful, or sublime, when we allow it to influence our way

50. See Kneller, *Kant and the Power of the Imagination*, 51–52.

51. Ibid., 52.

52. See ibid., 55. Kant argues this in section 42 of the *Critique of Judgement*. Kneller ventures that Kant's reticence to let the imaginative freedom express itself in art toward cultivating morality may stem from his views on obedience to the authority of the state and what he perceived as legitimate social change: "Too much freedom can threaten the established order, and good Burger that he was, Kant could applaud Frederick the Great's imperative 'Think for yourself!' and yet comfortably follow up with 'But do as you are told.' " *Kant and the Power of the Imagination*, 57.

53. Kneller, *Kant and the Power of the Imagination*, 64.

of being in the world, such that we are changed by it, there are moral implications, "and this is all the more so if we may even call upon others to take a similar interest."[54] Like the universal implications in the "Categorical Imperative" of the second *Critique*, by which human reason exhorts us to act as though we would at the same time will the action to be a universal law, the concern to take a subjective experience through aesthetic reflection, and call on others to be similarly interested, may result in a moral responsibility to the world, even if Kant was ultimately unwilling to boldly venture into the field of the impossible for the sake of the Other.

Cultivating interest and attentiveness also engenders responsiveness, as long as the attention is toward the external—what is outside the self. Attentiveness to the radically new can be wearying, as Krutch acknowledges, and threatening, if we assume Kant drew back from the abyss in an effort to retain confidence in a lawful order. But that he could see the capabilities of the transcendental imagination and believed he had to close it off because of the unlimited lawlessness that could be unleashed, gives a glimpse that it is there. A prior and independent ground of the possibility of all knowledge, especially of all experience, which occurs in us "behind our backs," unconsciously, as it were, is the very space Kant discovers outside or beyond those conditions, a space in which the imaginative freedom can run and "play"; to envision—to *produce*—a better world. Theology especially must consider the potential of the freedom of the imagination to give ethical significance to what is seen, and furthermore, to gain ethical significance from the visual arts. As we will see, Levinas was conflicted on whether this is possible, although his work betrays a longing and a poetic sensibility, something that Derrida recognized was Levinas's practice of aesthetics.

Emmanuel Levinas and the Problem of Aesthetics

In one of his later essays, Levinas laments the boredom inherent in society, the failure of the imagination with regard to our interhuman relationships. Technology and consumer culture have unleashed

---

54. Kant, *Critique of Judgement*, sec. 42, p. 132.

a big-brother type of uniformity: everyone eats the same food, wears the same clothes, uses the same smartphone. The modern period's turn to science and technological advancements as the arbiter of meaning has led to a crisis of meaning. I say this, of course, from a personal computer while listening to Mozart on my iPad. I must continually strive to avoid the infiltration of e-mails and text messages to be able to get anything done. The World Wide Web has ensnared us all, petty flies that we are, and in many ways it has sucked the marrow from us. The ubiquitous presence of screens and devices means that we are inundated with images hourly, daily: of clichéd personality traits, overly sexualized human beings, kittens doing cute things, kids doing cute things, celebrities, products, entertainment, escapism. Jean Baudrillard argued that this bombardment leaves us with a sense that real things have been displaced by their representation in advertisements, television, movie images, and caricatures: the real has become the *simulacrum,* in which the appearance of reality becomes reality itself, or it is difficult to tell the difference. For Levinas, this is reflected in the banality of disenchantment, when the thirst for the new gives way to the familiarity of the Same:

> The unknown is immediately made familiar and the new customary. Nothing is new under the sun. The crisis inscribed in Ecclesiastes is not found in sin but in boredom. Everything is absorbed, sucked down and walled up in the Same. The enchantment of sites, hyperbole of metaphysical concepts, the artifice of art, exaltation of ceremonies, the magic of solemnities—everywhere is suspected and denounced a theatrical apparatus, a purely rhetorical transcendence, the game. Vanity of vanities: the echo of our own voices, taken for a response to the few prayers that still remain to us; everywhere we have fallen back upon our own feet, as after the ecstasies of a drug. Except for the other whom, in all this boredom, we cannot let go.[55]

55. Emmanuel Levinas, "Ideology and Idealism," in *Of God Who Comes to Mind*, trans. Bettina Bergo (Stanford, CA: Stanford University Press, 1988), 12; see also Richard Kearney, "The Crisis of the Image: Levinas' Ethical Response," in *The Ethics of Postmodernity: Current Trends in Continental Thought*, ed. Gary B. Madison and Marty Fairbairn (Evanston, IL: Northwestern University Press, 1999), 13.

Once again, for Levinas, alterity is the reflection of the transcendence which rescues us from the constant thrum of "our own voices"—the vanity of my own face, the "selfie" taken in front of the Duomo in Florence, or worse, in front of the tragic accident (common, all too common these days). But in what ways might the alterity of the Other and the summons to responsibility be communicated, so that the smooth, shiny surface of the Same may be broken?

As we have seen, Levinas locates this summons in the face of the Other, especially the hungry, the sick, the imprisoned; the summons is not a linguistic call, a literal voice, but is rather an *optics*, a seeing, through which the disturbance of banal complacency takes place. If "seeing" is so important to his ethical project, why is there no corresponding aesthetics? While it would seem that Levinas would credit the arts with the task of aiding this encounter, or this disturbance, or at least with preparing us to recognize the significance of the Other when alterity presents itself, Levinas is conflicted in much of his corpus about the place of the arts in his ethical teaching. There are a few reasons for this, but we shall see that his admiration for the inherently aesthetic ways in which one of his closest friends, Maurice Blanchot, views the shape of human existence as a response to the space of art provides Levinas with a way to view art's redemption. This is simply to say that Levinas's concerns with art and visual imagery are valid (if hyperbolic) and should always be understood against his singular emphasis, on the Other who cries out in misery, toward whom and of whom I am hostage.

Perhaps the most obvious reason for Levinas's suspicion of images is the problem of idolatry. As a devout Jew, Levinas regards the Second Commandment with gravity: "You shall not make for yourself an idol, whether in the form of anything that is in heaven above, or that is on the earth beneath, or that is in the water under the earth" (Exod 20:4). Images of the divine are certainly forbidden here, but so too is any positive statement about the God who will always remain just beyond our grasp. Within this "just-beyondness" is the longing, the desire for God in which Levinas locates the this-world, right now, messianic task of attention to the Other. Kant was also concerned to uphold the integrity of the Second Commandment: in the third *Critique*, he writes,

A religion is never free from the imputation of idolatry, in a practical sense, so long as the attributes with which it endows the supreme being are such that anything that man may do can be taken as in accordance with God's will on any other all-sufficing condition than that of morality. For however pure and free from sensuous images the form of that concept may be from a theoretical point of view, yet, with such attributes, it is from a practical point of view depicted as an idol—the character of God's will, that is to say, is represented anthropomorphically.[56]

Hence, Kant's premise is that the only legitimate discourse of God is moral discourse. No image, and certainly no theoretical attribute, may be admitted of the supersensible: "morality must then conform to theology."[57]

Contemporary Jewish thought on aesthetics still prioritizes the Second Commandment, recognizing, as Melissa Raphael observes, that "images transmute life in time into the silence of an object caught in the faux eternity of a still, two-dimensional plane. But what is interesting is that Jewish art—like any good art—is actually very adept at refusing to donate the life of an image's object to art."[58] The Second Commandment as thought to be interpreted by Moses is a warning to

take care and watch yourselves closely so that you do not act corruptly by making an idol for yourselves in the form of any figure, the likeness of male or female, the likeness of any animal on earth, the likeness of any winged bird that flies in the air, the likeness of anything that creeps on the ground, the likeness of any fish that is in the water under the earth. And when you look up to the heavens and see the sun, the moon, and the stars, all the host of heaven, do not be led astray and bow down to them and serve them, things that the Lord your God has allotted to all the peoples everywhere under the heaven. (Deut 4:15-19)

56. Kant, *Critique of Judgement*, 288n7.
57. Ibid., 289.
58. Melissa Raphael, *Judaism and the Visual Image* (London: Continuum International, 2009), 20.

The commandments are delivered not as a list of rules but rather in the context of a covenantal relationship, in which God establishes a just society, one that values life, respect, and care. The Second Commandment here may be interpreted as an exhortation to never substitute the sign for the signified, since such leads to idolatry; but even more important, the Second Commandment "disallows any positive knowledge of God and awakens the longing for a God who is always beyond the limits of thought. Longing for God, truthful religion, in turn drives the task of redeeming the world, even when its messianic ideal might never be attained."[59]

Underlying this is Levinas's anxiety that human beings may be enchanted by an impersonal aesthetic or technological object and not drawn toward the face of the Other, that which opens toward the infinite. Paul Ricoeur reminds us that Edmund Husserl's notion of intentionality in Phenomenology is ontologically neutral: the "other" toward which consciousness intends can be anything capable of being represented. For Levinas, however, the order of the revealed world cannot bypass the Other in favor of an object.[60] If we become so enamored of the way being appears through an object and not in the suffering reality of human beings in need, we may neglect the primacy of care for the Other: "The mystery of things is the source of all cruelty towards men," he writes, and Judaism in its denunciation of the "infantilism of idolatry," which refuses to be subservient to the object or thing in the way that Christianity is, in its integration of "the small and touching household gods into the worship of saints and local cults."[61] "Judaism has not sublimated idols—on the contrary, it has demanded that they be destroyed."[62] The arts, perhaps especially visual art, may be self-referential rather than other-directed, substituting image for the transcendent.

---

59. Ibid., 30.

60. Paul Ricoeur, *Figuring the Sacred: Religion, Narrative and Imagination*, trans. David Pellauer, ed. Mark I. Wallace (Minneapolis, MN: Fortress Press, 1995), 120.

61. Emmanuel Levinas, "Heidegger, Gagarin and Us," in *Difficult Freedom*, trans. Sean Hand (Baltimore: Johns Hopkins University Press, 1990), 232–33.

62. Ibid., 234.

In this sense, Levinas's concern may be in the way visual art defuses the reality of the object and inverts the directionality of consciousness. He considers this explicitly in an early essay, "Reality and its Shadow." Written shortly after the war ended, in 1948, when the scale and extent of the crimes of the Nazi era were becoming apparent, this essay contains some of his most passionate arguments against art, particularly visual art. In fact, the editors of *Les Temps Moderne*, the magazine in which the essay first appeared, included a strongly worded preface in order to temper the possibility of negative reaction.[63] Levinas's passion here, however, reads more like a lament than a conclusion; seen through the eyes of his wartime experience, the high culture of European societies did nothing to prevent the suffering. Considered against the backdrop of emaciated bodies thrown into mass graves at Bergen-Belsen, the cultured class in Europe were no more attuned to their responsibilities by their aesthetic sensibilities, patronage of museums, and collections of art.

Art "is the very event of obscuring," Levinas writes, belonging neither to the order of revelation nor to the order of creation.[64] Here, he may be following Plato's famous wariness of images, by which the artist is merely an imitator of the "truth" and borrows the term "shadow," perhaps as a reference to the shadows on Plato's cave walls, the shadows that not only distort the real but also "charm" us into accepting their representations over what is for Plato real, true, or good. We are seduced by the consolation images offer, the image's "hold" over us, rendering us "in art, essentially disengaged, constitutes in a world of initiative and responsibility, a dimension of evasion. Here we rejoin the most common and ordinary experience of aesthetic enjoyment. . . . [I]t especially brings the irresponsibility that charms as a lightness and grace."[65] The "charm" leaves us

---

63. *Les Temps Moderne* 38 (1948): 769–70, cited in Aaron Rosen, "Emmanuel Levinas and the Hospitality of Images," *Literature & Theology* 25, no. 4 (December 2011): 376.

64. Emmanuel Levinas, "Reality and Its Shadow," in *Collected Philosophical Papers*, trans. Alphonso Lingis (Dordrecht, The Netherlands: Martinus Nijhoff, 1987), 3.

65. Ibid., 11.

disengaged, as the representations of objects in visual art are shadows disengaged from reality, a "doubling" of objects that leaves both the representation in the artwork and the reality of the object itself "ambiguous."

Richard Kearney argues that Levinas's concerns are "not directed against the poetic power of the imagination *per se* but against the use or abuse of such power to incarcerate the self in a blind alley of self-reflecting mirrors."[66] In chapter 3, we considered the problem of the seduction of the imagination from the standpoint of how commodification and consumer culture affect both the power of the work of art to challenge and surprise perception, as well as the content of the image to acquiesce to the "Same." Levinas wants to make it clear that alterity—the distancing of truth just a little farther down the road—is crucial to the ethical content of any concept, and so of any image or work of art, protecting the vulnerability of the Other from the violence of the Same.

Perhaps his warning should be read as another bulwark against Heidegger's optimism regarding art, especially as Heidegger associated "art" with "truth": "the actual reality of the work has been defined by that which is at work in the work, by the happening of truth."[67] In "The Origin of the Work of Art," Heidegger declares

---

66. Kearney, "The Crisis of the Image," 15.

67. See Hubert L. Dreyfus, "Heidegger on the Connection Between Nihilism, Art, Technology and Politics," in *The Cambridge Companion to Martin Heidegger*, ed. Charles Guignon (Cambridge, UK: Cambridge University Press, 1993), 298–99: "[G]eneralizing the idea of a work of art, Heidegger holds that 'there must always be some being in the open [the clearing] something that is, in which openness takes its stand and attains its constancy.'" Here Dreyfus cites Heidegger, "On the Origin of the Work of Art," in *Basic Writings*, ed. David Farrell Krell (New York: Harper and Row, 1977), 59. Dreyfus calls this constancy of openness in the clearing a "cultural paradigm" (à la Thomas Kuhn): "[A] cultural paradigm collects the scattered practices of a group, unifies them into coherent possibilities for action, and holds them up to the people who can then act and relate to each other in terms of that exemplar. Works of art, when performing this function, are not merely representations or symbols, but actually produce a shared understanding," 298. This is akin to the way Tillich understood the shifts in art in terms of its cultural reception, which is why he had such trouble with medieval and Renaissance art as relevant to a contemporary

that "[t]he art work opens up in its own way the Being of beings."[68] Without mentioning this essay by name, Levinas in his essay "Heidegger, Gagarin and Us" addresses so many points made by Heidegger that it seems unlikely that Levinas was not thinking of "Origin of the Work of Art" when he wrote it.

We noted earlier that a dimension of Levinas's invective against Heidegger pertains to Heidegger's anti-Semitism. It is difficult to remain neutral about one's philosophy, even with one as "great" as Heidegger, after physically witnessing the degradation and murder of his people and the loss of his own family to a government and ideology Heidegger seems to have appreciatively supported. Levinas's admiration for Heidegger's genius was strongly tempered by his mistrust of a philosophy that not only ignored ethics, for the most part, but also reinforced, in Levinas's mind, the very narcissistic totality that Levinas believed was behind Heidegger's racism. Paul Ricoeur notes this as well; while Heidegger took the gospels and Christian theology as points of departure for his thought, he completely avoids the Hebraic corpus, "which is the absolute stranger in relation to Greek discourse, he avoids ethical thinking with its dimensions of the relationship to the other and of justice."[69] Levinas did not write an autobiography, but in a short description of his life, in which he lists the places he lived, the Dreyfus Affair that shaped the questions of his youth, the friends who influenced him, and the positions he held, he notes as a last point: "This disparate inventory is a biography. It is dominated by the presentiment and the memory of the Nazi horror."[70] A soldier for his adopted France, Levinas was held prisoner

---

receptivity of the ultimate concern. Whether Heidegger thought of this more social and communal way of thinking about art is difficult to say, unless what Heidegger means by the truth of art as "the act which founds a political state" ("Origin of the Work of Art," 60) is really just a "cultural paradigm."

68. Heidegger, "The Origin of the Work of Art," 166. Originally published in 1950, it was published again in 1960, one year before Levinas wrote "Heidegger, Gagarin and Us."

69. Paul Ricoeur, cited in Salomon Malka, *Emmanuel Levinas: His Life and Legacy* (Pittsburgh, PA: Duquesne University Press, 2006), 170.

70. Emmanuel Levinas, cited by Michael Kigel in his translator's notes to Malka, *Emmanuel Levinas: His Life and Legacy*, xiv.

in a German POW camp fifty kilometers from Bergen-Belsen for five years, working as a woodcutter with the other Jewish inmates; he rarely spoke of those years, but that his work is so singularly focused on the priority of the ethical relation before subjectivity cannot but be deeply influenced by the loss of his and his wife's entire extended family and the guilt he always carried with him for surviving.

Levinas was born in Kovno, Lithuania, a city with a long history of Jewish presence, "one of the parts of Eastern Europe in which Judaism knew its highest spiritual development; the level of Talmudic study was very high, and there was a whole life based on this study and experienced as study."[71] His father operated a bookstore and encouraged the importance of Russian culture to his children and in his business. Levinas admits a profound debt to Russian literature, especially Tolstoy (he remembers hearing of his death as a boy), Gogol, Pushkin, and of course Dostoyevsky, whose work inspired him to pursue philosophy. The First World War made his family refugees when the Germans occupied Kovno; the family moved to Kharkov in the Ukraine and back to Kovno until Levinas left for the University of Strasbourg in France. There he met Maurice Blanchot, who was to become a dear and lifelong friend. Describing his influence, Levinas stated: "With him, very abstract notions opened up unexpected vistas, and things took on new life."[72]

Blanchot is known for his complex novels (*Aminadab* was named after one of Levinas's brothers who perished in the Shoah) as well as a philosophy devoted to the place of paradox and abstraction, using language to shatter language of its finality and order, pointing toward "the silence which is proper to it." William Franke observes, "Blanchot thinks in and around the paradoxical il-logic of what cannot be said, for it is nevertheless 'what must be said,' which he follows unflinchingly to some of its most excruciatingly difficult, indigestible implications. All the ways of unsaying are never nearly

71. Emmanuel Levinas, interview with François Poirié, trans. Jill Robbins and Marcus Coelen, with Thomas Loebel, in *Is It Righteous to Be? Interviews with Emmanuel Levinas*, ed. Jill Robbins (Stanford, CA: Stanford University Press, 2001), 24.

72. Ibid., 30.

enough to unsay our language sufficiently so as to liberate what it oppresses."[73] Language is never strictly referential and art is never strictly representational. The Other is unsayable for Levinas, because alterity is the past-all-graspness of the Other; art and language for Blanchot "are realized only as the approach of the unreachable."[74] The tendency toward the unsayable is palpable in these thinkers, in the attempt to express an insane time, when violence and apathy regularly eclipse peace and care. Leslie Hill acknowledges the appreciation both Blanchot and Levinas convey of the poet Paul Celan as one whose work transcends "the bipolar solidarity of immanence and transcendence, as an inscribing within the poem's separation from itself, thereby giving rise to the possibility of an encounter with the outside."[75]

Levinas gives a sense that art participates in the unsayable—"being present without being given"—in a particularly poetic essay on Blanchot, "The Poet's Vision."[76] Poetic language preserves alterity: it is "[t]he mode of revelation of what remains other, despite its revelation,"[77] providing presence and absence at the same time. Art "accedes to a different space: Night"[78] rather than the space of "Day," where we do our busy work and perform our political ambitions and think we are in control; art uncovers "in an uncovering that is not truth, a darkness . . . on which no hold is possible,"[79] "like a night manifesting itself in the night."[80] No longer interior, the space of art refers to the "exteriority of absolute exile." Given that Levinas has

---

73. William Franke, *On What Cannot Be Said: Apophatic Discourses in Philosophy, Religion, Literature and the Arts*, vol. 2 (Notre Dame, IN: University of Notre Dame Press, 2007), 428.

74. Maurice Blanchot, *The Space of Literature*, trans. Ann Smock (Lincoln, NE: University of Nebraska Press, 1989), 310.

75. Leslie Hill, " 'Distrust of Poetry': Levinas, Blanchot, Celan," *MLN* 120, no. 5 (December 2005): 992.

76. Emmanuel Levinas, "The Poet's Vision," in *Proper Names*, trans. Michael B. Smith (Stanford, CA: Stanford University Press, 1996), 131.

77. Ibid., 130.

78. Ibid., 129.

79. Ibid., 136.

80. Ibid., 132.

evolved his position on the arts in later years, we might wonder whether his earlier statement in his essay "Reality and Its Shadow," that art "is the very event of obscuring," may be read more optimistically. Levinas is appreciative of Blanchot's "new way of knowing" that leads him to realize "The essence of art from this perspective is the passage from language to the ineffable that says itself, the making visible of the obscurity of the elemental through the work."[81] While Levinas is initially concerned about Blanchot's indebtedness to Heidegger, he praises Blanchot for his "nomadism"—his "irreducible relation to the earth: a sojourn devoid of place . . . the I of the Eternal Wanderer, identified by gait rather than location, along the border of non-truth, a realm extending farther than the true."[82] Levinas juxtaposes Heidegger's confidence in the world art renders inhabitable (or endurable, as we saw with Nietzsche), the light "from on high" that makes this world, with Blanchot's "black light . . . a light that undoes the world, leading it back to its origin, to the over and over again, the murmur, the ceaseless lapping of waves, a 'deep past, never long enough ago.' The poetic quest for the unreal is the quest for the deepest recesses of that real."[83] Art *does* obscure, because it must thwart the logocentrism that has so captured the West.

Although Levinas, perhaps due to his painful past, was unable or unwilling to give the arts a pride of place, he writes an essay on the Jewish poet Paul Celan (1920–1970), considered the most important German-language poet after Rilke. Celan's work provides a searing witness to the atrocities suffered under the Third Reich. He was cruelly separated from his parents when they refused to leave their house and were deported, then later murdered, by the SS; Paul and a friend had been in a hideout against his parents' wishes. Celan survived the war, married, and was successful as a translator, poet, and essayist, living in Paris the rest of his life. He and his wife Gisèle lost a son soon after birth; another son was born, but not even the close bond that developed between he and Eric could mitigate the

81. Ibid.
82. Ibid., 136.
83. Ibid., 137, citing Paul Valéry's poem "Cantique des Colonnes," in Paul Valéry, *Oeuvres*, vol. 1 (Paris: Gallimard, 1957), 118.

demons that haunted him, exacerbated by little François's death. Celan suffered vicious episodes of depression and nervous exhaustion; from the mid-to-late 1960s, he was hospitalized several times and finally took his own life in the Seine. Such mental anguish also claimed the life of Primo Levi, another artist tortured by his survival of the camps. Levinas's experience intersects with Celan's; the loss of family and home, the forced labor camps, the refuge in France. It is possible that Levinas could appreciate Celan's artistic witness to catastrophe because he knew that this was from authentic experience. Levinas writes that Celan's poetry originates at the "pre-syntactic," "pre-disclosing," "pre-logical level,"

> the moment of pure touching, pure contact, grasping, squeezing —which is, perhaps, a way of giving, right up to and including the hand that gives. A language of proximity for proximity's sake, older than that of "the truth of being," [this seems to be a dig at Heidegger, whom Celan knew]—which it probably carries and sustains—the first of the languages, response preceding the question, responsibility for the neighbor, by its *for the other*, the whole marvel of giving.[84]

This is, Levinas notes, an opportunity for both "extreme receptivity" and "extreme donation," the giving of attention, the making of oneself into a sign, a gesture of recognition, all "in the movement that carries them toward the other."[85] If art can do this, perhaps art can contribute to the encounter with the stranger, the neighbor, fostering the habitus of witness, toward action borne by the recognition of infinite responsibility.

Celan for Levinas provides "Insomnia in the bed of being, the impossibility of curling up and forgetting oneself. Expulsion out of the worldliness of the world, nakedness of him who borrows all he owns"—the "spiritual act par excellence."[86] Here is artistic language, poetry as a "modality of the otherwise than being," the "ineluctable:

---

84. Emmanuel Levinas, "Paul Celan: From Being to Other," in *Proper Names*, 41. Emphasis his.

85. Ibid., 43.

86. Ibid., 45–46.

where the divine presence can be encountered. Hence, for Rahner, theology's dependence on conscious self-expression in reference to God might indicate that

> the most perfect kind of theology would be the one that appropriates the arts as an integral part of itself. We might then argue that the self-expression contained in a Rembrandt painting or in a Bruckner symphony is so strongly inspired and borne by divine revelation, by grace, and by the self-communication of God that it tells us, in a way that cannot be translated adequately in a verbal theology, what persons really are in the sight of God.[93]

Because of its transcendent subject matter, theology must not confine itself merely to texts. Human persons communicate in ways beyond the verbal; indeed, even speaking a language is a more expressive and multidimensional way of communicating than merely reading a language. Engaging images, sound, movement, and the broken discourse of poetry are the sort of habitus that calls on the emotions, reactions, memories, and dreams that are human experience beyond the merely rational. Theology cannot satisfy the rational impulse for measurement, observation, and certainty (all of which are even inadequate in the natural and physical sciences), so it must consider other arenas of human experience if, indeed, as Rahner asserts again and again, human experience is where God is found.

Rahner's thought, however, has been seldom examined for its aesthetic qualities, much less for its place in a theological aesthetics.[94] Toward the end of his life, Rahner investigated the relationship

---

93. Karl Rahner, "Art against the Horizon of Theology and Piety," trans. Joseph Donceel, in *Theological Investigations* 23 (New York: Crossroad, 1992), 163.

94. For work in this area, see Peter Joseph Fritz, *Karl Rahner's Theological Aesthetics* (Washington, DC: The Catholic University Press of America, 2014), in which "aesthetics" refers to "an account of the manifestation of being. . . . [I]f ontology asks what being is, aesthetics asks how being manifests itself," 11; in this sense, Fritz compares Rahner's theological project to that of Hans Urs von Balthasar. In short, Fritz's is not an examination of Rahner's use of aesthetics and art as a *resource* for theology. See also Richard Viladesau, *Theological Aesthetics: God in Imagination, Beauty and Art* (New York: Oxford University Press, 1999),

between theology and the arts. While Rahner did not search aesthetics for its import in theology to the extent of Paul Tillich, Rahner indicated that there is a future for doing theology from an aesthetic perspective or in using the arts to witness the Holy Mystery that is God. There is a profuse beauty in his worldview, in which God to be God is committed to a permeation of the created world, as both its "ground" and its "horizon." There is some of Heidegger's influence here, Rahner acknowledges: "Heidegger . . . surely he has taught us *one thing*: that everywhere and in everything we can and must seek out that *unutterable mystery* which *disposes* over us, even though we can hardly name it with words."[95] *Dasein* is constituted through both being-in-the-world and the fundamental mystery of existence, Being; Heidegger builds on and corrects Kant by asserting that the existence of unlimited Being is an *a priori* condition of possibility for every object and every consideration of speculative reason. *Dasein's* activity of existing finds no distance between the self and the world. For Rahner, God's self-communication can only be found through the world, and in our sensual knowledge, we have immediate access to God, because God is Godself the fulfillment of human beings: "All communication in the created order, in so far as this can be conceived or is to be found in traditional theology (*lumen gloriae*), must be understood in relation to the direct access to God as communication with his immediate presence."[96] This is because God is the tacit ground of the ecstatic movement of human knowledge and therefore, for Rahner, known unthematically in every sensible pursuit, in every

---

which incorporates Rahner's thought but is not a Rahnerian aesthetics per se; Thiessen, "Karl Rahner: Toward a Theological Aesthetics"; James Voiss, "Rahner, Von Balthasar, and the Question of Theological Aesthetics: Preliminary Considerations," in *Finding God in All Things: Celebrating Bernard Lonergan, John Courtney Murray, and Karl Rahner* (New York: Fordham University Press, 2007).

95. Karl Rahner, *Martin Heidegger im Gesprach*, ed. Richard Wisser (Freiburg and Munich: Alber, 1970), 48–49, translated by Thomas Sheehan in *Karl Rahner: The Philosophical Foundations* (Athens, OH: Ohio University Press, 1987), xi.

96. Karl Rahner, "The Hiddenness of God," in *Theological Investigations* 26, trans. David Morland (New York: Seabury Press, 1979), 235.

activity of knowing.[97] This relies on Thomas's "conversion to the phantasm"—*conversio ad phantasmata*—we can only arrive at the divine in our encounter with and in the sensible world, our relationships, our language, our history, and the actuality of our freedom.

Hence, the permeation of divine being in and through the sensible world is the condition for how we know anything about God; the activity on both "sides" is kenotic, each reflecting the other. Incarnation is a way to name the active involvement of God in the world. Here, for Rahner, the case may be made that art and the aesthetic as a mode of knowing are valuable theological resources. The act of seeing is "a kind of sensory experience of transcendence that serves as foundation and mediation in referring the sense-endowed spiritual subject to God."[98] In this sense, it follows "that even an image that does not have a specifically religious theme can be a religious image, when viewing it helps to bring about, through a sensory experience of transcendence, that properly religious experience of transcendence."[99] Rahner asserts that it is a "naïve theology" which assumes that transcendent experience is not possible unless the image is explicitly religious. He even denounces religious "kitsch" that is "unable to evoke in those who see it a genuine and deep religious reaction."[100] Furthermore, "the most perfect kind of theology," a theology that is "the total human self-expression," would be one that appropriates "sculpture, painting and music" as "an integral

---

97. Rahner relies on Thomas Aquinas's epistemology for this. Thomas, following Aristotle, had maintained that the entire objective content of human intellectual knowledge was derived from sense experience; the fundamental ideas on which the first principles of metaphysics rested must be derived from the mind's intuitive grasp of God, without which any intellectual activity would be impossible. See Gerald A. McCool, "Karl Rahner and the Christian Philosophy of St. Thomas Aquinas," in *Theology and Discovery: Essays in Honor of Karl Rahner*, ed. William Kelly (Milwaukee, WI: Marquette University Press, 1980), 65.

98. Karl Rahner, "The Religious Meaning of Images," trans. Joseph Donceel, in *Theological Investigations* 23 (New York: Crossroad, 1992), 158.

99. Ibid., 159.

100. Karl Rahner, "Art against the Horizon of Theology and Piety," trans. Joseph Donceel, in *Theological Investigations* 23, 167.

part of itself."[101] Rahner realized that much work needed to be done in order to relate art that is not explicitly religious to theology but seems confident that "Genuine art is the result of a well determined historical event of human transcendentality. . . . [Real artists] announce what is eternal in a unique manner in which their historical particularity and their longing for eternity are combined in a unity that constitutes the essence of the work of art."[102] Revealing a sensitivity to the originality of the artistic vision, he comments on Albrecht Dürer's famous *Feldhase* (*Field Hare*), a watercolor from 1502 (at the Albertina in Vienna) which features an unusually realistic rendering, down to the hairs of the rabbit's fur and the light reflected from Dürer's workshop in the rabbit's eye. While it may seem "a well-determined insignificant human experience," once one sees it "with the eyes of an artist, I am beholding . . . the infinity and incomprehensibility of God."[103]

101. Ibid., 163.
102. Ibid., 166.
103. Ibid.

CHAPTER FIVE

Beyond Language, Beyond Reason

Vulnerability, Art, and the Problem of Catastrophic Suffering

from **Descent from the Cross**

Moldy sack of flour, white
wineskin, swollen, the Savior
is removed from the stained wood, his head-
not-head fallen, drooping like
a small hot-air balloon
airless. One man clutches his arm
this ugly rag-doll,
staring at it in wonder,
in pity and fear. Others hold him
passing him one to the next their gazes
straying up and down.
A fat man adorned in a turban
stands to the side and observes,
satisfied with his own living belly.
Against the backdrop of the gloomy skies
another stoops over, letting
the sheet slowly drop.
Everything around is dark. The trees too.
Only the body shines.

No, not exactly. Try again. From the beginning.
Soft white flesh. As though
living, breathing, moving its arms,
even loving. Outside the frame,
one guesses they'll put him to rest in the ground.
Put him to rest? Will he rest? Eternal rest.
No. Not exactly.

—Tuvia Ruebner[1]

In summer 2014, West Africa experienced an escalation of an Ebola virus outbreak that primarily affected the nations of Sierra Leone, Guinea, Liberia, and Nigeria. A one-year-old boy named Emile Oumouno, who died in the village of Meliandou in Guinea in December 2013, was originally considered the first victim, but researchers continue to investigate other possible originating cases. As of March 27, 2016, the total number of deaths due to the Ebola virus in West Africa is 11,308, which may be a conservative estimate, since many cases in remote villages may not have been recorded.[2]

The outbreak in Liberia was declared "over" by the World Health Organization (WHO) on May 9, 2015, when forty-two days—the longest-known incubation period—passed without a confirmed case since the last was buried on March 28, but cases have continued to be reported as late as spring 2016. Resources in healthcare, media, and communication were inadequate to the task of containing a highly communicable health crisis after a long and costly civil war in Liberia. Healthcare workers often left their jobs in fear of acquiring the virus due to a shortage of protective gear; medical clinics were overwhelmed as there were simply not enough hospital beds, or even floor space, to treat the sick; those in need of medical care—especially prenatal—

---

1. Tuvia Ruebner, "Descent from the Cross," in *In the Illuminated Dark: Selected Poems of Tuvia Ruebner*, trans. Rachel Tzvia Beck (New York: Hebrew Union College Press, 2014), 139, excerpt.

2. The WHO discovered scores of bodies in a remote diamond-mining area of Sierra Leone in December 2014, one example of the difficulty collecting reliable data; see "Ebola: Mapping the Outbreak," BBC News, June 8, 2015, http://www.bbc.com/news/world-africa-28755033.

avoided clinics as the lack of resources often meant an increased chance of either being rejected for care or being infected with the virus. Since the first cases were confirmed in March 2014, unaffected nations considered these cases isolated incidents, underestimating the social, political, and economic implications of an outbreak of a disease in which the illness and the contagion grow in direct proportion. The governments of affected nations, for fear of losing economic investment in their countries and desperately needed work, downplayed the escalating crisis. The WHO did not declare the Ebola outbreak a "public health emergency of international concern" until August 8, 2014. At that point, it was finally recognized that mobility in terms of air and land travel threatened to make Ebola a global crisis; such a threat created ripples of panic in the United States and other areas of the world, provoking anxiety and consequent discrimination.

The reality of Ebola is terrifying, as the virus can replicate and kill with alarming speed once symptoms occur. The virus dismantles the sacred in the body, causing hemorrhaging and fluid loss which destroy vital organs and cause delirium, making it impossible to care for oneself. But beyond the physical consequences, the Ebola virus must be considered in its cultural reception, as a symbol that points toward both latent fears of the Other and the suffering of the Other to whom we are infinitely responsible. Being human, according to Emmanuel Levinas, refers to the Other as the primordial locus of subjectivity, even to the extent that I share the guilt of the burdens the Other suffers. Such is a means of accepting the burden of the vulnerability of the Other which "qualifies alterity itself."[3] While the inclination to escape this responsibility neglects the meaning of being human in the world, the desire to enter what is a never-ending task, that of openness to the very differences and uniqueness of the Other, is what makes me human, what makes a "self." The face of the Other is a summons to response: the vulnerability of the Other is the entry point of openness to the Infinite, where the unknown becomes a palpable matter of experience, and so where my responsibility, the practical trajectory of day-to-day life, is evident. But what is my

---

3. Emmanuel Levinas, *Totality and Infinity: An Essay in Exteriority*, trans. Alphonso Lingis (Pittsburgh, PA: Duquesne University Press, 2008), 256.

responsibility to the distant Other? The Other who is worlds away, who I will perhaps never physically meet? When images of the crisis disturb my complacency, how do I assimilate the catastrophe worlds away into my infinite responsibility?

For most of us in North America, the Ebola crisis and the complex socioeconomic and cultural history that led to it seem to be as far away from daily life and experience as whether there is life on Mars. In other words, this crisis and the related crises in West Africa do not affect me; it is a horrible news story relegated to the margins of the banter of all that must be accomplished today. The bills that need to be paid, pickups and drop-offs, the dishes in the sink . . . those whose daily lives add *survival* to such busyness, who live with death as ordinary, are immeasurably Other to my routine. "They do not think of death," writes Maurice Blanchot, "having no other relation but with death."[4] I know, intellectually, that such a relation with death is how the majority of humanity lives. Whether distant Other or Other in my proximity —those with crude cardboard signs on street corners, youth at-risk for police brutality, those struggling to cross the Mexican border just twenty miles away. The weight of such struggle—and too often the failure to survive—rarely enters the landscape of my vulnerability. The Other may be geographically near but is worlds away in the degree of difference between my white, middle-class privilege and those who must wonder, *will the cop who just pulled me over deem my skin color a threat?* How should I carry this distance?

The parameters of "otherness" have grown significantly since Levinas's lifetime; daily news feeds on a cell phone I carry with me mean that I am continually proximate to events which happened within hours, even if thousands of miles away. Am I infinitely responsible to these persons also? An aesthetics of vulnerability pertains to a sensitivity to the suffering of those Others who are distant, whether geographically, economically, culturally, or however alterity may be described; an aesthetics of vulnerability negotiates the images, art, and cultural artifacts that express the experience of the Other and hone my sensibility for the Other.

---

4. Maurice Blanchot, *The Writing of the Disaster*, trans. Ann Smock (Lincoln, NE: University of Nebraska Press, 1995), 40.

As overwhelming as it appears, I believe that the prophetic message in Scripture, the teachings of Christ, and the exhortations of thinkers such as Levinas and Blanchot all agree that yes, the scope of "infinite responsibility" is indeed wide enough to include both the geographically distant Other as well as the geographically proximate Other. Such is inherent in an aesthetics of vulnerability, in which sensibility and awareness are defined through particular concern for those most at-risk. The specific questions underlining the ethical "what must I do?" are not easily navigable; but the compass by which the prophets tell us to steer determines that our obligations to one another grow exponentially with the suffering that occurs in the world, no matter how far from my immediate experience. Indeed, the very intention of "infinite" in infinite responsibility is in the "past-all-graspness" of the task, which carries even the weight of the suffering of those I will never meet. Subjectivity is necessarily interdependent.

If we explore this in terms of the incarnation, which may be interpreted as a moment critical in the human testimony to divine proximity and therefore critical to understanding what it means to claim that there is reciprocity between the divine and created, we see that incarnation as referring to the dwelling of the infinite God in those who suffer must be broadened in scope, dilated, as a pupil opening to the light, rather than narrowed. Blanchot writes of such an eye in *Thomas the Obscure*:

> [U]seless for seeing, his eye took on extraordinary proportions, developed beyond measure, and, stretched out in the horizon, let the night penetrate its center in order to receive the day from it. And so, through this void, it was sight and the object of sight that mingled together. Not only did this eye that saw nothing apprehend something, it apprehended the cause of its vision. It saw as object that which prevented it from seeing. Its own glance entered onto it as an image, just when this glance seemed the death of all image.[5]

5. Maurice Blanchot, *Thomas the Obscure*, trans. Robert Lamberton (Barrytown, NY: Station Hills Press, 1988), 15.

The "cause of its vision" is the visual interruption of the Other. Georges Bataille writes that the mind is an eye: "[E]xperience has an optical framework, in that one distinguishes within it a perceived object from a perceiving subject, the way a spectacle is different from a mirror."[6] The "void" is always on the periphery of experience, signifying the alterity inherent in the unknown. Aesthetic experience is willing to assume the void in its seeking. Aesthetic experience begins with the eye insofar as the face is the subject of ethics as an optics, according to Levinas; the ethical begins in the visual. Hence the image makes possible a wide field that is outside the scope of ego-driven experience, beyond the nose of my perception, "outside the camp" as in Exodus: "Now Moses used to take the tent and pitch it outside the camp, far off from the camp; he called it a tent of meeting. And everyone who sought the Lord would go out to the tent of meeting, which was outside the camp" (Exod 33:7).

Maurice Blanchot similarly notes that divine proximity is often understood through the metaphor of distance; he quotes Isaiah 57:19: "Peace, peace be to him that is far off, and to him that is near, saith the Lord; and I will heal him."[7] Similarly, Jesus declares divine proximity in distance in the parable of the "Lost Son," which caps a series of parables on the art of losing, finding, and rejoicing. The son who has "traveled to a distant country" in an effort to spend the wealth he so brazenly demanded of his father—wealth that his father gave without so much as a word of caution or protest—is now destitute and has decided to return to his father so that he can at least eat, begins his journey home, rehearsing a little speech designed to fill his belly. My favorite line in the story, "But *while he was still far off*, his father saw him and was filled with compassion; he ran and put his arms around him and kissed him" (Luke 15:20), refers to the "far off" found in Isaiah. The wandering son does not need to be

---

6. Georges Bataille, *Inner Experience*, trans. Stuart Kendall (Albany, NY: SUNY Press, 2014), 125.

7. Maurice Blanchot, *"Paix, paix au lointrain et au proche,"* cited by Kevin Hart, *The Dark Gaze: Maurice Blanchot and the Sacred* (Chicago: The University of Chicago Press, 2004), 162. Hart translated this essay from 1985 that appeared in *De la Bible á nos jours: 3000 ans d'art* (Paris: Société des Artistes Indépendants, 1985), 53.

proximate to inspire the compassion of the father: the son is "still far off." The son has not yet had a chance to deliver his little speech of recompense, and we are never sure in the story whether the son has actually learned anything about the unreasonable demands he made or the failures he accrued. We are never sure whether the son will even remain in his father's house: for all we know, he hocks the robe and ring his father lavishes on him and returns to the same wanton spending as before. But the actions of the son are not central to the story; the focus is on the father, who has watched from a distance, possibly for years, for evidence that his son is still alive: one "who was dead, and is alive again, who was lost and is found."

In this chapter, we will examine how art and visual culture bring the distant Other into our proximate space, highlighting the tension between the Other in infinite alterity and the Other in visual proximity. This tension is also an aspect of the doctrine of incarnation, since God brings the distant Other into proximate space to reveal the scope of distance and alterity. The intuition of the early church that Jesus reveals the dwelling of the divine reflects a new realization of "where" God dwells. God dwells not in the self-sufficiency of Greek philosophical concepts of "the One" as distant because of the remoteness of divine perfection to our imperfection but, rather, God dwells utterly proximate to human beings, to daily life, suffering and death, while remaining transcendent, divine alterity "just-beyond" our grasp. We see this explored in the artistic interpretations of the *Gnadenstuhl,* or Mercy Seat, motif, in which the suffering of Jesus is reflected in the grief of the Father and the Spirit. The motif's persistence through centuries and across cultural boundaries reflects the early church's devotion to the God who dwells with us in our suffering, taking our burdens on Godself, even before the early church had a developed notion of trinitarian doctrine. In order to explore the meaning of this intuition, reflected in the persistence of a motif in art, we will first consider the devastation of catastrophic suffering, that which is "stronger than death": "the intensity of dying, the push of the impossible, the pressure of the undesirable even in the most desired."[8]

---

8. Blanchot, *The Writing of the Disaster,* 47.

The Problem of Catastrophic Suffering

The problem of catastrophic suffering is the most urgent and inescapable issue in theology today, as well as the organizing problem in rethinking issues in Christology. "Catastrophic suffering," as noted previously, refers to the sort of suffering that is not in and of itself beneficial in any way to the growth or education of human beings.[9] This is suffering which should not happen, suffering with no inherent purpose or goal, suffering that is unjust and unnecessary. Emmanuel Levinas called this "pain in its undiluted malignity, suffering for nothing. It renders impossible and odious every proposal and every thought that would explain it by the sins of those who have suffered or are dead."[10] There is simply no justification for such suffering; even if some good may result in its course, even if some may survive and have the opportunity to reflect on it or ascribe meaning to it, this meaning is neither justification nor explanation for "why" it happens.

Ivan Karamazov, of Fyodor Dostoyevsky's *The Brothers Karamazov*, rejects worship of God based on the prevalence of catastrophic suffering. In a chapter titled "Rebellion," Ivan delivers a series of arguments to his brother Alyosha that reject the notion that suffering occurs in order to move humanity closer to heaven, or, as John Hick put it, to "grow our souls." Alyosha is a novice in training with Fr. Zosima; his character is named after Dostoyevsky's own son, who died of an epileptic seizure at the age of three. Alyosha is deeply religious but not hypocritically so; he is innocent to the world's

9. Because I am attempting to explore the doctrine of the incarnation, I am primarily concerned in this project about the relationship between God and human beings; but it should be noted that the term "catastrophic" regarding suffering without inherent purpose also applies to the suffering of nonhuman animals and environmental destruction. For more on this, see Peter Singer, *Practical Ethics* (Cambridge, UK: Cambridge University Press, 2011), 16–122; Jacques Derrida, *The Animal That Therefore I Am*, ed. Marie-Louise Mallet, trans. David Wills (New York: Fordham University Press, 2008); Aaron Gross, *The Question of the Animal and Religion: Theoretical Stakes, Practical Implications* (New York: Columbia University Press, 2014).

10. Emmanuel Levinas, "Useless Suffering," in *Entre-Nous: On Thinking-of-the-Other*, trans. Michael B. Smith and Barbara Harshav (New York: Columbia University Press, 1998), 98.

depravity and Ivan loves him dearly. But in this chapter, Ivan wishes to open Alyosha's eyes to the horrors of the world that have taken away his desire to worship the God whom he believes intends the catastrophic suffering of children, even if for the "greater harmony." Ivan voices what many believers assume to be true: that even catastrophic suffering occurs for the "greater good," as part of the "divine plan," creating an environment in which virtue can flourish. Whatever "harmony," whatever "heaven" or worthwhile end toward which humanity and creation are headed will far surpass the suffering of the present moment. To Ivan, worshiping God requires trust in God's good intention when creating the conditions in which catastrophic suffering, like all suffering, occurs for our ultimate benefit.

After telling several stories of horrific abuse, including a story about a little girl beaten and forced by her parents to sleep in an outhouse and a young boy killed by a rich general's pack of dogs, Ivan's rhetoric has escalated to fever pitch. He cries:

> Do you understand why this infamy must be and is permitted? Without it, I am told, humanity could not have existed on earth, for we could not have known good and evil. Why should we know that diabolical good and evil *when it costs so much*? Why, the whole world of knowledge is not worth that child's prayer to "dear, kind God"! I say nothing of the sufferings of grown-up people, they have eaten the apple, damn them, and the devil take them all! . . . If all must suffer to pay for the eternal harmony, what have children to do with it, tell me, please? It's beyond all comprehension why they should suffer, and why they should pay for this harmony. Why should they, too, furnish material to enrich the soil for the harmony of the future? I understand solidarity in sin among adults. I understand solidarity in retribution, too; but there can be no such solidarity with children. And if it is really true that they must share responsibility for all their fathers' crimes, such a truth is not of this world and is beyond my comprehension. Some jester will say, perhaps, that the child would have grown up and have sinned, but you see—he didn't grow up, he was torn to pieces by the dogs, at eight years old.[11]

---

11. Fyodor Dostoyevsky, *The Brothers Karamazov*, trans. Constance Garnett (New York: Barnes and Noble Classics, 2004), 224–26.

Ivan's anger is born of witnessing the absurdity and utter uselessness of the suffering of the innocent. He is angry that the world is fashioned the way it is, that God as the world's architect did not create a plan for the world in which heaven is possible without the suffering of the innocent, and so he rejects this plan and rejects the divine architect as well.

The problem of reconciling catastrophic suffering with what the Judeo-Christian-Muslim tradition teaches of the God who loves humanity will never be adequately solved. In a rare essay on the subject, "Why Does God Allow Us to Suffer?," Karl Rahner considers four possible answers: (1) suffering is unavoidable in an evolving, finite world; (2) suffering comes from human sin as a product of human freedom; (3) suffering exists to test us and bring us to maturity; and (4) eternal life will countermand the suffering of this life. While admitting the element of truth in each of these, Rahner gives brief but articulate rebuttals to all four. Notably, he argues, "The children burned to death by napalm bombs were not going through a process of human maturing. Elsewhere, too, in innumerable cases there is suffering which is destructive in its effects, despite all good will to endure it in a human and Christian way, which simply demands too much from a person."[12] But because none of these formal, academic answers fully suffice, we are left with the incomprehensibility of the problem of suffering, as we are left with the incomprehensibility of God. Such incomprehensibility, such attention to the void, is more appropriate to the task of reflecting on catastrophic suffering in the passionate and poetic language of a homily he delivered to St. Michael's Church in Munich during Lent 1946:

> We prayed, and God did not answer. We cried, and he remained mute. We wept tears that consumed our hearts. . . . We would have shown him why we have every reason to despair because of his silence. We would have had endless material on file: the unanswered prayer for babies who starved to death . . . the misery of violated young women, of children who were beaten to death, of the exploited labor slaves . . . of those crushed by

12. Ibid., 203.

injustice, of the "liquidated," of the cripples, of those dishon-
ored. . . . [T]he essential answer that God gave to man . . .
which he gives by him himself becoming a beggar in this world,
by his becoming flesh and letting the cry of need rise from his
own tormented heart into the disconsolate silence of our distant
God . . . the eternal God didn't order us with harsh words to
continue praying until it pleased him to hear us in the coming
of his eternal kingdom, rather he let his eternal Word become
flesh to weep together with this lamenting choir: Lord, let your
kingdom come, the kingdom in which all dreams are ended and
you hear the weeping of the poor and the cry of need of all
human agony.[13]

Here, as earlier, Rahner appeals to the doctrine of the incarnation as
a way to enter the paradox between the hidden and present God,
between the God who does not answer the prayers of tormented
children and the God who becomes Godself "a beggar in this world."
Incarnation is the lens through which to address the incomprehensibility of the God to whom we address our prayers by name.

Indeed, *how* the problem of catastrophic suffering is addressed—
whether through practical theology's interest to offer solutions,
through moral theology's interest to make substantive decisions, or
liturgical theology's interest to lament—determines the contemporary relevance of theology as the study or contemplation of what it
may be possible to say of the identity or nonidentity of God. After
Auschwitz or Bosnia, is it possible to say anything about God? During Haiti's cholera epidemic? After the feminicides in Ciudad Juarez?
When twelve-year-old Tamir Rice is shot in Cleveland for playing
with a toy gun "while black"?

The present age witnesses the continuation of the terrible failure
of rational thought after the Western Enlightenment, and so the
terrible failure of much of modern thought in the West is evident in
the "new kind of barbarism," as Theodor Adorno describes, that
consistently sacrifices human lives and the health of the environment

---

13. Karl Rahner, *The Need and Blessing of Prayer*, trans. Bruce W. Gillette
(Collegeville, MN: Liturgical Press, 1997), 49, 55.

for the sake of power, wealth, and nationalism. This barbarism is obvious when we examine the colonial origins[14] and class retaliations that underlie the string of genocides in the twentieth century: the German colonial persecution of the Herero people in southwest Africa, persecution by the Young Turk government of Armenians during the First World War, Nazi persecution of Jews during the Shoah, the Soviet Union's imposed famine on Ukraine, the Khmer Rouge's killing fields of Cambodia, the rape and slaughter of Muslims in Bosnia, and Rwandan genocide—not to mention the massacres in El Salvador, Sudan, and Syria—and this is again only a partial list. The twentieth century was not a moment in the evolution of human reason's triumph but has rather been an unprecedented period in which the unqualified failure to recognize and name the atrocities as they festered and advanced amounts to a failure of education and educators, according to Adorno, "and barbarism continues as long as the fundamental conditions that favored that relapse continue largely unchanged."[15] Adorno notes Sigmund Freud's observation that civilization produces anti-civilization and reinforces it: genocides are not aberrations or anomalies in the course of modern history but are somehow born in the structures of human society. "All empires of humans are built on the destruction of the body,"[16] writes Ta-Nehisi Coates; empire is the illusion that there is, or can be erected,

---

14. An essay by Jürgen Zimmerer, "The Birth of the Ostland Out of the Spirit of Colonialism: A Postcolonial Perspective on the Nazi Policy of Conquest and Extermination," outlines the links between the German colonialism of South-West Africa and the Nazi interest to exterminate the Jewish people, in *Colonialism and Genocide*, ed. Dirk Moses and Dan Stone (New York: Routledge, 2007), 101–24. The genocide in Rwanda of Hutu against Tutsi is rooted in the postcolonial consciousness of the artificial race boundaries drawn by the Belgian colonialists, pitting tribe against tribe. French colonialism in Cambodia laid the foundations of Pol Pot's turn to Maoist communism and the justification for exterminating those deemed unnecessary to the society after Cambodian independence.

15. Theodor W. Adorno, "Education after Auschwitz," in *Can One Live after Auschwitz? A Philosophical Reader*, ed. Rolf Tiedemann, trans. Rodney Livingstone, et al. (Stanford, CA: Stanford University Press, 2003), 19.

16. Ta-Nehisi Coates, *Between the World and Me* (New York: Spiegel and Grau/ Random House, 2015), 143.

a bulwark to vulnerability. When those who live in the comfortable illusion of empire are awakened to the atrocities upon which their comfort is built, "their own vulnerability becomes real—when the police decide that tactics intended for the ghetto should enjoy wider usage, when their armed society shoots down their children, when nature sends hurricanes against their cities—they are shocked in a way that those of us who were born and bred to understand cause and effect can never be."[17]

In other words, modern society—modern Western society in particular—contains the roots of what allows and promotes such atrocities. Investigating the extent of Western culpability in the catastrophic suffering of distant Others reminds those of us who are privileged to benefit from the imperial and genocidal tendencies of Western practices that the infinite responsibility inherent in becoming human is extended in scope to those whom I will never meet. The Ebola epidemic, for example, was exacerbated by post-colonial distrust of the West, whether in terms of medicine, military action, and the borders of nations. We often pin blame on the leaders—Lothar von Trotha, Adolf Hitler, Pol Pot, Slobodan Milosevic, Ratko Mladic—in such a way that we fail to see how even ordinary citizens must share the burden of responsibility because we were silent and unquestioning when early stages of catastrophe cried out for rec-ognition and witness. Adorno calls for courage to face the deprav-ity in human history and society squarely and soberly: "One must come to know the mechanisms that render people capable of such deeds, must reveal the mechanisms to them, and strive, by awaken-ing a general awareness of those mechanisms. . . . [T]he only education that has any sense at all is an education toward critical self-reflection."[18] Barbarism is obvious when we see the horrific daily headlines; it is not so obvious in the way we continue our banal business, when we switch channels to escape the disquieting truth that the barbarians are us. The instinct of those in much of North American and European society seems to be to avoid con-fronting the horror that surrounds Western wealth, white privilege,

17. Ibid., 107.
18. Adorno, "Education after Auschwitz," 21.

for concepts as nebulous as "national security." We who are comfortable do not like discomfort. Education for critical self-reflection, and openness to what we may find in this process, is necessary to fashion a world without barbarism, in which catastrophic suffering is no longer tolerated.

Yet language has no words to describe the extent of the catastrophic suffering of the victims. Even the word "genocide" has a long and complex history. The term was coined to describe both the intention by the Nazis to eliminate an entire ethnic community and the systematic slaughter that followed. Theodor Adorno observes that elevating "genocide" to a concept cuts the unspeakable down to size: it becomes an institution to be prohibited, rejected, and debated. As a term of language, I can use it in all sorts of ways—at dinner parties, in a lecture, as the punchline of a joke, and in this book, without having the slightest idea what it means to experience it, to dig the graves, to smell the ash, to see the blood, and wonder if there is a God in a world in which "genocide" is possible. Placing huge inconceivable and unfathomable notions into neat and tidy definitions and terms to memorize carries the danger of assuming such notions can be conquered, understood, *known*. Eerily, Adorno anticipates the current debates on whether the mass killings in the Sudan can be defined as "genocide":

> The day will come when discussions will take place about whether some monstrous act falls within the definition of genocide; whether the nations have a right to intervene, a right of which they have no real wish to avail themselves; and whether, given the unforeseen difficulties in applying the term in practice, the whole concept of "genocide" should not be deleted from the statutes. Shortly thereafter, medium-sized headlines will appear in the papers: "Genocidal Measures in East Turkistan Almost Complete."[19]

Conceptualizing the unfathomable experience of victims of catastrophic suffering risks turning the lives of millions of the murdered, maimed, and displaced into neat phrases and scholarly essays such

19. Ibid.

as this one. Education for critical reflection, as noted earlier, is crucial to the recognition and witness that keeps the memory of the suffering from turning to dust and to any hope of preventing future massacres.

Yet the danger inherent in the typical processes of education—reading scholarly works, writing on them, delivering and hearing lectures—comes dangerously close to reifying the suffering, to assuming that we within the educational process would ever understand what it must be like to die alone in an alley, be tortured, or subsist on a death march or in a refugee camp simply because we have read about it or discussed it. The best we can hope for is that we be committed to awareness and the alleviation of catastrophic suffering as our infinite responsibility and find multiple ways, beyond language and text, to bear the weight of another's burdens. Often more than we can bear, witnessing to the suffering of others, as Ivan Karamazov does, is what the doctrine of the incarnation signifies. The existence of God is meaningless unless God suffers resisting the human empires that continue to slaughter. There is no God without such vulnerability and without such resistance.

The Suffering Other in Proximity

Casa Hogar Las Memorias is an HIV/AIDS hospice ten miles east of Tijuana, Mexico. The journey there winds through unpaved roads and barrios of homes patched with plastic tarp, corrugated tin, and cardboard in the community of La Morita. Strings of laundered towels and clothing drying in the sun add color against the expanse of arid ground, swaying in the wind like flags. Families join in communal markets, spreading items for sale on folding tables under canopies. Although the hospice depends entirely on donations and endures deterioration and loss daily, there is nothing somber at Casa Memorias; painted in bright colors and sprinkled with the giggles of caretakers' children, it feels more like entering a home than a care facility. Rooms are devoted to different levels of severity of illness, which means that sometimes the room housing the most critically ill is the most crowded.

Alberto had arrived only a few days prior to my visit, and the only bed available in the critical room was near the door to the outside, which was propped open for breeze. Without a screen on the doorway, flies lazed in and out. Alberto was too weak to swat them away, and so they continued to pester him. Having recently vomited on his pillow, no one had yet had a chance to replace it for him. These things I could do: swat away flies and give him pillows and sips of water. But I had trouble understanding his Spanish, which was muffled by his weakness and mild dementia. From caramel skin stretched taut over his bones, his wide eyes pleaded to me to relieve him of his pain: the very thing I could not do. I smiled stupidly and took his hand, but he didn't want to be touched—his pain was too pervasive, too intense. I stood facing him, nodding as he cried, absolutely helpless as he fell from broken words into silence. He died two days later.

I have visited AIDS patients in other ministries, but none were so close to death, dying in the "un-power" into which Alberto descended; Blanchot describes this dying that wrests from the present, always a step over the edge, that rules out every conclusion and all ends: "it does not free nor does it shelter."[20] "In death, one can find an illusory refuge: the grave is as far as gravity can pull, it marks the end of the fall; the mortuary is the loophole in the impasse. But dying flees and pulls indefinitely, impossibly and intensively in the flight."[21]

That night, at home, I needed faith that God is not bound by my failures to understand or appreciate the extent of his suffering. The infinite God cannot be restrained by my failures to do anything of service for him; faith in this Infinity clumsily guides through the field where my responsibility continues despite my limitations. It is precisely in my failure that my responsibility does not end. Faith in the unboundedness of God where catastrophic suffering occurs is indeed the extent (perhaps the *only* extent) of Jesus' cross as "salvific." But after seeing Alberto dying young and in such pain, how absurd to think that one dying could ever be salvific. Whatever we mean by the cross as "salvific," it must have something to do with the instinct of the early followers of Jesus that the divine dwells in

20. Ibid., 48.
21. Ibid.

the Witness Tent of John's gospel,[22] where there is only pain, heat, and flies.

John Caputo explains that desiring "love" or "God" is desiring an "unconditional event," the wholly Other, outside of experience, the "unconditional promise of the event contained" in "love" or "God," the "least bad" names we have "for the conditioned, empirical counterparts of something unforeseeable, unconditional, and nameless."[23] We long for the unconditional, for the unattainable, the "undeconstructible," and so divine infinity is "an unstable situation in which the finite keeps foundering, in which determinate conditions keep collapsing under the call of the unconditional event, in which constructions keep falling under the weight of the undeconstructible."[24] Such is what fuels theological thinking, observes Caputo; hence the paradox between the unsayable and what is said will never be resolved. Although a few words here have spoken of Alberto's suffering, there could never be a way to *say* his suffering in the depths of it, in the midst of his loneliness and fear in the night he died. There is only the promise of an infinite beyond the catastrophe of this death, a promise that indwells Jesus on the cross and provides hope in what Christians designate as "resurrection."

God's own *alterity* as distinct from finite creatures is then *incarnate*, shouldering the very catastrophe of intense and unjustifiable suffering. The paradox is that God by becoming incarnate in all who suffer catastrophe remains the Other who will forever transcend human comprehension and the interest to totalize and name the suffering of an Other. This paradox, however, also contains a mirror: reflected by the eternal incomprehensibility and alterity of God is our human but infinite responsibility to the very catastrophe of the suffering Other. If the promise of the incarnation of the Infinite in the suffering Other is authentic, my infinite responsibility to Alberto is authentic, never to end. My failure to comfort Alberto will always be

---

22. See John P. Keenan and Linda K. Keenan, *I Am/No Self: A Christian Commentary on the Heart Sutra* (Leuven: Peeters, 2011), 97.

23. John D. Caputo, *The Weakness of God: A Theology of the Event* (Bloomington, IN: Indiana University Press, 2006), 294.

24. Ibid.

with me, even as I believe that he is now with God, in the bosom of this infinity. The infinity of human responsibility is a reflection of the incomprehensibility of the God who shoulders the catastrophe of unjustifiable suffering in such a way that Christians use the word "incarnate" to describe it and point to the historical person of Jesus of Nazareth as evidence of this divine activity, evidence inherited with images from the very prophets of Jesus' own tradition.

Finding God indwelling and incarnate in Jesus of Nazareth, whether in the first century or in the twenty-first century, contradicts what we think we know about God, as well as what we think we know about ourselves. Encountering the divine embodied in Alberto, bed-ridden and abandoned by his family because he was gay and had AIDS, his face contorted in pain, means that I have been beholden to him in spite of myself. As Levinas argues, the structure of my subjectivity—how I understand myself—is already invested in this infinite respon-sibility before the encounter with the Other. The vulnerability of the suffering Other means that I may try to forget him, I may try to push his face from my thoughts, but even in that very attempt I am recog-nizing that his otherness, the worlds of agony he occupied far from my comfort and privilege, demands my response and my response constitutes any "self" I can have. The memory of him, and my recall-ing this memory, threatens to become a mere anecdote, a story in a sea of encounters, unless I am somehow able to assume, in the lan-guage of "meeting the God past all grasp," the infinite responsibility that contextualizes my subjectivity.

The Suffering of the Distant Other

Tuvia Ruebner, in the poem that began this chapter, describes the broken body of one taken off a cross in images that traverse time between events of more than two thousand years ago and the suf-fering endured today in circumstances as varied as human beings are themselves. Art—poetry, music, theater, visual art—enriches awareness of the depth of suffering in the world by simultaneously shattering and cultivating the distance of otherness, bringing the strange and daunting into the life experience previously unaffected by a physical or personal connection while also increasing awareness of the alterity of the Other. Art engages emotion that creates the experience our compartmentalizing and conceptualizing of the suffering had neglected or ignored. Such is the paradox of art: it is both the expression of an individual and a public discourse; it is both personal and communal, an exercise in communication that transcends complete comprehension, playing with the obvious and the subtle. In this sense, the experience of suffering is also paradoxical; all human beings will suffer but we will all fail to ever fully understand the suffering of another. As Harold Schweizer writes, "[A]rt is as autonomous, gratuitous, and irreducible to analysis as suffering. Both art and suffering can be diagnosed, and neither can be understood; both are purposeless and gratuitous."[25]

The doctrine of the incarnation is language that binds together the experience of catastrophe as well as the experience of those who witness catastrophe, since it means that even the divine has not escaped the catastrophe: God is not separate from or remote to the suffering of the disaster. Blanchot reminds us that the etymology of "disaster" refers to a "break from the star," a place of dis-order; "I call disaster that which does not have the ultimate for a limit: it bears the ultimate away in the disaster."[26] In this sense, Jesus' dying and death has no star; it is dis-order, a murder. If we are to understand Jesus' death through the lens of the catastrophic deaths of the millions before and after him, we must attempt to strip the interpretations of his death in Christian tradition from all the layers of triumph and destructive power that have built empires on his cross. The bare bones of articulating Jesus' death, what his death is as a catastrophe, as a disaster, is broken from the star of meaning, the guide of *telos* and purpose. If we Christians wish to say that God died *this* meaningless, senseless, absurd death, and that "incarnation" is language tracing the divine in the suffering of the disposable—those who die in the chasms of hunger statistics—then witnessing the death of Jesus reveals that God becomes incarnate where there is catastrophe.

25. Harold Schweizer, *Suffering and the Remedy of Art* (Albany, NY: SUNY Press, 1997), 2.
26. Blanchot, *The Writing of the Disaster*, 28.

Otherwise, we may commit the sin of *naming* the suffering of an innocent man, which deprives Jesus of his alterity and so deprives him of his divinity. To name Jesus' dying as though it was part of a divine "will" or "plan" may be the root of violence perpetrated in the service of the Christian religion: such provides a conquering of the unconquerable, a justification for that which must never be justified. Installing one murder into a "divine plan"—even if for the "salvation of the world"—is a convenient way to fit *more* murders into a divine plan. Once we have the power to name one human being dying in obedience to the glory of God, perhaps it is not too far a stretch to name another, and another, until we Christians glorify a truth that functions to acquiesce to the very destructive power that continues to torture, maim, and rob persons of life—prisoners in Abu Gharib, the indigenous and native peoples of lands before colonial empires, young black men in Tuskegee. At the foundation of every hegemony is the construction of a truth that fits the purpose of power. How often has Jesus' cross been invoked to claim salvific meaning as the justification and locus of divine appeasement?

It would be as if I in my whiteness and my privilege could claim I understood Alberto's dying. It would be as if I could claim there was purpose in it. An unspeakable absurdity. Albert came to Casa Memorias because he had nowhere else to go, nowhere else to die; but that there was Memorias and people who would welcome him and give him a bed so he would not die in the streets is evidence of a trace of the divine whereby we can crawl back from the nihilism that would otherwise secure us. That there was an end to his dying assures me that suffering has an end, even if the memory of his face, his dark eyes that tried in vain to convey to me what he needed, will never leave me.

If I were an artist, I would try to express this chasm between his suffering and my comfort, the place of refuge I occupy. So I rely on the work of others. Art reminds us of the purposeless and gratuitous passion of Jesus, who dies as one of the disposable people, one of the millions of destitute poor. The images in Ruebner's poem recall Jesus' isolation and humiliation and serve our attempt to witness and comprehend the death of Saah Exco, a young boy whose death by the Ebola virus was captured by National Public Radio photojournalist David Gilkey. Exco died in an alley in the densely populated and impoverished township of West Point, in the capital city of Monrovia on the coast of Liberia.

West Point is home to seventy-five thousand people on a small peninsula extending into the Atlantic Ocean; it is a tangle of corrugated tin shanties, brightly colored cinderblock structures, and muddy streets in which there are open sewers. For the children of West Point, the beaches many use as toilets—UNOCHA estimates that there are only four public toilets available in West Point[27]—are also playgrounds. Saah Exco was found wandering those beaches alone, naked and weak, having been denied access to a clinic because it was not equipped to handle Ebola patients. His mother and siblings were suspected Ebola victims. People who saw him kept a watchful distance until he wandered into an alley and a crowd began to gather. Clothing was passed to him and he struggled, frail yet persistent, to dress himself. The crowd, anxious with dread over a virus as contagious as it is misunderstood, could only view his deterioration (including the photographer, Gilkey, who admitted he was too paralyzed by fear to reach out to him), until his death.[28]

Saah's broken body, like the "ugly rag doll" in Tuvia Ruebner's poem, was observed in "wonder, pity and fear"—their gazes, and now my gaze, over him, "straying up and down," trying to make sense of a senseless image. Primo Levi's poem introducing *Survival in Auschwitz*

---

27. United Nations Office for Coordination of Humanitarian Affairs (UNOCHA) also estimates twenty to thirty cases of cholera and other waterborne illnesses reported weekly in Monrovia due to improper sanitation. According to a 2010 report by the United Nations Environmental Program (UNEP), water contamination is exacerbated by the Firestone Natural Rubber Plantation, an American company that is the second largest producer of rubber on the continent, 45 km away from Monrovia. Rubber is one of Liberia's top export commodities, according to the report; see *Africa Water Atlas*, Division of Early Warning and Assessment (DEWA) of UNEP, Nairobi, Kenya, 2010, p. 255.

28. See Matthew Silver, "The 10-Year-Old Boy Has Died, Probably of Ebola," NPR, August 21, 2014, http://www.npr.org/blogs/goatsandsoda/2014/08/21/342216397/the-10-year-old-boy-has-died-probably-of-ebola. David Gilkey, who since 2007 worked as a staff photographer and video editor for NPR, was killed in Afghanistan on June 5, 2016. He had witnessed tragedy all over the world, such as bombings in Gaza, the tsunami in Japan, and poverty following the devastation of Typhoon Haiyan in the Philippines. We are all indebted to the bravery of journalists such as Gilkey who keep the suffering of the world proximate.

reminds me that I watch him—"satisfied in my own living belly"—at a distance from his horror in every way possible; my color, my economic security, and my geography might as well place me in another solar system, another galaxy apart from this scene. My distance is unspeakable: it is too far from this child's suffering. I "live safe in my warm house," I "return in the evening to hot food and friendly faces."[29] I travel over this planet where Ebola and poverty cause immeasurable agony from the indifference of my computer, briefly engaged in concern, an interruption in workaday business. If I had actually been in that alley, I would have only watched in stupefied terror as well.

For most in the United States, it is hard to imagine the multilayered catastrophe of Ebola, from the physiognomies of pain, weakness, rapid fluid loss, and internal and external bleeding to the personal isolation, the orphaned children, and the socioeconomic consequences of nations unable to recoup losses. In addition to the well-known origins of crises in many African nations such as poverty, lack of clean water for sanitation, and insufficient medical facilities, the complexity of this tragedy has colonial and postcolonial roots. From the terrible centuries of the buying, selling, and torture of millions of persons for the slave labor that built the economies of Europe and North America to memories of Western medical experimentation on citizens of Congo in the race to find a vaccine for Polio, the factors that contribute to the current tragedy of Ebola reaches far back in the history of West and Central Africa.

Memories of colonial oppression have been preserved in stories retold for generations; such cultural memory of a people has led to protests in which communities declare that there is no Ebola or that it is another Western attempt to invade their lives, creating more segregation and isolation. Senegalese professor Cheikh Ibrahima Niang observes, "When people say that Ebola does not exist, they are rebelling against something. . . . [T]hey feel that they are treated with paternalism. There is a very important African metaphor that says a forest fire which has spread to a town or community needs to be fought at its origins. Barricading myself at home and stockpiling water for

---

29. See Primo Levi, preface to "If This Is a Man," in *Survival in Auschwitz*, trans. Stuart Woolf (Amazon Digital Services, 2013).

when it arrives will not put it out."[30] Blocking national borders, often artificial remnants of colonial intervention, and imposing medical practices that fail to understand local rituals and beliefs, are Western answers that may have initially exacerbated the problem and intensified the suspicion. Hence the strong postcolonial mistrust in these communities that Ebola is merely the name of another attempt by those with power to dismiss them as expendable, as easily replaced labor.

Much of the political violence on the African continent can be traced to the history of measuring and probing, segregating and naming, often performed in the service of Western science:

> Disease served as a social metaphor and fear about the sexual, social and political implications of racial mixing were often experienced in these terms: indigenous people represented the locus of sickness and were described as dirty, unhygienic vectors of disease that threatened to contaminate colonists . . . medicine was employed directly in the service of colonialism.[31]

Historians and sociologists commonly refer to Western medicine as a "tool of empire" in Africa, which in tacit ways continues to influence white reactions to persons of color today in the United States and Europe. The Ebola virus has entered discourse in the United States through the narrative of fear of the Other, a way to mask racist assumptions of what is "normal" or "healthy": for example, immigrant children from African nations other than those affected by Ebola have been harassed and labeled "Ebola kids,"[32] revealing

30. Cited in Malick Rokhy Ba, "Ebola-denial a Revolt Against Colonial Mindset: Expert," for AFP (Agence France-Presse), September 2, 2014, http://news.yahoo.com/ebola-denial-revolt-against-colonial-mindset-expert-054418266.html.

31. Karen Flint, "Medicine," in *Colonialism: An International Social, Cultural and Political Encyclopedia*, ed. Melvin E. Page and Penny M. Sonnenburg (Santa Barbara, CA: ABC-CLIO, 2003), 381.

32. Jon Herskovitz, "In Dallas, African Immigrants Worry about Backlash from Ebola Case," Reuters, October 5, 2014, http://www.reuters.com/article/2014/10/05/us-health-ebola-usa-immigrants-idUSKCN0HU00120141005. A Nigerian child in Connecticut was banned from her school, http://www.christianpost.com/news/connecticut-school-accused-of-racism-after-it-bans-nigerian-american-girl-from-class-amid-ebola-fears-128858/.

American ignorance that makes "Africa" into a monolithic entity with one culture and one ethnicity. Politicians in the United States and Europe have argued for bans on flights from West African countries, as well as the isolation of those returning from giving medical assistance there, tactics that only exacerbate the fear of the Other.

The cultural identity that has preserved the communities beset by Western colonial attempts to marginalize their uniqueness has tragically been a factor in the staggeringly rapid spread of the virus. In the cultures of Liberia, Nigeria, Sierra Leone, and in many others on the African continent, a rejection of Western individualism is necessary for community as well as for survival. It is therefore unthinkable not to hold or otherwise touch a sick person in need of comfort; as the Akan in Ghana say, "Alone is miserable."[33] The embrace is an integral part of religious practice throughout Liberia and Sierra Leone. After someone has died, the act of washing, kissing, and caressing the body is ritually performed by those with high status in the family or in society. It is customary to spend hours preparing the body for the afterlife, from trimming nails to braiding hair; Mattu Morru explains, "If someone is not buried properly, her ghost will return to haunt people."[34] Actions that identify the life and value of persons and relationships are now lethal in communities affected by the virus, threatening the very survival of cultural identity.

In October 2014, Jon Hamilton of National Public Radio news reported on the Very Reverend Herman Browne and his wife Trokon of the Episcopal Church of Liberia, who self-quarantined after caring for a friend with Ebola. The Brownes have been leaders in their church and community in educating about Ebola, but despite intellectually acknowledging the risks of caring for one with a highly contagious virus, Trokon Browne explained the difficulty maintaining a safe distance when a friend or family member is sick: "I cannot see my hus-

33. Mercy Amba Oduyoye, *Beads and Strands: Reflections of an African Woman on Christianity in Africa* (Maryknoll, NY: Orbis Books, 2004), 47.

34. Mattu Morru, from "Outbreak," PBS *Frontline*, episode produced by Dan Edge and Sasha Joelle Achilli, directed by Dan Edge, aired May 5, 2015, http://www.pbs.org/wgbh/pages/frontline/health-science-technology/outbreak/transcript-81/.

band sick and not touch him. . . . Ebola might as well kill us. So it's still very hard. Trust me, it's still very hard."[35] Added Reverend Browne, "Those who don't care and those who don't want to express their care are those who survive. Those who actually care are those who die. At the heart of it, for some of us with religious eyes, is an anti-care, anti-love message. And that can be very draining."[36]

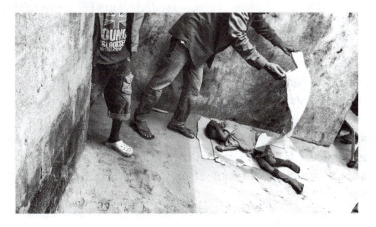

Can this photograph[37] adequately represent the agony of this child and the agony of witnesses powerless to act? Of course not; no image and no words will ever fully capture the experience of catastrophic suffering. The deficiency of language and images and the insufficiency of perception and awareness multiplies the suffering of victims and renders witnesses mute and catatonic. Adding to the devastation of this little boy's death is the devastation of being utterly unable to understand the depths of his agony and the paralyzing fear of the disease itself. Although surrounded by witnesses and photographed

35. Jon Hamilton, "Ebola in Church: A Reverend's Quarantine Spreads the Word," NPR *Morning Edition*, October 20, 2014, http://www.npr.org/blogs /goatsandsoda/2014/10/20/357399593/ebola-in-church-a-reverends-quarantine -spreads-the-word.

36. Ibid.

37. Photo credit: David Gilkey, "The 10-Year Old Boy Has Died, Probably of Ebola," *All Things Considered*, National Public Radio, aired August 21, 2014, http://www.npr.org/sections/goatsandsoda/2014/08/21/342216397/the -10-year-old-boy-has-died-probably-of-ebola.

in his last moments by an American journalist, no one held him while he died, no one cooled his feverish forehead, no one stroked his hair. We can only *approach* the catastrophe of his suffering, never comprehend it, by reminding ourselves of the complex history that led to it and the attempt to recognize and address those complexities, layers that describe my distance from him—geographical, ethnic, economic—will always be superseded by my failure to have any grasp of his suffering. Therein lies the infinite. I will not know the games he played when healthy, the way he looked at his mother or held his sister's hand. How do I explain that despite the chasm of difference and distance, I feel irrevocably changed by this photograph and the photographer's heartbreaking narration of powerless witness? Recalling Tuvia Ruebner's poem above, as a cloth is gently lowered over the boy's body, now completely spent of energy, completely depleted of life, "Against the backdrop of the gloomy skies/ another stoops over, letting the sheet slowly drop./Everything around is dark."[38]

This photograph and his story are compelling because I am to never forget him. My failure to traverse the distance between us is evidence of the infinity understood through both distance and intimacy. Levinas describes transcendence in reference to a relation with a reality infinitely distant from my own reality, "yet without this distance destroying this relation and without this relation destroying this distance"[39]—as a relation that depends on distance, I must neither confuse the boy's experience with mine, nor make him into an object, even if such indicates the inexplicable pull and power Saah Exco's story and dying have over me. The bond with the Other, Levinas writes, "is not reducible to the representation of the other, but to his invocation" that is "irreducible to understanding."[40] In other words, it is not mere being that joins us, as though our shared human nature is enough, but the distance and the call. The call, as

---

38. Tuvia Ruebner, "Descent from the Cross," in *In the Illuminated Dark*, 139.

39. Levinas, *Totality and Infinity*, 49.

40. Emmanuel Levinas, "Is Ontology Fundamental?," in *Entre Nous: On Thinking-of-the-Other*, trans. Michael B. Smith and Barbara Harshav (New York: Columbia University Press, 1998), 7.

Primo Levi writes, is to "Carve them into your hearts/At home, in the street/Going to bed, rising;/Repeat them to your children."[41] This invocation of the Other, which breaks through my complacency and is carved into my heart: this is what it means to be religious, writes Levinas, as "The essence of discourse is prayer."[42] The original meaning of "religion" is "to be bound," which seems to be Levinas's aim: "What distinguishes thought directed toward a thing from a bond with a person is that in the latter case a vocative is uttered: what is named is at the same time what is called."[43]

But what can this "call" mean? Have we in the West ignored the blight of Ebola because we have grown inured to the list of tragedies that are associated with all parts of Africa—starvation, genocide, civil war, AIDS, rape, and genital mutilation? Deadly viruses, rampant destitution: such is what happens *there*, in those countries, on the farthest planets. Is it possible to bring Saah Exco into my sphere of memory without victimizing him again, without adding to his tragedy by designating him as another anecdote of what happens *to them*, over *there*? Can he affect me without the power dynamic within the privilege of continuing with my day, crossing off the things on my to-do list, forgetting about him? Levinas warns us of the problem of possession that occurs in encounter, when the Other becomes an object of use, and his image captured in a photograph becomes an object to possess and display. Again, the depth of his suffering is neglected, creating a greater distance.

Considered further, I must ask whether my concern for his suffering is more precisely the interest to limit my involvement; he and the virus, the poverty, the layers of colonial and postcolonial manipulations that have placed millions in the absurd situations of child soldiers and child brides. I can keep Saah Exco at arm's length because he has died a world away, while hundreds of immigrant children from Mexico and Central America populate detention centers not an hour's

---

41. Levi, preface to "If This Is a Man." See also James Hatley's use of Levi's preface in *Suffering Witness: The Quandary of Responsibility after the Irreparable* (Albany, NY: SUNY Press, 2000), 11.

42. Emmanuel Levinas, "Is Ontology Fundamental?," in *Entre-Nous*, 7.

43. Ibid.

drive from here. They may not be dying, but they are afraid and alone, awaiting deportation, caught within the web of our society's and our government's failure to provide refuge from the drug wars for which our society and our government, again in layers of colonial and post-colonial manipulation, are responsible. Because I benefit from this postcolonial economy and the worldview of white society, my responsibility is bound to that privilege. Even if I am not specifically to blame for the colonial history, the racism and economic disparities that existed before I was born, I am responsible for them because I have profited from them. My infinite responsibility extends to the distant Other because my privilege is based on the history that has created the illusion of distance. James Hatley observes, "Levinas distinguishes between guilt, which is the burden I or the other may carry for our specific actions in regard to the other, and responsibility, which is the burden on me of the other's vulnerability to suffering. This burden imposes itself before any action on my part toward the other as other were even possible."[44] Guilt should refer to more than my specific actions; it is channeled into the responsibility measured in terms of ethical involvement: what am I willing to acknowledge, what comforts am I willing to forego or give up? How involved will I become?

The danger in keeping those who suffer catastrophically at either physical or intellectual arm's length is in their use for my own gain. I have already benefited from the history that has constructed the distance between the catastrophe "over there." Such is called "instrumentalization." Instrumentalization of the victims of catastrophic suffering also refers to the possibility that I may take some perverse voyeuristic pleasure from the weight of the numbers of the dead, the gravity of their situation, the hopelessness of their stories. Theodor Adorno writes persuasively on this point: art runs the risk of turning victims themselves into works of art:

> When even genocide becomes cultural property in committed literature, it becomes easier to continue complying with the culture that gave rise to the murder. One characteristic of such literature is virtually ever-present: it shows us humanity blos-

44. Hatley, *Suffering Witness*, 104.

soming in so-called extreme situations, and in fact precisely there, and at times this becomes a dreary metaphysics that affirms the horror . . . by virtue of the notion that the authenticity of the human being is manifested there.[45]

Adorno here refers to the way culture has a tendency to whitewash catastrophic suffering as somehow justifiable in the context of a medium that shows the "triumph of the human spirit"—trivializing terror into a neat package with beautiful people doing brave deeds. Bravery is abundant right now in affected areas of West Africa, where nurses and doctors continue to serve the sick and dying at risk of their own lives. But it is a "dreary metaphysics," indeed, if we consider that the manifestation of this courage is *why* catastrophic suffering occurs. Neither should catastrophic suffering a world away be understood to give my comfortable life gratitude and meaning; such an interpretation is the worst kind of theodicy.

Saah Exco's story was one of the few individual stories captured by the media during the Ebola crisis in summer 2014. I am still, months later, haunted by his image. Can there be discourse about him in that alley without trivializing, instrumentalizing, or sentimentalizing him? I imagine a little boy brave enough to attempt to dress himself when he was so weak that his arms could barely raise his shirt over his head, his persistence to live when many of his family had died. I would not be aware of his particular dignity had I not seen his photograph and heard the testimony of those witnessing his last moments. But his suffering surpasses my imagination, surpasses the image in the photographs, and his silence in death means he will never be able to represent himself, to discuss his experience or reflect on it. Saah Exco's dignity is not constituted in victimization by the history of colonialism and poverty: his alterity must not be defined only by his suffering, even though he suffers needlessly, catastrophically, and without purpose. He is more than a victim of Ebola, more than an unfortunate casualty of Western oppression, more than one of the uncountable and uncounted who succumb to preventable disease and malnutrition every year. Rather, his existence

45. Adorno, "Commitment," in *Can One Live After Auschwitz?*, 252–53.

is both prior to and indicative of something beyond, something infinite, which can only be learned in encounter, in the face-to-face. His face displaces my existence: his face demands something of me. In this disturbance, I confront something infinite, something beyond my capabilities, something I will never understand or resolve. In this disturbance by alterity, by his otherness, I am no longer free to be what I was; I am called to more than what I thought was good or ethical, again called to something infinite. He must be more than a statistic, more than a victim, more than a symbol or theme: he must be he himself, and this very reality is beyond my comprehension, drawing me deeper into the ethical responsibility which, according to Levinas, structures subjectivity, such that each human relationship is a relationship of equals that reveals infinite responsibility.

Levinas writes, "The Other as other is not only an alter ego. He is what I am not: he is the weak one whereas I am the strong one; he is the poor one, 'the widow and the orphan.' There is no greater hypocrisy than that which invented well-tempered charity. . . . [W]hat is essential is that he has these qualities by virtue of his very alterity."[46] Levinas states this not to create binaries of oppositions (weak vs. strong) but to underscore the alterity with which we confront each other; the alterity we experience in the encounter with the Other is the realization that the Other, the transcendent, will always be just beyond my grasp or comprehension.

The chasm of otherness between this boy and myself is reflected in the chasm between those who in terror were physically present in that alley but were unable to touch him during his collapse. The dichotomy between healthy and sick in which to be sick is a threat to the lives of the healthy makes the chasm of alterity impossible to cross. Part of the responsibility to witness is recognition of this chasm of difference and the utter inability to bridge it, to continue to witness and persist in the attempt to alleviate catastrophe. Levinas calls the face-to-face "an ultimate situation" because separation and transcendence "form the fabric of being itself": reflection on this encounter "involves a calling into question of oneself, a critical at-

---

46. Emmanuel Levinas, *Existence and Existents*, trans. Alphonso Lingis (Pittsburgh, PA: Duquesne University Press, 2001), 98.

titude which is itself produced in face of the other and under his authority."[47] Without this critical reflexive stance, the Other is merely one of my representations, an image for my amusement or dominance, for my well-being, which assimilates the Other into the self, the "Same."

Saah Exco and the countless others who have died nameless to me from Ebola, from AIDS, deserve that there is witness and desire to alleviate their suffering. Only "God" can suffer the agony of the Other, only the transcendent can intimately occupy the depth of his pain. Only God as Infinite, as beyond individuality and subjectivity, fully shares catastrophic suffering. God's very existence is bound to the dynamic of witness, responsibility, and kenosis. This is where the doctrine of the incarnation is understood, where it lives and makes sense, in the discipline of "letting go"—the emptying of the self for the Other—and engaged through praxis, in worship, spiritual discipline, and the work of justice but expressed through the sacred dimension of art. "Kenosis" is one of the ways the earliest followers of Jesus celebrated the divinity they experienced through him; it signifies the way to relationality, whether for divine or for human persons. Emptying the self of the false self attached to the things of an impermanent world grounds compassion. In Jesus, Christians find not only the revelation of how to empty the self for the Other as a human being but also that God to be God must be self-emptying and Other-oriented. This is the meaning of communion as *suffering-with* in terms of relationship or *suffering-as* in terms of incarnation. God shoulders the suffering, incarnating Godself through the unexpected: an ordinary peasant who died alone.

Witness and Theodicy

Witness here understood necessitates the overcoming of theodicy, the philosophical justification of evil and catastrophic suffering as necessary in some way to the divine will or "plan of salvation." Theodicy is the product of thinking about God in causal terms, as the

---

47. Levinas, *Totality and Infinity*, 81.

one who controls the forces and events of the world or universe. A virus with the destructive capability of Ebola, an earthquake that levels Port-au-Prince: theodicy's classical philosophical trajectory argues that God must have *wanted* such events to devastate human populations, and if God as the source of all good desired or allowed these events, God must have a "good reason" for being behind them. This leads to salvation theories: if Haiti didn't have voodoo in their culture, if the poor worked harder to bring themselves out of poverty, if people went to church, if they prayed better or more often—the victims could be spared such catastrophes, or they would see these catastrophes as educational opportunities that lead to salvation and a more comfortable and secure way of life. These are tired arguments, worn threadbare from overuse without critical reflection, hauled out on CNN by the token religious representative, most often Christian, every time there is another disaster.

Theodicy has onto-theological roots, conceiving God on the horizon of being, power, and causality, as if God were a cosmic power supply, John Caputo explains.[48] The fault in onto-theological thinking, and its by-product, theodicy, is that it justifies the un-justifiable—turning catastrophe and disaster, or "evil" in some definitions—into a good, something desirable, something *beneficial*. By justifying what is unjustifiable, onto-theological thinking has become the white oppressor's organizing cry: "you who are slaves, who die of malnutrition, who are the casualties of capitalism, suffer now because there is a better world beyond this one." The practice of theodicy, of justifying catastrophe and evil as belonging to the benevolent plan/will/act of God, has insidiously promoted more violence, more racism, more exclusion. James Cone writes, "Through cultural and religious imperialism, Europeans imposed their racist value system on people of color and thereby forced them to think that the only way to be human and civilized was to be white and Christian. It not only makes the oppressed want to be something other than they are but also to become like their oppressors."[49] Why

---

48. Caputo, *The Weakness of God*, 40.

49. James Cone, "Theology's Great Sin: Silence in the Face of White Suprem-acy," in *The Cambridge Companion to Black Theology*, ed. Dwight N. Hopkins and Edward P. Antonion (Cambridge, UK: Cambridge University Press, 2012), 144.

would the oppressed wish to become the oppressor?—because that's where the power is, especially power perceived as closer to the divine. Theodicy has turned the tables on those who suffer catastrophically, making Jesus' admonitions to prioritize the oppressed into something that rings hollow in the marble palaces of white Christianity; theodicy has no purpose in a Christianity that seeks to alleviate suffering, transforming unjust power structures into societies promoting equality and peace.

The placing of another's needs before my own is termed "substitution" by Levinas; more than sympathy or empathy, "substitution entails bringing comfort by associating ourselves with the essential weakness and finitude of the other; it is to bear his weight while sacrificing one's interestedness and complacency-in-being, which then turn into responsibility for the other."[50] Substitution is an essential aspect of the maternal relationship; for many mothers, assuming the overwhelming vulnerability of the newborn child is experiencing responsibility for another as something that exceeds the boundaries of what is reasonable or even possible. This is for Levinas the blueprint of *human* ethical interaction and so is not merely the domain of biological mothers. He writes, "In proximity to the absolutely Other, the stranger whom I have 'neither conceived nor given birth to,' I already have on my arms, already bear, according to the Biblical formula, 'in my breast as the nurse bears the nursling.'"[51] Assuming maternal identity in the care of a child means that maternal identity is forever after bound to the subjectivity of the self, even if the child dies. The Infinite is then approached indirectly as the perseverance of the human person in the face of an unfathomable Other, resisting the perhaps more instinctual tendency to be only for myself: "When can a positive sense be given to this negative notion? When I am turned toward the other [person] and called not to leave him alone. It is a turning contrary to my perseverance in being. This is the circumstance in which God has spoken."[52]

50. Jill Robbins, ed., *Is It Righteous to Be? Interviews with Emmanuel Levinas* (Stanford, CA: Stanford University Press, 2001), 228.

51. Emmanuel Levinas, *Otherwise than Being: Or Beyond Essence*, trans. Alphonso Lingis (Pittsburgh, PA: Duquesne University Press, 1998), 91.

52. Ibid., 101.

We have examined the problem that comes with witnessing the "dark field" of another's experience in catastrophic suffering. Such a void is a place of wildness—radical alterity from my own perceptions and experience—that is openness to alterity and so desire for the divine. Witnessing catastrophic suffering is a foundational experience of this alterity, since it places my own experience of the world in question and demands a response; whether one is indifferent or profoundly affected in witness, catastrophic suffering stakes a claim on all involved. In the divine-human relationship, the only response is substitution, as Levinas urges us to understand Isaiah 65:24 literally: "Before they call, I will answer; while they are still speaking, I will hear." He explains, "In approaching the other I am always late for the meeting. But this singular obedience to the order to go, without understanding the order, this obedience prior to all representation . . . this responsibility prior to commitment . . . [is] inspiration and prophecy, the passing itself of the Infinite."[53] Our response refers to the degree of ethical involvement; for Levinas, ethics as the language of response to the Other precedes any critical reflection. "Witness," asserts Levinas, "is humility and admission; it is made before all theology; it is kerygma and prayer, glorification and recognition."[54]

As kerygma and prayer, witness is more appropriate to the poetic and other forms of artistic discourse. Harold Schweizer recognizes that art is as "irreducible to analysis as suffering" while being essentially related to it: "[N]either art nor suffering . . . permit us to become pure, disinterested subjects of knowing in their presence."[55] Suffering and art are linked through a crisis of meaning and communication: "By virtue of its irreducibility to meaning or explanation, by its very refusal to function according to the laws of reason or logic, art acquires an opaque materiality like the body in pain."[56] Art, suffering, the question of God and the possibility of transcendent meaning are all experiences impossible to fully comprehend or articulate.

53. Ibid., 150. Italics in the original.
54. Levinas, *Otherwise than Being*, 149.
55. Schweizer, *Suffering and the Remedy of Art*, 2.
56. Ibid.

Theology is irresponsible unless it considers the persistence of catastrophic suffering as its context and art as a medium; as Adorno reminds us, "hardly anywhere else does suffering still find its own voice, a consolation that does not immediately betray it."[57]

The question before us now is whether visual art assists in, or takes the role of, prophetic witness in the possibility of the displacement of the self; might visual art act as prophetic exhortation? Art, especially visual, was historically undervalued in the West as a medium for theology until the twentieth century, when abstract art was explored by Paul Tillich as a way to dislodge the propositional truth claims of language and representation that formed the matrix in which two world wars, or indeed, any war, is described as "inevitable."

Art by its nature resists the easy interpretation. Theodor Adorno begins his *Aesthetic Theory* with the pronouncement, "It is self-evident that nothing concerning art is self-evident anymore, not its inner life, not its relation to the world, not even its right to exist."[58] This relates to Adorno's deliberately nebulous concept of authenticity, which he argues is impossible after Auschwitz: "[T]he authentic artists of the present are those in whose works there shudders the aftershock of the most extreme terror."[59] This "shudder" is the response to the suffering world that vibrates in the work of art genuinely attentive to the age of spiritual anxiety and ambiguity in which we live.

Max Paddison reminds us that for Adorno, art is related to a crisis of meaning that especially followed the horror of the Shoah: "Authentic art rejects handed-down meaning through negation, to the

---

57. Adorno, "Commitment," 252.

58. Theodor W. Adorno, *Aesthetic Theory*, ed. Gretel Adorno and Rolf Tiedemann, trans. and ed. Robert Hullot-Kentor (Minneapolis, MN: University of Minnesota Press, 1997), 1.

59. Theodor W. Adorno, "Jene zwanziger Jahre," in *Eingriffe, Gesammelte Schriften*, vol. 10, pt. 2 (Frankfurt: Suhrkamp, 1977), 506, translated by Max Paddison as "Authenticity and Failure in Adorno's Aesthetics of Music," *The Cambridge Companion to Adorno*, ed. Tom Huhn (Cambridge, UK: Cambridge University Press, 2004), 199.

effect that it appears to elevate meaninglessness itself in place of meaning, thereby becoming meaningful in spite of itself."[60] Nothingness, the nihil, becomes the frame of meaning. In this sense, Adorno understands "authenticity" in works of art to reflect awareness of the context that robs art of its authenticity: this paradox is the attempt of art to attain the pure, unmediated "truth" when all truth is mediated. So even the nihilist seeks meaning while claiming that there is none. Otherwise, works of art rely on traditionalist stereotypes, affirming accepted meaning as if it were unproblematic, conforming to the status quo.[61] Authenticity in art for Adorno thus pertains more to the paradox between coherence and incoherence, between integration and brokenness, than to an achievement of either: he writes, "[T]he more rigorously and ruthlessly works of art insist on their spiritualization, the further they distance themselves from what is supposed to be made spiritual."[62] Authenticity in art refers to a willingness to embrace the paradox and contradictions of the spiritually ambivalent contemporary world; if art is indeed possible, for Adorno, it lives in this tension.

The historical situation is inseparable from the artwork; the artist is compelled to respond to his or her own context. The context of the twentieth into the twenty-first centuries is both the inheritance of the modern period—the rise of science and decline of religion—and the proliferation of organized violence as well as corporate devastation of the environment and native communities implemented with unprecedented efficiency. For all gained through science and industry, there has been no corresponding mitigation of the suffering of human beings. The "reason" or "advancement of thought"[63] promised by the Enlightenment of the seventeenth and eighteenth cen-

---

60. Paddison, "Authenticity and Failure," 199.

61. See Ibid.

62. Theodor W. Adorno, "Art and the Arts," in *Can One Live after Auschwitz? A Philosophical Reader*, ed. Rolf Tiedemann, trans. Rodney Livingstone et al. (Stanford, CA: Stanford University Press, 2003), 373.

63. Max Horkheimer and Theodor W. Adorno, *The Dialectic of Enlightenment*, ed. Gunzelin Schmid Noerr, trans. Edmund Jephcott (Stanford, CA: Stanford University Press, 2002), 1.

turies is turned on its head when a chemist can casually stroll into his workaday laboratory and invent napalm. This contradiction, of ordinary people living in quiet suburbs and using technological expertise that results in mass suffering, indicates that "progress" has become regression. Indeed, taking seriously the trajectory of Western history, rationality, or at least the promise of science and reason, has collapsed into barbarism when from the technological advancements of detached drone warfare to the reliance on cheap and inhumane labor for the advancement of capitalism, the "progress" promised by the Enlightenment has only resulted in more suffering in human and nonhuman existence, not less. Adorno writes, "What the philosophers once knew as life has become the sphere of private existence and now of mere consumption, dragged along in an appendage of the process of material production, without autonomy or substance of its own. . . . Our perspective of life has passed into an ideology which conceals the fact that there is life no longer."[64]

Hence the "crisis of meaning" that engages the creative process: responding to the suffering world has always been integral to the artistic endeavor, but the specifics of time and place in the contemporary sense must include not only the escalation and intensification of the catastrophically suffering world but also the failure to adequately reflect on its impact on all of us. Art, poetry, music, and other creative endeavors may be our best hope for a way to begin this reflection, as Harold Schweizer argues, due to art's "refusal to function according to the laws of reason and logic. . . . Like the suffering body, the meaning of art is in its non-referential autonomous dimension, its own subjective temporality and irreducible particularity."[65] As that which mediates material and spiritual, amorphous and particular, contextual and general, abstract and figurative, art enhances our witness to the incommunicable and incomprehensible suffering of the Other. Art is where the emotional and non-rational intersect with the reflective and expressive.

---

64. Theodor W. Adorno, *Minima Moralia: Reflections on Damaged Life*, trans. E. F. N. Jephcott (London: Verso, 2005), 15.
65. Schweizer, *Suffering and the Remedy of Art*, 2.

The Gnadenstuhl *Motif in Art*

David Tracy observes that the only way human beings can comprehend redemption is through the "reality of the infinite, qualitative distinction between that God and this flawed, guilty, sinful, presumptuous, self-justifying self."[66] "Incarnation" may be understood in the divine traversing this field of distinction and otherness in an emptiness of no-self, such that mirroring the journey through this field is how the divine is incarnate in us. The exploration of this field means witness to those who catastrophically suffer through a heightened sensitivity to the alterity of the Other. Tracy notes that for Jürgen Moltmann, the cross represents divine identity with the forsaken and those who catastrophically suffer: "The cross, as cross, exposes the contradictions in the present, the non-identity of the present with God's Word, the need for a theological negative dialectics."[67] The cross is the event in which God takes the absurdity of catastrophic suffering into God's life and being and so is a moment in which we may witness God's solidarity with those who suffer. Otherwise, the cross is draped in triumph and perpetuates the violence that led to it.

Yet, the relationship between suffering and God from the perspective of the expression in visual art often occurs in a visceral and experiential way. Visual art illuminates something of both the ordeal of suffering and the depth of the divine witness to it; the *Gnadenstuhl* motif in visual art is a particularly poignant way of revealing the meaning of divine and human witness to catastrophic suffering. Recognizing that the popularity and development of the motif occurred alongside one of the greatest epidemics in human history, the bubonic plague, provides the historical context that facilitates a critical appropriation of the image when witnessing to the suffering of those from the Ebola and AIDS viruses today. Although the motif fell out of favor as did most depictions of Christian religious figures in the latter half of the nineteenth century, the emotional and theo-

---

66. David Tracy, *The Analogical Imagination: Christian Theology and the Culture of Pluralism* (New York: Crossroad, 1986), 415.

67. Ibid., 416.

logical impact of the image is profound, especially in person, whether one views the works in context (such as in a church) or in a museum gallery. The appeal of a medieval motif for Christology today occurs in an aesthetics of vulnerability, in an effort to glimpse that the emptiness of divine being is not absent from the absurdity of catastrophic suffering.

This exercise in interpretation is an experiment: relying on art to articulate the impact of the idea of incarnation is an attempt to take art seriously as material for theological investigation. The *Gnadenstuhl* or "Mercy Seat" or "Throne of Grace" motif in Christian art can then be critically correlated to contemporary Christology. *Gnadenstuhl*, as a name for the motif, derives from Martin Luther's 1534 translation of the Bible,[68] specifically Hebrews 4:16, "Let us therefore approach the throne of grace with boldness, so that we may receive mercy and find grace to help in time of need." Although little has been written about the *Gnadenstuhl* motif, regarding both its significance in the history of art as well as its potential significance in theological reflection, its compelling emotional presentation and fascinating combination of scriptural, doctrinal, and liturgical allusions deserves consideration in both regards.[69] In this motif, God the Father is usually seated, in early examples on a throne, and supports the dying or dead Christ, in some examples on the beams of a cross, in others without the cross

---

68. According to Wolfgang Braunfels, Franz Xavier Kraus identified this connection between Martin Luther and the term; see *Die Heilige Dreifaltigkeit*, Lukas-Bücherei zur Christlichen Ikonographie, Band 4 (Düsseldorf: L. Schwann, 1954), 35–37. In 1534, Martin Luther used *Gnadenstuhl* in Exodus 25:21-22 and translated Hebrews 4:16, "Darum laßt uns hinzutreten mit Freudigkeit zu dem Gnadenstuhl, auf daß wir Barmherzigkeit empfangen und Gnade finden auf die Zeit, wenn uns Hilfe not sein wird." Luther uses *Gnadenstuhl* in Romans 3:25 as well, translated in the NRSV as "sacrifice" or "place" "of atonement." See *The Luther Bible of 1534*, ed. Stephan Fussel, www.ccel.org/ccel/bible/ delut.all. html#i. The notion that the cover on the Ark of the Covenant held the same significance as the Christian altar, according to the motivation behind Luther's translation of *kapporeth*, is Braunfels's assertion.

69. François Bœspflug, *La Trinité dans l'Art d'Occident (1400–1460)* (Strasbourg: Presses Universitaires de Strasbourg, 2000) includes some history of the motif. This work continues the project begun in *Dieu dans l'Art* (Paris: Les Éditions du Cerf, 1984).

in a pietà-like composition. The Holy Spirit, usually represented by a dove, is between the Father and Son or among the figures elsewhere in the composition.[70] Whether or not the actual cross is present, the unifying thread of nearly all the works of art that utilize the *Gnadenstuhl* motif is the theme of a unity between heaven and earth in the passion of Jesus, such that his experience of catastrophic suffering affects all three divine persons. Just as heaven and earth join to praise God in the liturgy, emphasized in the Jewish mystical traditions that led to the insertion of the *Sanctus* in the eucharistic anaphora, heaven and earth join to mourn the death of the Son of God in solidarity with all those who suffer catastrophically. The shared passion of heaven and earth in the *Gnadenstuhl* motif is thus supported by a complex set of symbols that derive from Jewish Throne-Chariot or *Merkabah* mysticism[71] and the visions of Ezekiel, Isaiah, Daniel, and the author of Revelation.

---

70. The *Gnadenstuhl* motif, as nearly every artistic and textual description of the triune God, predominately uses "two men and a bird" to represent the three divine persons, sometimes even cloaking the Father in papal attire. For the purposes of this chapter, we will table these idiosyncrasies, evident in nearly all medieval art in the West, in the hope that new artistic interpretations, more inclusive and daring to contemporary sensibilities, might continue to arise. There have been attempts at inclusive interpretations; two examples, one from the past and one from the present: a twelfth-century fresco in St. Jakobus Kirche in Urschalling, Upper Bavaria, Germany, seems to show the Father and Son flanking a female Holy Spirit. It was covered up (of course) and later interpreted as the three angels who visit Abraham and Sarah in Genesis 18. In Port-au-Prince, Haiti, a mural from 1951 in the Episcopal Cathedral of Sainte Trinité depicts Christ, appropriately brown skinned, on a cross and God the Father as an enormous eye to his left and possibly the Spirit as a tree shading him to the right. All the murals in Sainte Trinité are gorgeously colored, vibrant reminders of the liberating value of theology in context; they were damaged by the devastating earthquake in 2010 and are still undergoing restoration.

71. *Merkabah* mysticism, explains Timo Eskola, is characterized by heavenly journeys and throne visions; Gershom Scholem is credited with identifying this as the earliest form of Jewish mysticism. In the two centuries before the common era, *Merkabah* mysticism was associated with Jewish apocalypticism. From Ezekiel's vision emerged a hymnic tradition focusing on the seraphim and angels' praise of God. See Eskola, *Messiah and the Throne: Jewish Merkabah Mysticism and Early Christian Exaltation Discourse* (Tübingen: Mohr Siebeck, 2001), 1–3.

Some awareness of the motif's place in the history of Christian art is necessary; the persistence of this motif through the latter half of Christian history pertains to the artistic ability to translate difficult and abstract concepts into visual expression. It is important to remember that the crucifixion of Jesus is seldom portrayed before the Carolingian period. The little Christian art that survives before the Edict of Milan, such as in the Catacombs, depicts Christ as the "Good Shepherd" or in other symbols.[72] The earliest depiction of Jesus on the cross dates from the early fifth century, in a carved ivory relief juxtaposing Christ's death with Judas's suicide:[73] Christ as innocent does not suffer, while Judas as guilty writhes in pain. With the Carolingian period, from around 780 to the tenth century, the cross is victoriously adorned in jewels and gold, and if Christ is present on the cross, he is not shown to experience pain.[74] But the Gothic period sees a new interest in depicting the reality of Christ's suffering by contorting the body as it would have hung on the cross and in showing the torment

72. Early Christians were mocked for their reverence of a savior who was crucified a criminal. This is evident in a first-century graffito from Rome in which a crucified man with an ass's head is worshiped by a man with his arm outstretched; the Greek text scrawled beneath reads, "Alexamenos worships God." See http://faculty.bbc.edu/rdecker/alex_graffito.htm for the graffito and a description by Rodney Decker. Richard Viladesau explores how the cross went from a symbol of disgrace to the primary symbol of Christian faith in *The Beauty of the Cross* (Oxford: Oxford University Press, 2006), 20–55.

73. *Christ's Victory on the Cross*, ca. 420–430, carved ivory panel, British Museum. See Richard Harries, *The Passion in Art* (Aldershot, UK: Ashgate, 2004), 10–11.

74. Charlemagne's motto had been *Renovatio romani imperi*; this interest to revive the Roman Empire in union with the Church is apparent in works such as the magnificent cover of the Lindau Gospels, ca. 870, now at the Pierpont Morgan Library, New York; the imperial crosses, such as the Lothair Cross, ca. 1000, which was made for the Ottonian emperor (originally thought to be made for Lothair II) and contained gems from Roman *spolia*, now at the cathedral treasury in Aachen, Germany. The reverse of the cross contains a crucifixion scene with possible trinitarian allusions. There are exceptions to the triumphalism that permeates the age, such as the wooden crucifix of Archbishop Gero at the cathedral in Cologne, ca. 970. For more on such exceptions, see Celia Chazelle, *The Crucified God in the Carolingian Era* (Cambridge, UK: Cambridge University Press, 2001).

reflected in Christ's face. As interest in portraying the Passion increases, so also does an interest in reflecting the agony of Christ into the countenance of heavenly figures that surround the uppermost area of the composition, such as angels, or the grief of the earthly figures, primarily Mary the mother of Jesus and John the apostle; Mary Magdalene frequently appears grasping the foot of the cross, a river of flowing red hair covering her face. The persistent theme of a unity of heaven and earth, whether in the nativity scene or in scenes of the ascension of Christ or the assumption of Mary, appears in the century before and continues through the Renaissance.[75]

The History of the Gnadenstuhl *Motif*

The earliest known *Gnadenstuhl*, a French manuscript illumination ca. 1120 from Cambrai, a region in north-central France,[76] appears in the missal at the *Te igitur*, beginning the canon of the Mass, immediately after the *Sanctus*. "*Te igitur clementissime Pater*" is written across the bottom of this illumination: "You, therefore, most merciful Father," turning to the Father through Christ in the Spirit. In a similar *Gnadenstuhl* from Cambrai,[77] the cross forms the "T" of *Te igitur*. The *Sanctus*[78] is derived from Isaiah 6:1-3, in which the prophet

75. In the thirteenth and fourteenth centuries, this is observed, for instance, in depictions of the nativity, the annunciation, the ascension, and the theme of the Augustinian *City of God*. Giotto's frescoes on the interior of the Capella degli Scrovegni in Padua, ca. 1305, are a good example, especially the *Crucifixion*, in which the dying Christ is surrounded by angels above and mourners below, both heaven and earth in pain. Duccio (1255–1319) also adopts this iconography in his *Crucifixion*, as do many other Italian painters in the fourteenth century.

76. Manuscript illumination, Bibliothèque-Médiathèque Municipale de Cambrai; see Fides Buchheim, *Der Gnadenstuhl: Darstellung der Dreifaltigkeit* (Würzburg: Echter, 1984), 22.

77. Manuscript illumination, Bibliothèque-Médiathèque Municipale de Cambrai, twelfth century. See Ibid., 18.

78. "Sanctus, Sanctus, Sanctus, Dominus Deus Sabaoth; pleni sunt coeli et terra gloria tua. Osanna in excelsis. Benedictus, qui venit in nomine Domini. Osanna in excelsis." "Holy, holy, holy, Lord God of Hosts; Heaven and earth are full of your glory. Hosanna in the highest. Blessed is he who comes in the name of the Lord. Hosanna in the highest." The question of when and where the

sees God "on a high and lofty throne," the train of his garment filling the temple, surrounded by six-winged Seraphim; "with two they covered their faces, with two they covered their feet, and with two they flew." This vision is the basis for the "angelic sanctification," or *Qedushah*, "an extremely ancient part of the Temple liturgy,"[79] and occurs three times in the Synagogue Liturgy: before the *Shema*, before the third of the eighteen benedictions, and at the end of the service. The *Qedushah* commences liturgical preparation for the presence of God; the *Sanctus* commences Catholic consecration of the Eucharist.

The connection between the *Qedushah* and the *Sanctus* is likely the hymns of the *Yorde Merkabah*, which are based on the vision in Ezekiel 1:1–28.[80] Ezekiel is at the River Chebar,

Gnadenstuhl, Cambrai, 1120

Sanctus entered the eucharistic anaphora is a matter of some dispute among historians of the liturgy, but there is little question as to its Jewish origins. See Bryan Spinks, "The Jewish Sources for the Sanctus," *Heythrop Journal* 21, no. 2 (April 1980): 168–79.

79. Ibid., 171.

80. See Ibid., and Edward Hardy, "Kedushah and Sanctus," *Studia Liturgica* 6, no. 4 (1969): 183: "In a number of Jewish forms the *Kedushah* of Isaiah 6 is combined with the elements from the mystic vision of the divine chariot (*Merkabah* as later called) in Ezekiel 1. The *Merkabah*-mystics loved to dwell on the adoration of the divine majesty by myriads of angels, as expressed in the *Chayoth* (living creatures) and *Ophanim* (wheels) of Ezekiel 1 (with further suggestions from such passages as Daniel 7)." Elements of Jewish *Merkabah* mysticism appear as early as Qumran community texts from the first century BCE, as well as the Ethiopic book of Enoch and the fourth book of Ezra. First Clement,

in exile in Babylon. In the midst of a storm, out of a flash of fire, glowing from within, appears the moving chariot or *Merkabah* of God: the apparatus is described in vivid detail as carved of precious stones, traveling in the thrill of constant movement.

> As I looked, a stormy wind came out of the north: a great cloud with brightness around it and fire flashing forth continually, and in the middle of the fire, something like gleaming amber. In the middle of it was something like four living creatures. This was their appearance: they were of human form. . . . [T]heir wings touched one another; each of them moved straight ahead, without turning as they moved. As for the appearance of their faces: the four had the face of a human being, the face of a lion on the right side, the face of an ox on the left side, and the face of an eagle; such were their faces. . . . Each moved straight ahead; wherever the spirit would go, they went, without turning as they went. In the middle of the living creatures there was something that looked like burning coals of fire, like torches moving to and fro among the living creatures; the fire was bright, and lightning issued from the fire. The living creatures darted to and fro, like a flash of lightning. . . . And above the dome over their heads there was something like a throne, in appearance like sapphire; and seated above the likeness of a throne was something that seemed like a human form. (Ezek 1:4-26)

Walter Wink observes that this vision is so overwhelming for Ezekiel that he can barely contain the description in language, so he con-

---

composed around 95 and reflecting Jewish influence, writes about the use of the *Sanctus* in early Christian worship, combining the language of Daniel 7 with the angelic hymn of Isaiah 6: "For Scripture says: 'Ten thousand times ten thousand stood by him, and thousands of thousands served him, and they cried out, 'Holy, holy, holy is the Lord of Hosts; all creation is full of his glory.' Let us also, then, being gathered together in harmony with intentness of heart, cry out to him earnestly, with one mouth, that we may come to share in his great and glorious promises. For he says, 'Eye has not seen, and ear has not heard, and it has not entered into the heart of humanity, what great things he has prepared for those who patiently wait for him.'" *The Letter of the Romans to the Corinthians*, or 1 Clement, in *The Apostolic Fathers*, 2nd ed., ed. and trans. J. B. Lightfoot and J. R. Harmer (Grand Rapids, MI: Baker Book House, 1992), 67.

tinually qualifies his words.[81] Here is the origin of the notion of the Son of Man, argues Wink: the manifestation of divine reality is in "something that seemed like human form" and Ezekiel is addressed by God as *Ben 'adham*, "child of the Human One."[82] God's revelation as a human to Ezekiel implies for Wink that "only God is, as it were, really Human, and since we are made in God's image and likeness, we are capable of becoming more truly human ourselves."[83]

The wheels symbolize the dynamism of God's throne, the seat of divine presence, roaming the earth. This insight would have been especially significant to a people in exile, as Ezekiel notes in 11:16, "I have been a sanctuary for them in small measure in the countries where they have gone." The "spirit of the living creatures was in the wheels" (Ezek 1:20 and 21) of the throne chariot, as the force of its mobility.[84] Wink describes the wheels, dome, and rainbow as "circular symbols of wholeness."[85] Ezekiel 1:22-28 describes a platform over the wheels; God's throne and Yahweh Sabaoth in human likeness is above the platform.[86] The chariot is powered by the cherubim, each with four faces—human, lion, ox, and eagle—and four wings, which seem to only be able to work in concert. Christians later assigned the iconography of four creatures to the four gospels: the lion is ascribed to Mark, the human to Matthew, the ox to Luke, and the eagle to

81. See Walter Wink, *The Human Being: Jesus and the Enigma of the Son of Man* (Minneapolis, MN: Fortress Press, 2001), 24.

82. Ibid., 26, 31.

83. Ibid., 26. Wink cites the thirteenth-century French exegete Isaac ben Judah ha-Levi: "Let us make man in that very image that the Holy One, blessed be He, showed to the prophets in the form of an anthropos." Ibid., 280n40.

84. Wink cites Bruce Chilton's observation of Ezekiel's vision: "[B]ecause Ezekiel saw the throne of God as heavenly rather than earthly, and as moving rather than static, he was able to have his vision in exile in Babylon rather than in the holy land. Ezekiel's vision in exile comes, then, at one of the critical points in Jewish history, when the very survival of faith hung in the balance." Wink, *The Human Being*, 25.

85. Ibid., 30.

86. This platform is visible in many manuscript illuminations of the *Gnadenstuhl*, even when the wheels and creatures are not present. It seems to be associated with the throne, as it does not appear when the throne is missing. Early association between the throne and platform can be seen in the German *Altarpiece with Gnadenstuhl*, ca. 1260, Staatliche Museen, Berlin.

John. In Scripture, the only other places that mention visions of God's throne and the surrounding cherubim occur in Ezekiel 10, Isaiah 6, Daniel 7, and in the book of Revelation, especially chapter 4.

Throne-chariot iconography in Christian art occurs as early as a manuscript illumination of the ascension in the Rabbula Gospels, completed in 586 at the Monastery of St. John of Zagba, which was presumably near Antioch in what is now Syria. Here, Christ appears in the heavenly mandorla, surrounded by different angels, including the fiery seraphim of Isaiah's vision and the wheels and tetramorph of Ezekiel's chariot vision.[87] In the Syriac liturgy, Ezekiel 1 is read during the feast of the Ascension. This intersection of theophany, angelic praise, and ascensions to heaven is integral to the phenomenology of *Merkabah* mysticism.[88]

The earliest depiction of the *Gnadenstuhl* motif places the faces of the four creatures in the four corners of the 1120 manuscript illumination; God the Father is enthroned, supporting the cross of Christ between his knees. The Father, Son, and Spirit are enclosed within a mandorla, an ancient symbol that appears frequently in the history of Christian art. Formed by the common area of two overlapping circles, the mandorla gets its name from the Italian word for "almond"; in Latin it is referred to as the *vescia piscis*.[89] Rendering the mandorla refers to the union of opposites, such as earth and heaven,

87. The Rabbula Gospels, 586, Biblioteca Mediciae Laurenziana, Florence. The fiery red wings of the seraphim beneath Christ's mandorla are covered in eyes, recalling the vision in the book of Revelation 4:6: "Around the throne, and on each side of the throne, are four living creatures, full of eyes in front and behind." Nothing is known about the artist Rabbula; the Monastery of St. John of Zagba is not mentioned in any other Syriac codex. The manuscript has been in the Laurentian Library in Florence since the late fifteenth to early sixteenth century. It also contains the earliest known manuscript illumination of Jesus on a cross.

88. See Josep Ribera-Florit, "Some Doctrinal Aspects of the Targum of Ezekiel," in *Targum and Scripture: Studies in Aramaic Translations and Interpretation in Memory of Ernest G. Clarke*, ed. Paul V. M. Flesher (Leiden: Brill, 2003), 152.

89. Aurelie A. Hagstrom points out that this combination of terms, *vescia*, meaning "vulva," and *piscis*, meaning "fish," "demonstrates that a *vescia piscis* is not only a symbol of the vulva of female genitalia but also is a symbol of a fish seen vertically." Hagstrom, "The Symbol of the Mandorla in Christian Art: Recovery of a Feminine Archetype," *Arts* 10, no. 2 (1998): 25.

matter and spirit, image and concealment. Ancient pagan applications of the shape are meant to represent the womb, the doorway into another world; Christians borrowed the symbol to depict Christ's birth into glory.[90] From the Rabbula Ascension to the early *Gnaden-stuhl*, the notion of incarnation refers to the "coincidence of opposites, beyond the grasp of reason, and there to seek the truth where impossibility meets me," as Nicholas of Cusa observed in 1453.[91]

Furthering the feminine symbolism, the location of the cross in the 1120 Cambrai illumination suggests a birthing stool, a way of depicting the idea that the Son is begotten of the Father, whose presence dominates the composition, as happens in several early examples of the *Gnadenstuhl*. The reference to a birthing position is enhanced by the placement of the cross or the corpus between the Father's knees or legs. Although here and subsequently the bearded Father figure is clearly male, we may recall that the early church fathers enjoyed bending language used to describe the Father. Excessive and poetic language bends conceptual categories to that which is "outside" rational expectations: "We must believe," asserted the fathers of the Eleventh Council of Toledo, "that the Son is begotten or born, not from nothing nor from any other substance, but from the womb of the Father (*de Patris utero*), that is, from his substance."[92] Lucas Cranach later makes the "birthing stool" connection more explicit in a *Gnadenstuhl* within a heavenly mandorla in which the Father's cape becomes a smaller mandorla that appears to birth to the Son in an *Ecce Homo* ("behold the man") position.[93] The radiant mandorla

90. Ibid., 26.

91. Nicholas of Cusa, *The Vision of God*, trans. Emma Gurney Salter (New York: Cosimo Classics, 2007), 43.

92. *The Symbol of Faith of the Eleventh Council of Toledo*, in *The Christian Faith in the Doctrinal Documents of the Catholic Church*, ed. J. Neuner and J. Dupuis (New York: Alba House, 1982), 102–6, http://www.fordham.edu/halsall/source /toledo.txt.

93. Lucas Cranach the Elder, *The Dying. Heinrich Schmitburg's Epitaph for his Father*, 1518, Gemäldegalerie, Berlin. Cranach here and in *The Trinity Worshiped by Mary and St. Sebastian* appears to follow a particularly northern European trajectory, with the Father clasping the "Man of Sorrows" by the shoulders or under the arms. He repeats the iconography of the Master of Flemalle (sometimes identified with Robert Campin) and executes several fine examples, one

contains an inscribed reference to the Sanctus: *"Sanctus Dominus Deus Saba[oth]."*

The Cambrai composition is further enhanced by the placement of the Spirit as a "Holy Kiss" connecting the lips of the Father to those of the Son, maintaining their connection even in the Son's death. The Spirit in this *Gnadenstuhl* is a vital part of the composition, as the posture of the dove echoes the shape of the cross, underscoring the Spirit's dwelling with Christ, becoming, as Jürgen Moltmann describes, Christ's "companion in suffering." "The Spirit is the transcendent side of Jesus' immanent way of suffering."[94] The Spirit sustains all those who suffer. In Ezekiel, this divine presence is understood in terms of *Shekinah*, according to the Targum to Ezekiel.

The symbolism pertaining to *Merkabah* mysticism in relation to the *Gnadenstuhl* is also apparent in what Erwin Panofsky termed the "Anagogical Window" of the Benedictine Abbey Church of St.-Denis, near Paris.[95] Its iconography is the result of the reform instigated by Abbot Suger (1081–1151; Abbot from 1122–1151). Trinitarian symbolism infuses many aspects of St.-Denis: in the central of the three portals of the West façade, the tympanum contains a relief of God the Father cradling a lamb above an enthroned Christ, surrounded by angels carrying the instruments of Christ's torture. The Spirit, as a dove, hovers directly over the Father. It can be argued that the iconography of this

---

in grisaille in 1430, now at the Stadelsches Kunstinstitut in Frankfurt. This iconography is often paired with an image of the Madonna and child; in an example from the mid-fifteenth century, the Master of the Darmstadt Passion, active in the Middle Rhineland, places the dead Christ without the cross on the lap of an elderly God the Father on one side of a diptych and Mary cradling the infant Christ in the same angle on the other; at the Gemäldegalerie, Berlin.

94. Jürgen Moltmann, *The Spirit of Life: A Universal Affirmation*, trans. Margaret Kohl (Minneapolis, MN: Fortress Press, 1992), 62.

95. The "Anagogical Window," or "The Quadriga of Aminadab," from the Chapel of St. Peregrinus, Abbey of St.-Denis, ca. 1140–1144. Available at http://vrcoll.fa.pitt.edu/medart/image/France/sdenis/windows/Anagogical/Sdenwind-Anagog.html. Erwin Panofsky calls this the "Anagogical Window" because of Abbot Suger's interest to follow pseudo-Dionysius's "anagogical approach," or "upward-leading method." See Panofsky, *Abbot Suger on the Abbey Church of St.-Denis and its Art Treasures*, ed., trans., and annotated Erwin Panofsky, 2nd ed. by Gerda Panofsky-Soergel (Princeton, NJ: Princeton University Press, 1979), 20.

tympanum echoes the *Gnadenstuhl* motif captured by the Anagogical Window.[96] As in the Cambrai appearances of the *Gnadenstuhl*, symbols of the four evangelists adorn the corners of the Anagogical Window; and elsewhere in the stained glass of St.-Denis, in the Chapel of St. Cucuphas, is a window devoted to Ezekiel's vision of the new temple in chapters 40–41.[97]

Iconography connects the throne-chariot experienced by Ezekiel to symbolism of the Ark of the Covenant as the locus of divine presence. Throne or "seat" imagery first appears in Exodus 25 in descriptions of the building of the Ark of the Covenant (Exod 25:21-22). First Chronicles 28:18 refers to the Ark of the Covenant as "a golden chariot of the cherubim that spread their wings and covered the Ark of the Covenant of the Lord"; Ezekiel chapter 10 connects the ark with the throne of God. The tent of the tabernacle is visible in the Anagogical Window behind the *Gnadenstuhl* and appears in several later versions of the motif, especially in manuscript illuminations. Of the window's iconography, Emile Mâle writes, "The Ark, the tables of the Law, and Aaron's rod, which marked the first covenant of man with God, are only symbols of another covenant that was definitive. The Ark appears as a pedestal for the cross."[98] Abbot Suger furnishes an inscription on the window: "On the Ark of the Covenant is established the altar with the Cross of Christ; Here Life wishes to die under a greater covenant."[99] With this, the complex imagery of God

---

96. Although she does not connect the trinitarian imagery of the Anagogical Window to the tympanum of the West Façade, Paula Lieber Gerson notes the importance of the Trinity to Suger. See Gerson, "Suger as Iconographer: The Central Portal of the West Façade of Saint-Denis," in *Abbot Suger and Saint-Denis: A Symposium*, ed. Paula Lieber Gerson (New York: Metropolitan Museum of Art, 1986), 192–94.

97. How exactly these windows were arranged in Suger's time is still an unsolved puzzle; see Louis Grodecki, *Les Vitraux de Saint-Denis, étude sur le vitrail au XIIe siècle, Corpus Vitrearum Medii Aevi, France*, vol. 1 (Paris: Centre National de la Recherche Scientifique, 1976); see also Madeline Harrison Caviness, "Suger's Glass at Saint-Denis," in Gerson, *Abbot Suger and Saint-Denis*, 257–72.

98. Emile Mâle, *Religious Art in France: The Thirteenth Century*, trans. Marthiel Matthews (Princeton, NJ: Princeton University Press, 1984), 180.

99. Abbot Suger, *De Administratione* 34, in Panofsky, *Abbot Suger on the Abbey Church of St.-Denis*, 75. It should be noted that Suger's medieval supersessionism

enthroned, the mystical chariot, and the Ark of the Covenant come together in the original usage of the term "Mercy Seat."[100]

The lid on the Ark of the Covenant is where God "will meet with you" (Exod 25:22). Although it can be translated as simply "cover" or "lid," the Hebrew *kapporeth* is used exclusively in the Hebrew Scriptures to refer to the "Mercy Seat" on the Ark of the Covenant. As a verb, it means "to pardon," or "to atone for," as in "to cover a debt"; hence, "Yom Kippur," the day in which sin is "covered," or expiated. Fasting and abstinence are practiced to prepare for encounter with God, asking that God be the one to "offer *kapparah*," an opportunity to start anew.[101] Kabbalists compared this to Moses' removing his shoes before the burning bush because he had approached holy ground. To come before the Mercy Seat is to meet God, and so Yom Kippur is the most joyous of the Jewish feast days, the day in which the priest was permitted to say the name of God, to participate in God's nearness, and to enter into the divine identity.[102] Exodus 25:18-22 describes the placement of the cherubim on the Mercy Seat: "The cherubim shall spread out their wings above, overshadowing the mercy seat. . . . There I will meet with you, and

---

is evident here and in other motifs depicted in the stained glass around St. Denis, including the depiction of Ecclesia and Synagoga, in which triumphant Christianity is contrasted with a humiliated Judaism. This symbolism can be found throughout Europe; for more on this, see chapter 6.

100. In Revelation 11:19, with the coming of the messiah, the ark is restored to its place within the heavenly temple. Louis Grodecki, however, believes that the window's iconography is meant to reflect Hebrews 9, which asserts that Christ is both the high priest who offers and the sacrifice itself, whose blood replaces that of goats and calves, sprinkled on the Mercy Seat. See Grodecki, "Les vitraux allégoriques de Saint-Denis," *Art de France* 1 (1961): 26–30. See also Mâle's assertion that the chariot is from the Song of Songs 6:12, from where the inscription under the ark, "Quadrige Aminadab," is taken. "Honorius of Autun, a contemporary of Suger, explained that Aminadab, standing in the chariot, is the crucified Christ, and the four horses of the *quadriga* are the four evangelists," *Religious Art in France: The Thirteenth Century*, 452.

101. See Michael Strassfeld, *The Jewish Holidays: A Guide and Commentary* (New York: Harper and Row, 1985), 111.

102. See Franz Rosenzweig, *The Star of Redemption*, trans. William W. Hallo (Notre Dame, IN: University of Notre Dame Press, 1985), 324.

from above the mercy seat, from between the two cherubim that are on the Ark of the Covenant, I will deliver to you all my commands for the Israelites."

In the temple cult, this was understood as the point of contact between God and humanity, the locus of divine presence on earth; Timo Eskola explains, "[T]he throne is a metaphor of mediation. It stands at the crucial point where heavenly holiness and earthly sinfulness meet."[103] In this sense, the mysticism of the Second Temple cult has a decidedly incarnational aspect, an embodiment in a place, through the experience of being forgiven; divine mercy and the locus of a throne are linked in Isaiah 16:5, "And in mercy the throne shall be established." *Merkabah* mysticism appears in the oldest apocalyptic literature. The book of Enoch has a wide span of authorship, dating from 300 BCE to the second century CE; fragments were discovered in Qumran, as were liturgical references to the *Qedushah*, which supports Gershom Scholem's observation that "the earliest Jewish mysticism is throne-mysticism."[104]

God places the "Son of Man" on the divine throne in the book of Enoch, specifically in the section known as the Book of Parables (1 Enoch 37–71), which uses the term "Son of Man" interchangeably with "Messiah" and "Chosen One" and is identified with Enoch

---

103. Eskola, *Messiah and the Throne*, 59.

104. Gershom Scholem, *Major Trends in Jewish Mysticism* (New York: Knopf Doubleday, 2011), 43. Scholem notes the importance of Enoch and Ezekiel to the development of *Merkabah* mysticism: "The first chapter of Genesis . . . and the first chapter of Ezekiel, the vision of God's throne-chariot (the '*Merkabah*'), were the favorite subjects of discussion and interpretation which it was apparently considered inadvisable to make public. . . . The *hayoth*, the 'living creatures,' and other objects of Ezekiel's vision were conceived as angels who form an angelogic hierarchy at the Celestial Court. . . . [T]he main subjects of later *Merkabah* mysticism already occupy a central position in this oldest esoteric literature, best represented by the Book of Enoch. . . . [T]he earliest Jewish mysticism is throne-mysticism. Its essence is not absorbed contemplation of God's true nature, but perception of his appearance on the throne, as described by Ezekiel, and cognition of the mysteries of the celestial throne-world. The throne-world is to the Jewish mystic what the pleroma, the 'fullness,' the bright sphere of divinity with its potencies, aeons, archons and dominions is to the Hellenistic and early Christian mystics." Scholem, *Major Trends in Jewish Mysticism*, 43–44.

exalted to heaven.[105] The Chronicler records that when Solomon became king, "he sat on the throne of the Lord and all the assembly bowed their heads and worshiped the Lord and the king" (1 Chr 29:20-23).[106] Moses also shares the heavenly throne in the theophany on Sinai; similarly, the *Life of Adam and Eve* from the first century CE associates Adam with the heavenly temple, the chariot, and the glory of God."[107] This relates to the idea that Adam was witness to Wisdom before the Fall: "The Lord showed him the pattern of Zion before he sinned" (2 Bar 4:3). Josep Ribera-Florit notes that this aspect of Jewish mysticism stresses the "Adam-Temple-Throne of Glory" pattern, which refers to seven things created before the world: "Torah and repentance, the Garden of Eden and Gehenna; the Throne of Glory and the Temple and the name of the Messiah."[108] Because Christians understand Jesus as the Messiah, this pattern was appropriated in Christian visual imagery from the Middle Ages through the Renaissance; the *Gnadenstuhl* motif is a salient example.

Divine Wisdom is also portrayed in the Bible as sharing the divine throne. Richard Bauckham writes that God's Word and Wisdom assist God in the world but neither as figures separate from or "external" to God, nor as created beings, angels, or semidivine entities; rather, Wisdom and Word are *intrinsic* to the divine identity: "they express God, his mind, and his will in relation to the world."[109] Roger Haight points to the Wisdom Christology inherent in Colossians 1:15-20: the "background of this hymn is the wisdom tradition, and

---

105. See Richard Bauckham, *Jesus and the God of Israel* (Grand Rapids, MI: Eerdmans, 2008), 169.

106. See Margaret Barker, "Beyond the Veil of the Temple: The High Priestly Origin of the Apocalypses," *Scottish Journal of Theology* 51, no. 1 (1998).

107. Josep Ribera-Florit, "Some Doctrinal Aspects of the Targum of Ezekiel," 156: "When we were at prayer, there came to me Michael the archangel, a messenger of God. And I saw the chariot like the wind and its wheels were fiery and I was caught up into the Paradise of righteousness and I saw the Lord sitting and his face was flaming fire that could not be endured. Many angels were on the right and the left of that chariot," *The Life of Adam and Eve*, in James H. Charlesworth, *The Old Testament Pseudepigrapha*, vol. 2 (New York: Doubleday, 1985), 266.

108. Ribera-Florit, "Some Doctrinal Aspects of the Targum of Ezekiel," 156.

109. Bauckham, *Jesus and the God of Israel*, 17.

in it Jesus Christ is identified with Wisdom," notes Haight, which echoes Proverbs 8:22 and the book of Wisdom 8:4, in which Wisdom is an "associate in God's works."[110] This is similar to 2 Enoch 33:4, "there is no advisor . . . My Wisdom is my advisor."[111] Wink observes that Wisdom inspired the prophets to be catalysts for change, entering "into holy souls and make them friends of God, and prophets" (Wis 7:27) as "God's emissary sent to those never invited to the banquet."[112] Wisdom shares the throne of God because Wisdom is how God is revealed. The persistence of throne imagery from the mystical traditions in Judaism through Christian appropriations points to the possibility of a Wisdom Christology that offers an understanding of Jesus as "exalted," as in the kenosis hymn. Wink argues that Wisdom is how Christians may see Jesus as "the Son of Man/ Human Being": "but not the only Human Being. In our Father/Mother's house there are many mansions, with rooms for Moses, Elijah, Enoch, Metatron, Melchizedek, and—why not blurt it out—everyone who has served to reveal the Humanchild since history began."[113]

Wink points to Wisdom as inclusive in Jesus' understanding; in Luke 7:35, Jesus identifies with the "tax collectors and sinners" as children vindicated by Wisdom.[114] Wisdom as feminine in Jewish mystical tradition as well as Scripture itself indicates the acceptance of feminine aspects to the divine and the interest to bend conceptual and linguistic references to the divine. At the Basilica San Fedele in Como, Italy, a thirteenth-century Gnadenstuhl fresco of the enthroned Father with the crucified Son is placed adjacent and parallel to a depiction of St. Anne, the traditional mother of Mary. Anne cradles a miniature adult Mary on her lap, while Mary nuzzles the infant Jesus. Despite its age, the fresco's colors are still vibrant, while their symbolism is unusual: rather than assign the traditional red to

110. Roger Haight, *Jesus: Symbol of God* (Maryknoll, NY: Orbis Books, 1999), 169.

111. See Bauckham, *Jesus and the God of Israel*, 166.

112. Wink, *The Human Being*, 89.

113. Ibid., 229. Wink's use of inclusive language creates the term "Humanchild"; in an effort to be inclusive to our Muslim brothers and sisters, we should add Hagar and Ishmael, Muhammed and Fatima, to his list.

114. Ibid., 89.

God the Father, Anne is draped in a magnificent red cloak lined in gold over a brownish undergarment. Mary is in cobalt blue over red, while the figure of the Father is draped in a reddish brown over a lighter golden brown garment. The fresco of St. Anne with Mary is set above a representation of Mary alone in a striped mandorla, draped in the reddish brown of God the Father over her blue cloak. It is rare to find her alone in a mandorla without her child and without context as an assumption scene. Also revolutionary is that the figures of St. Anne and God the Father are the same size and are enthroned in the same position; the figures on the respective laps are smaller in scale, out of proportion. The motif here treats the heavenly actions of the triune God as mirrored in the earthly actions of the heritage of mothers who brought Christ into the world, and recognizes the maternal aspects of the divine.

Masaccio's Gnadenstuhl

Tommaso (Masaccio, "little Tom" or "clumsy Tom") Cassai da S. Giovanni di Mone (1401–1428) borrows the St. Anne with Mary and the infant Jesus motif (also called *Anna Selbdritt* in Germany, where it was most popular[115]) but depicts the figures as more lifelike in their size relative to each other;[116] working with his mentor, Masolino da

---

115. *Anna Selbdritt* literally means "Anne herself the third" or "Anne with two others." Virginia Nixon does not comment on the San Fedele fresco or the Masaccio version and offers this on the role of St. Anne in Italy: "Generally speaking, in Italy Anne does not appear to have been seen in terms of a joint link with daughter and grandson. In Florence, where levels of salvation anxiety seem to have been relatively low and where, according to Richard Trexler, relationships with saints tended to follow the patron-client model that is based on chosen rather than blood ties, Anne was not viewed primarily in terms of her ties with Mary and Jesus, and she had no special connection with salvation." Nixon, *Mary's Mother: Saint Anne in Late Medieval Europe* (University Park, PA: Penn State University Press, 2004), 64.

116. Masaccio, *Virgin and Child Enthroned with St. Anne and Five Angels*, 1424. Tempera on panel, 175 cm x 103 cm. Galleria degli Uffizi, Florence. It is a matter of scholarly debate which elements of the composition are Masaccio's and which belong to the more senior Masolino. Because of the San Fedele fresco comparing St. Anne to God the Father, I find similar elements here that refer to the enthronement of the *Gnadenstuhl* motif. Here St. Anne is clearly enthroned

Panicale, in Florence, the enthroned figures—Mary as the center of the composition, at a natural or relative scale, can no longer fit on her mother's lap, so she gets her own throne—are surrounded by angels, including seraphim. St. Anne was considered a "protectress" of Florence, and a festival dedicated to her celebrated the religious role of the guilds that formed the economic structure of the city.[117] Here, Anne casts an aura of protection in an outstretched hand, a gesture that attempts to extend into our space. The work was executed at about the time Masolino and Masaccio were beginning the project of a series of frescoes in the Brancacci Chapel of the Madonna del Popolo in the Church of Santa Maria del Carmine in Florence. But Masolino soon left Florence for Hungary, and Masaccio, just twenty-four-years old, was left to work out his particular style on his own.

This style would transform painting in Florence and so aid in mapping the landscape of the Renaissance, with the notion that the natural world is central to the divine life, placing God within the plane of human existence. Such an artistic insight is one of the most critical testimonies to the meaning of the incarnation, in addition to opening the conceptual door to an alternative to the hierarchical thinking that defined the medieval worldview. The frescoes of the Brancacci Chapel feature scenes in the life of Peter, the patron saint of the chapel's patron, as well as the story of the temptation and Fall. Michelangelo spent hours studying these frescoes; their influence can be seen in the Sistine Chapel cycle on the Garden and Fall

---

as well as Mary; the desire of the artist to maintain a natural scale of the figures in the composition meant that it became difficult to address how both figures would be enthroned, so although Mary is sitting between her mother's knees, St. Anne does not appear to have a throne of her own. The figure of St. Anne is not affected by the same light that illuminates the Virgin and child; some art historians have believed this to be indicative that Masolino is responsible for the figure of Anne, while the advancements in the portrayal of natural light illuminating the figures belong to Masaccio. While this is possible, it is also possible that Masaccio intended for St. Anne to recede into a shadowy, otherworldly realm. The angels do not form a mandorla, but the curtain which they draw back is an element in *Gnadenstuhl* iconography based on the curtain in the temple that was drawn to protect the Ark of the Covenant.

117. See John Henderson, *Piety and Charity in Late Medieval Florence* (Chicago: The University of Chicago Press, 1997), 215.

but fail to attain the heartbreaking demonstration of the pain of loss in Masaccio's *Expulsion from the Garden of Eden*. Masaccio depicts Adam's face buried in his hands as if he cannot bear the sight of the world outside the Garden, but Eve's face is turned upward, a contorted gash, her eyes like wounds, her scream audible. This is surely one of the most visceral expressions of suffering in all of Western art, anticipating Edvard Munch and the Expressionists of the twentieth century. Contrasted with Masolino's *Temptation* in the Brancacci fresco cycle, which is rather banal, Masaccio made it possible for artists to be distinguished from mere decorators. His depiction of Eve here represents an original moment in the self-understanding of the human person in art, as she embodies the vulnerability of newly discovered mortality, trying in vain to cover her nakedness, now indicative of this vulnerability.

A short time later, Masaccio depicts his version of the *Gnadenstuhl* motif as a formidable fresco in the Dominican church of Santa Maria Novella in Florence in 1427, before his departure for Rome in 1428 and untimely death.[118] The work was to have substantial influence on the direction of Italian iconography for the next two hundred years. His friend Filippo Brunelleschi (1379–1446)—who also designed the dome on Santa Maria del Fiore after a hundred-year search for an architect who could complete it—likely supplied the precision with which the one-point perspective of the enormous illusionistic barrel vault behind the figures is constructed.[119] In 1568, Giorgio Vasari was so impressed with the illusion that he declared it appeared as though there was a "hole in the wall." Everything about the work reveals a new era emerging in creative expression. Considered the earliest surviving example of systematic linear perspective, the parallel lines recede from the plane of the picture's surface in a "vanishing point," in this case at the foot of the cross, at about the eye-level of the viewer, as though the viewer is present at the scene; all the figures, from the

118. Giorgio Vasari, in his *Lives*, asserts that Masaccio was murdered, perhaps poisoned, writing that the motive may be "either by reason of envy, or because good things rarely have any long duration"; see Andrew Ladis, *Victims and Villains in Vasari's Lives* (Chapel Hill, NC: UNC Press, 2015), 67.

119. See Rona Goffen, introduction to *Masaccio's Trinity*, ed. Rona Goffen (Cambridge, UK: Cambridge University Press, 1998), 20.

donors to the saints to God the Father, belong to the same scale. The space of the viewer and the space of the scene intersect.

Although the scene makes no attempt at a historical rendering of the crucifixion, Masaccio strives for realism by placing Mary and John on the same platform as the cross with the figures naturally proportionate to one another. Mary is depicted as a stern, elderly woman, stronger here than in the fainting spells she frequently undergoes in depictions of the crucifixion in both late Gothic and into the Renaissance. Masaccio has also resisted depicting her romantically as young and beautiful. In her composure amid the gravity of the moment, she turns toward us, breaking the surface of the picture plane with an admonition and an upturned hand, the opposite gesture of St. Anne in the Uffizi composition. Rona Goffen suggests that Mary here appears to warn the viewer, as a "confrere of the order of Preachers, who offers her sermon near the pulpit from which the Dominicans themselves addressed their flock."[120] I don't see her as preachy, just angry. It is an unusual look for Mary in art; I cannot think of another depiction of her with an analogous countenance. Mary rarely looks directly at the viewer in Christian art. She is usually looking up, down, at Jesus, or her eyes are closed. For a figure to look directly at the viewer—remember that she is just above the viewer's eye-line—is an extraordinary statement for this time. Her stare bores through the picture-plane. She wants us to pay attention; she wants us to remember this. She wants the death of her son to mean something. She is part of a larger statement Masaccio makes about death: death accompanies even the grandest and most glorious human achievements. What makes this mausoleum so striking is that it forbids the weepy sentimentality that will creep into Christian art by the late seventeenth century. Masaccio could at least have thrown a few angels in there to lighten the mood; but no, the angels are *outside* this scene. Even Mary's traditional celestial blue is missing, the color Masaccio chose for her in the crucifixion scene of his Pisa polyptych of 1426; here she is draped in black rendered with violet undertones.

Indeed, all the celestial iconography typical of the motif has been removed. There are no allusions to the heavens, no starry sky. The

120. Ibid., 18.

color palette is red muted through black and white, with some midnight blue in the Father's cloak and in some of the squares of the barrel vault: somber in such a way that it is difficult to tell whether the fresco itself has simply deteriorated of its own mortality (and historically its "care" has bordered on abuse) or whether this was Masaccio's intention all along. Although the scene at first glance may appear triumphalistic because of the grandeur of the architecture, the impression when viewed in person is rather that of entering a mausoleum.

At the time, Florence may have felt like a mausoleum, given the ravages of disease, war, and famine. The first occurrence of the bubonic plague in Florence occurred in 1348, just a year after a devastating famine, according to Giovanni Boccaccio's *Decameron*, written between 1349 and 1371.[121] That occurrence in Florence alone claimed three to four-fifths of its citizens, according to tax records, often at a rate of five hundred a day. We will probably never know the exact numbers of the dead, since the death rate was higher among the poor. Death would occur within three days of infection and inflicted considerable agony, emotional as well as physical; it turned Florence into "a living Hell," according to Wayne Rebhorn: "People are trapped inside a city of the dead, forced to endure endless repetitions of the same sterile events that only provoke depression and despair." Florence had become "a city whose structures have collapsed . . . in which people are fundamentally disconnected from one another."[122]

---

121. Boccaccio (1313–1375) lived in Florence two years before the plague struck there the first time; as one who "straddles two ages without being fully part of either," Wayne Rebhorn notes in his translator's introduction to the *Decameron*, Boccaccio anticipates the secular direction of the Renaissance in the late fourteenth century and writes movingly of both the emotional and physical effects of the plague in Florence. Of the former, he writes that the devastation was such that even families abandoned each other, taking "one utterly cruel precaution, namely, to avoid the sick and their belongings, fleeing far away from them," even parents from children. Boccaccio, *The Decameron*, trans. Wayne A. Rebhorn (New York: W. W. Norton, 2013), 7. See also Samuel Cohn, *Cultures of Plague: Medical Thinking at the End of the Renaissance* (Oxford: Oxford University Press, 2009), 95–97.

122. Wayne A. Rebhorn, introduction to Boccaccio, *The Decameron*, xxxviii.

One cannot read these descriptions without recalling the devastation of Ebola in West Africa.

The medieval plague occurred in two predominant forms: one form infected the bloodstream, causing internal bleeding and buboes in the lymph nodes which would ooze and bleed; it spread via contact with bodily fluids. The other form was pneumonic, infecting the lungs and becoming airborne when the patient coughed; this form spread more quickly and was detected in Florence. Dementia and disorientation occurred in both types because of the rapidity of fluid and oxygen loss. So many died so quickly that there was no way to bury the dead as they died, and bodies remained rotting in the streets for days. Families resorted to burial in mass graves. This meant that it was common to die without being administered last rites or consecration during burial; Clement VI granted remissions of sin to all plague victims because few could be attended by priests.[123] "And no bells tolled, and nobody wept no matter what his loss because almost everyone expected death. . . . And people said and believed, 'This is the end of the world,'" wrote a chronicler from Siena.[124]

If the 1348 plague was not enough, Florence was ravaged by war and economic crisis in the late fourteenth century. When papal legates embargoed the export of grain from the Papal States to Florence, people starved; in 1375, Florence rebelled and formed a league against the papacy which grew to include most of Tuscany. Two years later, Cardinal Robert of Geneva—later to become Avignon Pope Clement VII—Pope Gregory XI's legate in Italy, ordered a massacre which slaughtered as many as five thousand, seized women for rape, and "what could not be carried away, they burned, made unfit for use or spilled on the ground."[125] This is called the "War of Eight

123. Barbara Wertheim Tuchman, *A Distant Mirror: The Calamitous Fourteenth Century* (New York: Random House, 1978), 95.

124. Ibid. A visit to Siena shows the nascent outlines for an expansion to their cathedral that would have made it double the size of Florence's Santa Maria del Fiore but the plague took half of Siena's citizens; there were no workers and no taxes to complete the project.

125. See Tuchman, *A Distant Mirror*, 321–22. See also Samuel Kline Cohn, *The Cult of Remembrance and the Black Death: Six Renaissance Cities* (Baltimore: Johns Hopkins University Press, 1992), 274–80.

Saints" (1375–1378), after a group of eight who were tasked with dissolving the sovereignty of the pope and the church's attempt to extract taxes and expand the Papal States into Tuscany.[126] The entire government of Florence was excommunicated by Pope Gregory XI and the city placed under interdict; it maintained an antipapal spirit through the next century.

The plague returned to Florence as well, over and over during Masaccio's short life.[127] A particularly severe emergence of the plague occurred the year Masaccio was born. Another outbreak in 1411 may have been what killed Masaccio's father before he turned thirty; the plague may have been what killed Masaccio in Rome before he turned thirty. Masaccio grew up surrounded by death and memories of death. Rona Goffen argues that Masaccio's fresco represents the resurrection,[128] but I see no allusions to Jesus' resurrection; the thesis only works in a general sense, as a distant hope. Rather, we see an extended meditation on the place of death in a world governed by human achievement. Death personified began to appear in Pisa's Camposanto around 1336 with Francesco Traini's *Il Trionfo della Morte* (*The Triumph of Death*); Orcagna includes a similar personification on a fresco in Florence's Santa Croce, which may be dated to the plague years.[129] In Masaccio's *Trinity* fresco, the skeleton depicted in the trompe l'oeil tomb below the *Gnadenstuhl* could be a plague victim.

126. See R. C. Trexler, "Who Were the Eight Saints?," *Renaissance News* 16, no. 2 (1963): 89–90.

127. See John Henderson, *Piety and Charity in Late Medieval Florence* (Chicago: The University of Chicago Press, 1997), 359–60.

128. See Rona Goffen, "*The Trinity* and the Letter to the Hebrews," in Goffen, *Massacio's Trinity*, 37. She argues that the iconography reflects the Father's offering of Christ as the eucharistic sacrifice.

129. Barbara Tuchman in *A Distant Mirror* includes the Traini fresco as an example of art post-plague (Tuchman, *A Distant* Mirror, 124) following Millard Meiss's thesis in *Painting in Florence and Siena after the Black Death* (New York: Harper and Row, 1964), but that same year, Joseph Polzer identified political figures from Dante's *Inferno* that implied a date of 1331–1336. Meiss, in response, altered his argument; see Joseph Polzer, "Aristotle, Mohammad and Nicholas V in Hell," *The Art Bulletin* 46, no. 4 (December 1964): 466; and Millard Meiss, "Notable Disturbances in the Classification of Tuscan Trecento Painting," *Burlington Magazine* 113 (1971): 178–87.

If the skeleton is a personification of Death or the plague victim of death, the entire iconography is all the more extraordinary. In this mausoleum of a world, God the Father holds the cross in place, stronger than Death, even the death of his Son, and the dove links the figures, a bright white flash of wingspan, the only ethereal element in the composition.

This all begs the question: what inspired Masaccio to implement the *Gnadenstuhl* motif in such a revolutionary way? Indeed, why choose the *Gnadenstuhl* composition at all? He could easily have shown off the architectural play of perspective with the crucifixion alone; but the presence of the Father and the Holy Spirit make the composition a *Gnadenstuhl*. Examining the several versions of *Gnadenstuhl* that formed a pattern in Florentine painting in the half-century leading to this, we better appreciate the creative audacity of this composition. Masaccio would certainly have been familiar with the work of the Florentine di Cione brothers, Nardo (d. 1366), Andrea (also called Orcagna, "archangel," d. 1368), and Jacopo (d. 1398). Each of the brothers executed a version of the *Gnadenstuhl* motif and all were commissioned work for Santa Maria Novella. The brothers were admirers of Giotto's move toward realism and dimension, and so follow the direction begun by Giotto,[130] but none makes the sort of creative leap into naturalism taken by Masaccio. Their versions of *Gnadenstuhl* are similar in style: all rely heavily on gold leaf for heavenly symbolism; the Father is represented as close in age to the Son and draped in blue over a red garment, supporting the cross while enthroned.[131]

---

130. Giotto (ca. 1265–1337) was a Florentine and a contemporary of Dante Alighieri who, in the *Purgatorio*, suggests that Giotto was associated with the older painter Cimabue, which Giorgio Vasari spins into a more detailed narrative. Vasari also tells us that Giotto did work at Santa Maria Novella in the late thirteenth century on a fresco of the annunciation and the suspended crucifix. With Giotto comes an interest to move away from the Byzantine influence to show sacred figures as removed from the emotion and materiality of the natural world. Giotto's later works in the early fourteenth century were for Santa Croce, the Franciscan church and "rival" to the Dominican Santa Maria Novella.

131. Although he was not to become as famous as Andrea (Orcagna) and Jacopo, Nardo creates a triptych that features a *Gnadenstuhl* in the center panel: the enthroned Father raises his right hand in blessing and rests his left hand on

Masaccio's God the Father, however, stands on a platform with his right toes visible and is not enthroned; the Father does not float or hover above the figures as in every other depiction of the Father in the century prior. The cross is planted in rock rather than floating above ground, and the Father and Son are equal in height and proportion. There is simply no historical precedent in the motif for what Masaccio has accomplished in his interpretation of the iconography and its theological implications, primary among them that God has not abandoned this world. Ursula Schlegel surmised that an enthroned God the Father refers to heaven and a standing Father refers to earth; John Moffitt points to Matthew 5:34-35: "Do not swear at all, either by heaven, for it is the throne of God, or by the earth, for it is his footstool" which recalls Isaiah 66:1.[132]

---

his lap, clutching what is presumably a Bible and does not touch the cross. This triptych was constructed in 1365 for the Ghiberti Chapel for the chapter house of the Monastery of Santa Maria degli Angeli in Florence, dedicated to St. Romuald, founder of the Camaldolese order. Nardo died a year later. The triptych is now in the Accademia in Florence. Orcagna's version, ca. 1367, now at the National Museum of Warsaw, is differentiated from the others by a more emotive expression of the Father and the Father's hand clasping the side of the Son. Jacopo places a *Gnadenstuhl* in the central pinnacle panel of a massive altarpiece centered on the Coronation of the Virgin in the central panel, now at the National Gallery in London but originally commissioned for the Church of San Pier Maggiore in Florence. The work was completed in 1371, with the collaboration of Nicolò di Pietro Gerini, who died when Masaccio was thirteen. Nicolò executes his own version of the *Gnadenstuhl* in 1400, using a lighter, brighter color palette except for the deep midnight blue of the Father's cloak: the enthroned Father supports the cross with both hands while the cross is planted firmly in the stony ground, flanked by a wealthy merchant family of Prato, who occupy a much smaller scale than the heavenly figures. The work is at the Musei Capitolini in Rome. Also attributed to Nicolò di Pietro Gerini is a *Gnadenstuhl*, ca. 1400, at the Vatican Pinacoteca. Judging from the color palettes of these works and the significant differences between the compositions, it is hard to believe they are by the same artist in the same time frame, but the tangle of relationships and attributions from six centuries prior is never easy to unravel.

132. See Ursula Schlegel, "Observations on Masaccio's Trinity Fresco in Santa Maria Novella," *Art Bulletin* 45, no. 1 (1963): 27; and John F. Moffitt, *Painterly Perspective and Piety: Religious Uses of the Vanishing Point from the 15th to the 18th Century* (Jefferson, NC: McFarland and Co., 2008), 100. Schlegel observes,

Within the presumably Brunelleschi-designed vault, the scene appears to take place as a ceremony—perhaps as a funeral—in any of the magnificent Florentine cathedrals of the fifteenth century. Heavenly or otherworldly allusions are replaced by the complex harmonics and symmetry discernible through human reason; not content to remove the Trinity from this world, Masaccio underscores the earthly dwelling of the divine but does not refer to the beauty of nature, as will become Leonardo da Vinci's concern. Rather, God is found within a human construct, devised through mathematical relationships frozen into architecture. In other words, even though each face in the work displays a different quality of accomplishment, whether serene acceptance on the face of the Son, austere appraisal on the face of Mary, or sober conviction on the face of the Father, the message seems to be that the scene itself takes place within, rather than detached from, the human world, perhaps even taking place within the human person.

Mortality is bound to even this most remarkable of harmonies: is it Adam's skeleton in the trompe l'oeil tomb? Such has been the predominant interpretation.[133] Is this a new rendering of the Adam-Temple-Throne symbolism that sustains much of *Merkabah* mysticism? If the skeleton in the tomb is indeed Adam, the architecture of a temple is clearly supplied in this fresco, as is the Throne of Glory or

---

"Although God's throne is in Heaven, the scene depicted by Masaccio has nothing to do with the heavenly realm, but rather with a sacred place on earth." She also argues that the iconography is that of the medieval church while stylistically, the fresco belongs to the Renaissance (Schlegel, "Observations on Masaccio's Trinity Fresco," 26), which is surprising, given the advancements in the characterizations.

133. Again, there is dispute on this point; according to Goffen, "[T]hat he is indeed Adam is undeniable. According to tradition, the first man was buried at the site where later Jesus was crucified." Goffen, *"The Trinity* and the Letter to the Hebrews," 48. She also points to Agnolo Gaddi's fresco cycle in Santa Croce in Florence (1388–1393), which illustrates this legend. Goffen's theological interpretation is far different from mine, since she interprets the blood of the cross as necessary to Adam's redemption. While this interpretation would have been more standard in fifteenth-century Florence, given the revolutionary aspects of Masaccio's expression of the *Gnadenstuhl* iconography, I believe that Masaccio was playing with something more than the standard.

Mercy Seat, even without the traditional, literal allusions to the *Merk-abah* and the Ark of the Covenant, the temple curtain, the four crea-tures, and the seraphim. Furthermore, Masaccio's haloes, symbolic of a sacred designation, do not follow visual art's precedent; rather than merely function as golden circles around the head, the haloes here follow the tilting of the heads in a naturalistic way, as though they were hats with wide brims. Such deficiency in heavenly or hier-archical authority may have been one of the reasons the work was covered for three hundred years.

In a further indication of the dismissal of authority, the inscription above the skeleton's tomb is not in Latin but in Italian: "I was once that which you are, and what I am, you also shall be." In the thirteenth-century legend "The Three Living and Three Dead," three young nobles cross paths with three decomposing corpses, who tell them, "What you are, we were. What we are, you will be."[134] Neither did the plague discriminate: in Francesco Traini's 1336 fresco, a heap of corpses shows "crowned rulers, a Pope in tiara, a knight, tumbled together with the bodies of the poor."[135] Is such a notion replicated by Masaccio as an existential caveat to the living of impending death? or an Athanasian statement of incarnation? Or both: God occupies the sphere of human existence that we might become God; the divine lives, even in the palace of death.

---

134. Tuchman, *A Distant Mirror*, 125.

135. Ibid. We should also note that Masaccio would have seen the Traini fresco when he was in Pisa painting the altarpiece for Santa Maria del Carmine, the Carmelite church, presumably just before he returned to Florence, ca. 1426. Only eleven panels of the polyptych survive, scattered all over the world. The crucifixion scene, now at the Museo Nazionale di Capodimonte in Naples, re-veals both a young experimenter and an astute awareness of the different ex-periences of the emotion of loss. Mary is in profile to us, her hands clasped tightly, pleading; John the apostle stares vacantly toward the left, his hands curled next to his face; Mary Magdalene is wailing at the foot of the cross, her back to us, her arms outstretched. It might be interesting to note that Traini also constructed a version of *Madonna and Child with St. Anne*, 1340–1345, now at the Princeton University Art Museum, in which Anne is draped in bright red and her huge body provides a shelter of sorts for Mary and the infant Jesus on her lap. Masaccio's version displays some stylistic similarities.

The Gnadenstuhl *and the Vulnerable Divine*

Masaccio, *Trinity*

Masaccio juxtaposes the shock of mortality—the human withered to bone—against the genius of the new—in his time, the marvelous mathematical achievement of Brunelleschian architecture and artistic perspective, as well as his own choice to depict human bodies with demonstrable solidity and authentic emotion. This is the paradox of incarnation, of the divine *within* human innovation and creativity, divine power contained not in the heavens or in the literally interpreted celestial visions of *Merkabah* mysticism but in the creation of a barrel vault. Notoriously difficult to construct above ground, a barrel vault is rumored to have been envisioned by Brunelleschi, in plans as early as 1428, for the nave of the Church of Santo Spirito, which is across the Arno, over the Ponte Santa Trinita, from Santa Maria Novella. Brunelleschi's death occurred nearly twenty years later, in 1446, as the stone for the church's construction was being delivered to the site. The heady excitement of what seemed possible in architecture was preserved by Masaccio in his *Trinity* fresco; what became actual in Santo Spirito is a flat ceiling of similar design to the Church of San Lorenzo, also designed by Brunelleschi. Barrel vaults of the length of the nave of Santo Spirito or San Lorenzo were abandoned out of practicality, perhaps, since they press so heavily against their walls that the walls require continuous abutment to absorb the downward and lateral thrust. The renovation of St. Peter's in Rome about a century later, sparing no expense, constructs in the nave the most impressive

example in the High Renaissance: a barrel vault twenty-seven meters—eighty-nine feet—in length.

Masaccio's work, in which mathematical perspective places the
viewer and the work within the natural world, signals an end to the
so-called Gothic style; his bold choice to place the three Divine Persons within a world governed by human reason is a theological statement that was dangerous enough to be covered up in the late sixteenth
century when Giorgio Vasari was commissioned by Cosimo I de
Medici, Duke of Florence, with permission of the Dominican friars,
to renovate Santa Maria Novella. Vasari covered Masaccio's *Trinity*
with an altar and a painting of his own, the *Madonna of the Rosary*.
There is some scholarly dispute on Vasari's motivations, after having
written admiringly of the work in his *Lives*; Masaccio's *Trinity* was
concealed for nearly three centuries, when it was discovered during
another set of renovations in 1861. In 1883, art historians Giovanni
Cavalcaselle and Joseph Crowe wrote that Vasari's actions constituted
"an unpardonable sin"; others note that the altar was constructed so
as to preserve the work.[136] While Vasari may have been pressured by
the Medici to suppress the revolutionary aspects of Masaccio's iconography, it is also possible that the late sixteenth century was not
a time the Catholic Church wished to promote the leveling of hierarchy. But images are in some ways more difficult to cover than words.
Masaccio's *Trinity* fresco continues to challenge what we think we
know about God because it insists that the divine, and the suffering
of the divine, occurs in our space and in our time.

The suffering of the divine is expressed in a more emotive content
in the pietà version of the *Gnadenstuhl* motif, in which the cross is
absent and God the Father supports the dead Son. This version appeared in French and Burgundian court painting from the late thirteenth century, notably in the *Pitié de Notre Seigneur* by Jean Malouel,
ca. 1400.[137] Although considered by the Louvre as simply a pietà, this

---

136. See Goffen, introduction to *Masaccio's Trinity*, 12; Ornella Casazza,
"Masaccio's Fresco Technique and Problems of Conservation," in Goffen, *Masaccio's Trinity*, 70.

137. Jean Malouel, *Pitié de Notre Seigneur*, ca. 1400. Tempera (?) on wood, 64
cm diameter. Musée du Louvre, Paris. Painted for Philip the Bold, Duke of
Burgundy, whose coat of arms appears on the reverse of the work.

work follows the *Gnadenstuhl* theme of the Father seated, bearing the lifeless body of Christ in his arms. The dove gently connects the heads of the Father and Son; angels on the Father's left form a throne for the Father, their faces each mirroring in heaven the sorrow of the earthly figures of John and Mary. Mary tries in vain to meet the eyes of her dead Son, cradling his arm as she did when she held him as an infant. The intricate interplay of slender fingers and hands provides a fragility that accentuates their helplessness and compassion.

The pietà version of the *Gnadenstuhl* motif becomes popular in the fifteenth century and dominates the usage of the *Gnadenstuhl* motif in the sixteenth century, when El Greco paints *The Holy Trinity* in 1577 as the uppermost component of the High Altarpiece of Santo Domingo el Antiguo in Toledo, above a larger painting of the Assumption of Mary. Perhaps he intended the composition as a bit of tribute to the pietà of one of his influences, Michelangelo, who had died in 1564. Michelangelo's sculpture *The Deposition* (ca. 1547–1553) is said to contain a self-portrait of the seventy-two-year-old in the face of the towering, hooded figure who supports the twisted body of the dead Jesus, whose body is in a position similar to El Greco's Christ in *Holy Trinity*.[138] The *Rondanini Pietà*, Michelangelo's last, unfinished sculpture, is of a standing Mary attempting to support the body of the dead Christ. But El Greco in Toledo combines influences toward a unique style. He had likely seen the *Gnadenstuhl* while he was in Italy; he may have also been inspired, as was Tintoretto's

138. Michelangelo's marble sculpture of the *Deposition* or the *Florentine Pietà* is in the Museo dell'Opera del Duomo in Florence. He seems to have intended this work for his own tomb. Constructing the work caused Michelangelo considerable anxiety, and he attempted to destroy it. There is some question as to the identity of the hooded male figure supporting the weight of Christ. Could it be Joseph of Arimathea? Nicodemus? Both play a scriptural role entombing the dead Jesus. No scholarly theory seems to have considered the possibility that this follows the *Gnadenstuhl* iconography and that the hooded figure is God the Father. In a drawing for Vittoria Colonna, he places Mary in an enthroned position, with the dead Christ between her knees in a cruciform position similar to the *Gnadenstuhl* iconography; two angels attend on either side. For a summary of the scholarship on this piece, see Moshe Arkin, "'One of the Marys . . . ': An Interdisciplinary Analysis of Michelangelo's Florentine Pietà," *The Art Bulletin* 79, no. 3 (1997).

Lamentation, by Albrecht Dürer's 1511 woodcut of the Trinity, which features a *Gnadenstuhl* composition similar to El Greco's. In El Greco's magnificent manipulation of the weight and power of Christ's body, the Father's grasp of the Son prevents his tumble forward into our space, back on our earth, thereby indicating that he belongs in our world as well.

But in the work of an unknown German master, who may be the Master of Sankt Laurenz, in Cologne, of whom several devotional works have been attributed,[139] we see a depth of sorrow on the Father's face that few who execute the *Gnadenstuhl* motif attain. Painted roughly contemporary to Masaccio's *Trinity,* here is the quiet, steady ache of loss, with none of the allusions to the victorious achievement of salvation that often occupy the notions of other versions of *Gnadenstuhl,* such as in Albrecht Dürer's Landauer Altar of 1511.[140]

The Master paints this and other devotional works in the gentler *Weicher Stil* or "soft style" of the "International Gothic" that was popular at the turn of the fifteenth century. This style appears in devotional works and altarpieces, emphasizing emotion and subtle, thoughtful realism. The celestial theme is represented in the angels who surround the divine persons in their grief. As often appears both in works implementing the *Gnadenstuhl* and in depictions of the crucifixion, these angels hold the instruments of Christ's torture:

139. Unknown Master, German. *Trinity.* Active 1415–1430 in Cologne. Oil on oak panel. 23.2 x 15.9 cm. Wallraf-Richartz Museum, Cologne. Featured on the cover of this book, the panel is attributed to the Master of Sankt Laurenz, the pupil of the Cologne Master of St. Veronica; this small panel was possibly the left wing of a diptych, with the Mater Dolorosa in the right wing.

140. Albrecht Durer's *The Adoration of the Holy Trinity,* the Landauer Altar, 1511; oil on lindenwood, 135 x 123.4 cm, at the Kunsthistorisches Museum, Vienna. This was the third altarpiece he constructed after his return from Italy. Here is all the glory of a church triumphant; the dove flies with wings spread apart directly above the papal mitre of the elderly Father. Female saints to the left are led by a crowned Virgin; a genuflecting John the Baptist leads prophets and kings from the Hebrew Bible on the right. The patron, Matthäus Landauer, is being welcomed into heaven by a cardinal. A self-portrait of Dürer (he created many; in one, he compares himself to Christ) is the only earthly figure, off to the right side with an inscription testifying to his work.

the flagellation column, the scourge, the stick with the sponge, and the lance. This image captures the heartbreak of both the Father and the Son, reflected in different ways. Father and Son are nearer in age than other versions of *Gnadenstuhl* of this period in northern Europe, which began to favor an elderly depiction of God the Father. But this version shows a familial resemblance in their facial features, while the paleness of Jesus' skin separates the living from the dead. Rather than cloaking the Father in heaven's bright colors, or in the traditional red of Byzantine icons, this Master paints the Father in coal gray, and standing rather than seated. The black gash in Jesus' side is emphasized against his smooth flesh, bleeding into the darkness of dried blood which cloaks the Father, enveloping Father and Son in a shape resembling a mandorla, against the gold atmosphere. The Spirit's placement preserves their bond, as in the earlier versions of *Gnadenstuhl* that portray the Spirit as a "Holy Kiss" between the Father and the Son. The Father and the angels surround the dead Jesus in our space, in our time. One can only imagine the devotional impact of this image during the upheaval and plague years of the early fifteenth century. The tenderness of the relationship between the Father and Son is somehow comforting, even while it reminds us of the suffering of the tortured.

Here we see that God has met our failed imagination—*my* failed imagination, when at the bedside of the dying—with divine vulnerability, giving Godself over to the suffering of the innocent. I stood beside Alberto utterly helpless; the small group gathered at a distance from Saah Exco stood by, utterly helpless. We were, and continue to be, all mute and catatonic witnesses to catastrophe. But the artistic insight that the divine does not remain remote and isolated from the godforsaken, that the darkness which accompanies us is the dwelling place of God, maintains the possibility of vigilance to the suffering Other. Only art in its appeal to the senses can both articulate and encourage the experience of divine revelation, in which we stake our subjectivity in the suffering of the Other, the Other in proximity and in distance, the Other in plague past or plague present.

CHAPTER SIX

The Presence of the Absent God

Incarnation and Abstract Expressionism

God manifests not by incarnation but by absence . . . when he veils his face in order to ask everything, to ask the superhuman, of man.

—Emmanuel Levinas[1]

Doesn't just about everyone experience that same shudder of vertigo standing before one of those great paintings of Rothko's high maturity—the canvas poised neatly between self-possession and self-divulgence: it draws you out and gives Nothing back. Its presence, like that of a black hole, is of such density that you might lose your Self there. Mute totemic authority: like what it must have been like to stand before the Burning Bush. For those Rothkos do not make a statement; rather, they raise a demand, or more precisely maybe, a question. The kind of questions, though, that the kabbalists raised; the kind larger than the sum of their possible answers—nothing can exhaust them. There is a moment in looking at those paintings when we stop looking at them and they start looking at us—at, and if we are not careful, if there is not enough of us there, straight through us. We can't help ourselves: these Rothkos keep bleeding out of aesthetical categories and into ethical ones. Not, is it beautiful? But rather, how should one lead one's life?

—Lawrence Weschler[2]

1. Emmanuel Levinas, "Loving the Torah More than God," in *Difficult Freedom: Essays on Judaism*, trans. Seán Hand (Baltimore: Johns Hopkins University Press, 1997), 85.

2. Lawrence Weschler, "Expressions of an Absolute," in *Everything that Rises: A Book of Convergences* (San Francisco: McSweeney's Books, 2007), 47.

For those who have never seen one of Mark Rothko's immense color field paintings in person, it may be hard to appreciate Lawrence Weschler's appraisal, and it may be hard to understand the argument attempted in this final section of our investigation relating the doctrine of the incarnation and visual art through an aesthetics of vulnerability. Standing before one of Rothko's "signature" works is a unique experience in the viewing of great works of art; for this reason, it is pointless to reproduce here small black and white images of a work by Rothko, or Ad Reinhardt, Helen Frankenthaler, or even the black and white works of Franz Kline or Robert Motherwell. The immensity and power of Abstract Expressionism propel art into vistas beyond what is reproducible or illustrative. The subtleties of color in the works of Rothko and Reinhardt are particularly lost in grayscale copies in academic texts, resulting in the absurdity of spilled ink. When Jackson Pollock's *Lavender Mist* is reduced to the size of a two by three-inch grayscale copy in a book, it appears to be a sprinkling of mold; it seems unjust to bother at all. All these artists produced works on the grand scale, like the fifteen-foot frescoes found in Italian churches, when an artist envelops the viewer in the lives of the saints aggrandized to the proportions of actors on movie screens.

Authentic Abstract Expressionism can be imitated but never copied; these are works given to the possibility of encounter, bringing us to the event, astounding in their bearing. Standing before them, we see layers of paint, the thicknesses—sometimes creamy, sensual; sometimes hard-edged, annoyingly messy, gloppy—throwing shadows, revealing bare canvas in places, begging for touch in the untouchable roughness or silkiness of a piece. In person, we see that their colors are true, intended: unaltered by the limitations of publication or computer projection. We notice that the light around us is a significant enhancement of the way color and energy transition, since the work expands its own possibilities when the light moves or dims, or when it is overexposed in light too harsh. The thoughtful museum designer will place benches before certain works. Use them; stay awhile. The moment matters. The excitement of being out of daily routine, the agitation of the travel to arrive at this place—the train or the parking problems, gum on one's shoe—contribute to the feeling that there is something special involved here in making a ritual of seeing.

We have traveled to see something of a frozen performance, a performance that has happened once and yet continues to happen and is re-vitalized in every generation. Here we have an opportunity to see energy and activity on a two-dimensional plane, an unsolved puzzle in the perpetual state of being unsolved. We are silently asked to pay attention with only our eyes rather than numbly moving past all that rushes through our visual horizon. Abstract and nonfigurative works especially require stillness and tenacity, which is why this final section will focus on works from the era of Abstract Expressionism, in order to gain a visual sense of the ambiguity spoken by the poet Hölderlin: "Is God unknown? Is God open like the sky? I rather believe so. What is God? Unknown, yet rich with particularities is the view which the sky offers."[3] In these paintings, figuration and identifiable subject matter are indefinite or missing altogether, nursing life beyond language, reason, linear thinking, and logic, so there is only the mystery left, the space of the unknown that permeates human existence. Gershom Scholem reminds us that this mystery is essential to being human: "If humanity should ever lose the feeling that there is mystery—a secret—in the world, then it is all over with us. But I don't believe we'll ever come to that."[4]

An aesthetics of vulnerability to the mystery is where we exercise the muscle of vision to discern "ultimate" reality, the "ground of being," "God" in the naked exposure of the unusual, to train our sensibilities to be open to the threatening or new. Works such as these remind us that reality is never secure or static and that it is possible to experience a moment or event that suspends the known world through the interplay of color, line, form, and surface that refuses to name or define "reality." Viewing this art is an opportunity for prayer and innovative contemplative possibilities for the meaning of the incarnation. Before one of Rothko's fields of color, I am reminded of how I long for the sort of silence that is alive and tangible;

3. Cited by Maurice Blanchot in *The Space of Literature*, trans. Ann Smock (Lincoln, NE: University of Nebraska Press, 1982), 275.

4. Gershom Scholem, "With Gershom Scholem: an Interview," in *On Jews and Judaism in Crisis: Selected Essays*, ed. Werner J. Dannhauser (Philadelphia, PA: Paul Dry Books, 2012), 48.

imagelessness paradoxically guiding us through the "image of the invisible God" (Col 1:15). Meister Eckhart writes,

> Consider the origin of our being the Son of God: We have the same being that the Son has. How is one the Son of God, or how does one know that one is, since God is like no one? This is true. Isaiah says: "To whom do you compare him, or what kind of image do you give him?" (Isaiah 40:18) Since it is God's nature that he is like no one, we must of necessity come to the point that I form myself into nothing and form nothing into myself, and if I remove and throw out whatever is in me, then I can be placed into the bare being of God, and this is the bare being of the spirit. Everything must be driven out that is [merely] likeness, so that I can be placed above into God and become one with him, one substance, one being, one nature, and the Son of God. . . . [F]or no image reveals to us the Godhead or its being. If any image or any "similar" were to remain in you, you would never become one with God.[5]

Without the urgency to find symbol or system in Abstract Expressionism, we are released from the requirement to name or define the "real" and are better equipped to "form myself into nothing and form nothing into myself." To remove and discard whatever obstacle of the measuring and ritualizing invasion of the "real": to be on the bare field, the "desert of the real"—this from the character Morpheus in the film *The Matrix* (1999)—the state of the driving out of the real, in order to drive out images that obstruct the search for God, or imprison God within a single symbol or set of symbols. This opportunity—or discipline—cleanses the visual palette of the figuration that might become too secure, that might mislead us into assuming that the white male *is* God, to paraphrase Mary Daly. Every symbol must be abandoned, rediscovered, and interpreted anew, then abandoned again; and so I must "form myself into nothing and form nothing into myself" so that I may not remain with the image, so that the similar or familiar may not remain.

---

5. Meister Eckhart, "Sermon 76," trans. Frank Tobin, in *Meister Eckhart, Teacher and Preacher*, ed. Bernard McGinn, Classics of Western Spirituality Series (Mahwah, NJ: Paulist Press, 1986), 329.

This chapter will explore the enigma of presence and absence in modern art as a metaphor for the paradox of presence and absence of God in the doctrine of the incarnation. While the previous chapter focused on the traditional figuration and personification of the triune God, this chapter calls those very personifications into question. Reflection on this paradox means entering a space in which we attempt to un-name the system of naming that led to literal personifications rather than the metaphor that is "a function of the religious experience of an encounter with transcendence,"[6] as Roger Haight puts it. God—the unpresentable, the unnameable—refers Godself to the Other in a radical and irrevocable way. God, whose house is the unknown dark, is the matrix within which the impossible becomes possible, as well as the possible impossible; such is creation in an eternal falling and rising, the "Big Bang" and "Big Crunch" in astrophysics, the push and pull, expanding and contracting of that which never settles or progresses. Such is humanity as witness to the trace of the transcendent. The mistake, the failure that enables creative expression and movement is analogous to the exaltation of the vulnerability that binds all sentient life and the death that is both a limit and an absence of future limit.

The Image as Nightmare

The "persecuted truth" Levinas describes as "the only possible modality of transcendence" reveals the poverty and humiliation that are ontological modes of existence, not merely social conditions and so something surpassing metaphor. The mode of the presence of God for Levinas, as we have seen, is ambiguous; one moves from atheism to belief and back again, because "the idea of infinity requires separation, requires it unto atheism, so profoundly that the idea of infinity could be forgotten."[7] In the field of this separation is the distance necessary for the awareness of alterity that engenders relationship with the Other. There is a Hindu proverb, "I want to

6. Roger Haight, *Jesus: Symbol of God* (Maryknoll, NY: Orbis Books, 1999), 438–39.

7. Emmanuel Levinas, *Totality and Infinity*, trans. Alphonso Lingis (Pittsburgh, PA: Duquesne University Press, 2008), 181.

taste the peach, not to be the peach"; the taste maintains the distinc-tion, the asymptote, allowing unity without collapse. This is the profundity of the Hindu concept *advita*, that we are neither one, nor two, but not-two. The world is not another reality in addition to God, and neither is the world equated with God. Such is the hidden-ness of God, the withdrawal of the infinite, when reality is empty again. The Other appears, shows her face, but remains absent, the alterity, or separation of the Other, forever just-beyond my grasp.

In this sense, the Christian claim that in the incarnation God is *known*, or *seen*, is for Levinas a sacrilege to humiliation as the onto-logical mode of the transcendent, the humiliation in which the prox-imity of God is possible. Levinas cautions Christians that "the humiliation of the manifestation must already be a distancing," an "ambiguity."[8] "One may wonder whether the true God can ever discard his incognito, whether the truth which is said should not immediately appear as not said."[9] Christians must not hoard the presence of God for themselves; the direct presence of God is im-possible. But the absence of God is where the presence of God be-comes a possibility, a trace, "the proximity of God in the countenance of my fellowman."[10] Levinas's critique of Christianity encourages a reappraisal of the triumphalist element in naming the presence of God in the incarnation. Because Jesus did not draw attention to *himself* as the presence of God, because he turned attention away from himself toward others—especially toward the suffering and marginalized Other—we can say something of the possibility of the impossible, that God "is," that God is revealed to "dwell with the contrite and the humble" (Isa 57:15), the God of "the stranger, the widow, and the orphan."

Levinas is suspicious of the Christian doctrine of the incarnation in a way similar to his suspicion of the value of art, as we saw in chapter 4. Levinas does not find an end-point of transcendence in

8. Emmanuel Levinas, "A Man-God?," in *Entre-Nous: Thinking-of-the-Other*, trans. Michael B. Smith and Barbara Harshav (New York: Columbia University Press, 1998), 57.

9. Ibid., 56.

10. Ibid., 57.

Jesus Christ, and neither does he find an endpoint in the appreciation of art. Levinas is of course not Christian, but this is not why he is suspicious of the Christian doctrine of the incarnation. Rather, Levinas believes that Christian doctrine attempts to traverse historical contextuality and thus claim an unhistorical (eternal) truth, which risks removing Christians from the ethical demands of the present in favor of a realized future. He is concerned that Christians have instrumentalized the salvation they declare Christ brings in such a way that their focus is on a future as accomplished, sealed, and delivered rather than on the messianic exhortation of the prophets of the Hebrew Bible to repair the suffering world. This is because the "end" is infinite—it will always be just beyond our grasp. Levinas is unyielding in the primacy of ethical responsibility as both the foundation of subjectivity and the direction of the unending and infinite task set before me. He admits of no distraction, no assimilation, no repair of the initial rupture of the natural order of being initiated by the Other. One can understand why he is suspicious of any Christian claim to have seized on the definitive revelation of the divine. Such triumphalism is not only the antithesis of the Gospel but also the very root of the violence that culminates in the mass graves of the twentieth and twenty-first centuries.

To gain a sense of how firmly the Christian stake of the presence of God has been captured and entrenched in the minds and hearts of Europe, one can simply walk into Johanneskirche in Werben (now Elbe), Germany: a stained glass window from 1417 reveals the juxtaposition of *Ecclesia*, depicted as a beautiful woman riding a tetramorph, the four-creature symbol of the four gospels, crowned by a heavenly hand and holding aloft a battle standard and chalice, set against *Synagoga*, depicted as a frail, downcast, blindfolded woman riding a donkey, holding the head of a goat (symbolic of the devil) and a broken staff. Synagoga's crown has slipped off and has been replaced with a hand from heaven plunging a bloody sword into her head. In between these two windows is a crucifixion scene, the familiar motif of Jesus on the cross between his mother and the apostle John. This same iconography is found in central Europe, with notable examples in Münster Cathedral and Elisabethkirche in Marburg; in France, notable examples are statues on the façade of Chartres

Cathedral and Strasbourg Cathedral, in the stained glass of Abbot Suger's St.-Denis, and the Cathedral of St. Etienne in Bourges.

A large fresco by Giovanni da Modena (ca. 1421) in the San Petronio Basilica of Bologna fashions the crossbeam of Jesus' cross into arms and hands with which to crown Ecclesia, riding the tetramorph, and stab the head of Synagoga, riding a goat; the contrast between Jesus' sorrowful countenance and the violence performed by his figure through his cross is particularly repulsive. The version that combines Ecclesia and Synagoga iconography with the cross as weapon is unfortunately called the "Living Cross," *Croce briachale*, *Lebendes Kreuz*, or *Croix vivante*. Approximately three dozen examples survive across Europe, in some cases incorporating God the Father; I have, however, yet to find an example in which the Father is enthroned as in the *Gnadenstuhl* motif.

There are thousands of examples of the iconography of Ecclesia and Synagoga, which first appeared in the ninth century in northern France in psalter and missal illumination and became marble inlay on a baptistery, in oil paintings, on jeweled book covers, reliquaries, and even on portable devotional altars. We briefly touched on the importance of blood to medieval piety in chapter 3; in an example in the Strasbourg Cathedral in France, close to the German border, an inscription beneath the figure of Ecclesia read: *Mit Christi Blut überwind ich dich* ("With Christ's blood I overcome you") and beneath the figure of Synagoga: *Das selbig Blut das bindet mich* ("The same blood blinds me").[11] The habitual use of this motif in both the new construction and renovations of churches during the Middle Ages and Renaissance served to display what was a "properly ordered Christian world," according to Nina Rowe: "[T]he consistent joining of the motif to images of ideal male rulership on ceremonial entrances of the local ecclesiastical and secular lord, the bishop, suggests . . . Ecclesia and Synagoga as figures particularly appropriate to convey ideals of power relations to urban publics."[12]

11. See Nina Rowe, *The Jew, the Cathedral and the Medieval City: Synagoga and Ecclesia in the Thirteenth Century* (Cambridge, UK: Cambridge University Press, 2011), 234.

12. Ibid., 3.

Such political ramifications intended to "keep Jews in their place" became pervasive in the cultural attitudes and the theological interpretations that perpetuated an increasingly virulent brand of anti-Semitism. Rowe observes that this motif "suited a mental landscape where theologians had limited contacts with real Jews and could thus cleave to the Augustinian notion that Jews preserved Old Testament scripture for the good of Christians"; hence, when increased contact between Jews and Christians revealed the Jewish people to be "intellectually creative, financially successful, and sometimes openly contemptuous of the dominant Christian society,"[13] the realization that the Jews were not a defeated people resulted in more pronounced violence depicted in further developments of the motif. The iconography of Ecclesia and Synagoga became associated with representations of the intercessory and atoning import of Christ's passion, in order to show the separation between Christians and Jews in terms of salvation and damnation.[14] The images of Synagoga and Ecclesia were even used in theatrical productions that depicted the passion narrative. Debates on stage between Synagoga and Ecclesia were intended as an intellectual defense for the superiority of Christian belief, signifying the difference between righteousness and aberrance, between virtue and vice in general social terms.[15]

While the visual motif of Ecclesia and Synagoga is not the origin of Christian anti-Semitism—for this we can go back to the late first century—the motif concretized and conceptualized the theological paradigm that only Christianity has received the fullness of divine revelation, which in turn justified the methodical expulsion of Jewish populations from the cities of Europe in premodernity and culminated in the systematically efficient program of murder in modernity that manifested in the pogroms of Russia, the American and British refusal to accept Jewish refugees, and finally the Shoah. Besides its obvious influence on the history of Christian anti-Semitism, one can only speculate the sad extent of the influence of this motif on the development of the theology of the incarnation, especially in terms of a theology of presence that results in an idolatry of expectation and containment.

13. Ibid., 239.
14. See ibid., 241.
15. See ibid., 245.

Such images, and their tacit influence, cannot but lead to a "crisis of representation," what Derrida called the "end of logocentrism," or the end of belief in immediate access to meaning through language, or stable truths represented by words.

In this sense, the argument at hand will be for a theology of the incarnation advocated through abstract forms of art, especially the beyond-figurative Expressionism of the mid to late twentieth century. Tillich suggested that "the most expressive form of art today in connection with religion must be sacred emptiness; an emptiness which does not pretend to have at its disposal symbols which it actually does not have."[16] Sacred emptiness follows kenosis in an attempt to move beyond being when doing theology. When doing Christology, sacred emptiness is a foregoing of self for the sake of the Other: the doctrine of the incarnation may approach the possibility that "self" is expressed heteronomically, as a vehicle for reception of and responsibility for, the Other.

Art is only worthwhile for Levinas, as we have seen, if it contributes to the saying (*le Dire*), rather than the said (*le Dit*), in a way recalling the optical directionality of ethics. Art must never waver from serving the rupture that the Other opens toward infinite responsibility. Art may make "tragedy endurable," but art will never eliminate tragedy, nor will art in and of itself create justice. Art rather provides a vision for justice and a vision for why we want to endure, for what is worth preserving. When women marched for fair wages and more dignified working conditions in the Lawrence, Massachusetts, textile strike during January–March 1912, now known as the "Bread and Roses Strike," they cried out not just for bread to feed their families, but for roses, because the human soul desires beauty, especially in the midst of the deadening monotony of industrialism. Art and culture are integral to establishing a worldview that prioritizes the weak and vulnerable as well as lifting them up. If art promises to shape our consciousness of grief, as Blanchot believed, then art can draw us out of our *selves* and disturb the tranquil surface of the Same.

16. Paul Tillich, "Art and Society," in *On Art and Architecture*, ed. John Dillenberger (New York: Crossroad, 1987), 40.

Because art does not point to itself as definitive but toward an infinity of interpretation across cultures and contexts, a hermeneutics that multiplies exponentially with every passing era, art may be a resource for Christian theology. The experience of the presence of God in the person of Jesus of Nazareth in those who knew him was a response to the messianic responsibility which they found enacted in Jesus and urged in themselves. Jesus gives his followers the power to heal, to cast out demons, "authority over unclean spirits" (Mark 6:7), because Jesus shows us our own messianic potential. The messiah as Levinas describes is the just one "who has taken on the suffering of others. . . . The fact of not evading the burden imposed by the suffering of others defines ipseity [selfhood] itself. All persons are the Messiah."[17]

Renewing the Christian commitment to the doctrine of the incarnation, despite the dangerous paths of oppression justified by its use in the history of Christianity, requires the space of emptiness through which the "self" of Jesus pours out to purge truth claims or claims to divine presence in which we have reached the decisive end. If the language of incarnation is poetic rather than logical or ontological, "incarnation" signifies the humiliation that refers to emptiness and the non-knowing in which the phenomenon of material things might appear.

What Is Modern Art?

The first time we examine an Abstract Expressionist painting in class, students bristle and are often noticeably uncomfortable. They may sigh or roll their eyes or try to regain their composure and comfort level by "finding" the object in it. Rarely do undergraduates (with the possible exception of art or art history majors) allow the experience of the work to just happen, to view it silently, allowing the work to be what it is, without conjecture or speculation. They want to be "right" about what it "means." Learning to live in silence before a work of art is a discipline like any discipline. Granted, the setting is

17. Emmanuel Levinas, "Messianic Texts," in *Difficult Freedom*, trans. Sean Hand (Baltimore: Johns Hopkins University Press, 1997), 89.

wrong. A classroom seems out of context for the works we see; we should be walking down the spiral walkway of the Guggenheim in New York, which Frank Lloyd Wright intended to resemble an inverted ziggurat, or the massive former Bankside power station in London's Southwark neighborhood on the Thames that is now the Tate Modern. In comparison to the real thing, art shown on a projector is rather banal; a painting that spans an entire wall reproduced to a few inches in a book is anticlimactic.

But repetitive exposure to works that challenge our assumptions (even the assumption that many have that they won't "like" abstract art) prepares us for thinking abstractly in general. Even the transcending of abstraction in a monochromatic work reminds us that any naming of the identity of an object abstracts from the experience of it. Finding a cat in a painting is not finding an actual cat; it is finding the experience of a cat, or something that reminds us of an experience with a cat. Whether we have an actual cat before us or a painting that features a cat, both are "real" experiences of "catness." Language does this too; it purports to directly name experience, but by the time the name or identity has been given, the space between the naming and the intuition has only widened. This is what Jacques Derrida meant by *différance*, the deferral of meaning in language. We never get to the final meaning (there is no final meaning): "Between the too warm flesh of the literal event and the cold skin of the concept runs meaning. This is how it enters into the book. Everything enters into, transpires in the book. This is why the book is never finite. It always remains suffering and vigilant."[18] Acknowledging this space of difference, this forbidden space, between language and meaning, between object and representation, in visual abstraction, prepares for the doing of theology; even *is* theology, discourse on the sacred.

This is why I torture my students with the discomfort given through much of modern art.[19] The habit of exposure to visual ab-

18. Jacques Derrida, *Writing and Difference*, trans. Alan Bass (Chicago: The University of Chicago Press, 1978), 75.

19. A few remarks about the meaning of "modern" might be helpful. The term "modern" comes from the Latin *modo*, meaning "just now." In 1127, Abbot Suger's architectural program renovating the abbey basilica of St.-Denis near

straction teaches us to distrust the ability to name or identify. By the end of the semester, students (for the most part) gravitate toward abstract works, and works without any figuration, for the pure joy of the way that they shape vision—and the way they let us off the hook of certainty: we can just be there with the painting, we don't have to be "right" about it or know the history of its iconography. Students have compared viewing abstract art to being in the thick of a forest (or surfing "the tube," engulfed in a watery canopy—I teach in California).

Our vision is like a muscle that needs new forms of exercise. The first time I realized this, I was in high school playing Pictionary with my youngest brother, who is dyslexic, and my other siblings. He drew a door none of us could recognize: rather than the standard upright rectangle with a small circle in the middle on the left side, he drew a tall thin rectangle with two circles on either side: a door seen not from the front but from its edge. I have never looked at a door in the same way again. Joe grew up to become a Shakespearean-trained stage actor with spot-on comic timing. I am indebted to him, as I am to all artists, for tilting my perception. Such is the exercise of the muscle of vision that prepares for the radically new. This may have been what scared Kant when he realized the power of the imagination to be able to operate at a distance and even independently from the understanding. Breaking through the usual way vision operates does not come easily to those who learn "normally" or who see the world through the lens of the Same.

Paris resulted in an entirely new style that could neither be classified as classically Greek nor Roman. He called the style an *opus modernum*, a "modern work." By the late Renaissance, this style was referred to as "Gothic," initially as an insult, since anything after the fall of Rome, anything that resisted classical style, is crude and "barbaric." "Modernity," on the other hand, refers to the overwhelming cultural, social, scientific, economic, and political changes in the Western world experienced over the last 150 years. Reacting to all this is the "modernist" era in art, literature, and music, in which art becomes a question for itself, characterizing the arts in self-critique beyond concepts, theories, or genre-descriptions. While there are many modernisms, or schools of modernism, modernism in art is generally characterized by an interest to deviate from linear and rational thinking.

The lens of the Same has been the scope of the Western trajectory, as Foucault points out, to exclude "madness" from history and culture. In *The History of Madness*, Foucault argues that the establishment of reason as the engine of modernity frames "madness" as an opposing category: we know we are "sane" because we can deem the Other as "insane." Can we overcome the blinders of the rational, which purport to shield us from the uncertain and enigmatic? The cushion of confidence that maintains security is a vain attempt to thwart vulnerability. There is no such thing as security, and fear is the greatest obstacle to openness to the mystery which makes us human. But "it doesn't happen without victims," Dorothee Soelle writes of the necessity to adopt risk as essential to life; "Life that excludes and protects itself against death protects itself to death. If the 'window of vulnerability,' as it is called in military language, is finally closed and walled up, the supposedly secure people inside the fortress will die for lack of light and air. Only life that opens itself to the other, life that risks being wounded or killed, contains promise."[20]

How can we awaken from the desire for security and certainty, maintained in sleepwalking, mind-numbing routine, when the exclusions on which the Western worldview has been built continue to cloud vision's ability to see? James Elkins asks whether there are things which actually do exist but that we cannot see, like the letter in the Edgar Allen Poe story "The Purloined Letter" that hides in plain sight. Is it possible to think of something we want to see but that we cannot visualize? Can we have an idea of something and fail to form an image of it? Can we have an image of something and fail to see it?[21] Like the eyeglasses I can picture in my mind but that I cannot "see," although they are on the table in front of me?

Those of us who are able to see are biased to the reception of visual information; it seems natural, direct, close to an experience of the "real." Human visual experience is the entry point in comprehending and responding to the environment, the scaffolding of

20. Dorothee Soelle, *The Window of Vulnerability: A Political Spirituality*, trans. Linda M. Maloney (Minneapolis, MN: Fortress Press, 1990), 7. Emphasis mine.

21. See James Elkins, *The Object Stares Back: On the Nature of Seeing* (San Diego, CA: Harvest/Harcourt, 1997), 103.

awareness constructed prior to concepts and language. The cave paintings discussed in chapter 4 are the oldest preserved report on the world.[22] We think in pictures whether we are awake or dreaming; the imagination brings the pictures our eyes take of the world and re-creates them in the mind. We saw in chapter 4 that Kant struggled with how much power to ascribe to the imagination. Arthur Koestler famously argued that thinking in concepts emerged from thinking in images, "through the slow development of the powers of abstraction and symbolization, as the phonetic script emerged by similar processes out of pictorial symbols"; in visual art, abstraction returns us to this primal movement, reducing the "real" to elemental components or taking the "real" out of its context. One of the reasons that the popular assessment of modern art is often negative is because Western cultures tend to see images as direct reflections of the things in the world rather than as constructs or interpretations of them.

We are used to living in a highly regulated world, in which the transitions between form and emptiness are often regarded more as patterns in service of human beings than as fundamental ontological truths. The sun sits high in the afternoon sky; the moon will wax and wane, the day will come and go, the leaves that are green turn to brown. One of the innovations in modernity has been in the perception of time. Centuries ago, when journeys that spanned a continent took months, our bodies and sense of time were able to gradually adapt, but the advent of train travel disrupted our expectations of time. Technology that could put us from one end of a continent to the other in a matter of days necessitated reform in standards of time, resulting in the International Meridian Conference in 1884, which formulated global time zones. Today, the frequency of plane travel means that we are often unsure of the time where we are; the digital world even lifts us out of time. Modernity thus inaugurated displacement in never before experienced ways. While human beings have always been nomadic to some degree, the rapidity with which journeys take place today has forever altered the constitution of human

22. See Donis A. Dondis, *A Primer of Visual Literacy* (Cambridge, MA: MIT Press, 1973), 2.

beings with regard to what is fundamental to human perception: the rhythm of time.

Perhaps it is no accident that Einstein's fascination with the speed of trains gives us the theory of relativity. Whereas Isaac Newton theorized an absolute time, independent of perception, progressing at a constant and consistent pace throughout the universe, train travel and Einstein gave us the end of absolute time. With the speed of light as the only constant, time and space are relative to it: time slows down (widens or dilates) as a particle reaches the speed of light. Muons, particles created by the collision of protons from cosmic radiation with air molecules, travel at 99 percent of the speed of light; with a life span of two-millionths of a second, how do they reach the earth's surface from the upper atmosphere? Because of time dilation. Relativity theory opens up fields we will neither directly see nor directly experience. Modernity has had to reorient itself to the end of absolutes; even the speed of light as a constant is destined to be challenged in the future. Relativity is a metaphor for the modern imagination attempting to transcend the rational, calculable, sense perception observations of day-to-day existence.

Modern art embraced this sense of displacement and fragmentation, as well as this desire to transcend rationality. We might say that the popular worldview is still grappling with what modern art achieved in the twentieth century. Modernism in art can be said to be anticipatory of what becomes postmodernism in philosophy. Jean-François Lyotard writes that the "postmodern" is first "modern" in terms of its "just now." Lyotard writes, "What, then, is the postmodern? It is undoubtedly part of the modern. All that has been received, if only yesterday, must be suspected. What does Cezanne challenge? The Impressionists. What objects do Picasso and Braque attack? Cezanne's. . . . Postmodernism thus understood is not modernism at its end but in the nascent state, and this state is constant."[23] For Lyotard, "modern" is the art that "presents the fact that the unpresentable exists. To make visible that there is something which

---

23. Jean-François Lyotard, "What Is Postmodernism?," in *The Postmodern Condition*, trans. Geoff Bennington and Brian Massumi (Minneapolis, MN: University of Minnesota Press, 1979), 79.

can be conceived and which can neither be seen nor made visible: this is what is at stake in modern painting."[24] The "unpresentable" is back in business. The crux of the postmodern is welcoming a space for the unpresentable, opening to an emptiness that is both plenitude and abyss. Postmodernity ripens the ground for religion—if religions shed the positive propositional thinking that characterizes oppressive authority structures—to rise again in human consciousness the way it did when we were "born" in the caves of Lascaux thirty thousand years ago. The only way to offer recognition that what is acquired in the "sensible manifold" (ahh, Kant) but cannot be finally representable is through abstraction more jarring and obvious than the more subtle abstraction of words and language. The artistic hermeneutic transforms the relationship between the human experience of the world and the visual image.

Modern art welcomes this sense of the relative, the messiness and indeterminacy of an expected order by confronting regulated and habitual experience with objects out of proportion or out of context—Dada non-sense upending urinals for display by R. Mutt/Marcel Duchamp (1917); a teacup, saucer, and spoon sensuously covered in gazelle fur by Meret Oppenheim (*Objet*, 1936); trains blasting from fireplaces by René Magritte (*Time Transfixed*, 1938). For hundreds of years, images in the West had been constructed primarily on a correspondence model between image and subject matter, much like word and thing. When reality is perceived to be out of whack, when Einstein does not receive the Nobel Prize for his theory of relativity because the end of absolute time and space was too disconcerting (he received it, finally, in 1922 after being nominated for ten years, for his discovery of the law of the photoelectric effect, which introduces the concept of photons), the way reality is imaged changes too. Newton believed that reason can master the mechanics of the natural world, uncovering clearly discernible laws that can describe any process anywhere in the universe; Freud thought that his conclusions about the human psyche were universally applicable. But in modernism, which describes the movement of art and literature as a reaction

24. Ibid., 78.

to modernity, the messiness of a reality without a center, without the organizing structure of a centralized authority, means that mastery of reality, the drive that Gavin Hyman argued characterizes modernity in science and history, is no longer possible. We can no longer rely on a correspondence between thing experienced and thing expressed; we can no longer represent the thing as it is, and we can no longer rely on representing the way something is when it is absent. Modern art, and modernism in literature, reject that there is a fixed reality or a direct relationship between thing and image of the thing.

Modern Art and the Catholic Church

Christianity is currently in the process of contending with this "crisis of representation" in which the image and the original are no longer in direct or even corresponding relationship. Western cultures tend to regard images and language as direct reflections of objects, which makes the world known, graspable. Until the late nineteenth and into the twentieth century, images in Western art tended to confirm a correspondence model of language and object; this is why realism has been the dominant direction of artistic construction of images, which reaches an apex in the discovery of mathematical one-point perspective in the fifteenth century. This is why contemporary people who are not accustomed to questioning the correspondence model of language or image find any abstraction, or indirect correspondence, so confusing. But realism, even photographic realism, is also an abstraction; while we might think that realism intends to mirror reality, and that the absolute mirroring of reality is "proof" of the artist's skill, which therefore makes a painting "good," we are lulled into assuming that we are witnessing an objective reality, when we always witness an artist's interpretation of reality. And as we have seen, there are oceans of possible interpretations of the artist's interpretation, because art interprets the experience of reality; it shapes our way of seeing and our way of understanding it. In this sense, visual art, as is the case in all art forms, is a collaborative effort between artist and viewer, and is only successful—in the achievement of new and daring interpretations and experiences—through vulnerability on both sides of the equation.

Without vulnerability, representation becomes a crisis. The crisis was especially inescapable when Europe was decimated by two world wars, recession, famine, and genocide; a breakdown in authority meant a breakdown in the possibility of certainty. Despite this, until Vatican II, the Catholic Church officially tried to maintain its hold on neoscholastic textbook-style certainty.[25] With Rome as its center, the Catholic Church was once the world's most powerful patron of the arts. But this was often because of the way the clergy bound power to the artistic process, not because of any authentic encouragement of creativity or regard for the possibility that art may critique as well as interpret doctrine.

The Council of Trent ended in 1563; from the Counter-Reformation on, the curia increased its attempt to secure a visually "correct" performance of Catholic teaching in the art objects of church buildings.[26] What we name today as the Baroque became the dominant

25. Thomas F. O'Meara observes that in 1870, the year papal infallibility was pronounced as dogma, neoscholasticism was the intellectual and theological form "of all that was ultramontane": "Neo-Scholasticism after 1870 dominated Catholic philosophy and theology, art and political theory, and was the standard against which every Catholic intellectual movement from Vatican I through the First World War to Vatican II had to be measured." O'Meara, *Church and Culture: German Catholic Theology 1860–1914* (Notre Dame, IN: University of Notre Dame Press, 1991), 33.

26. After the Council of Trent, artistic freedom became more limited; Cardinal Paleotti issued *Discorso introno alle imagini sacre e profane* (Discourse Concerning Sacred and Profane Images) in 1582, which outlined the theory of Counter-Reformation art. In Seville, oaths of allegiance to the Eucharist and immaculate conception were required for admission to the academy of painting, and artists bristled with the awareness that the Inquisition was watching for the presence of unofficial teaching. See Nigel Aston, *Art and Religion in Eighteenth-Century Europe* (London: Reaktion Books, 2009), 30–31. Anthony J. Godzieba gives a more appreciative reading of Paleotti's treatise, arguing that Paleotti's interest to compare the artist to a preacher with "the task of teaching the articles of the faith and exhorting people to live virtuous lives" leads to an art for the populace, since images are "universally accessible to the learned and unlearned alike; indeed, 'painting replaces the word or supplements it.'" Although "Paleotti warns artists to avoid allegory, novelty, unrestrained invention, incorrect proportions, and genre scenes without biblical foundation or edifying value," Godzieba wants us to understand that this was in service of the characteristically Catholic theological

style from the late sixteenth to the middle of the eighteenth century. An emotionally excessive style, for the most part, the reinforcement of its aspects by the official church was a desire to defend Catholic faith against both a growing secularism and the emerging Protestant movement. This was the period in which art not only intended to communicate the stories and doctrine important to the faith but also intended to nurture and even deliver the experience of faith. Over such an extensive period, the style was bound to have high points—Caravaggio and his followers, such as Artemesia Gentileschi; Gianlorenzo Bernini, especially the *Ecstasy of St. Theresa* (1647); Diego Velasquez, Francisco de Goya—and its low points, especially in late Baroque, when the particular success of the emotional impact of images on the faithful began to turn into another form of authoritarianism and mass persuasion, with the Jesuits at the helm.

By the nineteenth century, in what is sometimes called "Academicism," religious images had degenerated into naïve institutionalism and mere illustrations intended to reinforce piety and dependence on church authority. The Papal States had dissolved in 1870; papal patronage of the arts declined as the Vatican's power waned. Meanwhile, the Impressionist movement in art pushed all the Catholic boundaries, especially in France, in its regard of nature as sacred. The Realist or Realism movement was even more antiestablishment than Impressionism; rebelling against the dramatic emotionalism of the late Baroque into the Rococo, as well as the elite academies and wealthy patrons, artists such as Gustave Courbet and Jean Baptiste Camille Corot focused on the life of the worker: the peasant toiling in the fields, in which every hardship is carved onto the subject's face and clothing. But the more widespread modernist movements in art became, the more the clerical church remained obdurate. The clerical church clung to the earlier standard of patronage in which

---

understanding of the sacramental nature of creation "that finite materiality can mediate transcendent divinity." Godzieba, "Caravaggio, Theologian: Baroque Piety and Poiesis in a Forgotten Chapter of the History of Catholic Theology," in *Theology and Lived Christianity*, ed. David M. Hammond, Annual Publication of the College Theology Society, vol. 45 (Mystic, CT: Twenty-Third Publications, 2000), 214–15.

authority dictates the subject matter but were only able to find mediocre talents willing to paint their requests, which resulted in sentimental and gaudy forms designed to placate the laity. Art produced in this period offers so little by way of correlation between the upheaval in world events and the Gospel that it is difficult to call much of what was produced "art." In 1932, speaking at the opening of the new Vatican *Pinacoteca*, Pope Pius XI condemned modern art as "unfitting for service in the church because it reverts to the crude forms of the darkest ages."[27] Pope Pius XII in *Mediator Dei* (1947) also condemned "those works of art, recently introduced by some which seem to be a distortion and perversion of true art and which at times openly shock Christian taste."[28]

In *L'Osservatore Romano* June 1951, Cardinal Celso Constantini, secretary of the Congregation for the Propagation of the Faith, attacked the modernist iconography in the Dominican church at Assy, Notre-Dame-de-Toute Grâce, and the Sacred Art movement led by the French Dominicans; that same month, Henri Matisse's Chapel of the Rosary for the Dominican sisters in Vence, France, was consecrated. A year later, in April 1952, Pius XII gave a speech to Italian artists designed to affirm "the promoters of the figurative arts"; in June, the Sacred Congregation of the Holy Office issued the Instruction "On Sacred Art," meant to be an official condemnation of the French Dominican movement. But it contained little intellectual force, primarily replicating the 1917 Code of Canon Law. In 1953, restrictions on the Dominicans meant the silencing of the periodical edited by Fr. Marie-Alain Couturier, OP (1897–1954), *L'Art sacre*.

Couturier was a founder of the Sacred Art movement as well as an artist whose stained glass and frescoes can be found in Assy, St. Sabina's in Rome, as well as the Dominican church in Oslo, Norway, St. Dominikus.[29] Couturier and his associate Fr. Pie-Raymond

---

27. *Acta Apostolica Sedis* 24 (1932): 335; Pius XI, Address, October 27, 1932.

28. Pius XII, *Mediator Dei* (1947), 195, http://w2.vatican.va/content/pius-xii /en/encyclicals/documents/hf_p-xii_enc_20111947_mediator-dei.html.

29. St. Dominikus was the first Dominican church built in Oslo after the Norwegian prohibition on Roman Catholic orders, which began in 1537, was lifted in 1897. Fr. Couturier went there to paint frescos and construct stained

Régamey were roundly criticized for commissioning non-Catholics—and, far worse, non-Christians and atheists—to implement the first examples of modern religious art in church buildings; his response: "This fact may be irritating, but at the present time it is undeniable. The Spirit breatheth where the Spirit will."[30]

Couturier brought together an astounding collection of artists: Chagall, Rouault, Leger, Matisse, Braque, Lipchitz—but particularly galling to the curia was a 1950 crucifix by Germaine Richier (1902–1959), an atheist who explained her work, "the cross has been taken with the suffering into the flesh. . . . There is no face because God is the spirit and faceless."[31] While this statement and the work has been criticized by theologians as antithetical to the doctrine of the incarnation,[32] one could also interpret both Richier's statement and

---

glass for the church soon after his ordination in 1928. See Grete Refsum, "The French Dominican Fathers as Precursors to the Directives on Art of the Second Vatican Council" (dissertation lecture, Kunsthogskolen Oslo, National College of Art and Design, December 8, 2000), 23. See also William S. Rubin, *Modern Sacred Art and the Church of Assy* (New York: Columbia University Press, 1961). I am indebted to these resources for the material in this section. I was fortunate to see Couturier's frescoes in person on a recent visit to Oslo; Sr. Else-Britt Nilsen eagerly led me around the church and community chapel and was very proud of the Couturier legacy. She showed me original drawing plans of the frescoes and a chalice that has an etching from a Couturier sketch. My hope is that Couturier's artistic contribution, as well as his willingness to encourage and experiment with new and daring art forms in sacred space, may secure a more obvious place in the Collection of Modern Art in the Vatican Museums.

30. Marie-Alain Couturier, *Sacred Art* (Austin, TX: University of Texas Press and the de Menil Foundation, 1989), 154; see also Refsum, "The French Dominican Fathers," 23.

31. "Art: Removal at Assy," *Time* magazine, April 23, 1951, 68.

32. See Cecilia González-Andrieu, *Bridge to Wonder: Art as a Gospel of Beauty* (Waco, TX: Baylor University Press, 2012), 137–46; R. Kevin Seasoltz, *A Sense of the Sacred: Theological Foundations of Christian Architecture and Art* (New York: Continuum, 2006), 340. Seasoltz also argues that the church at Assy "reflects such a disparity of styles that it is more like a museum than an integrated place for Christian worship." Ibid., 258. It might be noted that the centuries-old churches in Europe rarely display an integrated iconographic program; having existed often through several periods of Christian art, remodels, pieces removed to be distributed to museums, it is not uncommon to find, for example, Gothic

her work as indicative of the God who incarnates in all who suffer catastrophe. Indeed, her cross is a raw, nightmarish chaos of suffering, flesh seeming to melt off bones, bronze molded by the reports of the extent of the genocide in the gas chambers and ovens of central Europe that were at the time beginning to penetrate Western consciousness, the human being barely scratched out in personhood in the midst of disaster. I think also of the Nick Ut photograph of the nine-year-old Vietnamese girl, Phan Thi Kim Phuc, running naked from her napalmed village in 1972; and recently, rows of crude tents in temporary European refugee camps, in the January cold and the mud, which recall permanent slums in Mumbai in the rot and the mud, all places where the faces blur into crowds.

It has now been over sixty-five years since Richier's crucifix first appeared at the altar in Assy. Those familiar with the modern art forms that have influenced contemporary liturgical art may not realize the impact this must have had, in a time when Academicism was the norm for liturgical art. It was understandably shocking. Surprisingly, even the existentialist philosopher (and convert to Catholicism) Gabriel Marcel disapproved of the work, claiming he could not find in it "the victory of Christ over suffering and death."[33]

On October 11, 1953, in *L'Osservatore Romano*, Celso appealed for the "expulsion" and "barring" of all modernist works as they are a "true profanation" of the sacred. The following month, the worker priests in France were ordered not to accept any further recruits and to leave their work as the conclusion of a systematic program of restraint. In 1954, just days after Fr. Couturier's death, Yves Congar, OP, in the same year he was banished from teaching or publishing

---

altarpieces in chapels with Baroque ceilings or modern Stations of the Cross placed in Romanesque architecture. What is perhaps disconcerting at Assy is the emphasis on Christian saints and stories from the Hebrew Bible rather than the more traditional focus on Mary, Jesus, and the triune God.

33. Gabriel Marcel, "Le Pseudo-Christ de Germaine Richier banni de l'église d'Assy," *L'Homme nouveau* (July 29, 1951), cited by Rubin, *Modern Sacred Art and the Church of Assy*, 164. Rubin also provides another statement from Marcel: "[O]ne must not think that they [Couturier and Régamey] are . . . the authorized representatives of the Church." Rubin, "Lettre à La Table ronde sur le Christ de l'église d'Assy," *La Table ronde*, no. 43 (July 1951): 181–82.

following support of the worker priest movement, courageously published on the controversy at Assy: "[I]t is essentially by the celebration of the mystery of the body of Christ that a place becomes a church," praising Couturier's churches as examples of work produced through a simplicity and transparency "that asserts the Glory of God in the poverty of man."[34]

Aidan Nichols argues, however, that the Assy project was misguided. "If by 'sacred' art we mean, as the Dominicans of *L'Art sacré* did, an art that exists so as to serve and interpret the Church's faith and worship, it seems inappropriate to seek out practitioners among unbelievers. How can they be expected to have an interior understanding of the Bible and the Liturgy which Régamey himself called the principal pertinent sources of a Christian sacred art?"[35] Nichols offers the possibility that "sacred" art may refer to the human search for God or transcendence, thereby making the art of "unbelievers" acceptable as a form of religious art, but argues that it still belongs external to the liturgical space, in the atrium or even outside the church proper, and as such would supply "a question mark to which the holy images in the liturgical space could furnish an answer."[36] Such an argument is in line with the official Catholic tradition of excluding non-Catholics from the eucharistic table, as though there must be cordoned off a liturgical space reserved for Catholics, where they may exercise their special form of worship. This is the thinking that led to the removal of Richier's crucifix from the church by the bishop of Annecy.

But the instincts of Richier and Couturier seem to have been more consonant with the suffering around them; the patients at the sanatorium served by the church and other parishioners protested. One invalid wrote a letter describing the "suffering and pitiful Crucified [of Richier] as our Christ . . . like one of us."[37] Another wrote hop-

---

34. Yves Congar, *Priest and Layman* (London: Darton, Longman & Todd, 1967), 237; see also Refsum, "The French Dominican Fathers," 23.

35. Aidan Nichols, *Redeeming Beauty: Soundings in Sacral Aesthetics* (Aldershot, UK: Ashgate, 2007), 121.

36. Ibid.

37. Cited in Bernardi, "Der Streit um Assy," *Rheinischer Merkur* (May 3, 1951), in Rubin, *Modern Sacred Art and the Church of Assy*, 52. Rubin's research on the difference between the episcopal and lay reactions "is confirmed by my private

ing "that our Christ will be given back to us. If it cannot be placed over the altar [where it originally was], then let it be placed somewhere else in the church." William Rubin notes that after the removal of Richier's crucifix, "it was placed in the mortuary chapel, located in a chalet behind the church near the rectory. Visitors with a special interest were discreetly led to it."[38] It was finally restored to the Church of Notre-Dame-de-Toute Grâce in 1971.

The shift toward modernism in the Catholic Church thus had begun in more ways than one when John XXIII became pope. In 1959, after he called for an ecumenical council to be convened in Rome, he issued *Princeps Pastorum*, which among other things affirmed the direction of art related to modernist tendencies to incorporate the very primitivism that had been attacked by Celso:

> The Church . . . so full of youthful vigor, constantly renewed by the breath of the Holy Spirit, is willing, at all times, to recognize, welcome, and even assimilate anything that redounds to the honor of the human mind and heart, whether or not it originates in parts of the world washed by the Mediterranean Sea, which, from the beginning of time, had been destined by God's Providence to be the cradle of the Church.[39]

Perhaps it was a matter of their mutual attention to the poor and forgotten that, despite Pius XII banning Congar from teaching, John XXIII appointed Congar to the preparatory theological commission of Vatican II, which helped write "Message to the World," the first statement given by the Council, on October 20, 1962.[40] Couturier did

---

poll of forty-three members of the congregation at Assy, of whom only three had reservations about the Crucifix. The Vatican, it appears, tends to create an abstraction called 'the faithful' to which it then attributes its own official taste and attitude." Ibid.

38. Ibid., 52n34.

39. John XXIII, *Princeps Pastorum* (November 28, 1959), 36, http://w2.vatican.va/content/john-xxiii/en/encyclicals/documents/hf_j-xxiii_enc_28111959_princeps.html.

40. For an online translation of the Latin of "Message to the World," see https://vaticaniiat50.wordpress.com/2012/10/20/text-of-councils-message-to-world/. Pope John XXIII's vision of a "world church" is clearly evident, as is the interest to redirect the church toward service of the poor: "Our concern is

not live to see his vision influence the council; his friend Maurice Lavanoux, editor of the US journal *Liturgical Arts*, was allowed to distribute copies of his work to members of the committee that formulated *Sacrosanctum Concilium* (the Constitution on Sacred Liturgy).[41] A chapter on sacred art affirms a new relationship with artists, encouraging bishops and others in authority to seek out the best religious art that reflects the times. But the constitution also advises bishops to educate artists on appropriate artistic content and iconographical schemes. This is problematic, to say the least, and actually commits the same authoritative overreach for which it had previously apologized.

The more substantive change in the Vatican's attitude toward modern art was to come with the election of Paul VI. At the begin-

---

directed especially to the more humble, the more poor, the weaker, and, in keeping with the example of Christ, we feel compassion for the throngs who suffer hunger, misery and ignorance. We are constantly attentive to those who, deprived of the necessary assistance, have not yet reached a standard of living worthy of man."

41. See Refsum, "The French Dominican Fathers," 25. Lavanoux, head of the American modernist group Liturgical Art Society, was largely responsible for quelling another controversy, this time in Rome at the meeting of the First International Congress of Catholic Artists. The positive popular reception of the church at Assy was causing problems for Integrism, "a view common in the extreme right wing of the clergy and laity, is based on the concept of retaining absolute 'integrity' of the structure of the faith through detachment of the Church from the modern world," according to William Rubin (*Modern Sacred Art and the Church of Assy*, 16). Lavanoux, leader of the US delegation, joined with delegations from Holland, Austria, Peru, and Switzerland to defeat a motion made by the Integrists demanding an Index of Sacred Art, intending to suppress artistic exploration of modernism in liturgical art. Lavanoux and his supporters submitted a document that, among other things, included a denial of the necessity for a set of rules concerning sacred art, support for the use of reinforced concrete and modern building techniques for new churches, because "the world is too large and the various needs of the people in the world" deserve to be met, and a call to dampen "fanaticism in matters of sacred art," as it can lead to "decadence more sterile than the one we are now endeavoring to overcome." See "Preliminary Report: First International Congress of Catholic Artists," *Liturgical Arts* 19, no. 1 (November 1950): 4–6, in Rubin, *Modern Sacred Art and the Church of Assy*, 46–47.

ning of his pontificate, May 1964, he invited artists to Mass at the Sistine Chapel, trying to repair the strained relationship: "[I]n all sincerity and boldness we admit we have caused you pain, imposing imitation on you who are creators, giving life to a thousand new ideas and innovations. We said you must adapt to our style, you must be faithful to this tradition. . . . Forgive us for having placed on you a cloak of lead! And then we abandoned you."[42] In his address to artists at the close of Vatican II, 8 December 1965:

> To all of you, the Church of the council declares to you through our voice: if you are friends of genuine art, you are our friends. . . . You have aided her in translating her divine message in the language of forms and figures, making the invisible world palpable. Today, as yesterday, the Church needs you and turns to you. She tells you through our voice: Do not allow an alliance as fruitful as this to be broken. Do not refuse to put your talents at the service of divine truth. Do not close your mind to the breath of the Holy Spirit. This world in which we live needs beauty in order not to sink into despair. . . . [A]ll of this is through your hands. . . . Remember that you are the guardians of beauty in the world. May that free you from tastes which are passing and have no genuine value, from the search after strange or unbecoming expressions. Be always and everywhere worthy of your ideals and you will be worthy of the Church which, by our voice, addresses to you today her message of friendship, salvation, grace and benediction.[43]

Paul VI commissioned a crucifix staff (ferula) for his liturgical use as pope from the Italian sculptor Lello Scorzelli in 1963 and used it for the first time at the official closing of Vatican II. The body of Christ here is broken, emaciated, weathered, beaten. While the more

---

42. Paul VI, "The Friendship of Artists and the Church," addressed to artists attending a Mass in the Sistine Chapel, May 7, 1964. *The Pope Speaks*, vol. 9 (Huntington, IN: Our Sunday Visitor, 1964), 392–93.

43. Paul VI, *Address to Artists at the Closing of the Second Vatican Council*, December 8, 1965, /w2.vatican.va/content/paul-vi/en/speeches/1965/documents /hf_p-vi_spe_19651208_epilogo-concilio-artisti.html.

traditional contours of head and body remain compared to the Richier crucifix, the work is startlingly nontriumphal and so offering little
by way of communicating "the victory of Christ over suffering and
death." Scorzelli's ferula has been carried by every pope since and
placed on papal rosaries. Although clearly expressionist in style, Paul
VI must have felt that it reflected his statements above: "talent put
at service of divine truth"; even as difficult as this crucifix is to behold, it does not manifest "strange or unbecoming expressions."

Paul VI opened the Collection of Modern Religious Art at the
Vatican Museums in 1973. The collection is remarkable, consisting
of over eight hundred works occupying fifty-five rooms, the majority
of which were donated to the Holy See by artists and collectors, but
finding it on a visit can take some doing. There is no published
catalog of the works and little has been done to promote the collection's existence. So Paul VI opened the door (or the basement, so to
speak, since part of the collection is housed below the Sistine Chapel), and the relationship between the Catholic Church and modern
art continues on its awkward way.

The Path along the Precipice

I am walking alone along a narrow path. A steep precipice on one
side, it is a deep bottomless in depth, a depth bottomlessly deep.
Across on the other side are meadows, mountains, horses, people.
I am walking and staggering down along the precipice. I am in the
act of the danger of falling down, but I throw myself toward the
meadow, the horses, mountains, people. I whirl about in the vibrant life—but I must return to the path along the precipice. That
is my way, which I must walk. I am careful lest I fall. Once again
in toward life and people. But I must return to the path along the
precipice. Because it is my path, until I plunge into the deep.[44]

44. Edvard Munch, journal entry 12 in *The Private Journals of Edvard Munch: We
Are Flames Which Pour Out of the Earth*, ed. and trans. J. Gill Holland (Madison,
WI: University of Wisconsin Press, 2005), 20.

Edvard Munch (1863–1944) writes this in his journal; because he did not date his entries, and because he records memories or feelings, it is difficult to ascertain the time in which they were written. J. Gill Holland calls these entries "verbal art" that accompanies his visual art.[45] Munch's loneliness is palpable here, and the way that he describes the landscape of his life is reminiscent of Van Gogh's painting *Thatched Cottages in the Sunshine: Reminiscences of the North* (1890), in which a faceless blue-toned peasant in the lower right corner is separated from the warm hearths of a village by a rocky hedge fence. This isolation of Van Gogh and Munch from participation in conventional society is strewn throughout the bodies of their work.

Munch knew loss: his mother died when he was thirteen of tuberculosis; five years later, his older sister Sophie also succumbed to the disease—events his father considered divine punishment, intensifying his father's depressive illness. Another sister, Laura, was institutionalized for schizoaffective illness and his only brother died of pneumonia at thirty. His father, a physician, brought Edvard along to the army hospitals where he practiced, further surrounding the boy with images of trauma and pain. Munch suffered a nervous breakdown in 1908 after having wrestled with anxiety attacks and alcohol most of his life and spent nine months in a hospital. The treatment seemed to cure the alcoholism, but he retreated further from human contact, becoming a recluse, even avoiding his sister, Inger, whom he had painted sitting atop the bouldered rim of the sea in one of his greatest early works, *Summer Night*, in 1889. The horizontal boundary in this work threads through many of his works, a boundary that cuts through the person: there is a demarcation, there is an inside and an outside. The edge of the chasm, the expanse of a lonely field: such is the life of the one who occasionally *desires* the abyss. In the abyss is anonymity, where the self is without self, without obligation, without root or past. The place of wildness.

"Wildness" refers us to a place where the desire to order, to master and control, must be relinquished or emptied in order to allow creative energy to emerge. Munch believed this; he sought the isolation of the

45. See J. Gill Holland, introduction to Holland, *The Private Journals of Edvard Munch*, 4.

Norwegian wilderness for the freedom to walk the precipice. It was this edge—between society and solitude, between convention and madness—that he believed maintained his creativity. His painting is at times bright, stippled in sunlight, lovers on a bench in a corner, or twisted into one many-limbed creature; at other times melancholy, seemingly built from the embers after the fire is a distant memory. The edge, the precipice, is one which artists of the twentieth century walked with abandon. Wildness emerged in the landscape of art with Manet, Van Gogh, Turner: a wildness always tempered in vulnerability, always given just before the breakdown.

The term "wild," Roderick Nash reminds us, is a contraction of "willed," such that wilderness means "self-willed land"[46]—land which is not bent to the will of another. Venturing into the unknown dark, where forces are free of human interference, means the risk of eccentricity, the risk of being wrong, the risk of oddness in a bearing by which we may begin to imagine the radically new. In this risk of eccentricity is the beginning of art, the concretization of the awareness of a special or transcendent dimension of existence; it may also be the beginning of theology. The interest to enter the disturbing unknown, to relinquish control, to empty the self in a manner akin to the divine ontology of vulnerability we see active in the kenosis hymn of Philippians 2, opens the space of creativity, for the artist, as well as for theological experience and discourse.

"Wildness" is the quality of being unbounded or uncontrolled by human beings; "wilderness" is the place where wildness occurs and flourishes. Wildness and its corresponding wilderness have a long history in the humanities, arts, and literature as a metaphor for venturing into the unknown or subconscious. Wildness may also refer to an actual locus of experience, as in Henry David Thoreau's work, in which living close to the natural, untamed world heals him for human society. Artists in the twentieth century were attracted to primitivism as a way to seek a "pure" form of experience free from artifice, as when Picasso was drawn to African art and the totemic themes of ancient religions. Freud believed that suppressing the

---

46. Roderick Nash, *Wilderness and the American Mind*, 5th ed. (New Haven, CT: Yale University Press, 2014), 1–2.

critical faculty that typically governs our thoughts leads to creativity; civilization represses imagination. Jung searched the mythical archetypes embedded deep in the human psyche to unlock human potential. Hence, although they may manifest as a threat to being, we need not escape or manipulate the unbounded and dangerous. Paul Tillich observes, "Facing the God who is really God means facing also the absolute threat of nonbeing. . . . [T]he basic anxiety, the anxiety of a finite being about the threat of nonbeing, cannot be eliminated. *It belongs to existence itself.*"[47] If through the kenosis hymn we see the image of a God who is known through humiliation, in vulnerability, the God of a "persecuted truth," as Kierkegaard put it, as Levinas later puts it, then facing God means exposing our own bare skin to the untamed elements. This willingness to expose, to remove that which Adam and Eve hid behind before they were expelled from the Garden, the courage of emptiness, is the place where art is possible.

The advent of modern art saw a font of creativity in a place of wildness. The best of modern art occurs through laying bare the self in the sort of emptying by which the detachment or humiliation of self brings reality to vividness, to life: the emptiness that brings matter, works of art, into being. Modern Art struggled with representing the unpresentable in the face of absurdity and the threat of nihilism. "The feelings I had at the time of the war in '41 was that the world was coming to an end," observed Barnett Newman (1905–1970), "And to the extent that the world was coming to an end, the whole issue of painting, I felt, was over because it was impossible to paint flowers, figures, etc., and so the crisis moved around the problem of what I can really paint."[48] The immensity of suffering in the first half of the twentieth century was anxious for new forms of expression and lament. Tillich recognized this in Modern Art, which

47. Paul Tillich, *The Courage to Be* (New Haven, CT: Yale University Press, 2000), 39.

48. Barnett Newman, television interview with Alan Solomon, July 12, 1966, part of the "U.S.A. Artists" series on National Education Television, *Archives of American Art*, Alan Solomon files, transcript of Barnett Newman interview, March 20, 1966; cited by Mark Godfrey, "Barnett Newman's Stations and the Memory of the Holocaust," *October* 108 (Spring, 2004): 37.

he considered both religious and timely to meet the needs of the age. The early twentieth century saw two dominant areas in Modern Art: Cubists claimed that objects don't have absolute shapes or surfaces, rejecting the rules of perspective and embracing two dimensions of the picture-plane. Surrealists challenged linear and rational thought, attempting to unlock what they believed to be the superior reality of the subconscious mind. The Abstract Expressionists, appearing in the 1940s, took these precedents further, shunning figuration in a tacit response to the catastrophe that Newman describes as civilization—the world—coming to an end. Abstraction and visible distance are metaphors for theology's attempt to offer what Richard Kearney calls the "testimonial imagination," "the power to remember the oppressed, to represent the unrepresented, to put a name on the unnamable crime by recounting it in images."[49] We will consider this move away from the mastery of the object through figuration or positive affirmation by first discussing the rise of abstraction in modernist art which leads to the spiritual wildness of Expressionism, as well as the religious and theological implications of this movement.

We have seen in previous chapters that art precedes Logos: art served to communicate the experience of the sacred before the formalization of language and the written word. Our contemporary disconnection from the "explosive generosity of celebration" of the sacred that first made us human means a disconnection from the space of the paradox between absence and presence that first appeared thirty thousand years ago and has yet to be resolved or overcome. Maurice Blanchot reminds us that the distance between the origin and the expression, this distance which art explores, is that "contact that shatters all acquired form—what is essentially before; what is, without yet being."[50]

---

49. Richard Kearney, *Poetics of Imagining: Modern to Post-modern* (New York: Fordham University Press, 1998), 238.

50. Maurice Blanchot, "The Birth of Art," in *Friendship*, trans. Elizabeth Rottenberg (Stanford, CA: Stanford University Press, 1997), 10.

"Shattering all acquired form" describes the intent of the Abstract Expressionist movement in visual art, which by the mid-twentieth century, sought a more visceral and emotional response to the reality of the age than previous movements in art had allowed. The abstract as nonimitative, as disorienting, as transcending phenomena, is a place of wildness in which one may find refuge as Thoreau did at Walden Pond. Of the artistic achievement of his friend Mark Rothko, Robert Motherwell wrote, "[I]t breaks out of the riverbed of modern art through a shift in subject matter to the undreamed one in abstract art of poignancy before the unknown void. . . . [I]n essence Rothko's belief was *I feel* therefore *I am*; this is what his color expressed, even when it was ugly, as occasionally happened."[51] The Abstract Expressionists wrestled with that unbounded nothingness, in which one may find the nihil of human life as well as that emptiness, that space or *différance* of the radically new, charged with possibility. In this sense, the Abstract Expressionist art of Mark Rothko, Robert Motherwell, Helen Frankenthaler, Jackson Pollock, and Ad Reinhardt provides theology with an opportunity to experience wildness (and also, perhaps, in the vast expanses of their canvases, wilderness) for the sake of the self-emptying (kenosis) that opens one toward empathy, new forms of discourse on the sacred, attempting an exercise of the nonrational and a renunciation of the idolatry that comes from positivistic language. In short, we have another opportunity to explore the divine occupancy of the material world—or the material occupancy of the divine world—that is the doctrine of incarnation.

To illustrate why Abstract Expressionism turns away from the figurative symbol, Robert Motherwell tells the story of Franz Kafka's horror when he discovers that the original publisher of *The Metamorphosis*, Kurt Wolff, has commissioned an artist to paint something for the cover. Kafka writes to Wolff: "It occurred to me . . . that

51. Robert Motherwell, "On Rothko: A Eulogy," in *The Writings of Robert Motherwell*, ed. Dore Ashton with Joan Banach (Berkeley, CA: University of California Press, 2007), 273.

[the artist] might want to draw the insect itself. Please, not that—anything but that! The insect itself cannot be drawn. It cannot even be shown in the distance!"[52] Motherwell cites Alan Blunden's chronology of Kafka: "Kafka knows that the ambiguities of his fiction can only be accommodated in the mind, in the imagination: to draw his images is to resolve their ambiguity, 'take them literally'—and hence destroy them."[53] Resolving ambiguity is not the project of the modern artist:

> The subject matter was at once too "real" as felt and too ultimate in its existential concerns not to be betrayed by the domesticated beauty of the School of Paris, or by the graphic tradition of constructivism, or by the obviousness and pathos of the socially varied forms of realism, or by the fantasies and black humor of the surrealists. No, in the 1940's, with the Second World War, the atomic bomb, and the beginnings of the electric era now exploding, only a monumental ambiguity would do.[54]

Modern art embraced Kafka's sense of displacement and ambiguity, as well as his imaginative step beyond rationality. The artistic hermeneutic transforms the relationship, and so the alterity or distance, between the human experience of the world and the visual image. Rothko's color field paintings remind us of this space, as well as construct it: this is a no-place that is a moment of lifting (or sinking)—a place, space, pause or interlude, a "non-thinking" space in which we don't cling to definitions or doctrine as authoritative, controlling, or demanding, instead submitting to awareness that emptiness or Buddhist *sunyata* is a dynamic and creative openness to the interdependence that informs infinite responsibility to the wholly Other.

---

52. Robert Motherwell, "Kafka's Visual Recoil: A Note (for Dore Ashton)," in Ashton, *The Writings of Robert Motherwell*, 337.

53. Ibid., citing Allan Blunden, "A Chronology of Kafka's Life," in *The World of Franz Kafka*, ed. J. P. Stern (New York: Holt, Rhinehart, and Winston, 1980).

54. Ibid.

This "space" was real for Mark Rothko. In interviews, Rothko made the following statements: "Abstract art never interested me; I always painted realistically. My present paintings are realistic,"[55] and "I'm not an abstractionist. . . . I'm not interested in relationships of color or form or anything else."[56] How did the New York School of Abstract Expressionism define abstraction? Barnett Newman argued against the idea promoted by abstract artists that subject matter must be eliminated in favor of hard-edged geometric shapes and form; Newman and Rothko preferred soft, organic forms more compatible with human emotion and the teeming subconscious explored by the Surrealists.[57] In 1947, Rothko writes that he views shapes as "organisms with volition and a passion for self-assertion" that move "with internal freedom, and without need to conform with or to violate what is probable in the familiar world," having "no direct association with any particular visible experience but in them one recognizes the principle and passion of organisms" when his work contained stacks of small, hazy, horizontal rectangles, before he abandoned shape altogether in 1949.[58] The guidance of his early abstractions led him deeper into the tragedy of life which Rothko believed to be the basic concern of the artist, whether visual artist, poet, or musician.[59] It seemed that the more he abandons figuration or shape, the further he ventures into the tragedy; whereas the Cubists had worked from reality to abstraction, Rothko began with the void and worked toward reality.[60]

55. William C. Seitz, interview with Mark Rothko, January 22, 1952, cited in Anna Chave, *Mark Rothko: Subjects in Abstraction* (New Haven, CT: Yale University Press, 1989), 25.

56. Selden Rodman, interview with Mark Rothko, *Conversations with Artists* (New York: Devlin-Adair, 1957), 93, cited in Chave, *Mark Rothko: Subjects in Abstraction*, 25.

57. See Chave, *Mark Rothko: Subjects in Abstraction*, 25.

58. Mark Rothko, "The Romantics Were Prompted," *Possibilities* 1 (1947–1948), in *Writings on Art*, ed. Miguel Lopez-Remiro (New Haven, CT: Yale University Press, 2006), 59.

59. See Rothko, "Whenever One Begins to Speculate," ca. 1954, in *Writings on Art*, 109.

60. See James E. B. Breslin, *Mark Rothko: A Biography* (Chicago: The University of Chicago Press, 1993), 210–11.

"Only Abstract Art Can Bring Us to the Threshold of the Divine"

On February 25, 1970, the day Mark Rothko's Seagram murals were delivered to the Tate Gallery in London, Rothko was found in his apartment, apparently dead of suicide from an overdose of barbiturates and slashed veins. These works are named "Seagram" because they originated as a commission by the Canadian distilling company for the Four Seasons restaurant in Seagram's corporate headquarters on Park Avenue in midtown Manhattan. In 1959, a year after agreeing to the commission, he realized his mistake: "I accepted this assignment as a challenge, with strictly malicious intentions. I hope to paint something that will ruin the appetite of every son of a bitch who ever eats in that room. If the restaurant would refuse to put up my murals, that would be the ultimate compliment. But they won't. People can stand anything these days."[61]

Rothko had decided to "trap" those who were wealthy enough to eat in such posh circumstances "in a room where all the doors and windows are bricked up"—the same effect, Rothko realized, as in Michelangelo's *ricetto* in the Laurentian Library of the Medici family in Florence.[62] Rothko had visited Florence in 1959, soon after beginning work on the murals; the Laurentian's ricetto, or vestibule, features a famous tripartite staircase leading to the long reading room, lit by a series of smaller windows high above a two-tiered series of opaque windows in a tension that inspires awe. The effect of the small, high windows is similar to a skylight; light comes from above but moves laterally. The windows below without glass reject transparency, playing with our anticipations: the window that isn't a window. The two cases of stairs that flank the central case are without rail, open, and lead nowhere. That the elite would have no escape from the cavernous depth of an abyss without end. Rothko's Seagram murals achieved something of the abyss, the dramatic tension of

---

61. Mark Rothko, in a conversation with John Fischer, "The Easy Chair: Mark Rothko, Portrait of the Artist as an Angry Young Man," *Harper's* (July 1970), in *Writings on Art*, 131.

62. See Ibid.

being caught in confusion or ambiguity. But Rothko withdrew from the commission before the restaurant had a chance to ruin appetites.

The road to his breakthrough year of 1949, when Rothko fully committed his work to the complete lack of representation, was long and painful. He had studied under Max Weber, one of the first American artists to adopt Cubism, in the Art Students' League in New York, but Cubism did not suit him; Weber's influence pertained more to giving Rothko permission to focus on the spiritual aspect of painting.[63] While wanting to abandon figuration by the mid-1940s, he had trouble finding the conduit through which he could express his own ideas about the "tragic-religious drama" that he felt undergirded all the mythological and Surrealist subjects which had preoccupied him through the 1930s. With a job teaching children at the Center Academy in Brooklyn, a Jewish school, he learned to appreciate the purity of children's imagination. He writes,

> Painting is just as natural a language as singing or speaking. It is a method of making a visible record of our experience, visual or imaginative, colored by our own feelings and reactions and indicated with the same simplicity and directness as singing or speaking. If you do not believe this, watch these children work, and you will see them put their forms, figures and views into pictorial arrangements, employing of necessity most of the rules of optical perspective and geometry, but without the knowledge that they are employing them. They do so in the same manner as they speak, unconscious that they are using the rules of grammar.[64]

His observations of the way children abandoned themselves in their art, their immediacy, was one of the greatest influences on his art, which at the time was not going well. As Simon Schama notes, Rothko not only tried on Cubism for size but also the Expressionism of Georges Rouault, Max Beckman, and Munch, and none fit: it was

63. See Bonnie Clearwater, *The Rothko Book* (London: Tate Publishing, 2010), 12.

64. Mark Rothko, "New Training for Future Artists and Art Lovers," *Brooklyn Jewish Center Review* 14 (February–March 1934): 10, in López-Remiro, *Writings on Art*, 1.

"as if Rothko is burdened by an overload of competing influences."[65] In 1949, Rothko was forty-six; he had struggled for more than twenty years with his own artistic identity until he had a moment, akin to Jackson Pollock's moment in 1947, of realizing how to manipulate the paint to bring the "unpresentable" forward.

He defended the movement of the New York School toward abstraction through Arshile Gorky, Adolf Gottlieb, and Pollock as an inclination toward mythmaking, "and as such have no prejudices for or against reality. Our paintings, like all myths, do not hesitate to combine shreds of reality with what is considered 'unreal' and insist upon the validity of the merger."[66] "I adhere to the reality of things," Rothko asserted, while "enlarging the extent of this reality. . . . [I]f I have abandoned the use of familiar objects it is because I refuse to mutilate their appearance for the rigors of grace and life which they are too old to serve and for which perhaps they were never intended."[67] Surrealism and abstraction he called his "father and mother," but Surrealism's relationship to the visual information of the subconscious was no longer adequate to depict the tragic experience which is "the only source book for art."[68] James Breslin notes that Rothko's movement toward total abstraction was not an escape from the material world but an interest to crush the world of the familiar in the same way that he ground his pigments with a mortar and pestle; this allowed him to create his own colors.[69] This act of crushing into the radically new is echoed in Rothko's statement, "The familiar identity of things has to be pulverized in order to destroy the finite associations with which our society increasingly enshrouds every aspect of our environment,"[70] which Breslin interprets as Rothko's desire to bring the sensible world "to the edge either of dissolution or new beginning" in which "loss

---

65. Simon Schama, *The Power of Art* (New York: Harper Collins, 2006), 405.

66. Mark Rothko, "Letter to the Editor of the *New York Times*," July 8, 1945, in López-Remiro, *Writings on Art*, 46.

67. Mark Rothko, "I Adhere to the Reality of Things," (1945) in *Writings on Art*, 44.

68. Ibid.

69. See Breslin, *Mark Rothko: A Biography*, 245.

70. Rothko, "The Romantics Were Prompted," 58.

merges with liberation" and the "human and transcendent can be rejoined."[71] Along similar lines, Dore Ashton observes, "His insecurity in the interpreted world was probably the deepest force, driving him past its barriers throughout his life."[72] Such an insecurity in the interpreted world originates, perhaps, in *who* is doing the interpreting, who acts as arbiters of the apparatus of power and privilege.

If Surrealist and abstract art are his mother and father, Rothko admits an interest to rebel against them, as a child should rebel, and against the essentialism that drove the early detours into abstraction, in which a universal form of reality can be discerned merely with shape and color; this is perhaps why there was an interest among Cubists to return to neoplatonic notions of an eternal realm of Forms that determines all material substances. But Paul Cezanne, whose late Impressionism anticipates Cubism and who famously said that "all nature could be reduced to the cylinder, cube, sphere, and cone," wanted young artists merely to pay attention to forms in nature, not be dismissive of them. Similarly, Rothko repudiated abstract art's "denial of the material existence of the whole of reality. For art to me is an anecdote of the spirit, and the only means of making concrete the purpose of its varied quickness and stillness."[73] Rothko called himself a "myth-maker" alongside the similarly felt views of Newman and Clyfford Still, based on the desire to mine the tragedy "generic to all myths and times, no matter where they occur."[74]

Today, the Seagram murals are displayed in a special room at the Tate Modern tailored to his specifications: close to the ground and lit by diffused light. Remembering the Laurentian ricetto, this is the only way Rothko's paintings should be seen, as the architecture of an experience, rather than an occasional colored surface. Architecture is art we can enter, art we can get lost in, art that surrounds us in such a way that we become a part of the building, not just as something that we see but as something that reacts dynamically with the

---

71. Breslin, *Mark Rothko: A Biography*, 245.

72. Dore Ashton, *About Rothko* (New York: Da Capo Press, 1996), 4.

73. Mark Rothko, "Personal Statement, 1945," in *Writings on Art*, 45.

74. Mark Rothko, "Introduction to First Exhibition Paintings: Clyfford Still, 1946," in *Writings on Art*, 48.

whole person.[75] This is akin to the relationship we observed between the architecture and the figures in Masaccio's Trinity fresco: art is a total experience, both housing and offering forth the divine.

Viewing the Seagram murals reminded me of a visit to the Grand Canyon: no matter how many pictures we took, none captured what it felt like to be there, insignificant in the magnificence, enclosed by endless variations on red, umber, ochre in the striations of rock and light, as though my eyes couldn't possibly discern the range of color at their current evolutionary stage (too few cones). The Seagram murals, grouped in the way Rothko intended, have that effect. Are these floating squares walled-up windows or open rooms? Fresh, open wounds or dried blood, in the process of healing? Random or deliberate—so much is controlled, and yet there are tiny drips everywhere, allowed to appear, minute meteors against the fabric of space. But no contradictions, no oppositions: Rothko had achieved what Michelangelo achieved, a resolution of opposites with the polarities still intact and on the move. After an hour on the bench with the works, watching the visitors, their interactions, the shifting light, I was overcome with a sense of gratitude; the sadness of blue-grey undertones had melted into a rich simmer of joy. The fire and the embers together, incarnation of divine into matter and back again. The undercurrent of sorrow that always accompanies grace, as the scene from Isaac Bashevis Singer's play *Teibele and Her Demon*, when the widow Teibele questions Alchonon's study of Kabbalah:

> Alchonon: There are times when a soul must conceal itself and there are times when a soul must reveal itself.
> Teibele: And it's time for revelation . . .
> Alchonon: Invisible threads join together all matters. When you shake one thread, all the threads shake.
> Teibele: When do you study? In the middle of the night?
> Alchonon: Yes. Night is a time of rigor but also of mercy. There are truths which one can see only when it's dark.[76]

75. See Robert S. Jackson, "Michelangelo's Ricetto of the Laurentian Library: A Phenomenology of the Alinari Photograph," *Art Journal* 28, no. 1 (Autumn 1968): 56.

76. Isaac Bashevis Singer, *Teibele and Her Demon* (the play based on Singer's short story), with Eve Friedman (New York: Samuel French, 1984), 51.

The Rothko Chapel

The organic extension of the arrangement of the Seagram murals in the Rothko room at the Tate Modern is the Rothko Chapel in Houston. I had researched and read about the Rothko Chapel for two years before I finally went. The paintings Rothko created for the chapel appear on the internet and in numerous publications, so I had a basic idea of what was there. James Elkins introduces his book *Pictures and Tears* with testimony of those who have visited the chapel or seen the works before their installation, toward an intention to investigate reactions before powerful works of art: why do we have emotional reactions to images, or even to abstract works without figuration? More specifically, why do people cry before works of art? Even more specifically, why do people cry before the large color field paintings of Mark Rothko?

The Rothko Chapel exemplifies the dynamic of self-emptying, or kenosis, explored from the experience of the creative giving of the artist's self and an open receiving of the viewer/participant. Rothko was especially astute at the response he wished to elicit from the viewer. Schama observes that the image for Rothko is "forever evolving, even during the time of our looking . . . a done picture was a dead picture."[77] Every artistic medium depends on an audience; there is no incarnation without recognition; there is no "God" without relationship. The possibility of incarnation is intimately connected to the risk of isolation and insignificance. Such is the dilemma of the artist. As I prepared to visit the chapel, I wondered whether I was preparing to meet Rothko, to see his self-portrait. I wondered whether the suffering that haunted him in the last years of his life would be too difficult to face.

Elkins's own experience in the Rothko Chapel was not one of tears, but he writes honestly of his initial reaction:

> The place is obviously thick with emotion, or the promise of it. I can't explain why I didn't cry, except that I may have been too well armed with my research on the lore and philosophy of crying. Sometimes philosophy is like a levee, keeping back the flood

77. Schama, *The Power of Art*, 421.

of disorderly thoughts. Philosophers keep the levee in good repair, and that's why philosopher's tears are so rare: they're like the incipient cracks in the dike, leaking one drop at a time. Clearly the Rothko chapel is a dangerous place for philosophy. Orderly thoughts and preconceptions are under continuous pressure, and after enough time passes, they crumble and dissolve.[78]

I understand what he means; sometimes being an "expert" in a field often bars the visceral and emotional connections others experience when they encounter the artwork. Armed with reason and research, the philosopher and the theologian are rarely able to let the whirling dervishes loose, but even worse is when the academy tries to squeeze every drop of passionate writing or wide-eyed wonder out of us. There is, of course, the possibility that we may slip and fall on this wonder and fail utterly. Elkins acknowledges this several times in this book, blaming the academic study of art history for the "desiccated museum pedagogy" in which "students are taught to comb through archives and old books to see how the original viewers once responded. Their own reactions are typically ruled out of court. Such scholarship is necessary to build a sense of history and to avoid solipsism, but it is a bloodless pursuit."[79]

Bloodless, indeed—when the Rothko Chapel has open veins in its history. It is unbearable to appreciate the chapel from a purely intellectual or academic perspective. It is also unbearable to consider the doctrine of the incarnation or the emptiness of all things from a purely intellectual or academic perspective. Returning to art as a resource for exploring belief, doctrine, and philosophical ideas is necessary to keep the life and the blood pumping in theology. Because of this, I realized that seeing Rothko's paintings for a chapel reproduced only in books or on the computer was unfair to his work, especially when I believe so strongly in the personal experience of art, so I went to Houston even though it was August.

78. James Elkins, *Pictures and Tears: A History of People Who Have Cried in Front of Paintings* (New York: Routledge, 2004), 22.
79. Elkins, *Pictures and Tears*, 208.

Perhaps it was something of a pilgrimage. The nearest I could get to the chapel from my hotel by commuter train was a little over a mile walk. Although the temperature was 94 degrees, the walk was relatively pleasant, through residential neighborhoods, large shady oak trees, and the outskirts of St. Thomas University's campus. The red brick, octagonal—Rothko's way of merging East and West—chapel is marked by a low, small sign, making the building's architectural profile humble, blending easily into the neighborhood and the old trees. There is no outside decoration, no fanfare, no snack shop, no souvenir stand; the penetrating silence within begins outside the doors. A young woman sat on a bench in partial shade, reading. The sun glared above. The only sound was an occasional car and the cicadas humming so steadily that they contributed to the silence.

Barnett Newman's superb sculpture *Broken Obelisk*, 1967, rises its five tons from the water of a rectangular reflecting pool. The sculpture intentionally embodies contradiction: in its weight on water, in the way the monument has been torn in half, modern civilization far from civility, the antipode of progress, far from evolved. A phallic triumph toppled, deliberately rusted and ruined, yet suspended in the humid air. Dedicated to the life of Martin Luther King, Jr., the sculpture stands guard over the chapel in "its assertion of freedom, its denial of dogmatic principles, its repudiation of all dogmatic life."[80] Newman was an anarchist and believed that the sort of reception appropriate to his work "would mean the end of all state capitalism and totalitarianism." Concerning its message, Newman explained, "It is concerned with life and I hope that I have transformed its tragic content into a glimpse of the sublime."[81] Ironically, the Municipal Commission of the City of Houston initially blocked the desired dedication of the sculpture to King's memory in 1969, saying they did "not wish to bias its reception by the public" or use the sculpture as a memorial,

---

80. Barnett Newman, Interview with Dorothy Gees Seckler, *Art in America* 50, no. 2, in *Art in Theory 1900-1990: An Anthology of Changing Ideas*, ed. Charles Harrison and Paul Wood (Oxford: Blackwell, 2003), 784–85.

81. Cited in Joy Giguere, *Characteristically American: Memorial Architecture, National Identity, and the Egyptian Revival* (Knoxville, TN: University of Tennessee Press, 2014), 225.

as such would engender "current political questions."[82] It seems the sculpture achieved what it wrought—identifying the threat King posed to the established order.

John (1904–1973) and Dominique (1908–1998) de Menil, the patrons of the Rothko Chapel, were no strangers to the occasional tussle with Houston culture. Both were born and raised in Paris, moving to Houston during World War II to preserve her family's petroleum drilling business. They became prominent local art patrons. Her tastes in art were guided in friendship with Fr. Couturier while the couple was living in France; he inspired what became a huge collection. Fans of Rothko's for years, they approached him in 1964 about the possibility of housing the Seagram works in a Catholic chapel they wished to build on St. Thomas's campus. The conception of this project was influenced by Henri Matisse's Chapel of the Rosary in Vence, one of the sites important to the Sacred Art movement; the de Menils had already been benefactors of St. Thomas University, but when the Basilean fathers bristled at the prominence of Rothko's influence, the chapel site was moved off St. Thomas's campus to become an ecumenical center.

Philip Johnson, who had designed the de Menil's house and other projects for St. Thomas, was enlisted as architect. After the Seagram debacle, Rothko was attracted to the promise of artistic license and the opportunity to guide an architect on all steps of the process by which the works would be presented. Thus the chapel was to be an unprecedented collaboration of artist and architect, in which the art would be the focal point around which the chapel was built, rather than the other way around, as has historically been the case. The art was to be the material of the religious or sacred experience, rather than in the background as decoration. Dominique de Menil's address opening the Rothko Chapel on February 26, 1971, a year and a day after Rothko's death, was bittersweet in its assertion of Rothko's courage. Abstract art prevents our visual naivete, she observed, since we can no longer represent Jesus as the Renaissance masters did in today's age of visual clutter: "only abstract art can bring us to the

---

82. Ibid., 226.

threshold of the divine."[83] We must cleanse our religious visual palette in an age where contemporary devotional portraits of Jesus look more like bad jokes. Although I understood this, I was still hesitant when I finally entered the chapel, afraid to be disappointed.

There are fourteen paintings, as many as the Catholic Stations of the Cross—Rothko considered making such a connection explicit but then dismissed it—set in the octagonal structure; nine of the paintings are grouped in threes, with two sets that echo the triptych format of Christian altarpieces during the Middle Ages and Renaissance. The largest triptych, at the north wall, is what one first sees upon entering. The walls are a matte, mottled white, the floor a dark grey stone, and there are simple wooden benches arranged to face four walls. Light comes from an opaque skylight in the center of the chapel, filtering the sun's severity. Such diffused light was of the sort Rothko preferred his paintings to be seen; he had carefully orchestrated not just the placement of the paintings within the architecture but the entire environment in which they are encountered. The paintings themselves do not compete with anything in the chapel. There is no focal point or altar, there are no words or plaques on the walls, there are no photographs of the artist or donors. In other words, it is an artistic achievement that is unlike any other I have visited: although bereft of obvious elements of religious practice or symbolism, the space is sacred because of an abiding and penetrating silence that envelops the visitor. Absent of all distraction, all reference to any particular religion or culture, the paintings themselves do not embellish and are not extraneous: the environment is self-sufficient such that the paintings wouldn't make sense separated from each other or placed in another space.

I sat down at first in front of the north apse triptych. My fourteen-year-old daughter, Annie, was with me, and there was only one other person in the chapel besides the rather annoyed looking guard; I can appreciate Rothko's darker paintings better when there are fewer people around. My first reaction was a bit dissatisfied, as well as disoriented, possibly from the transition between the Texas heat and

83. Dominique de Menil, "Inaugural Address at the Rothko Chapel," in *The Rothko Chapel: Writings on Art and the Threshold of the Divine* (New Haven, CT: Yale University Press for the Rothko Chapel, 2010), 19.

the cool interior. A cloud must have moved and suddenly the light from the skylight was intense: even though the paintings are matte, which Rothko created by mixing hot rabbit-skin glue with pigment, there was an unsettling reflection on the surface of the north triptych. In remarks concerning how his paintings are to be displayed, Rothko noted the problems caused by viewing the works in severe light: "[I]f there is too much light, the color in the picture is washed out and a distortion of their look occurs. . . . [T]hey should not be over-lit or romanticized by spots; this results in a distortion of their meaning. . . . [A]bove all the entire picture should be evenly lighted and not strongly."[84]

James Elkins's first impression was that these works "were weak and frail, like that dusty black fabric that is stretched over old audio speakers. . . . [T]he pictures looked exhausted."[85] While it is possible that sunlight has faded the works, it seems more accurate to say that in the paintings, we witness the exhaustion of a man who had lived too long with profound sorrow, who had absorbed the tragedies of the first half of the twentieth century as though they were his personal memories. Elkins's observation of "dusty black fabric stretched over old audio speakers" also seemed apt until a group of clouds blessedly shielded the sun and the surface of the paintings took on a purple depth that was like the skin of an eggplant, untranslatable even in the best print photography. A diaphanous spot of maroon emerges from the purple in the left wing of the north wall apse triptych. This rising maroon is the closest to a "something" in these works but is so restrained that it is not a focal point. It does not manifest in several of the color plates that have been published. The red that underlies all these works—Rothko often relied on an initial wash of red over the surface of his canvases before he proceeded further—appears more explicitly here as light independent

---

84. Mark Rothko, "Letter to the Whitechapel Gallery, 1961," in *Writings on Art*, 145. Breslin notes that Rothko never had a chance to install the paintings in the Chapel. "'I do remember distinctly telling him,' said William Scharf, 'that Texas light was going to be frighteningly different from what he was contending with in mid-town Manhattan.'" Breslin, *Mark Rothko: A Biography*, 474.

85. Elkins, *Pictures and Tears*, 6.

of material context, light with no star, no source. Rothko's complicated layers of glazes enable alterations in tone with the movement in light. I had expected more darkness. But as the light outside changed, the paintings themselves took on the shifting possibilities of spectral waves, receding and moving forward. Here was a remarkable "depiction" of pregnant and plentiful silence, the sort of silence that requires surrender, a willingness to enter the work as it is.

The triptychs on the east and west walls, arranged like traditional triptychs from Western Christendom, embody the deepest and most consistent obscurity. Here the murky blackness is an arena of sorrow with no resolution. There is no resurrection panel or the comfort of a gilt aura to offset the suffering of the crucifixion that usually occupies a medieval or Renaissance triptych. The paintings on the northeast, northwest, southeast, and southwest walls are similar to each other but far from identical, using vertical brushstrokes that veer in randomness like a rain shower when the sun is out. The subtleties in the fields encourage the quiet. The borders of the paintings, deliberately fashioned in the color and appearance of crushed red grapes (here he uses rags instead of brushes for the effect), frame the blackness so as to cordon off the mortality we cannot help but confront: here is our discussion of death; here we will see the black syrup of a sleep that pulls us under consciousness—the mortality that pulsates under the surface of all that is material. "I would like to say to those who think of my pictures as serene, whether on friendship or mere observation, that I have imprisoned the most utter violence in every inch of their surface,"[86] wrote Rothko of the trend of darkness in his late works. Although predominantly matte, there is a glossy rectangle that hovers in a corner.

I think about my desire to fix things, about the Jewish mystical inclination to repair the world (*tikkun olam*), about the optimism that the world can be repaired. I wonder whether I can be courageous enough to use my own pain for good, to feel it without fear; Rothko's pain seems to emanate from these canvases, his confrontation with the abyss. These paintings manifest the blackness of the bruise that

---

86. Mark Rothko, in Breslin, *Mark Rothko: A Biography*, 355.

is Rothko's anger, which is entirely appropriate in this chapel, or in any space set apart for the sacred, an anger that is not given to Christian sacred spaces but should belong in them as opportunity for lament. Rothko was angry that the world prefers to escape the sorrow of everyday chaos rather than face the steady beat of the tragic that must accompany awareness of the transcendent. One child dies every three seconds of malnutrition and preventable disease . . . another explosion in Iraq . . . another teenager caught in gang crossfire in Chicago . . . another inoperable cancer diagnosis . . . nearly one in four of my female students will be sexually assaulted before she graduates . . . the beat of night and more night. I think Rothko was furious that he felt all this and others didn't, and he swallowed all the sadness of lost and battered lives. The restless wandering of a little boy who had trouble assimilating from Russia to Portland, Oregon: the only time Rothko believed he was in the right place was in his painting.[87] He was angry that he was alone in this hole. Painting

---

87. James Breslin writes of Rothko's identification with victims of pogroms in his native Russia: "One story that he did repeat involved an early memory of his family and relatives talking about a czarist pogrom. 'The Cossacks took the Jews from the village to the woods and made them dig a large grave. Rothko said that he pictured that square grave in the woods so vividly that he wasn't sure the massacre hadn't happened in his lifetime. He said he'd always been haunted by the image of that grave, and that in some profound way it was locked into his painting.' In another version of the story Rothko himself witnessed the digging of the grave and the ensuing massacre." Breslin comments that there were no pogroms in Dvinsk, where the Rothkowitz family was from: "Rothko certainly never witnessed such an execution. He may have heard adults discussing pogroms elsewhere, and he may have heard a story about a mass grave, but the mass grave was a phenomenon of the holocaust, not of pogroms." Breslin, *Mark Rothko: A Biography*, 17–18. Matthew Baigell connects Rothko's desire to identify with the victims of persecution in the past to his trauma in the present; Baigell cites Cathy Caruth: "Trauma describes an overwhelming experience of sudden or catastrophic events in which the response to that event occurs in the often delayed, uncontrolled, repetitive appearance of hallucinations and other intrusive phenomena." Caruth, *Unclaimed Experience: Trauma, Narrative and History* (Baltimore: Johns Hopkins University Press, 1996), 11; see also Matthew Baigell, *Jewish Artists in New York: The Holocaust Years* (New Brunswick, NJ: Rutgers University Press, 2002), 103.

was where Rothko believed he could draw the viewer into this hole with him. Matthew Baigell notes that the trauma that accompanied Rothko through his life refers to his tacit interest to bear witness "from the eruption of evil that is radically incurable—is itself somehow a philosophical and ethical correlative of a situation with no cure, and of a radical human condition of exposure and vulnerability."[88]

The chapel demonstrates the clarity of vision Rothko sought as he plowed through the pain inside and outside. "The progression of a painter's work, as it travels in time from point to point, will be toward clarity: toward the elimination of all obstacles between the painter and the idea, and between the idea and the observer,"[89] since pictures "live by companionship"[90] and the possibility of rejection or misunderstanding is always the risk taken by any form of communication. John Fisher points to Rothko's anger as contributing to his suicide, "the justified anger of a man who felt destined to paint temples, only to find his canvases treated as trade goods."[91] It may be that Rothko's anger originated in his loneliness. We are, each of us, alone in the deep places of our suffering, places no one else can fully understand or share; neither can we the living ever "know" the finality of death. Our hope can only be that the divine lives there too.

It occurs to me that Jackson Pollock could not have displayed like this; nor Franz Kline or Hans Hoffman—their works are usually too high-energy to be in such a space. I suppose that if they were so inclined, they could have created a space specifically for their work, or at least similar groupings, but it is hard to imagine their work creating the sort of contemplative environment that hastens the quiet. Barnett Newman, who was also raised Jewish, comes closest with his series of fourteen paintings titled *Stations of the Cross: Lema*

88. Baigell, *Jewish Artists in New York*, 104, citing Shoshana Felman and Dori Laub, *Testimony: Crises of Witnessing in Literature, Psychoanalysis and History* (New York: Routledge, 1992), 57–58.

89. Mark Rothko, "Statement on His Attitude in Painting, 1949," in *Writings on Art*, 65.

90. Mark Rothko, "The Ides of Art, 1947," in *Writings on Art*, 57.

91. Rothko and Fisher, "The Easy Chair," 138.

Sabachtani (1958–1966),[92] which are similarly best appreciated as a group displayed together in their own room. If one painting is taken out of this context (which often happens for exhibitions), the works do not make sense the way that they do together. When seen together, the effect is startling, with the eerie undercurrent that the familiar is being torn apart, and what is comforting and comfortable is being shredded: such is a valuable entryway into thinking about the cross for Christians. Newman explains that the Markan death-cry of Jesus, *Lema Sabachtani*, is

> the question which has no answer. This overwhelming question that does not complain, makes today's talk of alienation, as if alienation were a modern invention, an embarrassment. This question that has no answer has been with us so long—since Jesus—since Abraham—since Adam—the original question, *Lema*? To what purpose—is the unanswerable question of human suffering. Can the passion be expressed by a series of anecdotes, by fourteen sentimental illustrations? Do not the Stations tell of one event? The first pilgrims walked the Via Dolorosa to identify themselves with the original moment, not to reduce it to a pious legend; nor even to worship the story of one man and his agony, but to stand witness to the story of each man's agony: the agony that is single, constant, unrelenting, willed—world without end.[93]

Despite the specifically Christian reference, Christians should refrain from thinking that these paintings are meant for believers' contemplation of the paschal mystery. As we saw in Chagall's *White Crucifixion*, Newman's *Stations* are also meditations on the devastation of injustice and violence Christians have historically perpetuated. Regarding the paintings as a group, their black and white fields shift,

92. The *Stations of the Cross* are owned by the National Gallery of Art in Washington, DC, but are not currently on view. Each canvas measures 78 x 60 inches. A fifteenth work, *Be II*, joined the group of works when first displayed at the Guggenheim Museum in New York in 1966.

93. Barnett Newman, *Stations of the Cross: Lema Sabachtani*, ed. Lawrence Alloway (New York: Solomon R. Guggenheim Museum Foundation, 1966), 9.

sometimes gashed with bare canvas, a view of naked skin in one being tortured, the exposure of vulnerability. If the black field defiantly withstands the encroaching assumptions of white, if there is a glossy difference, there is the matte to break it up. Sometimes the "zips" or stripes are smooth, like intended diagrams, sometimes they are rough and chaotic, no blending or bleeding boundaries. The energy of these paintings is in the way they are able to hold hard, sliced edges against softer, brushed strokes in tension, like a taut string vibrating. Charles Riley writes that Newman's achievement is in locating silence in these works: as in a musical performance, "Newman was able to locate a still point not once but many times, and the result is one of the great ascetic experiences . . . in contemporary painting."[94] These still points, rests or silences, a "momentary focus on the spaces which separate people—'between the glance of their eyes' ";[95] a space as important as the brushstroke.

Both Rothko and Newman attempt to elevate awareness of the depth and chaos of the suffering that permeates this life and this world. The *Stations of the Cross* and the Rothko Chapel paintings exemplify the culmination of the move toward greater and greater abstraction, more profound minimalism, that reveals a new spiritual "language" in which the unsaid, the unsayable, are converted into a material experience. In the paintings of the Rothko Chapel, color as the activity of both harmony and discord moves so subtly as to be imperceptible. We are brought before the shifting purple void, we feel the radiant dark field, as well as the promise of harmony in the silence they inspire, in the movement away from representation or speech.

The Unsaying

On a recent visit to the Los Angeles County Museum of Art (LACMA), I was struck by how beaten-up *Number 15* (1950) by

94. Charles A. Riley, *The Saints of Modern Art: The Ascetic Ideal in Contemporary Painting, Sculpture, Architecture, Music, Dance, Literature and Philosophy* (Hanover, NH: University Press of New England, 1998), 58.
95. Ibid., 59.

Jackson Pollock appeared. The frame of *Number 15* looked as though it had been hacked, even split in places, the Masonite, or fiberboard, exposed in others. Despite the appearance the typical art patron of the 1950s, *Number 15* is not art for the pearls-and-white-gloves set, finely finished and polished. This was made by a man with a cigarette perched on his bottom lip, an inch of ash perilously suspended, his sweat and beard mixing with the common house paint that remained on his fingertips when he scratched his face. The tangled masses of drips on the Masonite reveal strain between the jagged ire of the artist and his careful and considered examination of what drip or spatter belongs where when. Pollock reveled in the space between the random and deliberate; he lived for its spell, and when he was there, he rarely noticed what was going on around him. The long drips of paint were an extension of the sticks he used, which were extensions of his fingers—without having to stop activity to reload paint the way one must stop to replenish a brush. His technique allows a feast of automatism, the "stream of consciousness" that doesn't pause for reflection or correction. In this way, Pollock was able to tap into the subconscious—or so he thought—in much the same way the Surrealists had.

Number 15 was given to LACMA by Pollock himself in 1951, toward the end of his drip period; it was never in the auction house nor in the wealthy collector's third house, but always here, a gritty painting viewed by a gritty public. This isn't one of his masterpieces, either. It is one of his smaller works, but the energy and sensuality are there; the drips build on each other in a raw dance, and there is anarchy throbbing in black and red behind the white. This energy, determination, and focus distinguish an authentic Pollock from a forgery. In an interview with the *New Yorker* in 1950, he responded to a critic's comment that his paintings did not have a beginning or an end: "He didn't mean it as a compliment," Pollock observed, "but it was. It was a fine compliment. Only he didn't know it."[96]

96. Jackson Pollock, interview with Berton Roueche, "Unframed Space," *New Yorker* (August 5, 1950): 16.

To experience a place "without beginning or end" is to experience what it means to traverse a place that has no path, prompting reflection on a life laid bare, as Lawrence Weschler indicated earlier: the "moment in looking at those paintings when we stop looking at them and they start looking at us—at, and if we are not careful, if there is not enough of us there, straight through us." In other words, the experiences engendered by abstract art are related to the willingness to engage these works long enough that the paradox between presence and absence, representation and withdrawal, clarifies what it means to topple the order of theoretical knowledge, when my compass is my knowledge of truth about the world, toward the Other as the compass of truth, and the affirmation that my perceptions are responsible.

As with art of Abstract Expressionism, we must be willing to interrupt our private knowledge of the world with the new, with embodied alterity. Because these, like all artworks, depend on the witness of the viewer, depend on the sensibility of the Other for affirmation, as well as the viewer's engagement with the alterity of the artist. Both artist and audience invoke disturbance of the order of theoretical knowledge, tearing at the fabric of our narcissistic default mechanisms. In the creative act, the artist desires relationship, a "trace of the other," even in works that have broken reliance on figuration; the mode of relationship is a place of negation. Persons can "lose" or empty themselves as both creators and observers of great works of art, which may explain why some weep in their viewing. One does not have to interpret what is "in" the abstract painting or even what the abstractions "mean"—scraping the surface of the representational exonerates the observer of having to construct a "self," a subjective standpoint. Here, Blanchot's "double mouthful of silence" is preserved: two alterities create something new and beyond both of them. Art that is only self-referential speaks to no one. Discourse desired with the viewer by Pollock, Newman, and especially Rothko is commenced in much the same way as prayer directed toward the ultimate: efforts toward the unseen, toward the unheard. Reverse this, and the same is true for the observer: the desire and openness to the vision of an Other, without easy linguistic or figurative referent in one's own experience, is a prayer directed toward the ultimate, the infinite.

In 1947, Rothko claimed that transcendental experience is possible when one leaves the familiar;[97] later, in 1961, he asserts, "[I]f people want sacred experiences, they will find them here. If they want profane experiences, they'll find those too. I take no sides."[98] His deliberate ambiguity regarding the meaning of his work is indicative of visual art, like poetry, searching for something that it cannot say, or for something it refuses to say. That Rothko is deliberately ambiguous about the meaning of his work may stem from his inner trauma, his identity with the pain of others, with the immensity of the suffering in the past of his homeland and his people. That he absorbed so much chaos might be an aesthetic sensitivity to vulnerability, which may have caused or come from depressive illness.

Blanchot and Levinas, the latter especially no stranger to the horrors of World War II, were able to maintain witness to vulnerability without slipping into despair through what they perceived as a "duty to live," a duty to persist despite the impossible task of responsibility to the Other. Blanchot writes, "How can there be a duty to live? The more serious question: the desire to die, too strong, it seems, to be satisfied with my death, and to be exhausted when I die, is, paradoxically, the desire that others might live without life's being for them an obligation. The desire to die absolves of the duty to live—that is, its effect is that one lives without any obligation (but not without responsibility, for responsibility is beyond life)."[99] Blanchot's interest in a language of the unsayable, a language without the imposition of the power of the Same, must be a language that preserves the alterity of the Other by venturing into the field of the outside, to shoulder the void and persist in spite of it. But in Rothko's case, depression exacerbated the void, as well as his guilt, perhaps because he was neither a victim of a pogrom nor of the Shoah. It was too much for him to bear; "suffering is suffering when one can no longer suffer it," observes Blanchot, describing the sort

---

97. Rothko, "The Romantics Were Prompted," 58.

98. Cited in "Art: Stand Up Close," *Newsweek*, January 23, 1961, 60, in Chave, *Mark Rothko: Subjects in Abstraction*, 195.

99. Maurice Blanchot, *The Writing of the Disaster*, trans. Ann Smock (Lincoln, NE: University of Nebraska Press, 1995), 10.

of suffering that is so limitless that even by dying, death is lost as a possible limit.[100] Such is the catastrophe, the suffering of which Dostoyevsky spoke.

It is up to the arts to "found a new hope," asserts Blanchot; "Hope is to be reinvented."[101] But not in the sense of the lofty, heavenly ideal: such is a "weak hope." Rather, there is hope when "it relates to what is always yet to come, and perhaps will never come. . . . [T]he more distant or difficult the object of hope is, the more profound and close to its destiny as hope is the hope that affirms it. . . . Hope is most profound when it withdraws from and deprives itself of all manifest hope."[102] Hope is most profound when it follows the uncertain, the improbable, the impossible in the relation with the Other, persisting because of the immensity of the task, not in spite of it. Comprehension must give way to the impossible, "to allow it to announce itself according to a measure other than that of power. What would this other measure be? Perhaps precisely the measure of the other, of the other as other, and no longer ordered to the clarity of that which adapts it to the same."[103] Blanchot excitedly asks, "[H]ow can we discover the obscure? How can it be brought into the open? What would this experience of the obscure be, whereby the obscure would give itself in its obscurity?"[104] This obscurity is the very exteriority of presence, the "passion of the Outside itself,"[105] the Outside of dualism. The arts cannot *say* this impossibility; rather, the arts answer to it, respond to it, witness to it, lay bare before it, "as attentive response in which the impatient waiting for the unknown and the desiring hope for the presence are affirmed."[106] Rothko was attentive to this impossibility, this "passion of the Outside" that leads to the alterity of the Other. Rothko paints what

100. Maurice Blanchot, "The Great Refusal," in *The Infinite Conversation*, trans. Susan Hanson (Minneapolis, MN: University of Minneapolis Press, 1993), 45.
101. Ibid., 40.
102. Ibid., 41.
103. Ibid., 43–44.
104. Ibid., 44.
105. Ibid., 46.
106. Ibid., 48.

Blanchot explores: in the unsaying is a submission to the Outside, the silence of emptiness or *sunyata*, in dynamic and creative openness to the interdependence between artist and participant that informs infinite responsibility to the Other.

The doctrine of the incarnation was, early in the Christian movement, intersected with the idea of kenosis, self-emptying, as a way to describe what it means to meet God in and through a human being. For the incomprehensible divine to be "contained" in a human person, breathing, suffering, moving, means a turn to the empty, the transcendence of boundaries between finite and infinite. Moving the idea of kenosis into conversation with ideas of "space" or "outside" and *sunyata* means that incarnation kenotically understood is the locus neither of presence nor of absence but as the foundation in which the colors of a Rothko pulse and intertwine with dynamism and life or with fear and despair—a space in which emptiness as interdependence is beyond what is possible and impossible or beyond what is possible or impossible. Non-duality is not that there are no dualisms. Non-duality sees beyond simplistic opposition. Regarding the world strictly through the lens of binary thinking misleads one into assuming that there is nothing other than the duality.[107] Thus might Derrida say that there are only "differences and traces of traces."[108]

Until Nietzsche in the late nineteenth century, Western philosophy, built largely on the edifice of Greek philosophy, has been marked by the search for the "one" underlying idea or truth that girds the diversity and multiplicity of what we experience. For Plato, this "one" is the only reality, and the changing and diverse world is

---

107. Paul Knitter puts it well: "Dualism results when we make necessary distinctions, and then take those distinctions too seriously. We turn those distinctions into dividing lines rather than connecting lines. . . . We not only distinguish, we separate. And one separation usually leads to ranking: one side is superior to and dominant over the other. Thus, we have the dualism of matter and spirit, East and West, nature and history, male and female, God and the world." Knitter, *Without Buddha, I Could Not Be a Christian* (London: Oneworld, 2013), 7.

108. Jacques Derrida, *Positions*, trans. Alan Bass (Chicago: The University of Chicago Press, 1981), 26.

illusory, not real. But it is this "Same" or essential unity-that-is-really-a-hegemony that Levinas argues is illusory; only in the preservation of alterity without recourse to the Same can we hope to sidestep the imposition of identity that prevents authentic relationship. With Derrida we see that even language does not provide this "Same" or unifying matrix in which to experience an Other. A doctrine, housed in words, has no single theological import that has a direct correspondence between signifier and signified. Doctrines are rather icons, windows into something sacred—"sacred" as signifier of what is impossible—what cannot be captured in language or in a painting.

A doctrine such as the doctrine of the incarnation is an intellectual bookmark for what is unknown but the elements played with—like colored confetti tossed into the air, then gathered and re-tossed, fistfuls of bright spots that suspend in unique randomness against the sky every time. Derrida seems to say that these confetti, these multidimensional signifiers of words caught in different contexts and used in ever-changing ways, will never be fixed or final, and that a doctrine will never achieve self-presence. These confetti, these signifiers, these drips in a Pollock painting, this blending of colors in a Rothko such that there is always one whisper of change as a color meets and penetrates another: this is where we can discuss "incarnation"—this is where incarnation discusses us—this is where presence and absence belong together, even if tossing fistfuls of the ideas connected to presence and absence will appear different against the sky every time.

Because of the work of Derrida, Levinas, and Blanchot—although each would bristle at the notion of contributing to the theological task—negative or apophatic theology is enjoying a resurgence of interest in postmodernity. The collapse of onto-theology and its attendant positivism accompanies the decline in confidence in the achievements of philosophical and theological rationality, according to John Caputo. He credits Derrida with exposing the limits of reason, such that mysticism doesn't merely pick up where reason's boundaries lie, as though "mysticism" becomes a repository for all we do not know (yet), the container for what we someday will be more sophisticated or highly evolved to understand. He explains,

> In deconstruction the delimitation of rationality is not made in the name of something deeper, but in the name of something other or new or novel, of an event rather than an abyss of Being. The stress is not upon nonknowing in the classical mystical sense, where that implies an even deeper, "learned" nonknowing, but rather nonknowing in the sense that we really don't know! Nonknowing is not an expression of a deeper truth; it means that we really don't know![109]

Acknowledging non-knowing is an acceptance of vulnerability that enters the sort of radical openness which Levinas believes we must prepare the heteronomous orientation: assuming non-knowing as a stance means a willingness to cleanse ourselves, repeatedly, of the imposition of the self onto the alterity of the Other, of the desire for certainty (which isn't the same as the desire for truth: truth is more complicated and elusive), and adopt the courage to embrace the possibility—the inevitability—of failure, absurdity, anxiety, and foolishness. A sense of the ridiculous, of play, of wonder: these are sorely needed in theology and are fed by all forms of art. "We can learn again to play," writes David Tracy. "In some games we, like Rilke, may even be fortunate enough to begin to sense our resonance with the play of the cosmos itself . . . outside the freedom of Watteau's fetes, Wordsworth's Lake Country, and Cooper's wilderness, or even outside the supremely natural games of the Taoist retreat and the Zen garden, we can all learn to play again."[110] Artists know that reinvention keeps them alive: constant experimentation and the willingness to fail, to risk the ridiculous and be fearless in the face of unsaying what was said.

"That's how we know we are alive," wrote Philip Roth in his novel *American Pastoral*, "we're wrong." The opportunity to be wrong is the opportunity to be alive, and being alive means adopting a habitus of non-knowing to explore new worlds of imagination.

---

109. John D. Caputo and Gianni Vattimo, *After the Death of God*, ed. Jeffrey Robbins (New York: Columbia University Press, 2007), 115.

110. David Tracy, *Plurality and Ambiguity: Hermeneutics, Religion, Hope* (Chicago: The University of Chicago Press, 1987), 17.

Levinas, with a sly grin, agrees: "The fact that philosophy cannot fully totalize the alterity of meaning in some final presence . . . is not for me a deficiency or fault. . . . [T]he best thing about philosophy is that it fails . . . for it thereby remains open to the irreducible otherness of transcendence."[111] The passage in *American Pastoral* explains the inevitable failure of perception regarding understanding other people; even when we try to meet people without expectations or prejudices, we still fail. "Since the same generally goes for them with you, the whole thing is really a dazzling illusion empty of all perception, an astonishing farce of misperception."[112] The option to lock oneself up and never leave one's room is just as absurd. Roth continues: "The fact remains that getting people right is not what living is all about anyway. It's getting them wrong that is living, getting them wrong and wrong and wrong and then on careful consideration, getting them wrong again. Maybe the best thing would be to forget about being right or wrong about people and just go along for the ride. But if you can do that—well, lucky you."[113] Replace "people" with "theology" or even "God" and we may get a sense of what Caputo means. Non-knowing is part of being alive. Shedding the skin of what we think we know allows a fresh new creature to emerge and wriggle away. Doing theology means that what we say about God will not be right, and most of the time it will be just plain wrong, but the living is in the doing of it, and the doing of theology, getting oneself up and thinking about God again, even when we are surrounded by the mud and the blood: risking the wrong is being alive. Art may be the place where theology can "go along for the ride" (or vice versa, and theology can take the arts for a spin), take the top down, let the wind roll in, and things can happen again—theology can breathe again.

---

111. Emmanuel Levinas, interview with Richard Kearney, in *Dialogues with Contemporary Continental Thinkers: The Phenomenological Heritage* (Manchester, UK: Manchester University Press, 1984), 58.

112. Philip Roth, *American Pastoral* (Boston: Houghton Mifflin, 1997), 35.

113. Ibid.

The Dynamic Interrelationship of Absence and Presence

Thirty spokes are united around the hub to make a wheel,
> But it is on its *wu* [nothingness] that the utility of the carriage depends.

Clay is molded to form a utensil
> But it is on its *wu* [nothingness] that the utility of the utensil depends.

Doors and windows are cut out to make a room,
> But it is on its *wu* [nothingness] that the utility of the room depends.

Therefore, regard you [being] as advantage, and regard *wu* [nothingness, non-being] as utility.[114]

Laozi writes here of the primordial nothingness, in which being and non-being, *you* and *wu*, material reality and emptiness, are mutually dependent.[115] "Wu in the first three verses is just emptiness, or the spaces in an entity, and these instances are used to introduce the last verse, in which wu and you are more general and abstract concepts. . . . [They] are a pair that cannot be separated,"[116] Xiaogan Liu explains. Might we also assert that the presence and absence of "God" or ultimate reality are mutually dependent? The landscape of reality is grounded by the immanence and transcendence of the God who is neither present nor absent, who is both present and absent. Through the lens of the Heart Sutra,[117] in which "form is emptiness, emptiness is form, form is not different from emptiness,

---

114. Laozi, *Daodejing* [*Tao Te Ching*], chap. 11, cited by Xiaogan Liu in "The Notion of *Wu* or Nonbeing as the Root of the Universe and a Guide for Life," in *Nothingness in Asian Philosophy*, ed. JeeLoo Liu and Douglas L. Berger (London: Routledge, 2014), 157. Liu's translation.

115. Xiaogan Liu, "The Notion of *Wu* or Nonbeing," 157.

116. Ibid.

117. The Heart Sutra, explains Joseph O'Leary, "is the distinctive foundational teaching of Mahayana [Greater Vehicle] Buddhism, this short text—only 280 syllables in the widely used Chinese translation from the original Sanskrit—is a package of spiritual and intellectual dynamite. The title refers to the *hrdaya*—'heart' or 'essence' of Perfect Wisdom." O'Leary, "Knowing the Heart Sutra by Heart," *Religion and the Arts* 12 (2008): 357.

emptiness not different from form," incarnation assumes the prospect of non-duality. Neither divine nor human, neither form nor emptiness is substantive in the sense of Greek philosophy, because they are each transitory, temporary. Emptiness is temporarily embodied in the forms we encounter: the cup is not a cup without the emptiness inside. This it is to contemplate the incarnation, since any material boundary is non-dual with what is beyond the boundary. The "horizon," of which Karl Rahner spoke, the distance, is also the ground, the condition of *ecstasis*, movement beyond the self. Moving toward another in the particularity of our history is essential to becoming subjects, or selves, or human: "Only this much is certain: man is in the presence of being in its totality insofar as he finds himself in the world."[118] For Rahner, God as the transcendental horizon of Absolute Being, is the necessary, universal, *a priori* condition of all possible human experience, and as such is the source of all knowledge and "anti-knowledge"; God is then the positive source of our not-knowing God—of our not knowing God as object—because of our epistemological limitations.[119] "God" as the source of not-knowing or unsaying may also be the source of the transitory movement of form, like the pure energy of light that shifts the color of the paintings in the Rothko Chapel.

Through abstraction and the transcendence of the image in visual art, one can also transcend expectations of what we assume that the

118. Karl Rahner, *Spirit in the World*, trans. William V. Dych (New York: Continuum, 1994), 62.

119. In this sense, we can understand that the Absolute Mystery of God is the guiding principle for Rahner's anthropology: see K. P. Fischer, *Der Mensch als Geheimnis: Die Anthropologie des Karl Rahners* (Freiburg: Herder, 1974) and Karl Rahner, "The Human Question of Meaning in Face of the Absolute Mystery of God," in *Theological Investigations* 18, trans. Kevin Smyth (Baltimore: Helicon Press, 1966). Mark C. Taylor notes that the Western view of God as object of thought or discourse stems from Cartesian dualism. "If man is defined as subject, everything else turns into object. This includes God, who now becomes merely the highest object of man's knowledge . . . an object of thought like any other." Taylor, citing J. Harris Miller, *Poets of Reality: Six Twentieth-Century Writers* (New York: Atheneum, 1969), 3, in *Erring: A Postmodern A/Theology* (Chicago: The University of Chicago Press, 1984), 22.

world is, of how things are supposed to look or how things are supposed to make us feel. Abstract visual art, perhaps more than any other visual art form, calls the viewer to become a participant in the moment of creativity, to enter a world not of the viewer's own determination or making. This is art that requires agency on the part of both the artist and the viewer; such agency is one of the reasons Abstract Expressionism is often called "action painting." Both the artist and the viewer participate in the disturbance. Donald Kuspit suggests, "Abstraction meant to enter the depth that representationalism could only suggest, as a nuance of the surface of objects. As such, abstraction worked against the charisma of the surface by disrupting the order which created it and which it reflected, particularly the hierarchical ordering of space and the objects in them."[120] Challenging and transcending spatio-temporal expectations frees us for the obscure.

In Buddhism, transcending such expectations lead to the truth of the interconnectedness and impermanence of all things; any attachment to either form or emptiness as the "true" reality is meaningless because of interdependence. As Jacques Derrida critiqued the traditional distinction between author and audience, so also Abstract Expressionism blurs dimensionality, time, and space, the distinction between artist and interpreter, and between subject and object, without center or unifying principle. Entering a space for the abstraction of reality is a way to experience that the "ultimate reality,"—merely a linguistic designation that refers to what promotes codependent origination—what Tillich refers to as the "ground of being"—cannot be expressed in words or concepts. A heightened sensibility of the catastrophic suffering of others or the sense of the interdependence of things are manifest in art in ways these are not manifest in reasoned explanations or the attempt at certainty in knowledge. The movement between what we do not know and what we know, between what we cannot say and what we can, between kenosis and

120. Donald B. Kuspit, "Abstract Expressionism: The Social Contract," *Arts Magazine*, March 1980, in *Abstract Expressionism: A Critical Record*, ed. David Shapiro and Cecile Shapiro (Cambridge, UK: Cambridge University Press, 1990), 190.

incarnation, is evident in Rothko and Pollock because it is still emotion, color, darkness, line, or an attempt at the pure form—the tangible—that enables this experience. Not prelinguistic, abstract art ventures beyond the linguistic and symbolic toward the emptiness at the heart of reality; "form is emptiness, emptiness is form." Theology, like art, and like doctrine, depends on the interaction and perhaps ultimate reconciliation (or not) of both form and emptiness; as Kukai, the Japanese founder of Shingon esoteric Buddhism, asserted, "The *Dharma* (truth) is beyond speech, but without speech it cannot be revealed."

The term *sunyata* is derived from the Sanskrit meaning "to swell." This is not a lifeless nothingness, a nihil (*abhava*), but a swelling, pregnant, "reality" that transcends the divisive polarity of being and nonbeing, cause and effect, time and eternity, as the "groundless ground" of all that is. Nagarjuna (ca. 150–250 CE), founder of the Madhyamika school of Mahayana Buddhism, asserted, "[I]f there were no emptiness, there would be nothing." Hence, "nothingness" and "emptiness" are not compatible or synonymous but are rather exclusive of each other: emptiness cancels nothingness, and I assume, vice versa. Nagarjuna teaches that *sunyata* cannot be reified or conceptualized. Masao Abe observes that this is the unobjectifiable; as such *sunyata* is not simply nothing as opposed to "a something": "Nothing as distinguished from something is still a kind of 'something' merely called 'nothing.' True Nothingness is beyond a mere nothingness, i.e., a negative nothingness, as distinguished from a somethingness."[121] *Sunyata* is neither a nothing nor a something but includes both; not mere emptiness, but fullness as the root and source of both being and non-being.[122] The term *sunyata* is merely a device for crossing a river; once the river is crossed, the device is discarded. Emptiness is not a theory or a doctrine or a practice. Neither is emptiness a form of causation, as though we could say, "emptiness causes creation"; rather, emptiness refers to the negation of the division that underlies dualism. All things are interrelated: the way to understand the extent

---

121. Masao Abe, *Zen and Western Thought,* ed. William R. LaFleur (Honolulu: University of Hawai'i Press, 1985), 197.

122. See Ibid.

of this is to deny any sort of dualism and promote the dynamism of interrelationship, of interdependence.

"Nirvana" refers to the dissolving of distinctions, perhaps more specifically the dissolving of divisive distinctions, what John Zizioulas identifies with sin. But we Western linear thinkers must understand that *sunyata* or emptiness is not the "goal" or end of Buddhist life but rather a point of departure from which Buddhist life and activity can properly begin. If *sunyata* is conceived as the goal, in the way that communion with God is the "goal" of Christian life, it is not conceived as presently within, behind, or beyond one's existence. *Sunyata* is only realized in and through the here and now in the awareness that there is no independent existence, no autonomous substance, no hierarchy of being, no center. A substance can never be the ultimate ground: if this were the case, a substance would be limited by differentiation, the differentiation between substantial oneness and the things which participate in that substance. This is also why *sunyata* is described as without "being" or under erasure. Heidegger described both "being" and "nothingness" as under erasure as well. The words themselves must be emptied. James Fredericks writes, "According to Nagarjuna, emptiness that is not completely empty is a false view of emptiness. In the same paradoxical way, the God that clings to an eternal transcendence, removed from creation, is not the true God."[123]

Masao Abe (1915–2006), the most important scholar of the Kyoto School's investment in Buddhist-Christian dialogue after D. T. Suzuki's death in 1966, compared the Christian appropriation of kenosis with the Buddhist notion of *sunyata*. Abe explains that *sunyata* has two aspects: wisdom and compassion, both of which are critical in regarding this world as the locus of reality. The Buddha emphasized dependent co-origination or relational origination, in which the divine and human co-arise and co-cease, as the "ultimate principle."[124] De-

---

123. James L. Fredericks, *Buddhists and Christians: Through Comparative Theology to Solidarity*, Faith Meets Faith Series (Maryknoll, NY: Orbis Books, 2004), 93. Emphasis mine.

124. Masao Abe, *Buddhism and Interfaith Dialogue*, ed. Stephen Heine (Honolulu: University of Hawai'i Press, 1995), 239.

pendent co-arising or conditioned arising (in Sanskrit: *Pratityasamut-pada*, "in dependence, things arise") is closely related to *sunyata*, the origin of all form and formless reality. Every rock in a rock garden is not simply a thing with a particular form but is uniquely and equally the self-expression, through the taking of form, of *sunyata* which is beyond every form.[125] If, however, the particular existence of the rocks here and now were not significant, the garden would express a dead nothingness. Abe explains, "In Buddhism it is emphasized that although everything and everyone has its own distinctiveness, we should not substantialize and become attached to it as if it were enduring but rather awaken to the reality that everything and everyone is equally nonsubstantial and empty."[126] This is another way of saying that "there are no separate individual existences" because "each existence depends upon something else."[127]

To put it yet another way, even samsara (the cycle of birth-death-rebirth; the phenomenal world) and nirvana (the liberation from suffering) are essentially interrelated, not separate ontological realms. Abe calls this "beyond the opposition between relativism and absolutism"[128]—everything is realized *as it is*, in its suchness, its *jinen*, its total dynamic, transitory reality. For Buddhists, nirvana is not an "impersonal" state as opposed to the material, and so, personal, state of samsara. Neither oneness nor variety should be prioritized over the other: this it is to know things as they are.[129] This affirmation of all things as they are is established through the negation of negation: the dominant-subordinate relationship among things in a dualistic sense is transcended in *sunyata*. For Abe, a personal God must be a God identical with all things, "including the sinful person, precisely because God is not a self-affirmative God

---

125. See Abe, *Zen and Western Thought*, 182.

126. Masao Abe, "A Rejoinder," in *The Emptying God: A Buddhist-Jewish-Christian Conversation*, ed. John B. Cobb, Jr. and Christopher Ives (Maryknoll, NY: Orbis Books, 1991), 175.

127. Shunryu Suzuki, *Zen Mind, Beginner's Mind* (New York: Weatherhill, 1998), 119.

128. Abe, *Buddhism and Interfaith Dialogue*, 78.

129. See Suzuki, *Zen Mind, Beginner's Mind*, 120.

(not one substance) but a completely self-emptying God. . . . [This] fulfills God's unconditional love to save everything without exception, including the unjust and sinful."[130] Because in Buddhism all can be "saved" or awakened to the Absolute Truth, it is unnecessary to predicate any self-interest in works of compassion. Whereas sin is a fragmentation, a separation, a judgment claim, such as "I have no need of you," compassion is necessary to realize the suchness of all things in an essential reciprocity. Writes Abe, "Through compassion realized in *sunyata* even an atrocious villain is ultimately saved, even evil passions are transformed into enlightenment."[131] Even the dualism between good and evil is transcended; Abe points to Matthew 5:45, "God makes the sun to rise on the evil and the good, and sends rain on the just and unjust."

In light of wisdom, realized in *sunyata*, all things are realized as they are; in light of compassion, the task for an awakened one is to help the unawakened realize their suchness and their interrelatedness to all things. Abe writes,

> [A]s the generation of "unawakened" beings will never cease, this process of actualizing the compassionate aspect of Sunyata is endless. Here the progress of history toward the future is necessary and comes to have a positive significance . . . whereas in wisdom realized in emptiness time is overcome, in compassion realized in emptiness, time is essential. . . . [I]n the endless process of the compassionate work of an awakened one trying to awaken others, Sunyata turns itself into vow and act through its self-emptying.[132]

The eye of wisdom sees all things in compassion, as they are; Abe asserts that even one who has attained nirvana cannot remain there, enjoying one's enlightenment while neglecting the suffering of those still caught in samsara: "To be completely unselfish, one should not

130. Masao Abe, "Kenotic God and Dynamic Sunyata," in Cobb and Ives, *The Emptying God*, 18.

131. Ibid., 32.

132. Abe, "The Impact of Dialogue," in Heine, *Buddhism and Interfaith Dialogue*, 60–61.

stay in nirvana but return to the realm of samsara to save one's fellow human beings who are suffering. . . . [I]n order to attain wisdom one should not abide in samsara; in order to fulfill compassion one should not abide in nirvana."[133] The dynamism of true nirvana is the interrelationship between nirvana and samsara.

As we examined in chapter 5, returning to the place of suffering and succumbing to the palace of death is what God does, is God in divine livingness; there is no aspect to human experience from which God is distant. God originates the movement between suffering and the promise of the cessation of suffering in the resurrection and suffers again in every hungry child. If kenosis is the way of exaltation in Christianity, the humility through which the early followers of Jesus identified his divinity, then kenosis has something to do with the way that God exists. The "duality" between exaltation and humiliation in the kenosis hymn is overcome because one, to be what it is, always transitions to the other: humility is the exaltation of subjectivity—the reality of the person—who must empty the self in order to "live" again, to be exalted. This may be why Abe asserts above that "the compassionate aspect of Sunyata is endless"—the humiliation, the vulnerability, is *life*—living-ness itself, and livingness is the fullness of interdependent existence. Emptiness, *sunyata*, continually empties as an object of attachment—it "is" by emptying into the livingness of form. "In the realization of true Sunyata, form is ceaselessly emptied, turning into formless emptiness, and formless emptiness is ceaselessly emptied and forever freely taking form."[134]

Similarly, Christians might see the incarnation as a ceaseless movement of the just-beyond, ungraspable infinite emptying into the suffering finite and thereby living and exalted as alive and then emptying suffering in resurrection. Blanchot considered this movement of divine emptiness as the being-ness of God: God has "emptied himself of his divinity in order that the world may be. But as nothing in God is more divine than this abdication, nothing can render God more present to us than this absence that is his most

133. Masao Abe, *Zen and Comparative Studies*, ed. Steven Hine (Honolulu: University of Hawai'i Press, 1997), 185.

134. Abe, "Kenotic God and Dynamic Sunyata," 28.

admirable gift, and that the world represents for us, essentially 'is.'"[135] But in order to recognize the ceaseless emptying of form and into form as the dynamic, oscillating, ambiguous activity of incarnation, Christians would have to rethink the positivistic character of the uniqueness of the incarnation, which deteriorates in the contemporary crisis of representation. Christians would have to raise vulnerability to the level of what exalts reality, what raises the dignity of all beings.

The Field of Boundless Emptiness

> I begin painting with a series of mistakes. The painting comes out of the corrections of mistakes by feeling. I begin with shapes and colors which are not related internally nor to the external world; I work without images. Ultimate unifications come about through modulation of the surface by innumerable trials and errors. The final picture is the process arrested at the moment when what I was looking for flashes into view. My pictures have layers of mistakes buried in them . . . layers of consciousness, of willing. They are a succession of humiliations resulting from the realization that only in a state of quickened subjectivity—of freedom from conscious notions, and with what I always suppose to be secondary or accidental colors or shapes—do I find the unknown, which nevertheless I recognize when I come upon it, for which I am always searching.[136]

Robert Motherwell here writes that the creative process is exposure to "a succession of humiliations," "layers of mistakes," "freedom from conscious notions" which opens the field of the unknown. Helen Frankenthaler also appropriates the mistake, the failure, as a moment in the life of a work of art. The mistake is the catalyst, the rabid energy of the means of making, in which one both manipulates and succumbs to where the media in a work of art will lead. Art ap-

---

135. Maurice Blanchot, "Affirmation (desire, affliction)," in *The Infinite Conversation*, 117.

136. Robert Motherwell, "Statement, 1947," in Ashton, *The Writings of Robert Motherwell*, 57.

pears when one releases attachment; as Hongzhi teaches, this is facing everything that may happen and letting go. Real mistakes are rare in this regard, since discipline is part of creating anything, but the mistake is part of the cultivation.

Hongzhi Zhengjue (1091–1157), a Chinese Chan monk, discusses Buddha nature as "an empty field, which lies immanent in us all," the potential of all sentient beings for awakening to the emptiness of all things. But this emptiness cannot be cultivated, only indicated, like a "finger pointing to the moon." We must "not allow our busy, mischievous thinking and conditioning to interfere with our own radiant clarity."[137] His teacher, Dōgen, was instrumental in bringing Zen to Japan; Dōgen echoes the teaching of Hongzhi when he called his life "one continuous mistake."[138] The mistake pertains to the interpenetration of the appearance of things with the emptiness of things, when we are lost in the empty field, in the vulnerability of being wrong about the interpretations we impose.

> The field of boundless emptiness is what exists from the very beginning. You must purify, cure, grind down, or brush away all the tendencies you have fabricated into apparent habits. Then you can reside in the clear circle of brightness. Utter emptiness has no image, upright independence does not rely on anything. . . . [W]e are told to realize that not a single thing exists. In this field birth and death do not appear. The deep source, transparent down to the bottom, can radiantly shine and can respond unencumbered to each speck of dust without becoming its partner. The subtlety of seeing and hearing transcends mere colors and sounds. . . . [E]verywhere turn around freely, not following conditions, not falling into classifications. Facing everything, let go and attain stability . . . so it is said that the earth lifts up the mountain without knowing the mountain's stark steepness. A rock contains jade without knowing the jade's

---

137. Taigen Dan Leighton, *Cultivating the Empty Field: The Silent Illumination of Zen Master Hongzhi,* ed. and trans. Taigen Dan Leighton, with Yi Wu (Tokyo: Tuttle Publishing), 3.

138. Ibid.

flawlessness. This is how to truly leave home, how home-leaving must be enacted.[139]

Getting lost, bumping into things, fumbling in the dark—such is the activity in deliverance from self-centeredness, as Keiji Nishitani points out, the "standpoint of *sunyata* is an absolute negativity toward the will that lies at the ground of every type of self-centeredness."[140]

In the end, I am moved by a mistake. Or, rather, a decision to succumb to a deliberate mistake, freezing a moment of ambiguity. In Helen Frankenthaler's *Wales*,[141] a swath of transparent brown in the lower right corner seems to be the result of mishandling or neglect, as though one was careless with her coffee, or has smeared dirt, making the stain worse in a futile attempt to clean it up, to make it seem as though an accident never happened. Against the other colors—a field of yellow as glaringly bright as that worn by Chinese emperors, clear purple at the edges reacting to the yellow, cobalt blue elbowing emerald green for balance—the brown is an earthy, muddy intrusion against the ethereal. Thin strips of bare canvas resist the color. The brown doesn't make sense, initially. And then it does . . . and then it doesn't. In this sense, Frankenthaler (and Rothko, as well) paint the shifting surface of the natural world, the appearances of the world in which the seething energy of molecules leave no final state in the seeming solidity of matter. The landscape of yellow is bordered, pushing through borders, but the brown is a tarnish; neither a border nor a landscape, nor a shape, since it struggles against definitive shape or scale. It may be counterintuitive to the one viewing it, but to the artist, the brown's encroachment represents the pure joy of impulse, "the quick tempest," to borrow a phrase from Nietzsche, and the courage to integrate failure, to experiment with rebellion, instead of wallow in the fear that avoids

139. Hongzhi Zhengue, "Practice Instructions," in Leighton, *Cultivating the Empty Field*, 30–31.

140. Keiji Nishitani, *Religion and Nothingness*, trans. Jan Van Bragt (Berkeley, CA: University of California Press, 1983), 251.

141. Helen Frankenthaler, *Wales*, 1966. Acrylic on canvas, 287.5 x 114cm. National Gallery of Art, Washington, DC.

it. This courage is where one may forget oneself and learn to give oneself over to the alterity of the Other, if the viewer is willing to go where the artist goes, as Nietzsche wrote to a friend a year before his nervous breakdown: "I lay physically for years at the gates of death. This was, positively, a place of good fortune. I forgot myself, lived myself down. . . . I think we are a pair of wanderers in the wilderness who are glad to have met each other."[142]

Frankenthaler's (1928–2011) marriage to Robert Motherwell (1912–1991) lasted from 1958–1971. She was a woman trespassing in the New York art world's men's club but held her own with raw strength and determination. She followed Pollock and was inspired by him but was not an imitator, spreading the thinned paint around her canvas with a mop or a house-paint brush in luxurious, overlapping stains, letting the organic journey of oil and pigment find their way through the bare canvas. She studied under Hans Hoffman, who was still breaking free from Cubism; she learned color from Rufino Tamayo, a muralist, but adapted color to her own style.

In a 1968 interview, she discusses her fascination with the corners of a canvas: "I've done different things at different times with corners, even using them or ignoring them or pretending they're not corners, or feeling very grateful that there are four corners, or painting as if the corners were miles beyond my reach or vision and that they were only centers of periphery, at other times feeling I want edges and limits defined. And you can fill or void centers."[143] The coffee-stained corner in *Wales* obliterates the definitions of borders; it allows her to break free of symmetry, long understood as key to what we respond to as "beauty." She was willing to juxtapose pure, brilliant color with a soiled corner. She explains her method:

142. Friedrich Nietzsche, *Selected Letters of Friedrich Nietzsche*, trans. Anthony M. Ludovici, ed. Oscar Levy (Garden City, NY: Doubleday and Company, 1921), 329.

143. Helen Frankenthaler, interview with Barbara Rose, 1968, part of the Oral History Program, started in 1958 to document the history of the visual arts in the United States. The transcript and partial recording can be found at the Archives of American Art, http://www.aaa.si.edu/collections/interviews/oral -history-interview-helen-frankenthaler-12171#transcript.

> When I first started thinking about color it was sort of out of
> perversity. In other words, say around '50 and '51, it occurred
> to me that something ugly or muddy could be a color as well as
> something clear and bright and a nameable, beautiful, known
> color. . . . [S]ometimes I think it came out of something very
> saving in me . . . . [I]f I have a pot of leftover green and a pot
> of leftover pink I will very often mix it just because I want to use
> it up. It's like leftover food in the icebox. And of course if it
> doesn't work on the picture, well, that's a loss. . . . I throw out
> I can't tell you how many paintings a year. For every one that I
> show there are many, many in shreds in garbage cans. But the
> attempt and the result is often from what's around and is avail-
> able that I can invent with. And people have often said that there
> seems to be so few materials around. Well, I have all the colors
> and all the tools and all the canvas, but I like . . . to play with
> the possibilities of the limits I've made for myself. . . . [I]t's the
> way a caveman might use the wall, and if you don't have a brush
> you use a pan, and if you don't have linen you use sailcloth.[144]

Shredding the works that don't work requires courage; playing with
limits, with the possibilities of limits, returns us to the Heart Sutra,
in which limits and boundlessness interpenetrate each other. Detachment from limits and the absence of limits, in attention to emptiness,
is where we can face the vulnerability in which we are able to love
our enemies, are willing to die before we kill what threatens us, sell
everything we have, embrace the leper, "bring in the poor, the crip-
pled, the blind and the lame" to our banquet (Luke 14:21).

Jesus' followers saw divinity shine through him even though he
was a failure as a messiah—he failed to take the destitute to the
promised land, failed to drive out the Romans and reclaim Israel—or
perhaps they saw divinity shine through him *because* he was a failure,
a misfit of society who faced death even in depths of fear so great
that he sweat blood before his arrest. He was a failure who persisted
through scorn and rejection, directing his final cry to his Father, to
our Father, to his Mother, to our Mother: *why have you forsaken me?*
He dies at this moment in Mark's gospel, under the weight of hu-

144. Ibid.

miliation, when he was weakest, most vulnerable. But because the death-cry in Mark is also a prayer, perhaps the iconic prayer of anyone in the midst of catastrophe, it is paradoxically the opening of emptiness, the surrender of the self, the utter loss of control. "We need to remember," Pope Francis stated at St. Patrick's Cathedral during his 2015 visit New York City, "that we are followers of Jesus. . . . [A]nd his life, humanly speaking, ended in failure, the failure of the cross."[145] Two months later, in Nairobi, Kenya, he detoured in the neighborhood of Kangemi, one of the poorest in the city, before speaking to a meeting with the youth in Kasarani Stadium: "When you don't understand something, when desperation hits you, then look at the cross. That is the great failure of God, that is the destruction of God, and it's a challenge to our faith. And this is hope, because history did not end in that failure. Rather it is in the resurrection of Christ that renewed all of us."[146] These remarks have caused a stir—as have Francis's actions toward inclusion and welcoming, his call for mercy, and his call to responsibility, especially toward the destitute poor—all these are failures in triumphalism, necessary failures that dismantle the closed system of authority.

American culture isn't big on failure. But to those who desire the abyss, failure walks the percipice of vulnerability. Acknowledging failure in the emptiness of honesty is how we chip away at the ego, at the presumption, at the assumption. White Americans—or those "who believe they are white" (to borrow a phrase from Ta-Nehisi Coates)—must acknowledge their privilege constructed along the blood-soaked path between past and present, so to empty finally the structures of power which have perpetuated, and continue to perpetuate, catastrophe. Levinas asks that we overturn the Western order, in which an already self-possessed subject encounters the

---

145. Francis, Transcript of Speech as Prepared for Delivery at St. Paul's Cathedral in New York, *Washington Post*, September 24, 2015, https://www.washingtonpost.com/local/social-issues/transcript-pope-franciss-comments-at-st-patricks-cathedral/2015/09/24/eaba43c0-6311-11e5-8e9e-dce8a2a2a679_story.html.

146. Francis, cited by Meghan J. Clark in "A Pilgrimage of Hope," *America*, November 30, 2015, http://www.americamagazine.org/content/all-things/pilgrimage-hope.

Other, in favor of understanding vulnerability as the condition for subjectivity and a responsibility to the Other that will never be fulfilled. Accepting this humiliation is to glimpse a trace of the divine, since the resonance of God's Spirit breathes in the field of night, the divine at the limit of the Other. Blanchot writes, "[W]ithout the incomprehensible mystery of the Other, we are incomprehensible to ourselves."[147] Here is the "event," the incarnate activity that makes the divine a servant, a victim of our vain attempts at control; the union of divinity and humanity, an incomprehensible unity "of all grandeur and baseness."[148] Such is "the mystery of the presence of the hidden God."

> God is unknown and nonetheless manifest. There where he is manifest, he has the qualities that render him, unknown, familiar to us. Familiar, he destines himself (and adapts himself) to what is foreign to him, and the more a thing is invisible the more it is destined to this manifestation of strangeness. But it becomes foreign to itself thereby, and foreign in the strangeness that renders it familiar to us; hidden as soon as manifest, hiding there where it shows itself. God is unknown, God is manifest. Unknown and open as the sky, he reveals himself in that which, showing him hidden, lets him appear as he is: Unknown.[149]

147. Maurice Blanchot, "Tragic Thought," in *The Infinite Conversation*, 96.
148. Ibid., 99.
149. Ibid., 103.

Select Bibliography

Abe, Masao. *Buddhism and Interfaith Dialogue*. Edited by Stephen Heine. Honolulu: University of Hawai'i Press, 1995.

———. *Zen and Comparative Studies*. Edited by Steven Hine. Honolulu: University of Hawai'i Press, 1997.

———. *Zen and Western Thought*. Edited by William R. LaFleur. Honolulu: University of Hawai'i Press, 1985.

Adorno, Theodor W. *Aesthetic Theory*. Edited by Gretel Adorno and Rolf Tiedemann. Translated by C. Lenhardt. London: Routledge, 1984.

———. *Can One Live After Auschwitz? A Philosophical Reader*. Edited by Rolf Tiedemann. Translated by Henry W. Pickford, et al. Stanford, CA: Stanford University Press, 2003.

———. *The Culture Industry*. Edited and translated by Rolf Tiedemann. London: Routledge, 1991.

———. *Minima Moralia: Reflections on Damaged Life*. Translated by E. F. N. Jephcott. London: Verso, 2005.

Amishai-Maisels, Ziva. "Chagall's *White Crucifixion*." *Art Institute of Chicago Museum Studies* 17, no. 2 (1991).

Ashton, Dore. *About Rothko*. New York: Da Capo Press, 1996.

Baigell, Matthew. *Jewish Artists in New York: The Holocaust Years*. New Brunswick, NJ: Rutgers University Press, 2002.

Bataille, Georges. *Inner Experience*. Translated by Stuart Kendall. Albany: SUNY Press, 2014.

———. *Prehistoric Painting: Lascaux or the Birth of Art*. Translated by Austryn Wainhouse. Geneva: Skira, 1955.

Bauckham, Richard. *Jesus and the God of Israel*. Grand Rapids, MI: Eerdmans, 2008.

Benjamin, Walter. *Illuminations*. Edited by Hannah Arendt. Translated by Harry Zohn. New York: Schocken Books, 1969.

Berger, John. *Ways of Seeing*. London: Penguin Books, 1973.

Blanchot, Maurice. *Friendship*. Translated by Elizabeth Rottenberg. Stanford, CA: Stanford University Press, 1997.

———. *The Infinite Conversation*. Translated by Susan Hanson. Minneapolis: University of Minnesota Press, 1993.

———. *The Space of Literature*. Translated by Ann Smock. Lincoln: University of Nebraska Press, 1989.

———. *Thomas the Obscure*. Translated by Robert Lamberton. Barrytown, NY: Station Hills Press, 1988.

———. *The Writing of the Disaster*. Translated by Ann Smock. Lincoln: University of Nebraska Press, 1995.

———. *The Blanchot Reader*. Edited by Michael Holland. Oxford: Blackwell, 1995.

Blum, Edward J., and Paul Harvey. *The Color of Christ: The Son of God and the Saga of Race in America*. Durham: University of North Carolina Press, 2012.

Boccaccio. *The Decameron*. Translated by Wayne A. Rebhorn. New York: W. W. Norton, 2013.

Bœspflug, François. *La Trinité dans l'Art d'Occident (1400–1460)*. Strasbourg: Presses Universitaires de Strasbourg, 2000.

Breslin, James E. B. *Mark Rothko: A Biography*. Chicago: The University of Chicago Press, 1993.

Buchheim, Fides. *Der Gnadenstuhl: Darstellung der Dreifaltigkeit*. Würzburg: Echter, 1984.

Caputo, John D., ed. *Deconstruction in a Nutshell: A Conversation with Jacques Derrida*. New York: Fordham University Press, 1997.

———. *The Insistence of God: A Theology of Perhaps*. Bloomington: Indiana University Press, 2013.

———. *Truth: The Search for Wisdom in the Postmodern Age*. London: Penguin, 2013.

———. *The Weakness of God: A Theology of the Event*. Bloomington: Indiana University Press, 2006.

Chave, Anna. *Mark Rothko: Subjects in Abstraction*. New Haven, CT: Yale University Press, 1989.

Christ, Carol P. "Why Women Need the Goddess: Phenomenological, Psychological, and Political Reflections." In *Womanspirit Rising: A Feminist Reader in Religion*, edited by Carol P. Christ and Judith Plaskow. San Francisco: HarperCollins, 1992.

Coates, Ta-Nehisi. *Between the World and Me*. New York: Spiegel and Grau, 2015.

Cobb, John B., Jr., and Christopher Ives, eds. *The Emptying God: A Buddhist-Christian-Jewish Conversation*. Maryknoll, NY: Orbis Books, 1991.

Cohn, Samuel. *Cultures of Plague: Medical Thinking at the End of the Renaissance*. Oxford: Oxford University Press, 2009.

Cone, James. *God of the Oppressed*. Maryknoll, NY: Orbis Books, 1997.

Crossan, John Dominic. *The Historical Jesus*. San Francisco: HarperSanFrancisco, 2009.

Derrida, Jacques. *Positions*. Translated by Alan Bass. Chicago: The University of Chicago Press, 1981.

———. *Writing and Difference*. Translated by Alan Bass. Chicago: The University of Chicago Press, 1978.

Dunn, James D. G. *Christology in the Making: A New Testament Inquiry into the Origins of the Doctrine of the Incarnation*. Grand Rapids, MI: Eerdmans, 1996.

Edelglass, William. "Levinas on Suffering and Compassion." *Sophia* 45, no. 2 (October 2006).

Elkins, James. *The Object Stares Back: On the Nature of Seeing*. San Diego: Harvest/Harcourt, 1997.

———. *Pictures and Tears: A History of People Who Have Cried in Front of Paintings*. New York: Routledge, 2004.

Eskola, Timo. *Messiah and the Throne: Jewish Merkabah Mysticism and Early Christian Exaltation Discourse*. Tübingen: Mohr Siebeck, 2001.

Franke, William. *On What Cannot Be Said: Apophatic Discourses in Philosophy, Religion, Literature and the Arts*. Vol. 2. Notre Dame, IN: University of Notre Dame Press, 2007.

Freedberg, David. *The Power of Images: Studies in the History and Theory of Response*. Chicago: The University of Chicago Press, 1989.

Freeland, Cynthia. *But Is It Art? An Introduction to Art Theory*. Oxford: Oxford University Press, 2001.

Godzieba, Anthony. "Caravaggio, Theologian: Baroque Piety and *Poiesis* in a Forgotten Chapter of the History of Catholic Theology." In *Theology and Lived Christianity*, edited by David M. Hammond. Mystic, CT: Twenty-Third Publications, 2000.

———. "'Stay with Us . . .' (Lk 24:29)—'Come, Lord Jesus' (Rev 22:20): Incarnation, Eschatology, and Theology's Sweet Predicament." *Theological Studies* 67, no. 4 (December 2006).

Goffen, Rona, ed. *Masaccio's Trinity*. Cambridge: Cambridge University Press, 1998.

de Gruchy, John W. *Christianity, Art and Transformation: Theological Aesthetics in the Struggle for Justice*. Cambridge: Cambridge University Press, 2001.

Haight, Roger. *The Future of Christology*. New York, Continuum, 2007.

———. *Jesus: Symbol of God*. Maryknoll, NY: Orbis Books, 1999.

Hart, Kevin. *The Dark Gaze: Maurice Blanchot and the Sacred*. Chicago: University of Chicago Press, 2004.

Hatley, James. *Suffering Witness: The Quandary of Responsibility after the Irreparable*. Albany: SUNY Press, 2000.

Heidegger, Martin. *Being and Time*. Translated by John Macquarrie and Edward Robinson. San Francisco: Harper and Row, 2008.

———. *Kant and the Problem of Metaphysics*. Translated by James S. Churchill. Bloomington: University of Indiana Press, 1962.

———. *Basic Writings*. Edited by D. F. Krell. San Francisco: Harper Collins, 1993.

Henriksen, Jan-Olav. *Desire, Gift and Recognition: Christology and Postmodern Philosophy*. Grand Rapids, MI: Eerdmans, 2009.

Hill, Leslie. "'Distrust of Poetry': Levinas, Blanchot, Celan." *Modern Language Notes* 120, no. 5 (December 2005).

Hurtado, Larry W. *Lord Jesus Christ: Devotion to Jesus in Earliest Christianity*. Grand Rapids, MI: Eerdmans, 2003.

Jackson, Robert S. "Michelangelo's Ricetto of the Laurentian Library: A Phenomenology of the Alinari Photograph." *Art Journal* 28, no. 1 (Autumn 1968).

Johnson, Mark. *The Body in the Mind: The Bodily Basis of Meaning*. Chicago: The University of Chicago Press, 1987.

Kant, Immanuel. *Critique of Judgement*. Translated by James Creed Meredith. Oxford: Oxford University Press, 2009.

———. *Critique of Pure Reason*. Translated by Werner S. Pluhar. Indianapolis: Hackett, 1996.

———. *Observations on the Beautiful and Sublime*. Translated by John T. Goldthwait. Berkeley: University of California Press, 2003.

Katz, Claire Elise. *Levinas and the Crisis of Humanism*. Bloomington: Indiana University Press, 2013.

Kearney, Richard. *Anatheism: Returning to God after God*. New York: Columbia University Press, 2010.

———. "The Crisis of the Image: Levinas' Ethical Response." In *The Ethics of Postmodernity: Current Trends in Continental Thought*, edited by Gary B. Madison and Marty Fairbairn. Evanston, IL: Northwestern University Press, 1999.

———. *Dialogues with Contemporary Continental Thinkers*. Manchester: Manchester University Press, 1986.

———. *The God Who May Be: A Hermeneutics of Religion*. Bloomington: Indiana University Press, 2001.

————. *Poetics of Imagining: Modern to Post-Modern*. New York: Fordham University Press, 1998.

————. *The Wake of the Imagination*. New York: Routledge, 1988.

Keenan, John P. *The Gospel of Mark: A Mahayana Reading*. Maryknoll, New York: Orbis Books, 1998.

Keenan, John P., and Linda K. Keenan. *I Am/No Self: A Christian Commentary on the Heart Sutra*. Leuven: Peeters, 2011.

Keller, Catherine. *God and Power: Counter-Apocalyptic Journeys*. Minneapolis: Fortress Press, 2005.

Kneller, Jane. *Kant and the Power of Imagination*. Cambridge: Cambridge University Press, 2007.

Knitter, Paul. *Without Buddha, I Could Not Be a Christian*. London: Oneworld, 2013.

Leighton, Taigen Dan, ed. and trans., with Yi Wu. *Cultivating the Empty Field: The Silent Illumination of Zen Master Hongzhi*. Tokyo: Tuttle Publishing, 2014.

Levinas, Emmanuel. *Basic Philosophical Writings*. Edited by Adriaan T. Peperzak, Simon Critchley, and Robert Bernasconi. Bloomington: Indiana University Press, 1996.

————. *Collected Philosophical Papers*. Translated by Alphonso Lingis. Dordrecht: Martinus Nijhoff, 1987.

————. *Difficult Freedom: Essays on Judaism*. Translated by Sean Hand. Baltimore, MD: Johns Hopkins University Press, 1990.

————. *Entre-Nous: Thinking-of-the-Other*. Translated by Michael B. Smith and Barbara Harshav. New York: Columbia University Press, 1998.

————. *Existence and Existents*. Translated by Alphonso Lingis. Pittsburgh, PA: Duquesne University Press, 2001.

————. *Humanism of the Other*. Translated by Nidra Poller. Urbana: University of Illinois Press, 2006.

————. *In the Time of the Nations*. Translated by Michael B. Smith. New York: Continuum, 2007.

————. *Is It Righteous to Be? Interviews with Emmanuel Levinas*. Edited by Jill Robbins. Stanford: Stanford University Press, 2001.

————. *Of God Who Comes to Mind*. Translated by Bettina Bergo. Stanford, CA: Stanford University Press, 1988.

————. *Otherwise than Being: Or Beyond Essence*. Translated by Alphonso Lingis. Pittsburgh, PA: Duquesne University Press, 1998.

————. *Proper Names*. Translated by Michael B. Smith. Stanford, CA: Stanford University Press, 1996.

————. *Totality and Infinity: An Essay in Exteriority*. Translated by Alphonso Lingis. Pittsburgh, PA: Duquesne University Press, 2008.

Lyotard, Jean-François. *The Postmodern Condition*. Translated by Geoff Bennington and Brian Massumi. Minneapolis: University of Minnesota Press, 1979.

MacIntyre, Alasdair. *Dependent Rational Animals: Why Human Beings Need the Virtues*. Chicago: Open Court Press, 1999.

Mâle, Emile. *Religious Art in France: The Thirteenth Century*. Translated by Marthiel Matthews. Princeton, NJ: Princeton University Press, 1984.

Malka, Salomon. *Emmanuel Levinas: His Life and Legacy*. Pittsburgh, PA: Duquesne University Press, 2006.

Marion, Jean-Luc. *God without Being*. Translated by Thomas A. Carlson. Chicago: The University of Chicago Press, 2012.

de Menil, Dominique. *The Rothko Chapel: Writings on Art and the Threshold of the Divine*. New Haven, CT: Yale University Press for the Rothko Chapel, 2010.

Merleau-Ponty, Maurice. *The Visible and the Invisible*. Edited by Claude Lefort. Translated by Alphonso Lingis. Evanston, IL: Northwestern University Press, 1968.

Morgan, David. *Protestants and Pictures: Religion, Visual Culture, and the Age of American Mass Production.* Oxford: Oxford University Press, 1999.

————. *Visual Piety*. Berkeley: University of California Press, 1998.

Motherwell, Robert. *The Writings of Robert Motherwell*. Edited by Dore Ashton with Joan Banach. Berkeley: University of California Press, 2007.

Munch, Edvard. *The Private Journals of Edvard Munch: We Are Flames Which Pour Out of the Earth*. Edited and translated by J. Gill Holland. Madison: University of Wisconsin Press, 2005.

Myers, Ched. *Binding the Strong Man: A Political Reading of Mark's Story of Jesus*. Maryknoll, NY: Orbis Books, 2008.

Nancy, Jean-Luc. *The Ground of the Image*. Translated by Jeff Fort. New York: Fordham University Press, 2005.

Nash, Roderick. *Wilderness and the American Mind*. 5th ed. New Haven, CT: Yale University Press, 2014.

Newman, Barnett. *Stations of the Cross: Lema Sabachtani*. Edited by Lawrence Alloway. New York: Solomon R. Guggenheim Museum Foundation, 1966.

Nietzsche, Friedrich. *The Birth of Tragedy*. Translated by Shaun Whiteside. Edited by Michael Tanner. New York: Penguin Books, 1993.

————. *Human, All Too Human*. Translated by R. J. Hollingdale. Cambridge: Cambridge University Press, 2004.

———. *Selected Letters of Friedrich Nietzsche.* Translated by Anthony M. Ludovici. Edited by Oscar Levy. Garden City, NY: Doubleday and Company, 1921.

———. "The Twilight of the Idols." In *The Portable Nietzsche.* Translated by Walter Kaufmann. New York: Penguin, 1976.

Nishitani, Keiji. *Religion and Nothingness.* Translated by Jan Van Bragt. Berkeley: University of California Press, 1983.

O' Leary, Joseph Stephen. "Emptiness and Dogma." *Buddhist-Christian Studies* 22 (2002).

———. *Questioning Back: The Overcoming of Metaphysics in Christian Tradition.* Minneapolis: Seabury Press, 1985.

Parry, Joseph D., ed. *Art and Phenomenology.* London: Routledge, 2011.

Peperzak, Adriaan T., ed. *Ethics as First Philosophy: The Significance of Emmanuel Levinas for Philosophy, Literature and Religion.* New York: Routledge, 1995.

Pollock, Jackson. "My Painting." In *Jackson Pollock: Interviews, Articles, and Reviews,* edited by Pepe Karmel. New York: Museum of Modern Art, 1999.

Purcell, Michael. *Mystery and Method: The Other in Rahner and Levinas.* Milwaukee, WI: Marquette University Press, 1998.

Rabinovitch, Celia. *Surrealism and the Sacred: Power, Eros, and the Occult in Modern Art.* Boulder, CO: Westview Press, 2002.

Rahner, Karl. "Art against the Horizon of Theology and Piety." Translated by Joseph Donceel. *Theological Investigations* 23. New York: Crossroad, 1992.

———. "Current Problems in Christology." Translated by Cornelius Ernst. *Theological Investigations* 1. Baltimore, MD: Helicon Press, 1964.

———. *Foundations of the Christian Faith.* Translated by William V. Dych. New York: Crossroad, 1990.

———. *The Mystical Way in Everyday Life.* Translated and edited by Annemarie S. Kidder. Maryknoll, NY: Orbis Books, 2010.

———. *The Need and Blessing of Prayer.* Translated by Bruce W. Gillette. Collegeville, MN: Liturgical Press, 1997.

———. "Poetry and the Christian." Translated by Kevin Smyth. *Theological Investigations* 4. New York: Seabury Press, 1974.

———. "The Religious Meaning of Images." Translated by Joseph Donceel. *Theological Investigations* 23. New York: Crossroad, 1992.

———. *Spirit in the World.* Translated by William V. Dych. New York: Continuum, 1994.

Raphael, Melissa. *Judaism and the Visual Image.* London: Continuum International, 2009.

Refsum, Grete. "The French Dominican Fathers as Precursors to the Directives on Art of the Second Vatican Council." Dissertation lecture, Kunsthogskolen Oslo, National College of Art and Design, December 8, 2000.

Ribera-Florit, Josep. "Some Doctrinal Aspects of the Targum of Ezekiel." In *Targum and Scripture: Studies in Aramaic Translations and Interpretation in Memory of Ernest G. Clarke.* Edited by Paul V. M. Flesher. Leiden: Brill, 2003.

Ricoeur, Paul. *Figuring the Sacred: Religion, Narrative and Imagination.* Translated by David Pellauer. Edited by Mark I. Wallace. Minneapolis: Fortress Press, 1995.

van Riessen, Renée D. N. *Man as a Place of God: Levinas' Hermeneutics of Kenosis.* Dordrecht: Springer, 2007.

Rothko, Mark. *The Artist's Reality: Philosophies of Art.* Edited by Christopher Rothko. New Haven, CT: Yale University Press, 2004.

——. *Writings on Art.* Edited by Miguel Lopez-Remiro. New Haven, CT: Yale University Press, 2006.

Rowe, Nina. *The Jew, the Cathedral and the Medieval City: Synagoga and Ecclesia in the Thirteenth Century.* Cambridge: Cambridge University Press, 2011.

Rubin, William S. *Modern Sacred Art and the Church of Assy.* New York: Columbia University Press, 1961.

Schama, Simon. *The Power of Art.* New York: Ecco/Harper Collins, 2006.

Schillebeeckx, Edward, with Huub Oosterhuis and Piet Hoogeveen. *God Is New Each Moment.* Edinburgh: T & T Clark, 1983.

Schlegel, Ursula. "Observations on Masaccio's Trinity Fresco in Santa Maria Novella." *Art Bulletin* 45, no. 1 (1963).

Scholem, Gershom. *Major Trends in Jewish Mysticism.* New York: Knopf Doubleday, 2011.

Schweizer, Harold. *Suffering and the Remedy of Art.* Albany: SUNY Press, 1997.

Seasoltz, R. Kevin. *A Sense of the Sacred: Theological Foundations of Christian Architecture and Art.* New York: Continuum, 2006.

Soelle, Dorothee. *The Window of Vulnerability: A Political Spirituality.* Translated by Linda M. Maloney. Minneapolis: Fortress Press, 1990.

Stauffer, Jill, and Bettina Bergo, eds. *Nietzsche and Levinas: "After the Death of a Certain God."* New York: Columbia University Press, 2009.

Suzuki, Shunryu. *Zen Mind, Beginner's Mind.* New York: Weatherhill, 1998.

Taylor, Mark C. *After God.* Chicago: The University of Chicago Press, 2007.

Thiessen, Gesa Elsbeth. "Karl Rahner: Toward a Theological Aesthetics." In *The Cambridge Companion to Karl Rahner,* edited by Declan Marmion and Mary E. Hines. Cambridge: Cambridge University Press, 2005.

Tillich, Paul. *The Courage to Be*. New Haven, CT: Yale University Press, 2000.

———. *On Art and Architecture*. Edited by John Dillenberger. New York: Crossroad, 1987.

———. *Systematic Theology*. Vol. 1. Chicago: The University of Chicago Press, 1951.

Tracy, David. *The Analogical Imagination: Christian Theology and the Culture of Pluralism*. New York: Crossroad, 1986.

———. *Blessed Rage for Order: The New Pluralism in Theology*. Chicago: The University of Chicago Press, 1996.

———. *Plurality and Ambiguity: Hermeneutics, Religion, Hope*. Chicago: The University of Chicago Press, 1987.

Vasko, Elisabeth. *Beyond Apathy: A Theology for Bystanders*. Minneapolis: Fortress Press, 2015.

Viladesau, Richard. *Theological Aesthetics: God in Imagination, Beauty, and Art*. New York: Oxford University Press, 1999.

Wertheim Tuchman, Barbara. *A Distant Mirror: The Calamitous Fourteenth Century*. New York: Random House, 1978.

Westphal, Merold. *Overcoming Ontotheology: Toward a Postmodern Christian Faith*. New York: Fordham University Press, 2001.

Wink, Walter. *The Human Being: Jesus and the Enigma of the Son of Man*. Minneapolis: Fortress Press, 2001.

Wyschogrod, Edith. *Emmanuel Levinas: The Problem of Ethical Metaphysics*. The Hague: Martinus Nijhoff, 1974.

Index

Abe, Masao, 289–93

Absolute Being, 287

Academicism (era in art), 112, 246, 249

Adorno, Theodor, 2–3, 99, 108, 113–14, 116–18, 167–70, 184–85, 191–93

aesthetics: definition, 3, 129; Kantian, 106, 130–31, 137; Levinasian, 139, 140–42; Rahnerian, 151, 153–54; theological, 90, 94–95, 94n13; of vulnerability, 4, 10–14, 48, 50, 53, 160–61, 195, 228–29

AIDS, 2, 171–72, 174, 183, 187, 194

alterity, xiv, xvi, 4, 6, 9–13, 17, 19, 24–29, 30, 34–36, 49, 56, 59, 66, 74, 103, 106, 113–14, 117, 118, 141, 145, 148, 159, 160, 162–63, 173, 175–76, 185–86, 190, 194, 231–32, 260, 279–81, 283–85, 297

angels, 41n5, 68, 86, 91, 108–10, 196n70, 198–99, 202, 204, 207n104, 208, 210n116, 211, 213, 223, 224, 225

animals, 10n22, 122, 125n10, 127; suffering of, 164n9

Anne, St., 209–11; *Anna Selbdritt*, 210–11, 213, 220n135

Anselm, St., xiii

Architecture, 219, 221, 265–66; of the Laurentian Library, 262–63

Aristotle, 29, 155n97, 216n129

Ark of the Covenant, xv, 195n68, 211n116, 220; in art, 205–7

atheism, 5n10, 27, 231

atonement, 195n68, 235

Baroque (era in art), 21, 245–46, 249n32

Bataille, Georges, 23, 48, 123–24, 162

Baumgarten, Alexander Gottleib, 129–30

beauty, x, xv, 9, 20n48, 21n50, 39, 89, 90, 94n13, 98, 102, 107n40, 115, 119, 122, 126–28, 154, 219, 236, 253, 297; and Kantian aesthetics, 106, 129, 130–31; distinction from the sublime, 135–38

Beckman, Max, 263

Being, x, 52, 55, 59, 70, 87, 89, 96, 114, 146, 150; of God, xiii, xv, 1, 26n62, 33, 43, 48, 53, 59, 66, 80, 86, 93, 155, 194–95, 230,